NEW SOUTH AFRICAN REVIEW 3

THE SECOND PHASE – TRAGEDY OR FARCE?

NEW SOUTH AFRICAN REVIEW 3

THE SECOND PHASE – TRAGEDY OR FARCE?

EDITED BY JOHN DANIEL, PRISHANI NAIDOO, DEVAN PILLAY AND ROGER SOUTHALL

WITS UNIVERSITY PRESS

Published in South Africa by:

Wits University Press
1 Jan Smuts Avenue
Johannesburg

www.witspress.co.za

Published edition © Wits University Press 2013
Compilation © Edition editors 2013
Chapters © Individual contributors 2013

First published 2013
ISBN 978-1-86814-735-9 (printed)
ISBN 978-1-86814-736-6 (digital)

Cover image: Thousands of striking mine workers demanding a wage increase demonstrate on 16 August 2012 on a hill near Lonmin's Karee Platinum Mine.
Photo by Gallo Images/*City Press*/Leon Sadiki

Project managed by Monica Seeber
Cover design and layout by Hothouse South Africa
Maps by Monica Seeber
Printed and bound by Paarl Media, Paarl

Contents

Preface

This third edition of the *New South African Review* indicates that our series of volumes featuring original chapters on issues of concern and interest to South Africa is coming of age, and is an established feature of the annual calendar (although for publishing reasons a new schedule will see it appearing in the first quarter of the year rather than the last). As ever, our chapters seek to present critical and progressive, yet varying, perspectives on current affairs, to encourage debate and diversity rather than conformity. Inevitably, for reasons of economy and practicality, there are numerous topics that we ignore or omit, and it may appear to some that our choice of issues is somewhat random, for although we as editors aim to discern common concerns raised by our contributors, we do not impose a theme upon them. We welcome suggestions of important issues, national or local, for inclusion in later volumes.

The *New South African Review* continues to be located in the Department of Sociology at the University of the Witwatersrand, Johannesburg, with John Daniel of the School of International Training in Durban having served as an additional editor of this and the two preceding volumes. We should like to thank the University for its financial support for the project under its SPARC Programme, and Professor Tawana Kupe, who served his final year as Dean of Humanities during 2012, for his constant support. Our colleagues in the Department of Sociology provide constant backing, while Ingrid Chunilall and Laura Bloem, our administrators, willingly undertake the numerous backroom tasks necessitated by production of the volume. Once again, we have received the enthusiastic support of Veronica Klipp and all her staff at Wits University Press, while Monica Seeber has exhibited her usual proficiency, combined with her kindly ability to harry recalcitrant contributors to stick to schedule. Finally, alongside our referees who unfailingly provide valuable and constructive comments, we thank all those who have reviewed our previous volumes and who have given us the encouragement to continue with this project on an annual basis.

John Daniel (School of International Training, Durban) and Prishani Naidoo, Devan Pillay and Roger Southall (all of the Department of Sociology, University of the Witwatersrand).

The Second Phase – tragedy or farce?

Devan Pillay

Hegel remarks somewhere that all great world-historic facts and personages appear, so to speak, twice. He forgot to add: the first time as tragedy, the second time as farce ...

(Karl Marx 1852)

The Marikana massacre of 16 August 2012 epitomised, in many ways, the tragedy of South Africa's transition to democracy since the heady days of 1994. If, on the one hand, the country is hailed as a 'miracle' of reconciliation, constitutional democracy and socio-economic progress in many areas, on the other hand it is a story of a dream deferred: rising unemployment and work insecurity; widespread poverty amid expanding inequality; increasing crime and corruption; sexual violence; rural decline and displacement; urban homelessness and slummification; state dysfunctionality and public disservice; corporate greed and ecological degradation of various kinds.

Much of this corresponds with the global picture of uneven (or enclave) development, and is captured by chapters in this volume and previous volumes of the *New South African Review*, as well as by the state's own National Planning Commission, which presents the social deficit as a problem of policy formulation and implementation. Marikana, however, exposes the scenario as a problem of global capitalism that still shows up in South Africa in a racialised form, embedded in a minerals-energy-financial complex based on cheap labour power – the hallmark of apartheid. Despite the coming to power of a democratically elected government supposedly representing the interests of the majority, Marikana has shown how, in the final instance, the state apparatus acts on behalf of a 'power elite', with the aid of subordinate classes beholden to its network of patronage, and with the aid of the mainstream media.[1]

The manner in which the African National Congress (ANC) and its Alliance partners responded – closing ranks around the tainted president Jacob Zuma – under the
guise of a 'second phase' of the 'national democratic revolution' to supposedly address
persisting historical imbalances, raises the question: has the tragedy of Zuma's first term,
which patently failed to address the essential features of the so-called '1996 class project'[2]
(namely, neoliberal, enclave development), now become a farce?

MARIKANA: THE TRAGEDY OF RACIAL CAPITALISM

Marikana is about the sociology of the triple transition (Von Holdt 2003): the inter-
twined transitions, to political democracy and elite pact-making; to globalised economic
liberalisation; as well as a much more complex set of social transitions in the wide range
of social spaces that constitute daily life, including the workplace, as ordinary people try
to reconstruct a new order amid the still burning embers of a racialised capitalist past
and present.

In other words, it is about the sociology of transnational corporations, investor
confidence, mineral extraction, global production and consumption processes, private
motor cars, ecological hazards, the repatriation of profits, high management salaries,
black economic enrichment, low wages, hazardous working conditions, migrant labour,
impoverished rural areas, fatherless households, informal settlements, municipal neglect,
state indifference, cosy corporatism, union oligarchy, rival unions, worker self-organ-
isation, working-class solidarity, cultural weapons, strike violence, police militarisation,
state violence, political opportunism, alliance politics, media bias … it is the story of
post-apartheid South Africa, distilled to its essence.

The savage power of the dominant class revealed itself in all its ugly nakedness on 16
August, as thirty-four striking mineworkers were mowed down by a police force acting on
the instructions of the economic and political elite. As Roger Southall's chapter shows, the
power elite may be fractured along racial lines and through various differentiated interests at the economic and political levels, and as such may not come across as a coherent
'ruling class'. Indeed, at the political level legitimacy is constructed through alliances that
carry the dead weight of past symbolism and allegiances, keeping in power a liberation
movement that has long ceased to be revolutionary. To remain alive this alliance needs
to breathe the oxygen of the 'national democratic revolution' ideological discourse that
seemingly excludes an economic elite that still resembles the old order. However, when
faced with a determined challenge from below, the power elite sees, crystallised before it,
its own true class interest. If, previously, the cacophony of petty squabbles struck discor-
dant notes, now the orchestration of raw power sang a coherent, if hellish, melody.

The Marikana tragedy exposed the interlocking common interest of the power elite,
and the disciplinary power of capital in the form of the minerals-energy-financial
complex. The key actors were, firstly, the British-based mining conglomerate Lonmin
(its owners and top management); secondly, a politically connected businessman who

sits on its board; thirdly, the ANC government (in particular the ministers of Minerals and Energy, and Police – with fingers pointing to the president); fourthly, the National Union of Mineworkers (NUM); and finally the Lonmin rock drillers, supported in part by the breakaway Association of Mineworkers and Construction Union (AMCU). In the background, initially unseen, were the loan sharks to whom many mineworkers were indebted, in order to make ends meet as they tried to support their families back home, and eke out a pitiful existence in the squatter settlement near the mine.

According to leaked e-mails, Cyril Ramaphosa, a Lonmin black economic empower-ment (BEE) shareholder and senior member of the ruling party, demanded 'concomi-tant' action against the striking mineworkers. In conversation with the Lonmin senior management, he used his political connections to ensure that strong action was taken against what he described as 'criminal' behaviour by workers engaged in an 'illegal' strike. The police hierarchy received their mandate from their political superiors, and gave it a savage interpretation. According to independent journalists and researchers, many of the police killings looked like premeditated murder (Alexander et al. 2102). In an interview with CNN on 8 January 2013, Ramaphosa denied that he initiated the violent action by police. He said he was concerned about the violence that had already happened, in which striking workers allegedly killed ten people, including police, security guards and fellow workers. These acts, he said, were criminal, and what he was calling for was action that would result in peace, not more violence. While the Farlam commission of inquiry appointed by President Zuma to investigate the killings will hopefully reveal the full truth, it seems clear that the minister of Police, Nathi Mthethwa, authorised the commissioner of Police, General Phiyega, to allow lethal force to be used. Ronnie Kasrils, former ANC minister of Intelligence, sums up the scenario:

> The people were hardly occupying some strategic point, some vital highway, a key city square. They were not holding hostages. They were not even occupying mining property. Why risk such a manoeuvre other than to drive strikers back to work at all costs on behalf of the bosses who were anxious to resume profit making operations (quoted in Alexander 2012: 175-6).

The question then remains: did President Zuma, as commander-in-chief, give the go-ahead in the final instance? It seems inconceivable that such a weighty decision, where ordinary public order policing rules were flouted, would have been left to a line minister. Alexander concludes that 'Zuma has not distanced himself from Mthethwa's judgment, so there is a high chance that he had prior knowledge of what would happen' (2012:176). In other words, the ANC itself is implicated from beginning to end – on behalf of trans-national capital, against workers, many of whom were still members of the ANC's biggest supporter within the Congress of South African Trade Unions (Cosatu), the NUM.

To repeat: Marikana is an expression of the tragedy of post-apartheid South Africa – the desperation of disempowered workers, living in squalid informal settlements and doing dangerous work deep underground, earning a relative pittance while the management and shareholders rake in millions each year (Lonmin's CEO Ian Farmer earned 325 times as much as the average mineworker, according to Alexander (2012: 177)). It is the tragedy of the minerals-energy-financial complex that underpins our economy, based on cheap black labour. It is also a tragedy of the state and the ruling party, which acted forcibly on behalf of the mine owners (having ignored the plight of the workers before), and seemed afterwards to justify the police actions. Indeed, police continued to harass and intimidate workers, seemingly to prevent them from testifying at the Farlam commission. The state also neglected the families of dead and injured mineworkers by not ensuring that they attended the hearings.

THE TRAGEDY OF ORGANISED LABOUR

Does Marikana represent the tragedy of organised labour in this country? Cosatu was formed in 1985 to champion the cause of the working class, and protect it from being hijacked by the political elite. While the federation remains a robust and vital defender of the poor and marginalised, it self-critically admits that it is in danger of becoming part of the elite. It spends too much time discussing narrow party-political issues, to the neglect of urgent organisational matters, including the increasing social distance between officials and members (Cosatu 2012a).[3]

Cosatu's largest affiliate, the NUM, was formed by Ramaphosa in 1982 to become the first union since the 1940s to represent black mineworkers. Originally from the black consciousness fold, the NUM joined Cosatu at its foundation and became the staunchest supporter of the ANC within the federation. The NUM has produced three successive general secretaries of the ruling party since 1991, namely Ramaphosa, Kgalema Motlanthe and currently Gwede Mantashe (all former general secretaries of the union). Like other affiliates, its close ties with the South African Communist Party (SACP) (its current president, Senzeni Zokwana, was elected chairperson of the party in 2012), instead of deepening a broader working class consciousness, have served to bind the union more closely to the conservative nationalism of Zuma's ANC.

This once-proud union became a victim of its own success in negotiating rights at the workplace and in enjoying the privileges of close ties with the ruling party. The cosy relationship with mine management meant that, often, the union would side with management against workers, whose unsafe conditions and low wages in relation to the highly skilled and dangerous work they did (sometimes for twelve to fifteen hours a day) had reached a point at which they took matters into their own hands. They went against the NUM's negotiated agreement, and embarked on a wildcat strike deemed 'illegal' by the NUM, management and the state. The workers were set up against a triumvirate of forces that they seemingly had little chance of overcoming.[4]

Yet conditions were such that the mineworkers could take no more. They were determined and highly organised – not by any union (the rival AMCU supported them but were not organising them). They drew on their own internal networks of solidarity and experience, and occupied a mountain-top far away from the Lonmin mine, determined to meet with management to negotiate their wage demands. Initially it was for R12 500 per month as an opening figure to bargain with but the refusal of management to negotiate with the workers, and the brutal massacre by police, solidified the R12 500 into a firm rallying cry. The workers refused to budge until they won that demand, and strikes spread to other platinum mines, and to the gold mines. This was an impressive display of raw working class power, against interminable odds. The victory came at great cost, as the wives and children of dead mineworkers asked why their husbands and fathers were killed over a wage demand. That question has yet to be fully answered by the Farlam commission.

For many, it is a tragedy that after the Marikana massacre Cosatu chose to close ranks behind Zuma and support his campaign for re-election as ANC president. Nevertheless, Cosatu's declaration on Marikana, drafted at its September conference, placed blame at the door of the police force for acting in the interests of mine owners (despite an intervention by the SACP general secretary, who placed most blame on AMCU, saying that the workers were misled).[5]

It was evident that the Cosatu central committee's decision to support Zuma was a close one. As part of the deal, the federation decided to push for decisive state intervention in a range of socio-economic areas (including strategic nationalisation, state ownership of land, capital controls and higher taxes for the wealthy) in order radically to address the triple challenges of unemployment, poverty and inequality. Prior to the Mangaung conference, Cosatu issued a Section 77 notice to the National Economic and Labour Council (Nedlac), signalling an intention to engage in mass action if these demands were not met (Cosatu 2012b).[6] It is clear that Cosatu has no intention of being a docile partner of the ruling party. But the labour federation must see urgently to its internal challenges before they become a tragedy.

THE TRAGEDY OF THE ANC

The December 2012 ANC conference in Mangaung ended with two notable outcomes – the widely welcomed election of Ramaphosa as the deputy president of the ruling party, and the adoption of the National Development Plan (NDP) as the guiding policy document of the party and government. Given the overwhelming majority (approximately 75 per cent) the Zuma slate received in the election for the National Executive Council (NEC), the outcomes of the conference were endorsed by the ANC's alliance partners the SACP and Cosatu – despite the latter's misgivings about the NDP as not being radical enough to transform the political economy and achieve its stated goals of eliminating poverty, reducing inequality and increasing employment, the key triple challenge facing the country.

The conference predictably confirmed the ANC's rejection of nationalisation as a policy goal, and re-elected Jacob Zuma as president. It also endorsed the 'second phase' of the 'national democratic revolution', ostensibly aimed at rapid transformation of the political economy, in order to address the historical imbalances caused by apartheid.

Given the jitters of the global investment community following the mine strike-wave, the ANC was determined to calm the markets, while pretending to take decisive action to address the problems of underdevelopment. It was, however, business as usual. If the 'first phase' was tragic from the viewpoint of the working class and marginalised, the second phase looks like it will be a farce. The NDP, despite noble-sounding rhetoric around inclusive growth and social protection, and some specific proposals that try to address issues of state incapacity, education, police militarisation and renewable energy, is in the end a mom-and-apple-pie document that fudges critical issues. In the final analysis it subordinates sustainable development to the export-driven growth priorities of the minerals-energy-financial complex. It is entirely in keeping with the first phase under Jacob Zuma, who tried to appease a range of contradictory interests, as long as the key interests of the power elite were secured:

- Firstly, the ANC tried to appease dominant (predominantly white) economic interests, domestically and globally, by continuing on a relatively conservative macroeconomic path based on the minerals-energy-financial complex. This path has historically been embedded within a system of cheap labour power and the exploitation of fossil fuels, making South Africa the most unequal country in the world, and one of the most polluted in terms of carbon emissions.
- Secondly, it tried to appease the economic aspirations of a rising black elite through black economic empowerment and affirmative action. While in principal necessary to correct historical racial imbalances, in practice it has often led to elite enrichment and cadre deployment – to the detriment of real wealth redistribution, efficient public services and effective implementation of government policy, particularly for the poor and marginalised.
- Thirdly, and most ominously, under Zuma the government appeased conservative interests that accord with his own background as a polygamous rural patriarch and ANC intelligence chief – attempting to undermine democracy by, for example, giving power to male traditional chiefs over rural women, and added power to securocrats.
- Finally, Zuma had to appease his alliance partners, the SACP and Cosatu who, along with the Youth League, played a major role in his ascension to power in 2007. These formations primarily represent the organised working class located in urban areas, and a development perspective that seeks the protection of workers' rights and greater state intervention in the economy. The SACP, however, has traded increased access to state power under Zuma for collusion (or silence) over a range of policies – from the 'secrecy' bill to calling for a law to prevent citizens from 'insulting' the president.

TRAGEDY OR FARCE?

In its support for Jacob Zuma's re-election as ANC president at Mangaung, Cosatu called for a 'Lula moment' during Zuma's second term of office.[7] Luis Inacio Lula da Silva, from the Workers' Party in Brazil, campaigned in 2002 against free market fundamentalism, and promised a real shift in power from the oligarchic elite to the working class and peasantry. At the time, Brazil occupied the dubious position of first in the league of countries with high social inequality. Once he was in office (from 2003), however, the power of international institutions and global financial markets, in concert with national elites, contrived to hem in his options. His first term saw Lula largely obeying the dictates of economic orthodoxy, with modest attempts at wealth redistribution, causing some left-wing factions to split away from his party.

During his second term, from 2006, however, Lula was much bolder. He embarked on a more substantial redistributive programme, which coincided with a commodities boom and increased revenues. Incomes for all classes rose significantly, and for the first time in many decades the wealth gap narrowed. Brazil is now no longer the most unequal country in the world – South Africa has knocked it off its infamous perch.

Lula achieved this through a number of initiatives, the most notable being expanding the *bolsa familia* (family allowance) programme and setting up the Zero Hunger programme, allowing everyone access to decent food, clothing and shelter. This came in the context of low utility prices, cheap public transport and, in some cities, innovative processes of participatory budgeting.

What impresses Cosatu most is that after re-election Lula re-composed his top team, and installed progressive economists to head the ministry of Finance, the secretariat of Strategic Affairs and the National Bank of Economic and Social Development. They implemented activist and redistributive fiscal and financial policies, moderated the economic orthodoxy of the central bank, and invested heavily in infrastructure, transport and energy, as well as in higher education.

Progressive social and economic policies were aimed at supporting local production, strengthening the domestic market, and reducing unemployment from 12.6 per cent to 4.7 per cent during Lula's term through expanding workers' rights, real wages and formal employment – not the opposite, as demanded by our own business class.

Of course, Lula, unlike his Bolivian and Venezuelan counterparts, was no revolutionary. Brazil still has high inequality, poverty, violence and landlessness. In its pursuit of rapid growth, it has degraded the environment, and trampled on indigenous peoples' rights in the Amazon forests. However, compared to decades of neglect by various oligarchic regimes, the Workers' Party has been a breath of fresh air for the working class and poor majority. By the time Lula left office in 2011 he was as popular as ever, paving the way for his successor, Dilma Russeff, to continue with his legacy.

Under Zuma, there have certainly been significant improvements in health and in industrial and trade policies. The scandal of Mbeki's HIV/AIDs policies was reversed. However, on close inspection it can be seen that many 'developmental state' policies began during the Mbeki era, and the Zuma administration continued with his conservative macroeconomic policies. In the meantime, widespread poverty persists, inequality has increased, corruption is commonplace, and our police have become more violent.

In the 'second phase' of the democratic transition, can Zuma do a Lula? Can he take on the vested interests in society – not just 'white monopoly capital', but also a rising black predatory elite that is diverting resources away from the poor? Can he appoint progressive people in key ministries to drive an inclusive developmental path? This, it seems, is what the SACP believes, and what Cosatu is hoping for. It is a vain hope.

Firstly, Zuma does not seem to have the drive to galvanise the country's energies into a coherent vision and sense of purpose. In fact, he is a threat to democracy, ready to appease backward sectors of society that want to undermine the hard-won democratic rights and freedoms embedded in the Constitution (by, for example, undermining the prosecutions authority, and introducing ominous legislation such as the Traditional Courts Bill and the Protection of State Information Bill).

Secondly, the president's personal conduct leaves much to be desired. The outrage of R230 million of taxpayers' money allegedly spent on his personal home, while his rural neighbours still wallow in poverty, leaves a bitter taste in many mouths. This makes it difficult for him to be a beacon of moral authority as is Mandela.

Thirdly, to build a democratic developmental state requires a coherent political movement to forge synergies with broader society, whereas the once-proud liberation movement seems more eager to march and defend the president's dignity than to mobilise society around a common vision. Unlike Brazil's Workers' Party, it no longer inspires as a vehicle for radical, democratic transformation – and its current leader is at the centre of division and disillusionment.

The thought of another seven years of Zuma at the helm fills many with deadened resignation. In the face of rising working class discontent, from Marikana to De Doorns,[8] the country desperately needs an inspirational leader to galvanise its citizens, and make them believe again. Zuma is no Lula.

Nevertheless, if it is fair to label the 'first phase' as a tragedy, is it fair to expect that the 'second phase' will be a farce? After all, despite his billionaire status and involvement in Lonmin, Zuma's new deputy, Cyril Ramaphosa, comes with impeccable credentials. He was one of the key architects of the country's Constitution, and is bound to defend the democratic rights embedded in it (see Butler 2007). He is likely to play a more pronounced role as deputy president after the 2014 elections, to the point of acting as *de facto* prime minister. Will he excite the imagination and unite the country around a new developmental vision, or will he act as the polished spokesperson of the power elite, protecting the essentials of the *status quo*? Indeed, is Zuma likely to sit back and allow this 'clever black'[9] to upset his apple cart?

These are questions that are likely to dominate the so-called second phase of the national democratic revolution. As the chapters in this volume indicate, the challenges are enormous, and are about the content of policies as well as their implementation. The first section, on power, party and class, contains a chapter by Roger Southall unpacking the power elite, while Susan Booysen looks more closely at the ANC as a party in decline. Paul Maylam compares the ANC/Cosatu/SACP Alliance with that of the National Party, and finds many similarities, while Ahmed Veriava and Prishani Naidoo take us into the world of subaltern politics, and the difficulties of building alternatives to the ANC.

The section on ecology, economy and labour argues for wage-led development (Dick Forslund), and for worker-centred nationalisation of a special type in the mining industry (Martin Nicol). William Attwell contends that the NUM and the South African Clothing and Textile Workers Union (Sactwu) pioneered broad-based BEE that brings tangible benefits to workers and their families, while David Fig argues against fracking for gas, and Jacklyn Cock engages with the politics of reform and revolution within the climate justice movement.

Under public policy and social practice, Vinothan Naidoo engages with the issue of cadre deployment and the politicisation of the public service, while Louise Vincent inter-rogates the tension between traditional cultural practices, such as male circumcision, and the Constitution. Shireen Motala gives a broad overview of the challenges in education, while Stephanie Allais looks at the changing policies of skills development. Finally, the vexing problem of health sector reforms is tackled by Laetitia Rispel and Julia Moorman In the final section, South Africa at large, Sanusha Naidu looks at South Africa within the BRIC network, punching above its weight, and John Daniel and Marisha Ramdeen peer into the troubled kingdom of Swaziland and it relations with South Africa.

With Zuma likely to be re-elected as president of the country in 2014, his uninspiring and tainted leadership suggests that the tragedy of unmet expectations may very well become a farce, as the radical rhetoric (cheered on by the SACP) increasingly bears little resemblance to actual practice. Meanwhile, workers and the marginalised continue to mobilise and organise, sometimes through Alliance structures, at other times indepen-dently. The most recent expression of alternative left politics is the Workers and Socialist Party (WASP), which emerged out of the ashes of Marikana, and is poised to contest the 2014 elections. But the ANC, the party of Nelson Mandela, remains popular among workers and the poor, even if they are increasingly unimpressed with its performance and voter turnouts are declining.[10] It will take a major crisis, and/or a credible alternative, for workers to conclude that the emperor has no clothes.

NOTES

1 Jane Duncan shows that in their coverage of Marikana between 12 and 22 August 2012 newspa-pers relied on business (including managers and owners of mines) for 41 per cent of their sources, and only 3 per cent on workers directly affected (with an additional 5 per cent from the NUM and 5 per cent from AMCU). TV coverage predominantly projected images from behind police lines, reflecting their viewpoint (see Alexander et al. 2012).
2 The term used by the SACP to describe the 1996 Growth, Employment and Redistribution (Gear) policy, which followed a Washington consensus free market logic.
3 For example, the general secretary of the NUM now earns around R1.4 million a year, which he justified as being 'market related' (*Mail & Guardian*, 18 May 2012).
4 Information based on workers' own testimonies, as recorded by Alexander et al. (2012).
5 Speech given by Blade Nzimande at Cosatu congress, as observed by the author.
6 Cosatu, although increasingly under the influence of the SACP, has to its credit maintained a rela-tively independent voice. It mounted opposition to a range of government policies that threaten democratic freedoms and impose increased burdens on the working class and which fail to take on

big capital, in favour of a much more assertive developmental agenda. Key affiliates such as the National Union of Metalworkers of South Africa (Numsa) also took on board ecological issues, and have promoted the idea of a socially-owned renewal energy sector that would directly challenge the basis of the minerals-energy complex. It looks likely, in the second phase, that organised workers will continue to vacillate between support for the ruling party and robust action against specific policies.

7   See Cosatu (2012a) for a discussion on the Lula moment, the essential features of which are presented here.

8   De Doorns, in the Western Cape, is where farmworkers began a strike for higher minimum wages (from R69 a day to R150) in 2012, and which exploded again at the beginning of 2013 as a result of employer intransigence and government inaction.

9   Zuma referred to critics who argued against the Traditional Courts Bill as 'clever blacks' who did not understand their own culture, having adopted alien 'white' culture (*City Press*, 3 November 2012). Later, he criticised black people who loved dogs more than people (and a few years back he attacked homosexuality). These utterances, which expose his social conservatism, are usually made to his traditional support base and in his mother tongue, isiZulu.

10   Recent surveys done recently by Wits University's Society, Work and Development Institute (SWOP) in 2008, and Cosatu in 2012, indicate declining but still substantial support among members for the ANC.

REFERENCES

Alexander P, T Lekgowa, B Mmope, L Sinwell and B Xezwi (2012) *Marikana: A View from the Mountain and a Case to Answer*. Johannesburg: Jacana.

Butler A (2007) *Cyril Ramaphosa*. Johannesburg: Jacana.

Cosatu (2012a) Secretariat Political Report of the 11th National Congress.

Cosatu (2012b) The Slow Pace of Socio-economic Transformation in South Africa (Section 77 Notice submitted to Nedlac, 11 December).

Marx K (1852) The Eighteenth Brumaire of Louis Bonaparte. http://www.marxists.org/archive/marx/works/1852/18th-brumaire/

National Planning Commission (2012) National Development Plan 2030: Our future – make it work. Executive summary. Pretoria: NPC.

Von Holdt K (2003) *Transition from Below: Forging Trade Unionism and Workplace Change in South Africa*. Scottsville: University of Natal Press.

PARTY, POWER AND CLASS

1

Party, power and class

John Daniel

After nearly two decades of democracy, South Africa seems full of foreboding – a sense that somehow the country is approaching the end of the immediate post-liberation era and that political and economic uncertainty beckons. The indicators are many and well known. The global crisis of capitalism, and its impact upon the economy in terms of reduction of overseas markets and inflow of foreign investment, resulting in slower growth, absorbs government, the private sector and the media every day. In turn, the gloom is heightened by growing appreciation in even the rarified quarters of Sandton and Pretoria/Tshwane that democratic South Africa has failed to address fundamental structural features of the apartheid economy. Inequality may have deracialised to some degree but it remains extreme, and the vast majority of the population (especially black Africans) continue to struggle for a living and inhabit a world of poverty. The dire consequences these continuities may have for democracy and stability are increasingly recognised, as South Africa grapples with a revolt of the poor, epitomised most explicitly by the billowing of 'service delivery protests' (which in 2012 reached higher levels than in any year since 1994), and which record a multiplicity of social ills – but above all would seem to express not merely a demand to be heard and for accountability from government, but also a growing impatience with things as they are.

Those who wield political or economic power (or both), and those who live comfortably in middle-class homes, are becoming increasingly aware of the insistent demands of the majority. Perhaps we are approaching an era in which the poor come to be recognised in ruling circles as 'the dangerous classes', who threaten to bring the foundations of the established constitutional and political order crashing to the ground. Too dramatic? Too dystopian? Hopefully, yes. Nonetheless, it is difficult to contest analyses that predict the crumbling of democracy and warn of the dangers of a lurch towards political authoritarianism unless some sort of radical changes are undertaken. From the right, the call is for a massive shake-up of labour law, to lower the cost of South African labour, and thereby to attract a new inflow of private investment. From the left, the call is for greater redistribution and higher wages and transfer payments to the poor in order to stimulate growth through increasing domestic demand. From government come calls for South Africa to become a 'developmental state' that can drive greater growth, equity and social justice through state-led initiatives and promotion of higher levels of investment. From the African National Congress (ANC) there are suggestions that the existing Constitution has become an impediment to development, and that a 'second phase' of the transition needs to be inaugurated. From Julius Malema come noisy demands for nationalisation, for the overthrow of the incumbent ANC-SACP-Cosatu Alliance, and for Africanisation of a still white-dominated economy.

It is possible to discern, amid the cacophony of these and other voices, an urgent need for concerted discussion about the distribution and use of power in South African society, and the resultant class structures that eventuate. The process of democratisation is often described as having featured an 'elite transition'; the incorporation of the hitherto racially excluded mass of the population into a democratised polity and the incorporation of a black elite into the task of running a largely white-owned corporate economy. Studies of black economic empowerment (BEE), though recognising the necessity of democratising the ownership and operation of the corporate sector, regularly complain about incorporation of black elites into existing corporate power structures rather than the deeper transformation of those structures. Even though it is recognised that there have been significant changes in South Africa's corporate structure since the early 1990s (through 'unbundling' of conglomerates, financialisation, globalisation), too often the characteristics of corporate power are asserted rather than investigated. Too little attention has been given to government-business relations and to the personal relationships these embody, with the result that the interface between political and economic power, and between black and white elites, tends to be left largely to speculation. It is thus that in this issue of the *New South African Review* we initially turn our gaze upon the issue of 'power': who wields it for whom, and how, and the consequences.

In the opening essay, Roger Southall seeks to understand the nature of South Africa's 'elite compromise' by asking whether it can be said that there is a 'power elite' and if so, whether it can be said to compromise a 'ruling class'. Arguing the virtues of 'elite theory', he draws his inspiration from the work of C Wright Mills, whose analysis of the power elite of the United States in the 1950s provided a valuable model for such studies elsewhere (across time and space). Fundamentally, Mills argued that to understand who holds power we need to explore who has the capacity to make decisions that have major consequences for the masses of ordinary people in society; and to understand this, we need to look at those institutions – political, economic and military – whose pinnacles comprise the 'command posts' of society. (It is not irrelevant to note, in parenthesis, that similar language is used by the ANC when in the various versions of its 'strategy and tactics' documents it speaks to its ambition to assume control over 'the strategic centres of power'.)

Southall proceeds to define South Africa's political directorate (those who occupy national level political decision-making positions) as those who have the capacity to make decisions that are both national and formative in their scope, whereas at what is equivalent to Mills's middle level of power (between elite and mass) forces such as provincial governments, Cosatu and civil society have far less capacity to shape policies, operating largely at the level of policy implementation and political lobbying, and otherwise enjoy only the ability to exert constraint.

Thereafter, Southall uses data from the 2011 edition of the invaluable *Who Owns Whom* to explore the contours of the corporate elite. In his conclusion, he proposes that there remain distinctly identifiable political and corporate elites, and that although BEE has ensured that there are certainly important overlaps between them, South Africa's power elite continues to exhibit fractures along lines of race; that the state and the ANC as the party that runs it are too diffuse to be unambiguously labelled in Marxian terms as the instrument of large-scale capital; and that although the idea of 'elite compromise' describes a reality, the political and corporate elites exhibit an 'uneasy co-existence' and consequently cannot be said to form a coherent 'ruling class'. Nonetheless, given that together they possess and exercise far more power than others in society and largely agree on the fundamentals of running a capitalist market economy, they can be said to constitute what Ralph Miliband (in the tradition of Mills) termed a *dominant* class. Southall concludes by proposing that, given the massive inequalities of South African society, the extent to which the elites prove able to respond creatively and constructively to pressures from below will determine the future course of South African democracy.

Southall's analysis is complemented by Paul Maylam's drawing out of parallels between the exercise of power by the apartheid-era National Party (NP) and the ANC. Maylam recognises fundamental differences in the popular legitimacy and goals of the two parties as both movements and governments. Nonetheless, he argues that it is possible to track similar tendencies in their respective histories. Both built up multiclass alliances under an umbrella of nationalism, each having to manage ideological tensions and class divisions in order to acquire power; the NP's pre-1948 and the ANC's pre-1994 electoral campaigns both embraced ambiguity in economic policy (incorporating socialist, capitalist and statist elements); both were to find it more difficult to hold these alliances once they were in power when the former enemy (for the NP, foreign-dominated monopoly capital; for the ANC, apartheid) had seemingly been vanquished. Both abandoned socialist elements in their agendas once they faced the task of ruling, while using the state machinery to provide employment and upward mobility opportunities for their constituencies. The NP's promotion of Afrikaner capitalism has been matched by the ANC's efforts to promote a black capitalist class through BEE. Finally, in both cases, once they had moved into government, the multiclass alliances they had constructed before assuming power were to come under increasing strain as they served the interests of individual component classes differentially, the NP favouring those of Afrikaner capitalists, the ANC of a growing black elite and middle class at the cost of its mass constituency. Just as, consequently, the NP class alliance eventually fractured, so the ANC is now facing the daunting task of keeping its own diversely composed support together. The possibility is that it may face the threat of losing its electoral hegemony much sooner than generally anticipated.

This possibility is contested by Susan Booysen, who argues that although the challenges the ANC is facing as a government are indeed eroding its support, it nonetheless displays very considerable capacity to regenerate its political power. It does this through seven mechanisms. First, building upon its status as a liberation movement, the ANC continues to present itself as representing the political aspirations of the broad spectrum of South Africans. Second, it counters pervasive evidence that its policies have become non-revolutionary through its continued promotion of the notion that it is 'a disciplined force of the left'. Third, it pursues parallel processes of inter-party (electoral and liberal) democracy and internal democracy-*cum*-democratic centralism. Fourth, the ANC continues to manipulate 'struggle speak' and 'struggle theory', using the notion of 'a two-phase revolution' to explain why the government has failed to realise the goals of economic liberation. Fifth, the ANC continues to enjoy an 'extended liberation movement dividend' insofar as popular opinion views the party as the best custodian and guarantor of the 1994 promised land. Sixth, it manages to balance the two worlds of 'elections' and 'other times', with levels of citizen opposition to the ANC receding during periods of electoral mobilisation. And seventh, the ANC is enabled to use state power as a source of patronage to compensate for any loss of support that results from its failures in service delivery and transformation. Booysen concludes that the dissection of the seven mechanisms for the regeneration of the ANC's political power suggests substantial vulnerability and fragility amid continuous ANC power.

State power is also used to confront and demobilise popular protest. In a personal reflection upon their involvement in the successes, failures and limitations of the Anti-Privatisation Forum (APF), Ahmed Veriava and Prishani Naidoo explore the dynamics of one of the 'new social movements' that have arisen around the struggles of the poor since 1994. Social movements, Veriava and Naidoo propose, are seen as emerging out of the failure of the liberation movement in government to act as a meaningful vehicle for advancing the daily interests of the mass of ordinary people who, ironically, constitute the ANC's major constituency. Having adopted neoliberal strategies such as the introduction of pre-paid water meters to link payment to delivery of services even from those who cannot (or claim they cannot) afford it, the government is then met with popular resistance which, in turn, is met by the calling-in of the police. Throw in allegations and outcomes of corruption and inefficiency by local councillors and administrators, and you have the combustible mix which, in recent years, has seen local protests taking place all over the country. It does not, however, follow automatically that the social movements arising around such particular struggles will result in the coming together of a wider initiative of greater political significance. For instance, although the APF managed to secure various gains, some of which became incorporated (and reshaped) into local government policy, ultimately little was won. Twelve years after it was formed, the APF had largely withered away, having failed to overcome internal factionalism and the difficulties of linking sustained community activism to the slower pace and uncertain outcomes of legal engagement with the authorities through the courts. In spite of the 'empty adoption' of socialism as a goal, the politics of the APF was in the end stranded in governmental terrain.

The 'new social movements' seek to offer an alternative to the fading politics of the established liberation movement, or – as Veriava and Naidoo put it – to become a new political force on the left. During 2012, we were to see the emergence of the Democratic Left Front as a focus for such aspirations, and one that seeks to make an impact in the elections of 2014. However, whether or not it (or any other such vehicle) will be able to overcome the ANC's ability to 'regenerate itself in power' remains highly doubtful, given the limitations of the social movements as they exist at the present moment. How to coordinate and unify social movements into a coherent political initiative capable of challenging ANC hegemony remains a dilemma that may well only be resolved if and when the liberation movement itself dissolves into competing factions.

Together, these four chapters raise major questions about the nature of the contemporary South African state and the quality, mechanisms and outcomes of ANC rule. They confirm the serious challenges posed by the structural legacy bequeathed to the ANC in 1994 combined with the ruling party's contested response to the dilemmas it has faced and is facing. Whether the ANC is using its power to promote the interests of incumbent economic and political elites, or those of the mass of the population, constitutes the key question posed to observers and citizens regarding the prospects for and of democracy.

CHAPTER 1

The power elite in democratic South Africa:
Race and class in a fractured society

Roger Southall

The major debate that took place from the 1970s between liberal historians and their Marxist-revisionist opponents revolved around whether there was a functional relationship between the policies pursued by successive South African governments and the interests of capital.[1] On the one hand, the liberal historians argued that there was considerable contestation between political and economic power holders; on the other, the Marxian-revisionists proposed that the relationships between them were broadly compatible, with changing political policies reflecting the changing interests of dominant elements of capital across different eras.[2] Inevitably, the debate was inconclusive but there was nonetheless to be a considerable convergence around the idea that, from the mid-1970s, the mounting costs of the National Party's rigid adherence to key tenets of apartheid were increasingly costly to large-scale capital, which, during the 1980s, came to exert significant pressure upon the government to enter into negotiations with the African National Congress (ANC).

From this broad agreement have flowed two assertions. The first is that the sustainability of South African capitalism requires the overall compatibility of what Sampie Terreblanche refers to as the systems of political legitimation and economic accumulation. From this perspective, the economic strains brought about by political crisis required the transition from white minority rule to a 'liberal capitalist version of democratic capitalism' (Terreblanche 2002: 456). The second assertion is that the transition to democracy was brought about by an 'elite compromise' structured around the concession of political democracy to the incoming ANC in return for its acceptance of the existing contours of capitalism. Although allowing for the expropriation of property by the state subject to market-value compensation and due process, the post-apartheid constitutions entrenched the rights of private property. This signalled that any government seeking to address the highly unequal, racially structured ownership patterns of the pre-democratic era whereby whites dominated the economy, would do so incrementally. The ANC was soon to find it appropriate to quietly discard (or at least to postpone to an unspecified distant future) commitments to socialism, and to abandon nationalisation in favour of market-driven policies. The move from the social democratically-inclined Redistribution and Development Programme (RDP) to the pro-market Growth, Employment and Redistribution (Gear) strategy in 1996 is but the most widely acknowledged marker of the conversion of ANC policy makers to capitalist economics.

The notion of elite compromise suggests an identifiable level of overall interest between South Africa's incoming political and established economic elites. When Tom Lodge sought to divine 'Who rules South Africa?' his answer was unremittingly political: 'A political movement governs, and has real power ... to reshape political and economic life', yet he managed to conclude that the ANC government was probably better for business than any of its immediate successors (Lodge 2002: 19-31). Similarly, accounts of business-state relations under the ANC have tended to depict contested, yet overall collaborative, relationships which have ensured that the economy has been kept on a relatively even keel (Taylor 2007). Similarly, Bill Freund (2006), when discussing how the ANC has used state power to promote black entry into the bastions of white capital, talks of 'the emergence of a new power elite' as if there is a relatively unproblematic convergence of political and economic power.

Whether or not they are compatible, none of these approaches is wrong. They all seek to illuminate how power is distributed and exercised in democratic South Africa. Interestingly, however, they remind us that the large body of work discussing post-apartheid political economy has been overwhelmingly empirical, and – as if the work of the neo-Marxists in the 1970s has been largely forgotten (or simply pigeonholed as referring to the pre-1994 era) – there has been remarkably little theorising about the nature of the state in democratic South Africa.[3] Perhaps to some considerable extent this reflects the limited applicability to South Africa of much theorising about the post-colonial state constructed, as the latter heavily is, around the unequal relationships between foreign capital (which usually retains its local predominance) and those who have inherited political power.[4] Although, as we shall see, it is arguable that large-scale capital has sought to create a 'subaltern class' in South Africa, the latter's political economy still differs fundamentally from those of most post-colonial societies (certainly in Africa) by the existence of a long-established, locally based and powerful private sector dominated by massive corporations. This, in turn, is why most analysis of power in the post-1994 South African political economy has been versed in terms of 'elites' rather than of 'class', with the implication being that elites can be identified by the role they play in heading political and economic institutions. Even so, for all the many references to elite domination in post-apartheid South Africa, and for all the widespread generalisations about 'elite compromise', there has been no concerted attempt to explore whether South Africa has a 'power elite', and if so from where it draws its power, how it exercises it, and whether it can be said to constitute a 'ruling class'. What follows is merely a preliminary attempt to address such issues by drawing from elite theory, driven by the view that our greater understanding of how power is exercised and distributed has major implications for the nature and quality of South African democracy.

ELITES AND DEMOCRACY

The relationship between rulers and the ruled under democracy is always problematic. In the well-known words of Abraham Lincoln's Gettysburg address, democracy is the rule of the people, by the people, for the people. However, this skips over the difficulty of how people are to rule over themselves in large-scale societies, where face-to-face democratic decision making by citizens is impossible. Democracy's answer has been that the people should have periodic opportunities to choose and replace their leaders, and if elected leaders are perceived as failing to rule on behalf of the people, then the people can respond by throwing the rascals out. However, the apparent simplicity of this argument merely raises a whole host of difficult questions that have kept political philosophers busy across the generations. What methods of selection or election of leaders are most democratic? What prevents elites, once elected, from changing the rules to ensure that they can hang on to power? How can elites be rendered accountable between elections? How can the people choose sensibly between competing elites, all of which disclaim self-interest, in an age when selling politics appropriates the techniques for selling soap?

These and many other questions crowd in on attempts to decipher the relationships between ruling and ruled. Broadly, the diverse answers that are given fall into two broad traditions (with considerable crossover between them).

First, there is a large body of 'elite theory' which argues that 'the history of politics is the history of elites' (Prewitt and Stone 1973: 4). Societal goals are established by the elite and accomplished under their direction. This does not mean that societies do not change, only that most change comes about as a result of changes in the composition of the elite. History is thus the interminable struggle among elites to control society, resulting in a circulation of elites, with established elites giving way to new ideas and interests. The relationship between elites and the masses thus remains one of domination. Elites and counter-elites may mobilise support from the masses, but ultimately the latter are largely pawns used in elite interests or observers of elite behaviour. Certainly, in democracies, under conditions of universal suffrage and competitive elections, the people have the opportunity to choose between elites, but after elections elite domination will reassert itself, not least because the elite is organised and the masses are not. Even in democratic political parties, elites will rise to the top. Elites will therefore retain their advantages despite advances in democratic thinking and techniques.

In contrast to this gloomy view, a more optimistic 'pluralist tradition' proposes that elites within democracy are seriously constrained. Elites fight among themselves, thereby imparting very considerable power to the people as to who should rule, and how. Political parties and 'pressure groups' impinge on the autonomy of elites to shape society, and as they compete among themselves they are compelled to take mass desires and wants into consideration, knowing that if they don't their chances of being elected to power, or keeping it, will be severely limited. Further, even though political parties and pressure groups will develop their own elites, the latter will themselves be subject to popular constraints within their sphere of action. Thus, rather than there being a simple division between elites and the mass, society is ordered into a hierarchy of elites, blurring distinctions between elites and people. Finally, elites are constrained by constitutions, which insist that societies are ruled by laws as well as by men, and that elites remain ultimately accountable.

It is important to recall that elite theory is not the exclusive property of conservative theorists. For instance, it is central to Leninist thought that only a political vanguard can make a political revolution. Nor does elite theory prescribe that the powers of elites will be unchanging. As noted by C Wright Mills (1956: 20), one of the foremost elite theorists of modern times, any attempt to insist that a ruling class or elite is omnipotent across all epochs of history and across all nations will end up in tautology, and the extent to which rulers have power is subject to considerable historical variation. In other words, the extent to which societies are dominated by elites is subject to empirical verification. This should remind us that elite theory is not normative theory (telling us how society 'should be' governed), but it does raise hugely important questions about the kind of society we want. In short, if it is true that there is a tendency for democracy to transform into elite rule, how should we attempt to counter it?

An important further consideration is that it is necessary to take both elite theory and pluralism beyond the political, for modern democracy operates within the context of advanced capitalism. Mills (1956: 23) argued that the development of capitalism had seen a progressive enlargement and centralisation of the means of oppression and exploitation, of violence and destruction, as well as the means of production and reproduction. This had led to the rise in power in the US of the 1950s not only of corporate elites, presiding over historically unrivalled productive power, but also of military elites, who wielded greater destructive power than their counterparts in any previous era. The 'corporate chieftains' and 'warlords' had joined together with a 'political directorate' which was increasingly detached from the formal constraints of democracy to form a power elite whose occupation of the 'command posts' of society enabled them to make (or not make) decisions that affected the everyday lives of ordinary men and women. This did not mean that the power elite constituted a ruling class in the Marxist sense, for the political and military holders of power possessed considerable autonomy from the economic domain. It did, however, mean that 'the power elite today involve[d] the uneasy coincidence of economic, military and political power' (Mills 1956: 276), a convergence later to be elaborated on by Dwight Eisenhower who, when he stood down from the US presidency, warned of the dangers of the rise of a 'military-industrial complex'.

Famously, Mills argued that the application of pluralist theory to US society described only a 'middle level of power' featuring a world of congressional and state politics and of small firms that romanticised comfortable notions of how power had been distributed in earlier centuries. Undue attention to middle levels of power obscured the new structures of power brought about by the processes of centralisation and bureaucratisation wedded to increased technological capacity. The reality was that the middle levels of power – those, for instance, of small property, state and city politics, labour unions, consumers, and white-collar groups – were increasingly dominated from above, whereas at the bottom of the heap the diversity of publics beloved by pluralist commentators had been reduced to a 'mass society' that was very largely the recipient of information from above, with little capacity to answer back and little autonomy from major institutions dominated by the power elite.

The relevance of these various considerations to contemporary South Africa is that, for many observers, the country's move from apartheid to democracy was an 'elite transition', brought about by a compromise deal between the established white elites (capitalist and National Party) with an incoming ANC liberation elite (for example, Bond 2000). For Terreblanche (2002), the outcome was a 'democratic capitalism' from whose benefits the large majority of black South Africans was excluded: apartheid has gone, but the new democratic forms merely obscure a circulation of elites.

Today's South Africa may be distant in time and space from 1950s America, but the value of returning to Mills lies in the simultaneous simplicity and directness of the questions he posed about the US of his time. Is it meaningful to describe South Africa as having a 'power elite'? If so, what is its shape, and what are the bases of its power? What are its interests and commonalities, and does it constitute a coherent 'ruling class'? Finally, what does its existence and mode of rule imply for South African democracy? What follows is a preliminary stab at answering such questions in the hope that it may provoke more detailed research.

ANALYSING SOUTH AFRICA'S POWER ELITE

Underlying the notions of South Africa's 'elite transition' is the implication that the pre-1994 power elite was fractured along political and economic lines. Notwithstanding tensions between conservative and reformist elements within the political elite revolving around security issues, large-scale capital was broadly united behind FW de Klerk's efforts to forge a deal with the ANC. The arrival of democracy introduced a circulation of the political elite, with the ANC assuming the dominant position in the initial post-1994 political coalition, enabling it to extend its control over the levers of political power at different levels (national, provincial and local). Meanwhile, notwithstanding important efforts by large corporations to protect their interests by drawing key individuals from the ANC into the corporate elite, the democratic settlement was based simultaneously upon the confirmation of the capitalist basis of accumulation and the consolidation of corporate power.

There is widespread recognition of major continuities between the apartheid and democratic orders regarding the distributions of benefits between different racial segments of the population. Despite significant efforts by the ANC governments to tackle poverty and inequality through the extension of a battery of social grants and pensions, the economy today remains profoundly unequal. There *has* been some welcome change – with modest growth since the transition, there has been a small improvement in the economic status of the general population, and a shift in income patterns away from whites towards blacks. For instance, although white average per capita incomes increased by 61 per cent between 1993 and 2008, African average incomes increased by 93 per cent over the same period.[5] Yet although such gross statistics indicate something of a deracialisation of income patterns, perhaps the principal beneficiaries of this have been those in a growing (although still small) black middle class and those among the black labour force who have retained, or obtained, formal employment (despite the extensive informalisation of employment within the private sector). Thus, according to Zwelinzima Vavi, general secretary of the Congress of South African Trade Unions (Cosatu), fully 50 per cent of the population lives on just 8 per cent of national income (*Business Report*, 21 December 2011).

What all this adds up to is that in analysing *who holds power* in South Africa we need to look closely at who has the capacity to make the *decisions* that structure the continuations of patterns of such inequality. This demands that we examine institutions.

Mills saw in 1950s America a triangle of power linking the political directorate, the corporate chieftains and the warlords, the last-mentioned having challenged civilian dominance of the political-economic system with the rise of the US to the status of a world power. In contrast, in South Africa, although the heavy involvement of leading industrial corporations in the building of a local armaments industry during the 1970s and 1980s led to the development of a reciprocal relationship between the military and business, and hence to the local equivalent of the US military-industrial complex (Simpson 1989), the senior military never approached equality with either the topmost rank of politicians or those who predominated over the economy. There was, to be sure, a period in the 1980s when, under PW Botha, the authority of the Cabinet was subordinated to a state security council, under whose authority significant civilian structures were militarised as the regime engaged in counter-revolutionary warfare at home and abroad. However, the senior military were put back in their place with the assumption of the presidency by De Klerk.[6] Subsequently, under the ANC, although there has been some movement of personnel from senior military ranks into the political and economic spheres, the military has remained subordinate to the civilian government. Although financial subsidies have continued to be pumped into the two major loss-making military-related parastatals (Armscor and Denel), the overall role these play within the economy has declined, as has the involvement of large-scale capital in the armaments industry. Democratic South Africa, in other words, is not threatened by a military-industrial complex. However, as we shall see, there are those who propose that it has remained under the yoke of a minerals-energy complex (MEC) that laid down the predominant path to capital accumulation under segregation and apartheid.[7]

In light of the above, we may conceive of the power elite in South Africa as those who occupy the commanding positions within the polity and the corporate sector; and by 'commanding positions' we mean those whose decisions (commissions or omissions) have major consequences for masses of ordinary people – as citizens, employees, consumers, taxpayers, grant recipients or whatever – who have little or no chance of changing them.

SOUTH AFRICA'S POLITICAL DIRECTORATE

Lodge (2002:22) portrays the South African 'governing class' as composed of 'presidents, premiers, members of cabinets and executive councils and – in the most extended sense – parliamentarians as well as the heads of civil service departments'. He sees the political movement from which the large majority of them are drawn as representing an amorphous social alliance (organised labour, black entrepreneurs, an emergent managerial class, the rural poor, and a multiracial intelligentsia) within which no group is dominant: all struggle for influence. Command of the state invests politicians and administrators with considerable autonomy, albeit an autonomy constrained by social actors, ideology, moral beliefs and perceptions of the possible. Meanwhile, the state has its own interests, and although its performance has probably been better for business than any of its predecessors, it is by no means 'a government wedded to the interests of the private sector' (Lodge 2002: 29). Indeed, the government continues to see business as representing a constituency other than its own, and it may often have considerable differences with it (Lodge 2002: 29-31).

Insofar as this description portrays the cut and thrust of daily political life in South Africa as depicted in the media, it is unobjectionable. However, apart from its uncanny resemblance to what Mills describes as the goings-on at the middle level of power, it fails to elaborate different levels of power and interest within the political movement and government while subscribing to a rather uncritical view of business-state relations as essentially pluralistic and undifferentiated.

In any government there is of course a hierarchy of power and authority flowing downwards from president or prime minister through the Cabinet (or equivalent), ruling party or coalition, and civil service. In this context, who makes what decisions (and ensures their implementation) becomes critical. In the ANC's South Africa, there is substantial agreement that, under Thabo Mbeki, the Office of the President underwent a major expansion in size and influence and, likewise, that the ANC caucus in Parliament was reduced, very largely, to voting fodder, not least because of top-down interventions to inhibit the capacity of parliamentary committees to hold the executive to account. There has been no major reversal of these trends under Jacob Zuma. Indeed, if anything, they have been extended, for instance through the location of the new Ministry of Performance Monitoring and Evaluation within the Presidency, and the imposition of a three-line whip on ANC MPs when the highly controversial Protection of Information Bill was put to Parliament in November 2011. Meanwhile, although Zuma characteristically has attempted to balance the wide diversity of interests represented within the ANC by expanding the Cabinet, there are manifestly inner and outer circles of political power at the topmost level.

The inner circle has normally been composed of the president, deputy president and those who have been appointed to the most powerful ministries. It was precisely Zuma's marginalisation by Mbeki within the inner circle from around 2000 that led to the ensuing battle between them. Those included within the inner circle will change with circumstance (although holders of major portfolios such as Defence are likely to be a constant), but they are principally clustered around the Presidency and the Ministry of Finance (notably Planning, Trade and Industry, Minerals and Energy), which together determine the major outlines of economic and financial policy. They are joined by select ministers who, although not necessarily heading ministries that rank particularly highly, wield significant political influence within the party and Alliance (we might instance, under Zuma, Blade Nzimande, whose particular importance as general secretary of the South African Communist Party extends well beyond his portfolio of Higher Education). Furthermore, as party factional interests have increasingly penetrated the state machinery, and state power has been used to fight internal party battles, so have ministries within the security cluster, notably Intelligence, risen in political stature and (it would appear) have been incorporated within decision making at the highest political levels.

The outer circle of political power would appear to have two principal elements. First, it is composed in major part of those national ministers not included within the inner circle. This does not mean that these ministries are not important in their own terms, for no one would deny the consequence of portfolios such as Education and Justice. However, whether their occupants find themselves within the inner circle will depend heavily upon their political weight and circumstance. Second, this outer tier would also seem to include individuals who enjoy major political influence and/or hold high position within the ruling party. Additionally, the highest circles of political power are, necessarily, sustained by the topmost ranks of the civil service, who join them in constituting the equivalent of Mills's political directorate (notwithstanding the tensions that seem so common between ministers and their directors general, the most high-ranking government bureaucrats).

It is notable that this particular identification of the political directorate gives greater priority to the state than it does to the ruling party, whereas – particularly in its immediate post-Polokwane mood – the ANC insisted that it was pre-eminent, and claimed to demonstrate this when, in September 2008, it 'recalled' Mbeki from the presidency. As it happened, Mbeki chose to obey the injunction (although, constitutionally, he could have put the decision to a vote of no confidence in Parliament). It is clear that, with the rise of the ANC 'party-state' the relative power of party and state will fluctuate and Booysen (2011: 369-372) sees the party assuming considerably more weight under the Zuma presidency. Certainly, the post-Polokwane dynamic whereby government actions were heavily influenced by President Zuma's battle to secure his (contested) return as president of the ANC at the party's congress at Mangaung in December 2012 points to party considerations playing a significant role in official decision making in particular instances. A major example of such instances is the deal between Cosatu and the ANC to suspend the government's introduction of 'e-tolling' to Gauteng motorways in May 2012 (this following the formation of an unlikely alliance between Cosatu, the Democratic Alliance (DA), business interests and an 'Opposition to Urban Tolling Alliance' that pressed its case through a combination of demonstrations and court action).[8] It is, however, generally occupancy of a state position which provides individuals with the capacity to make key decisions. Individuals within government may be constrained by broad party policies, but the extent to which these limit the autonomy of decision makers in practice is limited, for official party resolutions are usually subject to variant interpretations,[9] with ministers consistently claiming that their actions, whatever they are, have been determined in accordance with the party line.

Ultimately, the political power elite is defined by the nature of its decisions. Generally, these are both *national* in their implications and *formative* in that they shape policy and outcomes, sometimes in the teeth of opposition from even within the ruling party. The classic instance remains the government's adoption of Gear in 1996. This significant shift from the broadly social-democratic tenor of the RDP to a much more vigorously pro-market policy was announced at short notice to startled ANC MPs from above, and was declared to be non-negotiable. Subsequently, the broadly pro-market thrust of economic policy has been maintained, notwithstanding its assuming more politically correct guises. Although, in recent years, the government has come to adopt a more interventionist posture centred around increased state spending on infrastructure, this would appear to follow as much from the failure of private investment flows to live up to expectations and to create jobs as from the ANC's consequentially assertive emphasis upon the virtues of a 'developmental state'.

Apart from exercising their authority over non-national spheres and being subject to considerable (state and party) control from above, provincial premiers and their executive office holders, along with those presiding over local government, have far more limited scope to shape policies, and are largely restricted to the sphere of implementation, thus tending to be judged in their success by the efficiency of their 'delivery'. Together with the broad body of the Tripartite Alliance (which links the South African Communist Party (SACP) and the Congress of South African Trade Unions (Cosatu) to the ANC), they appear to operate at the equivalent of Mills's middle level of power, where their influence over the elite is largely one of *constraint*. In individual instances, such as a particular industrial relations dispute with either state or private employers, bodies like Cosatu and its individual unions may be popularly portrayed as exercising 'veto power'. However, this term – beloved by American pluralists – fails to capture the fluidity that normally obtains in power relationships. Trade unions may use their strategic weight to secure gains for their members, yet they can rarely dictate terms to either government or employers, and they end up in a situation of bargaining. Similarly, there were many within the ANC and the Alliance who despaired at the tragic consequences of Thabo Mbeki's insistence that HIV did not cause AIDS, but they felt powerless to contest the resulting policy decisions openly. It was only after various judgements in the Constitutional Court ruled government policy unconstitutional and civil society mobilisation rendered the presidential line politically costly, that doubters within the Cabinet felt sufficiently brave to compel Mbeki to withdraw from the fray and for government to shift its ground in conformity with scientific rationality. Similarly, although the unprecedented combination of protest against the Protection of Information Bill between the parliamentary opposition, civil society groups and the media interests contributed to the government re-drafting its content significantly during 2011, this was equally an outcome of its belated recognition that an unchanged Bill would be thrown out by the Court.

This particular instance suggests that the one institution that may have *veto power* over government is the higher judiciary, culminating in the authority of the Constitutional Court. Does this mean that those who sit on the Constitutional Court should themselves be included within the national power elite? Certainly, the Court has handed down significant judgements declaring state actions to have been unconstitutional. During 2011, it was apprehension that a case brought by activist Terry Crawford-Browne would likely result in the Court's instruction to the president to institute an inquiry into the notorious 1998 arms deal that resulted in the government's taking pre-emptive action, announcing the establishment of a judicial inquiry over whose terms of reference it would have greater control than if these had been laid down by the Court itself. However, although the Court has on occasion adopted formative positions, instructing government (at different levels) to take particular courses of action, its capacity to enforce such judgements has in practice proved limited.

Mills was largely silent on the role of the Supreme Court in the US, although the thrust of his argument suggests that he thought its capacity to constrain the power elite had diminished with the rise of the military-industrial complex. In contemporary South Africa, I would argue, the high judiciary – more independent than it was under apartheid – remains alongside, but outside, the power elite. Worryingly, however, there are mounting indications that the political directorate is increasingly restive with constitutional constraint, and will take what actions it can to erode the veto powers of the Constitutional Court and to diminish the state's public accountability under the Constitution.

THE CHANGING SHAPE OF SOUTH AFRICA'S CORPORATE STRUCTURE

The composition of the political elite is relatively easy to identify because politicians are the focus of concerted attention in the media. In contrast, identification of those who form the corporate elite is considerably more difficult, not least because many leading corporate power holders prefer relative obscurity and are skilled at hiding behind their high suburban walls. There are classic questions to be confronted. How do we relate wealth to power? As Mills stressed, the modern corporation is the fount of wealth, but it does not follow that the wealthy are automatically the makers of key decisions, for some will be passive shareholders and have their wealth managed for them. In South Africa, as in other contemporary capitalist societies, control of corporations has to a considerable extent moved away from the owners of capital to managers, the most senior of whom are the ones who actively exercise corporate power. Again, private ownership of large corporations has largely given way to institutional ownership, with bodies like banks, unit trusts and pension funds holding significant investments in the actual companies that make things or dig minerals out of the ground, suggesting a shift of power and influence to asset managers and those who make investment decisions.

The corporate structure has evolved around an MEC that by virtue of its weight and linkages has played a determining role throughout the rest of the economy. The origins of the MEC lay in gold mining. After exhaustion of surface gold deposits, the economies of scale required by deep mining demanded enormous amounts of investment and led to an early concentration of capital. By the early 1930s, the fifty-seven goldmining companies were, with minor exceptions, controlled by six finance houses or groups. The conglomerate forms that developed thereafter were extensions of this oligopoly. Subsequently, notably during and after the 1960s, the economy gravitated away from its dependence on gold and diamonds to a range of other raw and processed materials, with the growth, *inter alia*, of coal, ferrochrome, platinum, vanadium and copper mining. The smelting, refining and supply chain activities required by these served as a major stimulus to manufacturing, which developed more around primary production than import-substitution production of consumer goods under the shelter of protection (Fine and Rustomjee 1996: 96-118).

Apartheid provided the conditions for the greater concentration of capital, as the major mining houses diversified further into manufacturing, as finance capital diversified into both, and as English and Afrikaner capital steadily merged their interests with each other and foreign capital. A further development was a greater interpenetration of private capital and the parastatals, of which the major ones – Eskom, Transnet, Sasol and the Industrial Development Corporation (IDC) – had themselves played a dominant role in lubricating the wheels of the MEC. By 1981, over 70 per cent of the total assets of the top 138 companies were controlled by state corporations and eight privately owned conglomerates spanning mining, manufacturing, construction, transport, agriculture and finance. Further concentration was to come as, with mounting political crisis, foreign companies disinvested and sold their assets locally. Unable to invest widely abroad during late apartheid, the conglomerates invested their excess capital by buying local assets that were often distant from their core business. By 1990, just three conglomerates – Anglo American, Sanlam and Old Mutual – controlled a massive 75 per cent of the total capitalisation on the Johannesburg Stock Exchange (JSE). However, the opening up of the economy through the transition to democracy brought about a dramatic change in the

capital market. First, the conglomerates chose to 'realise shareholder value' by an exten-
sive process of 'unbundling'. Second, the opening up of the economy encouraged major
South African corporations to go global alongside a (limited) inflow of foreign capital
(Southall 2010).

The non-core assets of the conglomerates were largely taken up by institutional investors, both public (for instance, the Public Investment Corporation) and private (pension
funds), as well as by new black beneficiaries of various state black economic empowerment (BEE) schemes, players who were, in turn, backed by the banks and institutional investors themselves. Unbundling had a significant effect upon the big three and
the other major conglomerates. Most notably, whereas in 1992 Anglo controlled some
eighty-six JSE-listed companies, by 2008 it had become a more focused miner with
holdings of more than 25 per cent in only four: AngloGold Ashanti, Anglo Platinum,
Kumba and Tongaat Hulett. A proportion of the unbundled assets were taken up by the
renewed inflow of international capital. Against this, from 1997, amid a general relax-
ation of exchange controls, the government granted permission for some of the largest
South African companies – notably, Billiton, South African Breweries, Anglo American,
Old Mutual and Liberty Life – to move their primary listings from the JSE to London,
thereby facilitating their evolution into major multinationals. In short, the transition
provided the conditions under which significant domestic funds could exit South Africa
and foreign capital could come in, this facilitated by Johannesburg's moving to become
the continent's primary financial centre for global capital. Indeed, the growing financialisation of the South African economy (the growing influence of the banks and private
investment institutions) has, in the view of some, seen the shift from the dominance of
the MEC to that of a minerals-energy-finance complex (MEFC). The appropriateness of
this term is indicated by Table 1.

By late 2010, there were some 405 companies listed on the JSE, with a market capitalisation of R5 772 billion. Of these, the top twenty by market capitalisation were as follows:

Table 1 indicates that although the degree of concentration of ownership has reduced
considerably since the early 1990s, and though 'unbundling' has made a significant
impact upon company rankings, the extent to which the JSE remains dominated by a
small number of companies – with just five corporations responsible for over a third of
total market capitalisation and the top ten responsible for over half – remains very high.
Meanwhile, further examination reveals that out of the top twenty, eight operate in the
minerals and energy sector directly; six operate in the financial sector; two in mobile
telecoms; and the other three in brewing, tobacco and multimedia, demonstrating the
continuing domination of the corporate structure by companies directly engaged in the
MEC. This is illustrated by Table 2, which indicates that, together, mining and finance
account for over half of the total market capitalisation of firms on the JSE.

Table 1: Top twenty companies on JSE, November 2010

Company	Market capitalisation (R billions)+	Percentage of total JSE market capitalisation
BHP Billiton	559	9.7
British American Tobacco	523	9.1
Anglo American	416	7.2
SAB Miller	373	6.5
MTN Group	228	4.0
Total % market capitalisation top five	*2099*	*36.4*
Sasol	202	3.5
Compagnie Fin Riche	202	3.5
Anglo Platinum	174	3.0
Standard Bank Group	162	2.8
Naspers	144	2.5
Total % market capitalisation top ten	*2983*	*51.7*
Kumba Iron Ore	128	2.2
Impala Platinum	128	2.2
AngloGold Ashanti	125	2.2
FirstRand	113	2.0
Vodacom	99	1.7
Absa	93	1.6
GoldFields	83	1.4
Old Mutual	76	1.3
Nedbank	64	1.1
Sanlam	55	1.0
Total market capitalisation top twenty	*3947*	*68.4*
Others (385)	1825	31.6
Total	5772	100.0

+ 1 billion = 1000 million

Source: Adapted from *Who Owns Whom* 2011: 45-50

Table 2: Market capitalisation of sectors as percentage of total JSE market capitalisation

Minerals and energy	
General mining	19.6
Platinum and precious metals	6.9
Gold mining	4.5
Other mining	3.3
Integrated oil and gas	3.6
Subtotal	*37.9*
Finance	
Banks	8.4
Life insurance	3.2
Investment services	1.2
Other finance	1.5
Subtotal	*14.4*
Industry and construction	*14.0*
Tobacco	*9.1*
Brewers	*6.5*
Telecoms	*6.2*
Retail	*4.1*
Other	*7.8*

Calculated from table of same name, *Who Owns Whom* 2011: 50-51. Allocation of some categories to sectors is inevitably arbitrary.

But how do we translate such information into identifying a corporate power elite, and what is the latter's relation to the holding of private wealth?

WEALTH, INCOME AND POWER IN SOUTH AFRICA'S CORPORATE SECTOR

It is more difficult to identify the powerful within the corporate structure than within the state. The political directorate was defined as those whose positions enable them to make decisions that have national-level implications, whether to decide economic policy, introduce a national health insurance system, sign a multibillion arms deal at taxpayers' expense with international arms companies, or increase social security benefits. In contrast, the decisions made by those who run South Africa's corporate sector may well have direct implications for the citizenry as a whole (the supply and pricing of electricity being one highly pertinent example), but more often decisions by major corporate power holders are likely to relate to particular economic sectors, their national effect being considerably more indirect. However, the corporate elite across the parastatal and private sectors make a multitude of investment and pricing decisions that have enormous consequences for citizens as employees, workers and consumers. The key difference, of course, between decisions made by power holders in the parastatals and those in the private sector is that the former are meant to be made in the public interest, whereas the latter are made in the interests of private shareholders and the bottom line.

An introduction to the contours of the corporate elite is provided by two sets of data that can serve as proxies for power.

First, we can identify the super-rich and link it to their key investments. In 2010, the wealth of the country's twenty richest men (only one woman made the top 100) according to disclosed shareholdings amounted to R102.6 billion.[10] At the top of the 'rich list' was Indian steel magnate Lakshmi Mittal, who owned 52 per cent of steel corporation ArcelorMittal, which had a market capitalisation of R33 billion in 2010. Second, and the richest South African, was mining executive Patrice Motsepe, worth R19.9 billion through his stakes in African Rainbow Minerals and Sanlam. Third was De Beers chairman Nicky Oppenheimer, based on his 2.5 per cent stake in Anglo American, worth R10.7 billion, but this excluded the Oppenheimer family's 40 per cent stake in diamond miner De Beers (delisted in 2001) and the Tswalu Kalahari Reserve, the largest private reserve in the country. Overall, the Oppenheimer family's wealth was listed as around R35 billion, ranking the family the 154th richest in the world.[11] Thereafter came:

- a list of highly placed individuals, for instance, Christo Wiese (R7.3 billion, nearly R6 billion of it held in Shoprite); Des Sacco (R5.1 billion, held in Assore Ltd); Stephen Saad (R4.2 billion, held in Aspen Pharmacare Holdings); Laurie Dippenaar (R3.05 billion, held in FirstRand); and Adrian Gore (R1.9 billion, in Discovery Holdings), who represent a mix of long established and more recent entrepreneurial wealth.
- the Ackerman family trust (R4.58 billion, held in Pick n Pay); and the Rembrandt trust (R4.4 billion held in Remgro Ltd), the investment vehicle of Johann Rupert (son of Anton Rupert, who started the Rembrandt group in the 1940s). Johann Rupert also holds a separate R672 million holding in Remgro;
- alongside Motsepe, three highly prominent black businessmen, Tokyo Sexwale (R1.9 billion, held in the Mvelaphanda Group and Mvelaphanda Resources); Cyril Ramaphosa (R1.55 billion, held largely in Assore – a mining holding company, the Bidvest Group and Standard Bank); and Lazarus Zim, coming in at number twenty with a fortune of R1.4 billion, largely held in Mvelaphanda Resources and Northam Platinum. Together, Motsepe, Sexwale, Ramaphosa and Zim represented the peak of the BEE elite (*Who Owns Whom 2011*: 59).

The majority of individuals located in the top twenty, and likewise in the top 100, held positions as chief executive officers or non-executive chairmen or directors in the companies in which they had major financial interests. At the very top, in other words, ownership was by no means cleanly separated from control, especially when around a 20 per cent holding in companies is likely to offer *de facto* control of voting on company boards.

The second set of data refers to the remuneration of the best paid directors. This indicates that it pays far better to be successful in the private sector than in the parastatals. In 2010, the top fifteen JSE-listed directors earned a total of R622 million compared with R1.024 billion in 2009 (the latter including a spectacular pay-out of R411 million by BHP Billiton to Chip Goodyear, who retired as CEO at the top of the commodity boom). In contrast, the top fifteen earners in state corporations earned a paltry R103 million in 2010 compared with R105 million in 2009. All the top earners are CEOs or senior executives, with those in the private sector reaping R143 million in performance bonuses and R123 million in gains in share prices, and some also picked up golden handshakes. Thus Pine Pienaar, who resigned as CEO of Mvelaphanda, and topped the list with a total income of R63.07 million, received a termination benefit of R34.45 million on top of a performance bonus of R22.38 million. Meanwhile, the R35 million paid to four parastatal CEOs who were unseated (Khaya Ngqula, SAA; Dali Mpofu, SABC; Siyabonga Gama, Transnet; and Jacob Maroga, Eskom) included handsome pay-out elements (*Who Owns Whom 2011*: 64-65).

The excessive remuneration paid to corporate high-flyers (publicly justified by the supposed need to reward their services in a globally competitive market for scarce skills) has caused outrage in a country where so many people are desperately poor (Pine Pienaar earned R37 500 an hour in 2010, more than most South Africans earn in a year).[12] Criticisms are given further bite by the continuing racialisation of incomes. In 2010, there was just one black (Jabu Mabuza, an executive of Hoskens Consolidated Investments), among the top twenty earners in the private sector, in contrast to the five whites among the top twenty earners in the lower-paying public sector in the same year. Yet income disparities along racial lines are merely an indicator of the deeper racialisation of wealth. Reports by two different private research companies found, variously, that just 7 per cent (Empowerdex) and 18 per cent (Trevor Chandler and Associates) of the share capital on the JSE was owned by black people in 2010 (SAIRR 2009-10: 279). More generally, however, we know too little about the wider distribution of wealth, the fundamental problem being that the government does not collect data relating to the ownership of assets (ranging through land ownership, holdings in shares and bonds, ownership of houses, and consumer durables), and multiple other difficulties such as lack of information regarding ownership of foreign assets, unincorporated businesses and unlisted corporations present themselves (Aron and Muellbauer 2004). Nonetheless, we may assume that there has been some challenge to racial disparities since Van Heerden (1996) using, largely, estate data, found that whites owned 90 per cent of South Africa's personal wealth. By 2011, according to Schussler (2011), net private ownership of assets (bonds, houses, shares, non-residential property) stood at R73 712 for Africans, R139 655 for coloureds, R360 838 for Indians and R952 511 for whites, which, if true, suggests a considerable narrowing in wealth distribution over the past two decades. However, just as Van Heerden (1996) found that 20 per cent of whites held more than 70 per cent of wealth in the early 1990s, so it is likely that ownership of wealth remains highly skewed towards the rich, not merely among whites, but also among the other former apartheid racial categories.

In drawing all this disparate data together we can venture the rather unsurprising proposition that the value of the financial investments of the rich and the remuneration of the top directors reflects corporate power, and that this is strongly weighted in favour of companies in mining and finance (including holding companies). The investments of fourteen out of the top twenty in the 2010 rich list are overwhelmingly held in mining and financial interests, and fully sixteen out of the top twenty earners are, similarly, directors of companies in mining and finance, the four exceptions being Paul Adams and Nic Durante of BAT, Graham Mackay of SAB Miller and James ('Japie') Basson of Shoprite. It is to be recalled that although wealth very easily translates into power, private wealth is generally diversified into different vehicles, as the rich entrust their wealth into the hands of institutions, large companies and their directors.

According to *Who Owns Whom* (2011: 43) fully 81 per cent of JSE market capitalisation was controlled by institutions (inclusive of major companies), up from 74.3 per cent in 2003 (the first year for which the calculation was made). This confirms that, although, as noted above, the very rich retain significant control over certain companies, ownership in South Africa has nonetheless become largely separated from direct control. This is underlined by the fact that only just over 8 per cent of the JSE's market capitalisation in 2010 was held by director-controlled companies (defined as directors holding in excess of 26 per cent of firms' market value with no other dominant shareholder). However, separation of ownership and control does not indicate a significant disjunction of interest between the very wealthy and their wealth managers. Shareholder activism in South Africa is generally reckoned to be even more limited than in most countries with developed corporate structures, and institutions that have the financial leverage to exercise control only rarely object to their directors rewarding themselves handsomely. Furthermore, although the South African corporate structure is the most advanced in Africa, in global terms it is not only relatively small, but also heavily concentrated in a few areas within the single city of Johannesburg. It is probable that the very wealthy and the directors of major companies live, work and play closely together, and have a highly developed sense of community of interest (communicated to a wider audience, for instance, via the weekday business programmes broadcast at peak hours on major radio stations). But how does corporate power relate to political power? To what extent is South Africa ruled by a coherent power elite?

THE SOUTH AFRICAN POWER ELITE: COHERENCE OR DISJUNCTION?

The suggestion early in this chapter that by the 1990s there had been a convergence among Marxist-revisionists and liberals around the idea of 'elite compromise' was in essence that the capitalist elite had had enough of apartheid and wanted to replace it with democracy. Terreblanche (2001) depicted this as the system of political legitimation falling in line with the mode of economic accumulation: the ANC gained control of the state under conditions of liberal democracy in exchange for accepting the existing structure and rules of capitalist economy. Nonetheless, even if we accept this paradigm, it remains remarkably difficult to decipher how economic weight is translated into political decisions. Let us recap the arguments of this chapter, and see how they fit together.

It is accepted that South Africa has distinctly identifiable political and economic elites. David Welsh (2009) has argued convincingly from the liberal position that the NP's adherence to apartheid strictures came at considerable cost to large-scale capital and to economic growth as a whole, although he demonstrates equally that, although capitalists only moved reluctantly into the embrace of majority rule, they had little direct influence over the ruling party. Whether or not we accept his interpretation *in toto*,[13] he makes it abundantly clear that the NP embodied a highly diverse set of political, religious and ideological interests, and was by no means the direct instrument of capital, Afrikaner or otherwise. Similarly today, the ANC is composed of a myriad jostling interests and factions, ranging from political conservatives to declared communists, from black business interests through 'tenderpreneurs' to the ANC Youth League, yet overall declaring itself the protector of the 'the people' and the poor. The ANC, in short, is most certainly *not* the tool of large-scale private capital, which is still overwhelmingly representative of white wealth and controlled by white directors. For a start, the ANC government's economic policy has involved numerous decisions and thrusts that have run against the direct interests of major business interests. The introduction, for instance, of new-order mineral rights under the Minerals and Petroleum Resources Development Act of 2002, which imparted to the state the ownership of all minerals in the ground, deeply upset large-scale mining capital, and there are other key areas (around the laws governing employment and which private employers deem to be 'inflexible') where the government espouses positions that are subject to constant criticism by business, big and small.

At the heart of the differences between the ANC and business is that the corporate structure is still highly racialised. During 2011, this was highlighted by the breakdown of the attempt to combine the interests of emergent black business and large-scale capital within one organisation, Business Unity South Africa, with accusations of racism by the former met by protestations of goodwill from the latter. Whatever the reality, the separation signalled severe tensions that will probably reverberate within the ruling party. Nonetheless, despite continuous sparrings around race, there are also major crossover points between government and large-scale white capital, although the extent to which there is a coherent 'black business elite' with distinctive interests remains an issue for concerted research.

BEE represents a strategy whereby the ANC has sought a deracialisation of capital, and whereby large-scale capital has sought to increase its leverage by creating a subaltern black capitalist class. A widespread critique of BEE is that its principal outcome has been to create a small grouping of very wealthy black businesspeople rather than to spread the benefits of capital ownership more widely, while simultaneously entrenching cronyism and corruption. Prominent black businesspersons who have made it to the top (notably Cyril Ramaphosa and Tokyo Sexwale) continue to wield significant influence within the ANC and presumably voice the interests of large-scale capital within the councils of the ruling party. Similarly, not only have the parastatals served as a platform for black managers to move profitably to the private sector, but state corporations also work very closely with large-scale capital, as instanced by Eskom's energetically proactive stance in favour of nuclear power. Again, crucial to a collaborative state-business relationship are the activities of state bodies such as the Industrial Development Corporation, the Development Bank of Southern Africa and the Public Investment Corporation, which direct huge investments into the path of private capital, and which, by their acquisition of shareholdings in major corporations, play a major role in the making of investment decisions.

Mills (1956: 276) identified an 'uneasy coincidence of economic, political and military power' in 1950s America rather than a coherent *ruling* class. Subsequently, Miliband (1969) was to assert that although a plurality of elites in capitalist society might constitute a *dominant* class, this did not necessarily make them a *ruling* class. The question, he asserted, was not whether this class had a substantial measure of political power and influence, but whether 'it also exercises a much greater degree of power and influence than any other class; whether it exercises a *decisive* degree of political power; whether its ownership and control of crucially important areas of economic life also ensures its control of the means of political decision making in the particular environment of advanced capitalism' (Miliband 1969: 45). To become a ruling class, a dominant class had to translate its dominance into the effective control of the state and its policies.

In today's South Africa, reflective of the country's divided history, there is an uneasy coexistence of largely racialised political and corporate elites who, though differing on lesser-order issues, agree upon major fundamentals or latter-day 'common sense' centred around the functioning of the market economy, with large corporations (especially those that dominate the JSE) exercising '*disciplinary*' power through their capacity to choose to invest or to withhold investment, and even to export capital in response to government policies.[14] If in post-1994 South Africa, therefore, we choose to argue the strong claim that the state is the committee of the ruling class, then we simultaneously need to admit that the latter is a committee that remains significantly divided by the inherent factionalism of ANC politics and perceived differences between the government and business (and within business?) along lines of race. Indeed, the disjuncture between the major concentrations of power within the political and corporate elites allows considerable space for other less powerful forces within society. At the middle level of power, notably at provincial and local levels, ambitious factions jostle for influence, money and tenders, whereas opposition parties, trade unions and civil society groups lobby the ANC and government around matters of class, sectional, and general interest within an untidy but lively democracy.

Power remains grossly unevenly distributed within South Africa and, unsurprisingly, continues to favour the powerful, and the country remains one of the most unequal in the world, even though liberal democracy has to some limited extent brought about a deracialisation of inequality. Whether the elites have the political will and economic guile to respond creatively to pressures from below by promoting more socially and racially inclusive growth will determine the future course and fate of South African democracy.

NOTES

1   Key texts in the debate included Davies et al. (1976), Bozzoli (1981) and Lipton (1979, 1985).
2   This exaggerates the polarity between the two positions. A survey of the power elite at the height of apartheid indicated that the political and economic power holders agreed on the basic principles of white rule while differing around tactics, yet Heribert Adam (1971), the author, was scarcely a Marxist.
3   For instance, there has as yet been no equivalent of the 'Kenya debate' of the 1970s and early 1980s which sought to illuminate and theorise the relationship between the post-colonial Kenyan state, the emergent African bourgeoisie and corporate capital (see, *inter alia*, Leys 1975, 1996 and Swainson 1977).
4   As Leys noted some time ago, the theory of the post-colonial state rested heavily on the argument of Hamza Alavi's (1972) notion of the 'over-developed' state. This argued that, on the basis of a colonial state which served the interests of metropolitan capital and had no roots in colonial society, incoming post-colonial political elites inherited military and administrative apparatuses that were 'over-developed' in relation to other classes.
5   Annual per capita incomes have increased from R46 486 for whites, who constitute just 9 per cent of the population, and R5 073 for Africans, 79 per cent of the population, at 2000 prices in 1993 to R75 297 and R9 790 respectively in 2008 (SAIRR 2009-10: 252).
6   See Welsh (2009: 467-475) for details of De Klerk's major showdown with rebellious senior officers of the South African Defence Force from late 1992.
7   For elaboration of the evolution and development of the MEC see Fine and Rustomjee (1996).
8   The e-toll saga (which is far from over) invites serious analysis regarding how decisions are made and how power is exercised, and for whom. Clearly the government seriously underestimated the depth of popular resistance to e-tolling. After making a major concession to the taxi industry (which would be exempted from tolls), it ultimately conceded suspension of e-tolling following a deal between Cosatu and the ANC that in effect took the decision temporarily out of government hands. Given Zuma's need for Cosatu's support at Mangaung, he could not afford a major confrontation with labour. However, the indications were that the government remained determined to introduce e-tolling in some form, at a later stage. A recent court judgement in the government's favour (just prior to this book going to press) has reopened the door to e-tolling, and has raised the issue of whether the very diverse coalition of interests that opposed it will remain united.
9   Thus Lindsay (2012), for instance, argues how, despite overarching laws supposedly defining BEE, in practice the different arms of government have different understandings of BEE, as well as different goals.
10   The 'rich list', published annually in the *Sunday Times*, is compiled by the research staff of *Who Owns Whom*. Concentration on the top twenty, rather than the entire 100 wealthy people who compose the list, is by no means entirely arbitrary. In 2011, the top twenty accounted for more than 70 per cent of the wealth of South Africa's richest people (*Sunday Times*, 4 September 2011). Note that other individuals, such as entertainers, sports stars and owners of unlisted businesses may conceivably have been as rich as those in the top 100, but if so, their wealth was not visibly invested on the JSE.
11   The Oppenheimers announced their decision to sell their 40 per cent stake in De Beers to Anglo American for US$5.1 billion in November 2011, severing a connection it had had with the company since Ernest Oppenheimer seized control of it from the company of Cecil Rhodes in 1927.

12   For an invaluable review of the entire issue of executive remuneration, see Crotty and Bonorchis (2006).
13   We might well argue that even if capitalists found apartheid increasingly costly, the overwhelming majority viewed it as preferable to the ANC and the perceived prospect of socialism.
14   It was reported in early 2012 that South African corporate cash deposits were sitting at over R500 billion, with companies reluctant to invest in major new investments within South Africa, in considerable part because of lack of confidence in government policies and capacities.

REFERENCES

Adam, H (1971) The South African power elite: A survey of ideological commitment. In H Adam (Ed.) *South Africa: Sociological Perspectives*. Oxford: Oxford University Press.

Alavi, H (1972) The state in post-colonial societies. *New Left Review*, 74, 1972, pp.59-81.

Aron J and J Muellbauer (2004) Revised Estimates of Personal Sector Wealth for South Africa, The Centre for the Study of African Working Economies, Oxford University, Paper 224.

Bond P (2000) *Elite Transition: From Apartheid to Neoliberalism in South Africa*. Scottsville: University of KwaZulu-Natal Press.

Bozzoli B (1981) *The Political Nature of a Ruling Class: Capital and Ideology in South Africa 1890-1933*. London: Routledge and Kegan Paul.

Booysen S (2011) *The African National Congress and the Regeneration of Political Power*. Johannesburg: Wits University Press.

Crotty A and R Bonorchis (2006) *Executive Pay in South Africa*. Cape Town: Double Storey.

Davies R, D Kaplan, M Morris and D O'Meara (1976) Class struggle and the periodisation of the State in South Africa. *Review of African Political Economy*, 7: pp.4-30.

Fine B and Z Rustomjee (1996) *The Political Economy of South Africa: From Minerals-Energy Complex to Industrialisation*. London: Hurst.

Freund B (2006) State, capital and the emergence of a new power elite in South Africa: 'Black economic empowerment' at national and local levels. Paper to Harold Wolpe Trust Tenth Anniversary Colloquium, 'Engaging silences and unresolved issues in the political economy of South Africa', 21-23 September, Cape Town.

Leys C (1975) *Underdevelopment in Kenya: The Political Economy of Neo-Colonialism*. London: Heineman.

Leys C (1976) The 'overdeveloped' post colonial state: A re-evaluation. *Review of African Political Economy*, 5, 39-48.

Leys C (1996) *The Rise and Fall of Development Theory*. London, Bloomington, Indiana, and Nairobi: James Currey, Indiana University Press and East African Educational Publishers.

Lindsay D (2011) BEE reform: The case for an institutional perspective. In Daniel J, P Naidoo, D Pillay and R Southall (Eds) *New South African Review 2: New Paths, Old Compromises*. Johannesburg: Wits Univeristy Press.

Lipton M (1979) The debate about South Africa: Neo-Marxists and neo-liberals. *African Affairs*, 78: pp.57-80.

Lipton M (1986) *Capitalism and Apartheid: South Africa, 1910-1986*. Aldershot: Wildwood House.

Lodge T (2002) *Politics in South Africa: From Mandela to Mbeki*. Cape Town and Oxford: David Philip and James Currey.

Miliband R (1969) *The State in Capitalist Society:The Analysis of the Western Power System*. London: Weidenfeld and Nicholson.

Mills CW (1956) *The Power Elite*. New York: Oxford University Press.

Prewitt K and A Stone (1973) *The Ruling Elites: Elite Theory, Power and American Democracy*. New York, Evanston, San Francisco, London: Harper & Row.

Simpson G (1989) The politics and economics of the armaments industry in South Africa. In Cock J and L Nathan (Eds) *War and Society: The Militarisation of South Africa*, Cape Town: David Phillip.

Schussler M (2011) www.Economists.co.za (March).

South African Institute of Race Relations (2010) *South Africa Survey 2009/2010.* Johannesburg: SAIRR.

Southall R (2010) South Africa: From short-term success to long-term decline? In Daniel J, P Naidoo, D Pillay and R Southall (Eds) *New South African Review 1, 2010: Development or Decline?* Johannesburg: Wits University Press.

Swainson N (1977) The rise of a national bourgeoisie in Kenya. *Review of African Political Economy*, 8, 39-55.

Taylor S (2007) *Business and State in Southern Africa: The Politics of Economic Reform.* Boulder: Lynne Rienner.

Terreblanche S (2002) *A History of Inequality in South Africa 1652-2002.* Scottsville and Sandton: University of Natal Press and KMM Review Publishing.

Van Heerden J (1996) The Distribution of Personal Wealth in South Africa. *South African Journal of Economics*, 64, 4, 278-291.

Welsh D (2009) *The Rise and Fall of Apartheid.* Johannesburg and Cape Town: Jonathan Ball.

Who Owns Whom in South Africa (2011) 31st edition. Johannesburg: Who Owns Whom.

CHAPTER 2

The ANC circa 2012-13:
Colossus in decline?

Susan Booysen

INTRODUCTION

Nineteen years into formal state power, the African National Congress (ANC) – by 2012-13 and in the presidency of Jacob Zuma – had reached the point where its political power remained formidable but, by all available indicators, beyond its peak. In the wake of the Mangaung elective conference, ANC leadership structures were taking stock of where the leadership battle had been taking the movement. There were two strands in this assessment process. The Zumaists publicly proclaimed that the ANC was stronger than ever, united, and at the pinnacle of its achievements. By contrast, others in the ANC expressed concern about Zuma's leadership, the quality of governance and, in particular, organisational weaknesses that had compounded deficits in government.

This raises questions as to how the ANC has been going about building and regenerating its power since political liberation. The process of shedding – being 'beyond peak' – has been far from fatal; the ANC retains a huge buffer of power, inclusive of popular and electoral support, over all party political rivals. Yet, the apparent turn to shedding power, rather than further accumulating and consolidating it, poses the challenge of identifying and dissecting the processes or mechanisms through which, and the manner in which, the ANC has been regenerating (even if imperfectly) its power. The unpacking of ANC power through these 'mechanisms' also helps concretise assessments of ANC strengths and weaknesses, of the state of ANC power, circa 2012 going into 2013.

This chapter has two objectives: conceptually, to identify and expound on such mechanisms; and analytically, to assess the state of ANC power regeneration in 2012-13 through the seven mechanisms that the analysis brings to the surface (Figure 1). Some of these mechanisms were automatically bequeathed to the ANC through the predominant political culture (given the ANC's status as former liberation movement) while others were consciously designed and nurtured. Some are common to South African political parlance while others were coined in the context of power (re)generation in ANC operations. It is hoped that the collective consideration of the mechanisms will contribute to an understanding of the ANC and the generation of political power, and in particular of the specifics of ANC power in the current political conjuncture.

The research and conceptualisations are largely anchored in the author's book, *The African National Congress and the Regeneration of Political Power* in which the primary organising principle and the framework for analysis are the mechanisms as they emerge over time and across domains of power. The chapter recasts and synthesises the book's analysis up to the early 2013 post-Mangaung period.

The mechanisms represent the operational principles in the ANC's project for the regeneration of its political power as party-movement and party-in-government. The mechanisms are: first, the ANC as *embodying the identity and aspirations of a large proportion of South Africans*; second, *casting the ANC as disciplined movement of the left*; third, *propagation of the two-phase transition* towards the 'national democratic society'; fourth, *drawing on the extended liberation movement dividend*; fifth, *parallel democracy and internalisation of opposition*; sixth, *the two worlds, of elections and 'the rest of the time'*; and, seventh, *control over state power* for generating hegemony and patronage, besides delivery.

The mechanisms apply across the four domains of ANC power: the ANC organisationally, in relation to the people, in multiparty politics and elections, and in state and government. The ANC uses the mechanisms for the retention and regeneration of its political power which it gained courtesy of political history (including the battles against colonialism and apartheid), political culture and movement ethos-tradition post-1994 governance.

This chapter first positions the ANC in the contemporary power stakes and then delves into this set of general assertions about the state of the ANC.

THE ANC AND 'POLITICAL POWER'

A review of ANC political power across the domains or 'faces' of organisation, people, elections and state shows the complexities of the ANC's retaining a vast amount of power, yet simultaneously suffering losses and decay and working to counteract them. By the end of its centenary year, the ANC as party-movement and party-in-government was working at retaining its organisational stature (defensively and reactively) and at achieving the greater realisation of its ideals in government (often meekly and stated in terms of anticipated and long-term fruition). The ANC had, by all indications, moved beyond its peak in power, imperfect as its realisation of this power since 1994 has been (Booysen 2011: 480-498).

Power leverages the ANC's ability, for example, to remain legitimately in control as government, to effect decisions and to gain compliance. There was no doubt that by 2012-13 the ANC was still firmly in charge of the 'balance between control and consent that governs the relation between ruler and the ruled', in the phrase used by Chabal (1992:5) to minimally define political power. The ANC's period in formal political power – state power – had not only transformed South African politics, the people and the state, but had also further legitimised the ANC's hold. It also brought changes which transformed the movement itself. After eighteen years plus in power, the ANC had become an organisation vastly changed from the one that waged the anti-apartheid liberation war and the one that governed South Africa in the early post-apartheid years. Power changed the ANC in ways that, by 2012, were undermining but not fatally derailing its potential for sustained power.

The foundation of contemporary ANC power remains its status as liberation movement, yet after close to twenty years in government its power extends well beyond this base. Through its being elected to govern and to occupy the positions of government and state power, a layer of power follows in which the ANC needs to be *seen* to be making progress in pursuit of ideals shared by the party and the people, or being *believed* to be better able to do so than opposition parties. Indubitably, although the ANC had a considerable amount of delivery to show, basic (previously existing or newly generated) social needs often remain unfulfilled. South Africans also expect continuous delivery, and they expect *their government* to be working for them in exchange for the power bequeathed. Power gives leaders and incumbents financial rewards; the status associated with position in the ANC and with representing the ANC in state and government brings power, prestige and privilege (Booysen 2011). In the process of governing, however, many of the representatives, bureaucrats and political deployees associated with the ANC also became corrupted in ways that triggered ANC self-deprecation, and disrespect for the movement. A second vulnerability was that the ANC leadership (often factional throughout the times of Thabo Mbeki and Zuma) triggered scorn through its appropriation of the 'right' to own the movement in the name of a faction constituted through manufactured or manipulated conference majorities. But in both the Mbeki and Zuma epochs the ANC was also shown to be organisationally resilient, capable at critical times of reinventing itself, and sustaining the impression that it was capable of some form of regeneration that would match the demands of the time.

The essential 2012-13 question, in terms of pivotal organisational power, is the extent to which the status of the ANC – as the commanding party and with its status as a liberation struggle icon – was a guarantor of access to private and corporate funding. The ANC's Pallo Jordan, for example, has argued that the ANC's current problems are anchored in its past failure to deal sufficiently with issues of public morality (Jordan 2008). Patronage is a serious consideration. Blade Nzimande, ANC-SACP, has said that it is the reason for

many political actors in the ANC to *not* express themselves or to mobilise against incumbents in internal ANC power struggles, for they fear that the incumbent would retain
power and cut their access to power and patronage (see Xundu 2009). The ANC has in
fact become a party of patronage, networked into a state of patronage.

The ANC acknowledges its weaknesses: careerism and the pursuit of individual power
and prestige (despite the '100 years of selfless struggle' centenary slogan) rather than the
unambiguous commitment to selfless service and overwhelmingly noble character of *the
ANC as liberation force in government*. Yet, despite its weaknesses, its internal wars and
its complex policy-ideological positioning, it remained the strongly dominant (and only
declining to a small degree) party political force in South Africa.

Democratically derived power comes from mandates and reservoirs of support that let
governments and their party political leaders get on with the job of governance. Electoral
mandates are crucial expressions of affirmative popular orientations. In South Africa
they constitute a periodic litmus test that tracks and summarises the ANC's popularity.
The trust and loyalty of the people are crucial to giving the ANC and the government
continuing power. Without these forms of power, governments rule by force, coercion,
outright violence or extensive propaganda and the manipulation of information in favour
of the governing party. The ANC has steered clear of force and coercion despite being
no stranger to manufacturing consent and limiting dissent through the enforcement of
discipline in intra-movement behaviour; in the extensive and state-aided promotion of
the dictums of its rule (such as the two-phase revolution-transition, continuous struggle
for liberations); and in flirting with the control of information (Booysen 2011).

Figure 1: Seven mechanisms in the ANC's regeneration of political power

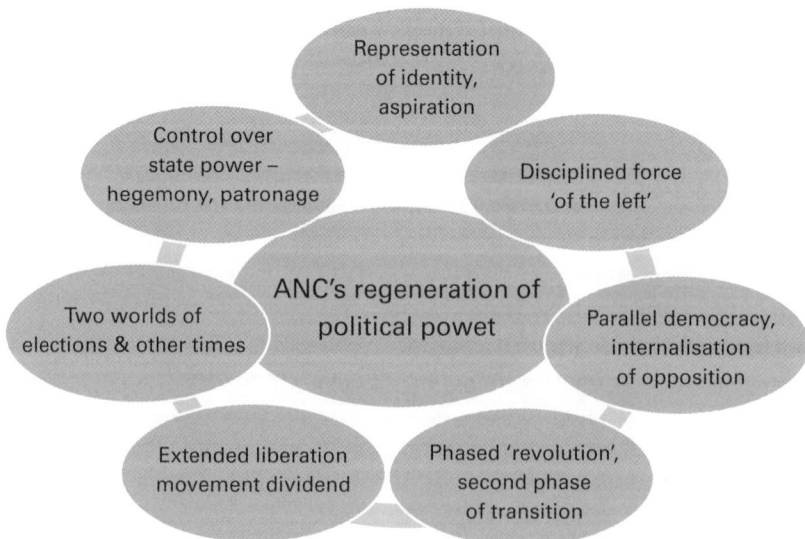

Table 1: Application of the mechanisms for the ANC's regeneration of political power across four domains

Seven mechanisms for the regeneration of ANC political power	Organisation	People	Elections	State
Representing struggle and post-struggle identity and aspirations	A	A	A	B
Disciplined movement 'of the left'	A	C	C	C
Parallel democracy and internalisation of opposition	A	A	B	C
Two-phase revolution and second transition	C	A	B	C
Extended liberation movement dividend	C	A	A	B
Two worlds of elections and 'other times'	B	C	A	C
Control over state power for hegemony and patronage	A	C	C	A

Key: A: strong presence /use; B: not predominant, but important; C: also evidence of usage.
(Source: Booysen 2011; continuous 2012 monitoring by the author.)

The sections that follow here present, in broad brushstrokes, a selection of trends in the operation of the mechanisms up to early 2013. The focus is, first, on establishing successes in the mechanism contributing to the (re)generation of ANC power. The second focus is on complications that have been arising, undermining the ANC's regeneration of political power, and it thus encompasses points of weakness, decay and uncertainty about the longer-term full capability for regeneration. The mechanisms are interdependent and the sections also highlight main points of conjunction.

REPRESENTING IDENTITY AND ASPIRATIONS

The ANC's symbolical representation of the political identity and aspirations of a broad spectrum of South Africans – often irrespective of their sense of celebration of, or their desperation with, the movement – offers one of the most potent mechanisms of continuing ANC power. In many ways the ANC is synonymous with the struggle against apartheid-colonialism (despite the objections of the Pan Africanist Congress of Azania and the Black Consciousness Movement). The ANC's occupation of the position of top-power is an unbroken reminder of an identity that encompasses dignity and human rights – even more so in comparison with the pre-liberation past. This mechanism has a first-order status and an impact (hitherto overwhelmingly positively) on ANC power across the domains of organisation, people, elections and state (see Table 1).

The ANC is determined to ensure that this mechanism remains alive. It continuously brings struggle history into the present (see Zuma 2012), albeit realised below par in its 2012 centenary year. It projects current struggles for improved government as the second phase of ongoing transition, which it theoretically distinguishes from a 'second stage of the transition' (see mechanism four). The ANC (2012b: 2) argued that the 'transition in the current South African context refers to a single and ongoing transition from apartheid colonialism to a National Democratic Society. The moment we are moving into is therefore best understood as a second phase of this transition.' The ANC thrives on being the longest-existing and most trusted agency for transformation. In the January 2012 Mangaung centenary celebrations, the ANC projected itself as the full embodiment of struggle history (there is only occasional recognition of the other movements, for example on Human Rights Day 2012, formerly Sharpeville Day). This ANC orientation is largely reflected in popular dispositions – where the ANC has no effective challengers for the status of liberation icon.

Complications become evident, however, in the three current ANC problems of quality of cadreship, state institutional-capacity problems to bring policy and ideals to fruition, and the ability of deployed cadres to bring home the delivery offerings that closely match the liberation benchmarks. The discussion of the complications associated with the other mechanisms has frequently related back to these three interactive core ANC problems.

The quality and motivation of cadreship has been under discussion at least since 1998 (Ngculu 2012) and has found expression in the document 'Through the eye of the needle' (ANC 2001). Issues of morality and commitment to serve dominated, and found frequent expression in organisational f(r)actional battles, which have been superimposed onto state institutions (Booysen 2011: 357-403). ANC cadreship often showed up in power mongering and influence peddling, rather than unambiguous service. This reality did not escape the eye of the people, but also did not destroy the ANC's bond with the people. The movement kept its link with the people alive by pronouncing (albeit selectively) against leaders' and ordinary members' corrupt or self-centred demeanour. This was done in discussion documents, conference resolutions and public speeches, in its reliance on the visibility of the work of those ANC leaders who had not succumbed, and in continuous internal scheming for the replacement of leaders.

THE ANC AS A 'DISCIPLINED FORCE OF THE LEFT'

The notion of being 'a disciplined force' (of the left) has been crucial to holding the ANC together and facilitating its positioning as a powerful party-movement, especially in the period since 2007. The building blocks of the disciplined force of the left, and its revolutionary rhetoric, had appeared as far back as in documentation around the Morogoro (1969) and Kabwe (1985) conferences, although the components first really started hanging together in the ANC 2006 January 8th Statement. The rhetoric builds up from there onwards and the *de facto* rallying calls flow thick and fast in the period from

2010 to 2012. The higher the manifestation of internal contest, and the more pervasive the evidence that the ANC was on a non-revolutionary path, albeit in government with an extensive social security-social wage presence, the more fervent were the reminders of the (claimed) status of 'disciplined force of the left' (see ANC January 8th Statements, 1990-2012).

The ANC's membership and support are massive and its organisational politics often substitutes for national-level contestation. It has a diverse, 'broad church' character. There are many leaders and associated groupings (often amounting to factions) that vie for control over the organisation and enclaves of the state. The ANC's evident willingness to enforce discipline, albeit partial and largely against factions agitating for leadership change, has helped to contain outbreaks of outright and divisive organisational warfare (and, on occasion, policy or ideological disputes). In the times of the ANC Youth League (ANCYL) 2011-12 revolt, however, discipline also served to foster factional dominance. In the early phases of Zuma's bid to retain the ANC presidency he was in effect pitched against the Youth League of Julius Malema – the only ones brazen enough to openly defy the ban on campaigning for Mangaung – while also directing the enforcement of the ban (Booysen 2012d). The operation of this mechanism, that of the disciplined force, is mainly evident in the domain of the ANC as organisation. Its effects are also evident in ANC power in the other three domains identified in this analysis (Table 1).

The ANC's organisational culture of respect for elders and deference to leadership in general aids the application of the 'disciplined force', and directly relates to acceptance of 'democratic centralism' (see, for example, ANC 2000). The ANC's emphasis on discipline has a long history. In documentation on the Kabwe conference it was noted, for example, that 'comrades deployed in forward areas should be the "cream of the crop"', with high political understanding, exemplary discipline and sense of responsibility (ANC 1985).

Democratic centralism is widely accepted as the glue that helps hold the mass of the organisation together. It entails the acceptance of the collective wisdom of the leadership (after internal deliberation), and the belief that the organisation – including through contests and conflicts – will self-correct and emerge on an even keel and in control (Booysen 2011; also see Asmal 2007).

Gumede (2005:301) quotes the ANC's Jabu Moleketi in arguing that democratic centralism, and specifically the principle that everybody should support the leadership's decisions, ensured ANC cohesion in the days of exile. The ANC's turn to the armed struggle helped steer it towards democratic centralism. Its reorganisation as an exiled liberation movement aimed at seizing state power, and its links with the South African Communist Party (SACP), influenced the ANC to adopt communist-style bureaucratic methods of operation and a vanguard Leninist strategy, with democratic centralism as its organising principle (see Johnson 2002).

The ANC embraces democratic centralism not simply as the rule of the organisational elite over the masses. It prides itself on placing a premium on internal debate – even if this sometimes amounts merely to hosting the occasion. Control and central coordination are strong (also see Butler 2006; Giliomee et al. 2001:172-173; Pretorius 2006). Zuma

(2008) explained that in democratic centralism: '… once the organisation has taken decisions they are binding even to those who did not advocate them. In the ANC we put the organisation above the individual, the unity of the organisation is central and must be protected at all times.'

Democratic centralism entails that once the leadership has been accepted by the membership, the leadership rules, until another round of movement elections (indirect, mediated by branch delegates) takes place. It is the responsibility of the leadership and cadres to give effect to decisions. Internally, debate may continue after decisions have been taken. Lodge (2002:161) points out that in earlier ANC days democratic centralism, in combination with 'a constitutionally prescribed prohibition on factionalism, made it very difficult for any organised mobilisation to assert itself against leadership policy'. If democratic internal debate does not resolve matters, it is the leadership rulings that will have to be accepted and publicly defended.

The ANCYL's revolt had the potential to undermine the mechanism. It made public the processes of internal organisational challenges and accountability. Its series of challenges threatened to move the ANC from its anchors of liberation and ideological credibility, especially insofar as Malema, then the ANCYL president, wanted to capture the ideal of 'economic liberation' from the mother body and build himself as a cult figure (Booysen 2011: 156). Malema erred in overstepping the 'disciplined force of the left' line. He and his grouping assumed that the League was invincible in its right to be kingmaker but they blundered by attacking incumbent emperors of the 'disciplined force'. The assault unsettled the ruling strata and activated the ANC disciplinary apparatuses. The externalisation of these internal battles (see ANC 2011a) highlighted the extent to which the ANC, this 'disciplined force', had been succeeding in keeping contests and conflicts away from public dissection.

The run-up to the ANC's 53rd national elective conference at Mangaung in 2012 *generally* challenged the notion of 'disciplined force of the left' – courtesy of discipline being equated with *not* challenging the incumbents for positions. In a series of resolutions from 2010 onwards, the National Executive Committee (NEC) condemned premature campaigning, arguably with a view to affording incumbents the space in which to pursue policy and governance without the distraction of leadership contests. The resolutions culminated, effectively, into *no campaigning* for ANC elections: the nomination process that formally commenced in October 2012 was given as the start of campaigning (Booysen 2011: 64). Hence, in the name of internal discipline, incumbents were the *de facto* campaigners.

The delegitimisation of internal dissent and external debate on policy issues further help to preserve the ANC's disciplined movement character. The cases of Andrew Feinstein, Pregs Govender, Barbara Hogan and Ben Turok (see, for example, Brown 2009:8) illustrate the limitations of ANC internal debate. All four cases related to resistance or protest against controversial ANC operations and legislation, ranging from the arms deal to control of access to state information. The ANC's assertion that there is only one centre of power in the Tripartite Alliance, the ANC, and the fusion between state and party (as for example in ward committees, provincial executive committees (PECs) and the National Executive Committee (NEC) of the ANC ruling over Cabinet and provincial executives) means, furthermore, that ANC 'internal discipline' directly sets the parameters of debate and public participation.

The notion of direct (intra-party) democracy is evident in ANC leaders' reference to the ANC as 'the parliament of the people' (see Lodge 1999). In the aftermath of Polokwane 2007, intense factionalism, sensitivity to and suspicion of dissent and criticism prevailed (Sefara 2009). The ANC's toxic response to the disaffiliation of the Congress of the People (COPE) from the ANC was evident in its ruthless countermobilisation to gain intelligence on who was deviating and to exorcise them from positions and opportunities. It was done under the mantle of action against ill discipline, and 'inability to accept the will of the majority' (as established through a partly authentic, partly manufactured conference and later NEC majority). The ANC's Kaizer Mohau (2008) noted: 'this is ill discipline and … counter revolutionary' (also see Southall 2000). The ANC's primary objective was never to banish the COPE defectors for the sake of punishment. It was, rather, to contain National General Council (NGC) fallout and discourage future ANC splits.

It was a sign of the changing ANC, however, that democratic centralism had started losing some of its hold (Booysen 2011: 91-92). It seemed no longer to be a core value to many of the members, and especially among the leadership corps, as substantiated by Gwede Mantashe (2010), reporting to the Durban NGC:

> Infighting and destructive contestation in the structures of the ANC remain one of the many challenges facing the movement. The influence of money in our processes has the biggest potential to change the character of the movement from being people-centred and people-driven in all the processes, to one where power is wielded by a narrow circle of those who own and/or control resources. This is at the centre of the resurgence of factionalism in the movement where contestation is neither political nor ideological but driven by narrow interests.

The lines between discipline and succession contests were blurring. By the time of Mangaung it was nearly impossible to force the Polokwane genie back into the bottle. Evidence of new 'ill discipline' (others would say unsuppressed internal democracy) was manifested in dissident conferences and parallel branches in provinces and the Youth League. The manufacture of high membership figures and conference majorities to support factional slates were the biggest game in the ANC town.

The contradictory ideological positionings of the ANC were playing out in the run-up to Mangaung. The rhetoric of the ANC remained intensely left, as it had been in the days of Morogoro and Kabwe, but in effect the ANC had made substantial moves to the right of the ideological spectrum. There were national-socialist orientations evident in the fusion of party and state, growing emphasis on the role of the state and state enterprises in a developmental agenda, extensive party and family patronage networks at the centre of state delivery efforts, and the creation of patriotic capital ('resource nationalism') with black economic empowerment overtones.

PARALLEL DEMOCRACY AND INTERNALISATION OF OPPOSITION

The ANC commonly operates in two concurrent, occasionally intersecting democratic frameworks – in the inter-party liberal democratic domain, *and* in the internal democracy-democratic centralism mode. 'Parallel democracy' is thus evidenced in the ANC leadership's direct engagement, with both members and other supporters, in actions that do not get channelled through electoral processes. The ANC's relationship with 'the people' is complex and goes beyond voting. It is carried by a layer of discourse and engagement that has little bearing on electoral politics and the formal rules of the game. It is part of the ANC's powerful democracy that runs alongside electoral politics. This is the world of the ANC engaged with *its* people. Politically, the ANC uses between-election periods to ensure that, come election time, it will not be in electoral trouble.

The ANC rates highly the ability to appeal directly to the 'people' (the bulk of the population and in particular black Africans), and has enjoyed substantial patience and trust in its standing with the masses. Trust remains strong but is also fragile – largely due to corruption, occasionally perceived disdain for 'the masses' and absentee representation (Booysen 2011: 86-125). A more amorphous point of connection concerns the interfaces between party-movement and state. Several interfaces were cultivated in the Mbeki era – and the Zuma administration continued using them in adapted and elaborated styles, ranging from executive rule in the provinces to local ward committee operations.

Organisationally, the ANC, with the mechanism of 'disciplined movement', channels much of activist input and dissent directly into the movement's systems to deal with criticism of, and challenges to, leadership. There is emphasis on the right to differ, but equally on the obligation to keep differences internal. The ANCYL was disciplined for taking dissent and criticism into the public sphere. Tripartite Alliance summits that regularly followed in the Zuma period in the wake of critical public exchanges by the Congress of South African Trade Unions (Cosatu) reduced the impact of internal differences. It remains likely that even the fallout from the dominant ANC faction's far-reaching construction of Zuma's Mangaung majority (Booysen 2012e) will remain internal to the ANC. This is *one* of the ways 'internalisation of opposition' is used as a mechanism for the regeneration of ANC power.

The 'internalisation of opposition' (Booysen 2012a; 2012b; 2012c) is popularly manifested when communities erupt in protest yet, come election time, often overwhelmingly return the ANC to power. This mechanism redirects criticism and dissent away from the electoral arena. The essential script is: first vote ANC and then, during between-election periods, protest to get more attention and better action (Booysen 2011: 126-173; 2012b).

Effective internalised opposition is equally evident in the Tripartite Alliance. Many policy and succession contests *that mattered* unfolded here. Party politics was an important yet separate and comparatively marginalised show. The ANC often condemns alliance contestation, yet it is a substitute for externalised, inter-party fights (Booysen 2011: 448-452). Intra-alliance exchanges play an opposition role in challenging ideas and policies. It benefits the ANC's project to retain power in legitimising dissent and criticism (coming from sources with credibility), yet electorally redirecting the critiques back into the ANC.

With the SACP in Zuma times increasingly integrated into government, and claiming credit for the bulk of 'Zuma-ANC' policy initiatives (modest, often state-interventionist, and by early 2013 mostly still far from being realised), Cosatu's 'responsibility' grew. The period was characterised by several instances of acrimonious ANC-Cosatu contestation. For example, Cosatu named some Cabinet members benefiting from tender corruption (see Mbanjwa 2009). Both Cosatu and the SACP spoke out on elite enrichment and public sector corruption. This internal contestation did not spiral out to map space for externalisation or a split, although the 2012 levels of suppression of intra-alliance contestation raised questions about the sustainability of alliance politics as effective internal opposition. The mechanism mostly helped to ensure that dissatisfaction with the ANC would not become available for capture by opposition parties or split-away tendencies. Come election time – as again happened in local election 2011 – Cosatu converted its patriotic between-elections opposition into ANC election support. Debates anchored in ANC branches in preparation for its policy conferences also serve the function of internalisating opposition. These debates, however, were often twinned with succession battles and attempts to discredit counter-factions (see for example, Cronin 2009a; 2009b; Malema 2009).

The COPE phenomenon was contentious to the ANC in that COPE externalised internal ANC problems and placed them in the domain of multi-party democracy. It crossed the separation between the two parallel layers of democracy in South Africa (Booysen 2009a). COPE's prospects for continuing to take support from the ANC were diminished when the ANC's core power project held, and COPE gradually faded from 'challenge' into being 'another micro-party'.

The ANC was experiencing complications in continuously nurturing this power mechanism. Polokwane 2007 opened a Pandora's box for the ANC. In its battle of Mangaung (Booysen 2012d) the ANC struggled to get the lid back on. Polokwane had unleashed a wave of energy that regenerated organisational fervour. It bestowed heightened and continuous factionalism (although the specific factions changed and the ANC mother body or dominant faction also denied their existence); free-for-alls in mobilisation to secure enclaves of power in the party and the state; and rejection of the idea that movement elders were supreme in wisdom and authority (yet with hierarchical ascendancy as a primary driving force). The ANC leadership, 2007-13, suppressed challenge and discontent, yet proxy alliances, leaked plots and 'underground' mobilisation for power and kingmaking were rampant. These included plans to make post-Mangaung amends for the brutal intra-ANC factionalist ascent of December 2012.

Simultaneously, the ANC's cushioning through the blanket extension of popular trust was showing evidence of thinning out. The popular outbursts of Marikana, De Doorns and Sasolburg demonstrated that the ANC was not in full control of its own destiny. Its policy proposals had largely become reactive and defensive. The paradox of the ballot and the brick was also displaying signs of weakening. There was a tangible popular sense of budding despondency that the ANC does not (sufficiently) care, and that corruption and public mismanagement were happening at the expense of heightened community returns on policy implementation and service delivery. The possibility nevertheless persisted for now that these sentiments would not soon find lethal traction in electoral politics.

THE 'TWO PHASE REVOLUTION', 'SECOND TRANSITION' AND 'SECOND PHASE OF THE TRANSITION'

The 'two phase revolution' is a long-standing ANC tool for the explanation of a phased, imperfect transformation (see Booysen 2011: 457-458). The use of the term the 'second (phase of the) transition' gained momentum in the wake of the ANCYL's pejorative appropriation of 'economic liberation' in its 2011-12 revolt against the mother body. It held the mother body to account, despite being shadowed by personal beneficiation (also see Radebe 2012).

The ANC national policy conference of June 2012 defeated the 'second transition' and aligned with the 'second phase of the transition', as part of the ongoing movement towards the National Democratic Society. This was a blow to what was seen as a predominantly Marxist phrasing of the 'second transition'. The 'second transition' parlance stood in the context of the ANCYL, in the time of Malema, positioning itself as a force to correct the ANC's purported over-emphasis on political liberation at the cost of the economic side. The conference delegates reckoned that 'second transition' was a denial of the ANC's continuous economic transformation efforts, in the first eighteen years plus, of the democratic dispensation (see ANC 2012b).

In its 1984 Constitution, the SACP describes the main content of the National Democratic Revolution (NDR) as 'the national liberation of the African people in particular, and the black people in general, the destruction of the economic and political power of the racist ruling class, and the establishment of one united state of people's power in which the working class will be the dominant force and which will move uninterruptedly towards social emancipation and the total abolition of exploitation of man by man' (Slovo 1988). The 'second transition' was intended as the ANC's shorthand explanation as to why poverty, inequality and unemployment were persevering. Limited policy renewal – as revealed in the June 2012 policy proposals and December 2012 resolutions – showed that the ANC desperately needed policy ammunition for its regeneration of political power. The proposals generally revealed modest renewal, paired with the recirculation of ideas that originated in, for example, the ANC's 2002 and 2007 conferences, and new proposals that were not to the scale of the policy problems. The most significant-seeming (yet ambiguous) turn was in the form of the National Planning Commission's National Development Plan, which had been adopted by Cabinet a few months earlier.

In the days of the difficult relationship between Cosatu's Zwelinzima Vavi and the then incumbent president, Mbeki, Vavi had argued that the Alliance was in a dismal state because of the ANC's arrogance in dealing with its partners. This arrogance was manifested in 'the insistence that the NDR should only be a bourgeois revolution, and the argument that we must strengthen capitalism as the basis for socialism. And it appears most brutally in the clamour from some quarters to smash strikes, privatise, cut taxes and weaken popular organisations' (Ka'Nkosi 2002). Joel Netshitenzhe (2000) illustrated the ANC's paradoxical worlds of using revolution-speak in the contexts of non-violent politics and liberal democracy (also see Prevost 2006) when he cautioned Cosatu that union militancy could undermine the NDR and the socialist revolution itself. Krista Johnson's (2002) remarks on the ANC's mixture of revolutionary and counter-revolutionary discourse, which blends insurrectionism, militarism and reform, remain pertinent:

> Ironically, one still finds the use of Marxist methodology or terminology in ANC circles or as the predominant mode of expression in ANC pronouncements. Indeed the ANC leadership still uses the language of insurrectionism and militarism while pursuing an agenda of reform. It still has militaristic, top-down concepts of organisation, even though the terrain is no longer that of warfare.

The ANC worked hard to assiduously present the contemporary struggles as the continuation of the liberation struggle – even if the battle by 2012 comprised the ANC struggling against its own internal tendencies and compromises, the legacies from South Africa's colonial-apartheid past, and prevailing global currents of ideology and finance. To some extent the ANC was absolved from responsibility for the deficiencies of its own period of governance – countered by evidence of arrogance in power and corruption in government and lukewarm reactions to help counter these problems.

On a lesser scale, the 2004-12 civil society upheavals were seen as 'the same form of civil society activism that mounted heroic protests against the apartheid regime', with the difference that 'our country today is governed by revolutionary agents for social change that understand the importance of a historical context …' (Mavimbela 2009:13). This statement was part of a growing barrage of pronouncements on the *revolutionary* character of contemporary ANC struggles, largely *in government*. Many of the community (or 'service delivery') protests amounted to intra-ANC ructions that spilled over into the public domain. Insofar as the protests amounted to rebellion against social deprivation, the ANC's proclamation of revolutionary action-in-progress could serve to reassure and to keep the hope alive that the transformation train would still pull into the local station.

The ANC's NGC 2000 meeting paid tribute to the 'body of cadres that consistently and tirelessly perform the necessary revolutionary duties. This is the clear cadre core that is committed to the revolution and on which the movement largely relies' (ANC 2000). Yet the ANC's cadreship problems were profound (ANC 2000):

… we have not sufficiently increased the number of those revolutionary cadres of the movement committed to the transformation agenda. Political activism among most of our members has drastically declined, leaving wide scope for such tendencies as careerism, rampant self-interest, corruption and other anti-people activities to thrive. The political culture, tradition and values of our movement have, in some instances, been deeply eroded. Our membership is mainly engaged in activities of the ANC when it is time to have AGMs, conferences or during election campaigns. A comprehensive review of our political education work since the unbanning indicates that our programme has not been able to produce enough cadres grounded in the politics, organisational values and culture of the movement.

The unrelenting cadreship problems increased the need for effective deployment screening to try and ensure that the pursuit of the 'second phase of the transition' would retain credibility in the face of cadre antics. The overwhelming 2012 evidence (ANC 2012c) confirmed the earlier ANC (2002) secretary general's verdict:

2002: The 1994 breakthrough opened up new opportunities for material and social advancement through positions in the public and private sector and for economic empowerment ... The occupation of positions of power and the material reward this offers could create some 'social distance' between individuals and constituencies they represent … This could render some in the revolutionary movement complacent, concerned with maintaining their positions and even indifferent to the conditions of the poor.

2012: The internal strife revolves around contestation for power and state resources, rather than differences on how to implement the policies of the movement. This situation has shifted the focus of the cadres and members of the movement away from societal concerns and people's aspirations. These circumstances have produced a new type of ANC leader and member who sees ill discipline, divisions, factionalism and in-fighting as normal practices and necessary forms of political survival.

The ANC's 2012 centenary celebrations offered the opportunity to rekindle the connection between 'struggle struggles' and post (political) liberation struggles clouded by cadre ethics-commitment. The Zuma 2012 centenary addresses (for example, Zuma 2012) were frequently overshadowed by concurrent intra-ANC contests. Still, the 'struggle speak' has frequently found resonance in South Africans' patience with the ANC and the high esteem in which they still hold the movement, affording it much (albeit less fervent) long-lasting trust, and continuing to believe (despite growing cynicism) that the ANC remains the most credible agency to entrust with delivering the 'better life for all'. The ANC has been the beneficiary of the 'extended liberation movement dividend'.

'EXTENDED LIBERATION MOVEMENT DIVIDEND'

There is a great and continuing belief among ANC members and supporters that the party-movement is the best custodian and guarantor of the 1994 Promised Land. Even if the ANC's 'best' is sometimes unimpressive, the ANC remains their party-movement of choice. They have been largely comfortable to give the ANC extended time to bring home the full liberation effect although the ANC's stature is being gradually undermined by persistent revelations of corruption and flawed leadership (see Booysen 2011: 487-489).

The ANC's insistence that the struggle was only entering the second phase helped sustain the liberation movement dividend. This mechanism also closely articulates with that of the ANC's representing the identity and aspirations of large numbers of South Africans.

The 'extended liberation dividend' highlights the existence of a voting population that is reluctant to penalise the ANC electorally (in substantive ways that impact nationally) for sub-optimal performance in government (Booysen 2012b). This grace phenomenon is nurtured through the ANC's continuous reassurances and citations of evidence that progress is consistent. This keeps alive much of the liberation struggle character of the movement and helps to ensure that opposition parties – especially the Democratic Alliance (DA) – have few chances of severely denting the ANC's electoral standings.

The extended liberation movement dividend primarily works in the domain of the people in relation to the ANC organisationally (Table 1). Its effect is, however, evident in election results and it affords the ANC-in-government additional space to improve its delivery repertoire, although the need to uphold the benefit places strains on the organisation to keep on justifying and proving that the current struggle is part and parcel of the second phase of liberation.

The ANC's relationship with 'the people' is a complex one. It constitutes an alternative and non-electoral sphere of democracy – the 'parallel democracy' explicated above. For the ANC this is the heart of democracy. The relationship is constantly expressed – whether through consent and expressions of popular support or in adversarial protest and challenge in the between-election periods. It is an honest form of engagement at times when the people do not feel obliged to protect 'their ANC' (and especially their ANC-in-government) against opposition party and media attacks and revelations. Goodwill and trust are the foundations of this relationship (Booysen 2011: 86-125). Contemporary politics raises the question of how long popular trust will prevail in conditions of deficits in ANC commitment and the ANC government's realised capacity to address popular needs more consistently and equitably. Popular goodwill towards, and trust in, the ANC are not bottomless (yet by 2012-13 they had not revealed signs of fatal decline) and depend on ANC dexterity in selecting manageable but meaningful government priorities and persuading the people that it governs as well as is organisationally and governmentally possible.

South African voters, close to twenty years after 1994, continued to treasure the five-yearly opportunities to re-embrace the moment of 1994. They celebrate their franchise and the (indirect) power that they exercise through the vote. The trauma of the apartheid past and the antithesis of the 'miracle election of 1994' (see Waldmeyer 1994; Harris 2010) still sustain their reaffirmations of the ANC. This electoral embrace, however, contrasts with expressions of discontent with the ruling party. Following election 1994, there was widespread talk of patience with government. After election 1999, it was not unusual to hear people and government alike talk about apartheid having been constructed over decades, and that it would not be possible to overturn its effects in the space of a few years, or to 'build Rome in a day'. By 2012-13, these discourses had deflated. Many doubts were being expressed about the ethical directions and integrity of the ANC – yet the bulk of the active South African electorate were re-issuing the extended dividend.

TWO WORLDS – OF ELECTION TIMES AND 'OTHER TIMES'

The ANC enjoys the substantial benefit of election times and between-election periods constituting, for the majority of South Africans, two different worlds. In the one world, citizen opposition to the ANC is vibrant (expressed in critiques, debates, between-election dissent and protest); in the other, this opposition recedes as elections approach (see Booysen 2011; 2012c). The transfer of voter discontent into the electoral arena in South Africa remains the exception rather than the rule. ANC members and supporters band together in between-election periods and exercise opposition through protest and other critiques of the ANC and ANC-in-government. Yet, come each election they return the ANC to power – up to 2011 there were few deviations from this rule. Elections in South Africa are largely the time for reaffirmation of the ANC's and the struggle's 1994 victory.

The 'two worlds' phenomenon, along with 'identity and aspiration', 'parallel democracy' and 'extended liberation dividend' (Table 1) facilitate understandings of the above 60 per cent electoral performances of the ANC despite conditions of sub-optimal government performance, deficient socio-economic transformation and doubts about organisational ethics.

Elections overwhelmingly remain the time of closing of the ranks against a party political enemy of choice. Elections, time after time and at least until national-provincial election 2009 and local election 2011, brought the bulk of the mobilised electorate to restate ANC support (see Booysen 2010; 2012b). In the national elections zone, voters have consistently endorsed the ANC by between 62 and 70 per cent, calculated nationally. Despite support-level setbacks in national-provincial election 2009 and local election 2011, the ANC remained firmly in charge. Up to local election 2011, only a few had abstained from voting. As Kimmie (2012) points out, however, the tendency to abstain had a notable effect on the ANC's 2011 result. Abstention was a form of loyal resistance, chosen over switching electoral support to an opposition party.

Instead of electoral punishment of the ANC, waves of protest enveloped many parts of the country. Especially from 2004 onwards (also see Ruiters 2003), protests became ingrained as part of the electoral cycle and as a pressure release valve that allowed voters at election times to again cast pro-ANC ballots. The protests materialised in the context of unabated unemployment, persistent poverty and increased inequality, accompanied by reports of far-reaching local government failures (see Powell 2012) and a global reces-sion that was taking a toll. Many communities were demonstrating feelings of despera-tion, *after* having returned the ANC with substantial electoral majorities. Opposition parties up to 2013 have had marginal space to enter this ANC-people relationship. The ANC could still rely on a good election campaign – especially if targeted against a well-profiled 'enemy' (Booysen, 2009b) and positioned as protection of the liberation and post-apartheid gains – to help deliver convincing electoral performances.

A sense of tangible vulnerability nevertheless prevailed, centred on whether the ANC could transform its governance project sufficiently, bring definitive turnarounds and thereby secure electoral belief in times beyond the liberation dividend. When would voters start holding the dominant and governing party to account electorally for the shortfalls and failures in government delivery? When would the electorate seriously start punishing the ANC-in-government for practices of corruption and mismanagement? When would an opposition party be judged to be more deserving of popular trust than an imperfect ANC?

The ANC thus benefits substantially from the two-worlds phenomenon. It confirms that the electoral game has been a cyclical celebratory event, largely affirming the move-ment that remains adored even if it has also shown itself to be manifestly fallible. The ANC makes severe mistakes, yet in seamless election rhetoric explains the 'challenges' in terms of the ongoing struggle against decades or centuries of injustice – with the opposi-tion parties, or the media and other critical voices, now the proxies for the past struggles.

STATE POWER FOR HEGEMONY AND PATRONAGE

Control over state power – and the associated leveraging of patronage and hegemony – compensates for power that the ANC has been forfeiting in the process of falling short on delivery and ultimate transformation. The mechanism obviously works primarily in the state domain, but it also affects the ANC organisationally (Table 1).

The ANC, towards the mark of twenty years in power, was going increasingly to rely on government performance to ensure continuous electoral prowess (in contrast with the preceding period in which the ANC would be guaranteed support – to some extent, at least, irrespective of actual performance). The ANC's history and identity, along with the demonstrably positive changes effected in its time in state power, have for now sustained it. The mechanism of state power is also bolstered through the dispensing of patronage and other opportunities. Good performance and reputation in the state helps to build hegemony which is also enhanced through the use of state power to control information and public agendas.

Hence the ANC would have to maintain a hold over state power to reinforce both tiers of 'parallel democracy' in which it operates – the electoral and comparative party power world on the one hand, and the ANC in its own world of relations with the people, its organisational world, and the Alliance world on the other. The ANC had to use state institutions to leverage policy implementation and delivery. Its task was vastly compli-cated by the fact that much of its organisational wars for intra-ANC strategic advantage over rivals were playing out in exactly the state-institutional domain where it had to invest in its own political future (Booysen 2011).

In Polokwane, the ANC resolved that its deployment committee needed to be strength-ened, given that the ANC 'remains the key strategic centre of power, which must exer-cise leadership over the state and society' (ANC 2007b). With a view to implementing the 1997 resolution on deployment and strengthening collective decision making and consultation on deployment of cadres to senior positions of authority, the conference instructed the incoming NEC to review the political management of the deployment process. The 2012 Mangaung missive had a slight change of tone (ANC 2012c: 28), also focusing on the substance of the deployees: 'Going forward, we should ensure that no cadre is deployed into a position without any proper training and preparation. Massive political education and academic training of ANC members is therefore crucial for the survival of the ANC as a progressive force and its success as a capable governing party.'

It had become imperative to substitute for some of the aspects of post-liberation deployment that had detracted from ANC performance in government. Judging by state-ments and initiatives in the *early* Zuma administration, there was a stronger sense than before that 'now was the time' to get things right. The *early second* Zuma term parroted the theme, now noting that other urgent issues had consumed the president's first term and that Zuma needed his second term to bring home the promises. The Zumaists argued nevertheless that the National Development Plan and the infrastructure development plan (both long-term projects with still uncertain outcomes) were proof of a fruitful first term.

There was doubtful substantiation of the early ecstasy with a new, committed and caring epoch that Polokwane had been argued to introduce. The ANC-to-government gap had been closed under Zuma, but intra-ANC and Alliance contests were directly transposed onto the state. In 2011-12 it caused a variation on the theme of governance paralysis that had been linked to the 2007 succession struggle. Now it combined with an even more wide-spread lack of sufficient state capacity, slow realisation of turnarounds, increasing evidence of state corruption and bad governance that would lessen the prospects for state proficiency, and the ANC losing central control over local enclaves of state-business convergence. By 2011-13, the Zuma administration was pushed to prove that it had what it would take to implement suitable and timely responses to the vexing policy and governance problems.

Employment-deployment issues caused the ANC's local election 2011 list problems. Upon announcement of candidate selections from the community-generated (but prin-cipal-vetted) lists, candidates turned on one another. ANC offices were stormed and some branches and regions sent delegations to Luthuli House. In many cases, nominations would have guaranteed employment for candidates (also see Yendi 2011). The ANC's Mangaung battles for delegate status were also anchored in gaining or keeping access to power and position.

By 2012-13 the ANC was thoroughly entrapped in deliberations over 'redeployment', the soft alternative to sacking and often the alternative to 'purging'. There was recognition that the ANC's performance in government was increasingly and directly affecting its longevity in state power. Yet loyalty to comrades was the other side of the coin – with power-bloc construction and an aversion to alienating potentially powerful ANC players and their followers frequently an unspoken bottom line. Maharaj (2011), by then presidential spokesperson for Zuma, illustrated the aversion: 'We don't like to drop a person. And that is a good quality. It is an error on the right side of history. We wouldn't be what we are if we don't care for people …'

Personal beneficiation of political and bureaucratic functionaries through their closeness to state political power is not the only motivation to be in public service anywhere and certainly not in South Africa under the ANC either. All employment brings remuneration and employment benefits. These benefits alone make loyal and other ANC cadres scramble and contest for deployment. However, political and public sector employment also brings opportunities for legal-and-fine, legal-but-inappropriate, and illegal or underhand personal enrichment. 'Crude cronyism' extended this repertoire. Such opportunities are accessed by virtue of office-holding and by family or business interests close to those in office (Booysen 2011: 387-392). The existence of in-groups and out-groups in ANC ranks is closely associated with leveraging opportunities which have made positions in public institutions, political office and the bureaucracy launch pads for affluence.

The ANC was also continually sensitive to criticism from opinion makers in broader society, and hyper-sensitive about the mass media and its role in public agenda-setting. As in the Mbeki days, the Zuma ANC (and the SACP, circa 2012) reacted vengefully when potentially influential persons criticised it and its government. The media was under continuous ANC scrutiny, with Parliament stealthily moving towards the introduction of a tribunal or other means of limiting the role of the media as an 'opposition force' that often held sway over public opinion. Parliament passed the Protection of State Information Bill and the National Council of Provinces (NCOP) suggested further amendments. In the context of the ANC's often being seen to be under siege politically – even if not electorally – it was important for the ANC to contain projections of itself as anything but the always virtuous liberation movement-party that would be engaged for decades to come with the task of completing the liberation project.

The ANC's control over state power is simultaneously its biggest asset and crudest liability. Crucial questions are whether the ANC can retain credibility and extend delivery; whether the syndrome of 'now it's our turn to drink from the trough' will ensure that the people get water while elites feast (ANC 2012d).

CONCLUSION

The operation and relative statuses of the seven mechanisms for the ANC's regeneration of political power tell a tale of a complex project that often straddles at least two political worlds (election times and 'other' times), two ANC organisations (the formal ANC and one wracked by warring factions), an ANC that straddles time zones (struggle history is continually, often justifiably, relocated in the present to ensure that the present will be framed by historical ANC struggle), two phases of struggle and revolution-transition (with South Africa located in the open-ended second part of both), and two ways of relating to state power (delivery and transformation versus target for self-enrichment).

South Africa carries the immense burden of structural problems bequeathed by colonialism and apartheid. The ANC reaps credit from this because it helps to explain the extended liberation movement dividend. The 'world' of the ANC as the disciplined movement (of the left) is still holding out, albeit in a faction-riddled world that frequently meshes with the ANC's nowadays patronage-driven hold on state power. The notion of the two worlds of election times and other times is also holding out, with rising questions about the sustainability of the divide, and with elections consistently showing up decay in the relationship. There is a close connection between this divide and the parallel non-electoral level of democracy – where the ANC is still afforded the space to deal with problems beyond the gaze of electoral contest. The ANC's two-phases of the transition-revolution is the volatile space that bridges the movement and the state, where the ANC is under pressure (and not performing well on the face of it) to show new and definitive initiatives to take the transition forward.

The analysis of the seven mechanisms for the regeneration of the ANC's political power suggests substantial (if as yet unquantified) vulnerability and fragility – amid extensive and lasting ANC power – and shows the ANC's immense strengths and advantages in regenerating power. They are daunting to competitors. Yet, there are penetrating complications. There is uncertainty as to how exactly change from the ANC as 'clearly positioned liberation movement in power' to 'wracked monolith delivering despite leadership focusing on personal power and position first, delivery and transformation second' is making an impact on how the people of South Africa relate to the ANC. The tipping points include people's trust in the ANC, their belief in the credibility of the ANC's policy and governance initiatives, and their willingness to shelter the ANC in election times. Cumulatively, the amalgam of mechanisms reflects the reality of change in and around the ANC, and highlights the certainty that the ANC's finely-tuned balancing act is volatile, fragile and in need of nurturing, but circa 2012-13 it is still working.

REFERENCES

African National Congress (ANC) (1985) Second national consultative conference: National preparatory committee composite and organisational report (section 5), http://www.anc.org.za/show.php?id=140 [Accessed 12 July 2012].
ANC National Executive Committee (NEC) (1990-2012). January 8th Statements for the period, http://www.anc.org.za/list.php?t=January%208th%20Statements [Accessed 13 July 2012].
ANC (2000) People's revolutionary movement for transformation (Section 2), ANC discussion papers, http://www.anc.org.za/show.php?doc=ancdocs/ngcouncils/docs2000/section2.html [Accessed 2 September 2009].
ANC (2002) Secretary general's organisational report, Stellenbosch, December 2002, http://www.anc.org.za/ancdocs/history/conf/conference51/index.html [Accessed 2 September 2009].

ANC (2007a) Declaration of the ANC 52nd National Conference, 20 December 2007, Polokwane, http://www.anc.org.za/ancdocs/history/conf/conference52/declaration1220-07.html [Accessed 12 January 2008].

ANC (2007b) ANC 52nd congress, Polokwane, resolutions, http://www.anc.org.za/ancdocs/history/conf/conference52/index.html [Accessed 1 September 2009].

ANC (2012a) Second transition? Policy discussion document for the ANC 4th National Policy Conference, Gallagher Estate Midrand, 26-29 June.

ANC (2012b) Report and recommendations on strategy and tactics of the ANC, ANC 4th National Policy Conference, Gallagher Estate Midrand, 26-29 June 2012, http://www.anc.org.za/docs/reps/2012/report_%20tactics.pdf [Accessed 2 July 2012].

ANC (2012c) Organisational renewal: Building the ANC as a movement for transformation and a strategic centre of power. Discussion document towards the National Policy Conference. Version 9, 10 April 2012. Johannesburg.

ANC (2012d) Interview with senior ANC official granted on condition of anonymity. Johannesburg, 1 March.

Asmal K (2007) The ANC will 'heal itself'. *Mail & Guardian*, 30 November-6 December 2007: 7.

Booysen S (1997) Life in the New Democracy: Focus on Elections, Government and Priority Issues. Research paper. Johannesburg: Matla Trust.

Booysen S (2009a) Congress of the People: Between foothold of hope and slippery slope. In Southall R and J Daniel (Eds) *Zunami: the 2009 South African Elections.* Johannesburg: Jacana with Konrad Adenauer Stiftung.

Booysen S (2009b) Nothing works like an enemy: the African National Congress in and after election 2009. *EISA Election Update* 4. Johannesburg: Electoral Institute of Southern Africa.

Booysen S (2010) Party opposition perpetually on the verge of promise – South Africa's election 2009. *Journal of African Elections* 9 (1): 80-109.

Booysen S (2011) *The ANC and the Regeneration of Political Power.* Johannesburg: Witwatersrand University Press.

Booysen S (2012) The regeneration of ANC political power, from the 1994 electoral victory to the 2012 centenary. In Nieftagodien N, A Lissoni and J Soske (Eds) *100 Years of the ANC.* Johannesburg: Witwatersrand University Press.

Booysen S (2012b) 'The ballot and the brick' – enduring under duress. In Booysen S (Ed.) *Local Elections in South Africa: People, Parties, Politics.* Stellenbosch: Sun Media.

Booysen S (2012c) The ANC and its mechanisms for the regeneration of political power. Political Studies colloquium, Nelson Mandela Metropolitan University (NMMU), Port Elizabeth, 24 April 2012.

Booysen S (2012d) *The ANC's battle of Mangaung.* Tafelberg Shorts e-books. Cape Town: Tafelberg.

Booysen S (2012e) Heyday of ANC unreason. *Sunday Independent*, 2 December 2012.

Brown K (2009) ANC lambasts Hogan for 'thinking out aloud' on policy. *Business Day*, 12 June 2009: 1.

Butler A (2006) How democratic is the African National Congress? *Journal of Southern African Studies* 31 (4): 720-736.

Chabal, P (1992) *Power in Africa: An Essay in Political Interpretation.* Basingstoke: Macmillan.

Cronin J (2009a) Should we nationalise the mines? *Umsebenzi Online* 8 (20), 10 November. http://www.sacp.org.za/main.php?ID=3128 [Accessed 24 July 2011].

Cronin J (2009b) A reply to Julius Malema, *politicsweb*, 25 November, http://www.politicsweb.co.za/politicsweb/view/politicsweb/en/page71619?oid=152353&sn=Detail [Accessed 24 July 2011].

Giliomee H, J Myburgh J and L Schlemmer (2001) Dominant party rule, opposition parties and minorities in South Africa. In Southall R (Ed.) *Opposition and Democracy in South Africa.* London and Portland: Frank Cass.

Gumede W M (2005) *Thabo Mbeki and the Battle for the Soul of the ANC.* Johannesburg: Zebra Press.

Harris P (2010) *Birth – The Conspiracy to Stop the '94 Election.* Cape Town: Umuzi.

Johnson K (2002) Liberal framework or liberation framework? Comparing liberal and vanguardist understandings of the reorganisation of post-apartheid South African society. Paper presented at the 10th Codesria general assembly, Kampala, Uganda, 8-12 December 2002.

Jordan P (2008) A letter to Comrade Mtungwa, an old comrade and dear friend. Address to the Platform for Public Deliberation. University of Johannesburg. 14 November.

Ka'Nkosi S (2002) Left digs in for long war with the ANC. *Sunday Times*, 28 July 2002: 4.

Kimmie Z (2012) The ANC's performance in the 2011 local government elections. In Booysen S (Ed.) *Local Elections in South Africa: People, Parties, Politics*. Stellenbosch: Sun Media.

Lodge T (1999) *South African Politics Since 1994*. Cape Town: David Philip.

Lodge T (2002) *Politics in South Africa from Mandela to Mbeki*. Cape Town: David Philip.

Maharaj M (2011) The other side of the coin. Interview with S'thembiso Msomi. *Sunday Times Review*, 17 July 2011: 1.

Malema J (2009) Julius Malema replies to Jeremy Cronin, *politicsweb*, 19 November, http://www.politicsweb.co.za/politicsweb/view/politicsweb/en/page71619?oid=151679&sn=Detail&pid=71619 [Accessed 24 July 2011].

Mantashe G (2010) State of the Organisation Report. ANC National General Council meeting. Durban, 20-24 September 2010.

Mavimbela V (2009) After the revolution: new goals, new strategies. *Sunday Times*, 6 September 2009: 13.

Mbanjwa X (2009) Mass action possible despite talks – union, http://www.iol.co.za/index.php?set_id=1&click_id=13&art_id=vn20090609051407103C949317 [Accessed 15 June 2009].

Mohau K (2008) The ANC shall never be defeated! 22 October, on http://www.mail-archive.com/yclsa-eom-forum@googlegroups.com/msg00327.htm [Accessed 30 July 2009].

Netshitenzhe J (2000) The NDR and class struggle: An address to the Executive Committee of Cosatu. *The Shop Steward* 9 (1), March, http://www.cosatu.org.za/shop/shop0901/shop0901-06.html [Accessed 17 September 2005].

Powell D (2012) Imperfect transition – local government reform in South Africa 1994-2012. In Booysen S (Ed.) *Local Elections in South Africa: People, Parties, Politics*. Stellenbosch: Sun Media.

Pretorius L (2006) Government by or over the people? The African National Congress's conception of democracy. *Social Identities* 12 (6): 745-769.

Prevost G (2006) The evolution of the African National Congress: From revolutionaries to social democrats? *Politikon* 33 (2): 163-181.

Radebe J (2012) ANC's new policy document: Why the second transition? Statement by the head of the ANC NEC policy sub-committee on the release of policy discussion documents, 5 March 2012. http://www.moneyweb.co.za/mw/view/mw/en/page295025?oid=563515&sn=2009+Detail [Accessed 24 March 2012].

Ruiters G (2003) *Debate 9*, Debate Editorial Collective, Johannesburg.

Sefara M (2009) Sauer Street: No real space for open debate. *The Sunday Independent*, 13 December 2009: 14.

Slovo J (1988) The South African working class and the national democratic revolution. *Umsebenzi* discussion pamphlet, http://www.sacp.org.za/docs/history/ndr.html [Accessed 28 January 2012].

Southall R (2000) Conclusion. In Southall R (Ed.) *Opposition in South Africa's New Democracy*. Johannesburg: Konrad Adenauer Stiftung.

Waldmeyer P (1997) *Anatomy of a Miracle*. London: Penguin.

Xundu X (2009) Crush patronage, says Nzimande. *Sunday Times*, 22 October 2009: 4.

Yendi S Y (2011) ANC's jobs for axed comrades plan. *City Press*, 1 May 2011: 1.

Zuma J (2008) Closing address to the ANC Youth League Congress, 29 June, http://www.polity.org.za/article/anc-zuma-closing-address-to-the-anc-youth-league-congress-29062008-2008-06-2 [Accessed 5 September 2009].

Zuma J (2012) Statement of the National Executive Committee of the African National Congress on the occasion of the Centenary Celebration of the ANC, 8 January 2012. http://www.anc.org.za/docs/jan8/2012/0108.pdf [Accessed 20 January 2012].

CHAPTER 3

Fragile multi-class alliances compared: Some unlikely parallels between the National Party and the African National Congress

Paul Maylam

In an interview in 2000, the eminent South African historian Martin Legassick argued that ' … the whole issue of class is completely relevant. The main issues in South Africa at the moment are being fought over within the Tripartite Alliance' (2002: 124). He went on to bemoan the growing marginalisation of class analysis in South African historiography. It is well known that there has been a shift away from what can be loosely called the 'political economy tradition' in historical writing – a glance through the contents pages of *South African Historical Journal* volumes over the past few years reveals hardly any articles at all written in that tradition. The reasons for this shift have often been stated. As Geoff Eley has put it: '"Materialist" explanations based primarily on the economy and social structure now seemed to oversimplify the complexities of human action. Previously attractive structuralisms now seemed "reductionist" or "reductive" in their logic and effects' (2008: 316-17).

The purpose of this chapter is not to decry the fresh lines of inquiry opened up in the past two decades such as gender, popular culture, belief systems, memory, and representations of the past but, rather, to lament the seemingly overhasty sidelining of the political economy tradition. It is possible to utilise class analysis without being reductionist, determinist or essentialist. I share Daryl Glaser's view that:

> For materialist class analysis to work it must be reasonable to suppose the following: that economic-material interests show up in, or influence, a range of behaviours, that they will on occasion do so unconsciously and will not necessarily engender class consciousness, that they can help explain the existence and persistence of non-class collectivities, and that collectivities formed on the basis of material interests will challenge the formation and maintenance of other kinds of collectivity (2001: 128).

Materialist analysis, it can be argued, has a particular salience in these times when corporate power is greater than ever in much of the world, given the growing corporate control over the mainstream media and the capacity of corporations to influence electoral politics through the funding of political parties and candidates.

I propose to argue in this chapter that such a line of analysis is especially apt for an understanding of post-apartheid South Africa. Moreover, as revisiting some of the earlier writing in the materialist tradition can aid this understanding, I propose to revisit in particular the work of Dan O'Meara on Afrikaner nationalism and the National Party (NP). What relevance, one might ask, can this possibly have to post-apartheid South Africa, given that the NP has ceased to exist and Afrikaner nationalism is virtually dead? The very idea of drawing any kind of comparison between the pre-1994 and post-1994 history of South Africa is offensive, wholly improper, thoroughly perverse, and open to serious objection. It would indeed be perverse to draw a straight comparison between, on the one hand, a government that presided over a system of institutionalised, entrenched racism – a system characterised by brutal repression, the denial of basic freedoms, relentless exploitation and ruthless dispossession – and, on the other, a government that has dismantled this system and established a democratic order shaped by a much-admired constitution. Yet despite these fundamental differences, it is possible to detect some similar tendencies and trajectories in the respective histories of the two movements. The key notion here is that of the multi-class alliance – the notion that shaped O'Meara's analysis of Afrikaner nationalism and the NP, and a notion that is applicable to the history of the ANC-led government since 1994. In both cases the differing class interests within the alliances gave rise to tensions, conflicts and fragmentation, especially as one particular class gained the upper hand, pursuing its interests at the expense of its subordinate allies.

BUILDING MULTI-CLASS ALLIANCES

Before acceding to power in 1948 and 1994 respectively, the Afrikaner nationalist movement and the ANC more or less succeeded in building multi-class alliances under an umbrella of nationalism. Both movements were, however, beset by internal ideological tensions and class divisions. Neither was able entirely to eliminate these tensions, but each did manage to bridge the divides to the extent that it could establish a support base strong enough to acquire power. It is thus necessary to show how each movement built its alliance.

Before the 1940s, the Afrikaner nationalist movement was beset by internal tensions. There were the ideological differences between the Hertzogites, who favoured an essential white unity while allowing for Afrikaner cultural autonomy, and die-hard nationalists who demanded an Afrikaner-controlled republic. There were, too, class tensions between Afrikaner capitalists, relatively small but growing in number, and based mainly in the Cape, and subordinate groupings – a petit bourgeoisie and a working class, who were located mainly in the north and were mistrustful of the capitalists (hereafter the term 'Afrikaner' is used to denote white Afrikaners) (O'Meara 1983: 221).

O'Meara shows how the process of building an Afrikaner multi-class alliance required the inculcation of a sense of victimhood and exclusion directed against those elements deemed responsible for the marginalisation of Afrikaners. All classes of Afrikaners felt themselves to be marginalised. Apart from a few exceptions, Afrikaner entrepreneurs fell largely outside the big business sector, comprising only about 5 per cent of all non-agricultural business undertakings in the country in 1938-39. As the industrial economy grew from the 1930s, smaller Afrikaner businesses struggled to compete, lacking sufficient access to capital. As Afrikaners moved to cities during this time of industrialisation they found themselves dominating the unskilled white labour sector, taking on jobs that paid lower wages than those enjoyed by their semi-skilled English counterparts. The alternative for these urbanising Afrikaners was to swell the ranks of the lumpen proletariat; by 1931 most of the 300 000 so-called 'poor whites' were Afrikaners, constituting about one-quarter of the Afrikaner population (O'Meara 1983: 51-52, 82; Giliomee 1979: 150-53). It was estimated in 1936 that the average per capita income of Afrikaners was about 60 per cent of that of other whites (O'Meara 1996: 74).

'This presumed relative economic deprivation of all Afrikaners,' argues O'Meara, 'stood at the core of the new Afrikaner nationalism of the 1930s and 1940s' (1996: 76). Nationalist mobilisers made it quite clear who was to blame for this deprivation – it was a combination of imperialism and capitalism, for which full responsibility lay with the British. In their view, the South African economy was controlled by British imperial interests building a system of monopoly capitalism that marginalised all members of the *volk*. Monopolies excluded Afrikaner entrepreneurs and exploited Afrikaner workers. This rhetoric was not always uniform, though. Some nationalist mobilisers directed their attack not at capitalism in general, but only at foreign-controlled capitalism that marginalised Afrikaners (O'Meara 1983: 34, 55, 89, 150-54). At the same time there were elements within the nationalist movement who were critical of the capitalist sector in more general terms. In the mid-1930s, for instance, the future prime minister, JG Strijdom, called for the newly purified NP to 'combat capitalism', proposing that the mines be nationalised and the power of banks be curtailed (O'Meara 1983: 51).

Herein lay a fundamental tension within the emerging Afrikaner multi-class alliance. At the forefront of Afrikaner nationalist mobilisation was a group with a particular concern to further the growth of Afrikaner capitalism – this was known as the Afrikaner economic movement. A key moment was the 1939 Ekonomiese Volkskongres, a gathering convened by the Broederbond. Here the dominant message was that nationalism and capitalism were perfectly compatible: they were merged into the notion of *volkskapital-isme*, according to which the *volk* would challenge the foreign domination of capitalism and develop a capitalist system that would advance the interests of all Afrikaners. To this end, the Reddingsdaadbond (the Rescue Action Society, hereafter RDB) was formed to win the support of all Afrikaners for the economic movement. The RDB created a fund that would supposedly be used for the benefit of all Afrikaners, although in the event only 10 per cent of this fund went towards relief for 'poor whites'. Most of it was invested in Afrikaner businesses, especially Federale Volksbeleggings, a new investment house. By the mid-1940s, the RDB had become ever more supportive of larger Afrikaner companies (O'Meara 1983: 107-11, 137-43; Giliomee 1979: 156-57).

In the years before the 1948 NP election victory there was indeed significant growth in the Afrikaner capitalist sector. The Afrikaner share of private sector operations rose from 5 per cent to 11 per cent between 1939 and 1950. Between 1938-39 and 1948-49, the number of Afrikaner business undertakings rose by 350 per cent, from 3 710 to 13 047, while turn-over increased by more than 500 per cent. Most of this growth was in manufacturing and commerce, with Afrikaner-owned manufacturing concerns growing from 1 239 to 3 385 in the same period; but Afrikaners still remained largely excluded from the mining sector (O'Meara 1983: 181-82; Giliomee 1979: 159). In 1942 the Afrikaanse Handelsinstituut (Afrikaans Commercial Institute, hereafter AHI) was formed, with the task of giving advice and information to Afrikaner businesses and facilitating cooperation between them. In time it set up local chambers of business. Although there were some tensions within the AHI between larger and smaller undertakings, the body was held together by its shared enmity towards foreign-dominated monopoly capital (O'Meara 1983: 143-47).

Within the nationalist movement there were thus these differing interests, tendencies and outlooks. During the 1940s the movement was able, to a considerable extent albeit not completely, to bridge these internal divides and build a multi-class alliance. Nationalist mobilisers, headed by the Broederbond, besought Afrikaners to stand together. Readily aware that internal class divisions threatened this unity, they appealed to Afrikaners to place supreme value on their shared cultural identity and sense of nationhood. At the same time, the mobilisers assured aspirant capitalists, as well as workers and the unem-ployed, that their best interests would be served if they joined the nationalist cause, a cause that would create entrepreneurial opportunities for Afrikaners, protect Afrikaner workers against foreign capitalist exploitation and black competition, and provide jobs for the unemployed (O'Meara 1983: 71-73; 1996: 41-43).

This multi-class alliance remained, though somewhat fragile, one that enabled an NP election victory in 1948 by the narrowest of margins. The party did enough to win sufficient electoral support among different sectors of the Afrikaner population: farmers, capitalists, the petit bourgeoisie, workers and the unemployed. As O'Meara has put it, the NP 'mobilised each group on the basis that they were discriminated against as Afrikaners, a condition which would end only when all Afrikaners were united in a single political movement' (1983: 243). A particularly interesting aspect of the NP's 1948 elec-tion platform is that it was not only crudely racist (promoting apartheid) and fiercely anti-communist, but also anti-capitalist. The party manifesto called for growing state control of the mines, banks, retail monopolies, land companies and other strategic industries (O'Meara 1996: 28, 34).

Is it possible to discern parallels between the ANC up to 1994 and the NP before 1948? Like the NP, the ANC succeeded in building a multi-class alliance under a nationalist umbrella. The ANC, as did the NP, had to manage internal ideological tensions and class divisions, although the common experience of repugnant racial discrimination tended to diminish the class differences. Neither organisation was able to eliminate these tensions entirely, but each did manage to bridge the divides to the extent that it could establish a support base sufficient to acquire power – in the ANC's case this was more than sufficient, as its electoral support in 1994 was much stronger than that of the NP in 1948.

In the decades before 1994 (and after) there were two main sources of tension within the ANC. One was the ideology of Africanism, representing a position that was ardently nationalist in that it rested on a narrow, racially exclusive notion of who could legitimately claim to be 'African'. Africanists were generally anti-communist, essentialist, and tended to deny the existence of internal class differences. This ideology was promoted by the Youth League from the time of its founding in 1944, and gave rise to the breakaway of the Pan Africanist Congress (PAC) in 1958-59. It was an outlook not shared by those who were less concerned about racial exclusivity and were more open to socialist thinking.

Class differences were at the root of the second tension. In the early decades of its existence the ANC was deemed to be a predominantly petit-bourgeois organisation that paid little heed to the needs of the black working class. Only in the 1950s did the ANC begin to take working-class organisation more seriously. From the 1950s the ANC was able to operate more or less as a 'broad church', allowing for some internal ideological diversity and held together by a deep-seated common enmity towards the apartheid order. The Freedom Charter was sufficiently vague, ambiguous, and open to different interpretations to satisfy (and dissatisfy) both socialists and those with a more liberal inclination. The two-stage theory of the South African Communist Party (SACP), one of the ANC's alliance partners, was a compromise that also served to bridge ideological differences. Moreover, the leadership style of Oliver Tambo, ANC president from 1967 to 1990, did much to paper over any cracks within the movement. With some skill, he managed to prevent different tendencies from gaining the upper hand, while not articulating clearly his own position. Himself a Christian, he showed great respect towards communists and, while always emphasising the national struggle, he showed an awareness of class issues (Callinicos 1999: 143-48).

That the ANC in opposition was able to hold together should not belie the existence of differing tendencies within the movement before 1994. Although for the first forty or so years of its history the ANC paid little attention to worker organisation and action, from the 1950s it began to take this constituency more seriously. In 1955, the South African Congress of Trade Unions (Sactu) was launched as the trade union wing of the Congress Alliance. At its Morogoro conference in Tanzania in 1969, the ANC issued a declaration that suggested it was moving in a socialist direction:

> Our nationalism must not be confused with the classical drive by an elitist group
> among the oppressed people to gain ascendancy so that they can replace the oppressor
> in the exploitation of the masses … Meeting the economic needs of the masses of the
> oppressed people … cannot be effectively tackled unless the basic wealth and the basic
> resources are … not manipulated by sections or individuals be they white or black
> (Iheduru 2004: 6).

In the early 1980s, large sections of the black trade union movement were becoming
wary of organisations like the ANC and its internal wing, the United Democratic Front
(UDF) (founded in 1983), afraid that workers would be used by populists as pawns in
political campaigns, but when Cosatu was formed in 1985 the worker movement became
much more closely aligned with the ANC. In March 1986 there was a comradely meeting
between the ANC and Cosatu, with the former stressing the importance of worker emancipation (Baskin 1991: 73-74, 92-95). This alliance seemed to confirm an ANC commitment to socialism. On his release from prison in 1990, Mandela firmly declared that 'the
nationalisation of the mines, banks and monopoly industry is the policy of the ANC and
a change or modification of our views in this regard is inconceivable' (Marais 2011: 97).
An ANC discussion document on economic policy, compiled in the same year, further
suggested a leaning towards socialism: policy would be geared towards state intervention and strategic planning, reducing inequality, raising corporate tax rates, unbundling
conglomerates, and prioritising redistribution as the means of achieving economic
growth (Marais 2011: 99-100).

The economic policy to be adopted by a future ANC-led government was never clear-
cut but, rather, a site of contestation. In the apartheid era, an African business class had
been slow to develop and hardly carried much political clout. The African Chamber of
Commerce had been founded in 1955, to be succeeded later, from 1964, by the National
African Federated Chambers of Commerce (Nafcoc). Nafcoc's aims and plans appeared
to have been modelled on the early operations of the incipient Afrikaner business class:
mobilising the savings of Africans to generate capital for African entrepreneurs (à la the
Afrikaner economic movement), and establishing the African Bank of South Africa in
1975 (à la Volkskas) for the same purpose (Southall 1980: 48-49, 55-59). Given the political
and economic conditions in South Africa, however, this African business class was never
able before 1994 to make the strides that its Afrikaner counterparts made before 1948.

It is uncertain how much influence the African business class wielded within the ANC
but there is no doubt that within a year or two of the ANC's socialist-leaning declarations
of 1990 there was a significant change of direction. Although this shift was much sharper
and more far-reaching than that of the Afrikaner nationalist movement in the 1940s,
there were still parallels between the two.

In 1991, Mandela announced to a US audience that the private sector would play a
decisive role under a future ANC government, and that conditions would be created
to attract foreign investment. The shift in his thinking appears to have solidified at a
meeting of the World Economic Forum at Davos in Switzerland in February 1992 where

he was much influenced by delegates from the Netherlands, China and Vietnam. They were all sympathetic to the socialist cause, but stressed to him the necessity of a country's accepting private investment, as the old Soviet model had died. Mandela returned to South Africa holding the view that '[w]e either keep nationalisation and get no investment, or we modify our own attitude and get investment' (Sampson 1999: 434-35). Not long after Davos, new ANC policy guidelines were drawn up. 'Growth through redistribution' was to be abandoned, and in the months leading up to the 1994 election thinking shifted towards the prevailing neoliberal orthodoxy (Marais 2011: 100-01). In the same year, the ANC itself moved into business when a group of its leaders, including Nelson Mandela and Walter Sisulu, founded the Batho Batho (the People's) Trust. Out of this trust would come Thebe Investments, which over time would acquire sizeable stakes in the financial sector (Southall 2008: 288-89).

Notwithstanding the obvious huge differences between the two, there was one similarity between the NP's 1948 election campaign and that of the ANC in 1994 – each was characterised by ambiguity surrounding economic policy. The NP, as we have seen, campaigned on a platform that contained socialist elements, albeit crudely racist, at a time when many at the head of the Afrikaner nationalist movement were looking ahead to a capitalist future. Similarly, the ANC's election campaign in 1994 was characterised by a certain ambiguity. On the one hand, it envisaged the state playing an enhanced role: extending the provision of welfare, creating jobs through public works programmes, presiding over land redistribution, and curbing monopoly capital. On the other hand, this was not a thoroughly radical programme: the need for a 'thriving private sector' was recognised; nationalisation was barely mentioned; and support for tariff reduction implied liberalisation. It was a programme designed to appease the working class and unemployed as well as the business sector (Lodge 1994: 30-32; Southall 2007: 207). But, as had the NP after 1948, the ANC-led government would, after 1994, lean heavily away from the more radical elements of its programme.

STRAINS WITHIN THE MULTI-CLASS ALLIANCES

Both the NP and ANC built multi-class alliances before acceding to power. Each alliance had held together over decades in the face of a common enemy – foreign-dominated monopoly capital and African nationalism in the case of the NP, and the brutal apartheid order in the case of the ANC. Once in power, however, each found it more difficult to hold its alliance together, as one particular class grouping within the alliance saw its interests served better by its governing party than did other, subordinate, classes.

NP government policy after 1948 clearly favoured capitalist interests, especially those of Afrikaner capital. An early indication of this was the second Ekonomiese Volkskongres, held in 1950, just two years after the election. The gathering was dominated by Afrikaner capitalists, whose interests were at the forefront of deliberations. The petit-bourgeois agenda was sidelined; and the problem of poor whiteism was deemed to have been solved. The primary task ahead was identified as advancing the Afrikaner capitalist sector (O'Meara 1983: 248-49).

This advance would be rapid, made possible by significant state support. Afrikaner farmers, a key NP constituency, benefited from government policies that ensured favourable prices for farm produce and a secure supply of cheap labour. Afrikaner-owned companies prospered, advantaged by the awarding of government contracts and mineral concessions. The Afrikaner financial sector grew as government departments and municipalities moved their accounts to Afrikaner institutions. For instance, the total amount of funds deposited in Volkskas doubled between 1948 and 1952 (O'Meara 1983: 249-50; Giliomee 1979: 166-75).

It might be argued that the NP government did fulfil part of its 1948 commitment to 'socialism', albeit a warped version of it, by pursuing a policy of nationalisation. State capitalism was expanded significantly, with the public sector's stake in the economy almost doubling between 1948 and 1973. The real objective, though, was not to pursue socialism, but to further the interests of the Afrikaner business class. The parastatals were used to counter non-Afrikaner dominance in the capitalist sector. Afrikaner businessmen were appointed to executive and managerial positions in the parastatals and would hold interlocking directorships in private companies and parastatals, facilitating business transactions between the two (O'Meara 1996: 79-80).

According to O'Meara, in the first fifteen years of NP rule '[f]ar and away the major beneficiaries were the members of a new class of urban Afrikaner financial, industrial and commercial capitalists. This group had blossomed from an embattled infancy to potent adulthood under the benevolent care of the NP government' (1996: 139). Within two decades, Afrikaner capitalists had become more capitalist than Afrikaner, with the nationalist message ceasing to have so much hold, its purpose served. By 1970 Sanlam had become the country's second biggest corporation behind Anglo American; and by the late 1970s Afrikaner capitalists had acquired a significant stake in the mining sector (Adam 1979: 178; Southall 2007: 204).

While the NP government prioritised the advancement of Afrikaner capitalist interests, it was also able for the most part to look after the concerns of its other Afrikaner constituencies, thereby ensuring its growing electoral dominance from the 1950s. Small businesses could prosper, the government's severe repression of black labour keeping down costs. Afrikaner workers and the unemployed also benefited. Afrikaner businesses took on Afrikaner employees and there was a rapid increase in the number of Afrikaners employed in the civil service. As more Afrikaners moved upwards into white-collar jobs, there was a corresponding decline in the number of them stuck in the lowest white income brackets (O'Meara 1996: 76, 81, 136-40).

Although all classes of Afrikaners benefited from NP rule, this did not prevent strains developing within the multi-class alliance. There was some disillusionment among sections of the Afrikaner working class as the NP abandoned its 1948 election promises to increase state control over the mines, strategic industries and banks. Tensions developed between, on the one hand, the Afrikaner petit bourgeoisie based in the Transvaal and

Orange Free State and, on the other, Cape financial and agricultural capitalists. In 1964, Federale Mynbou, a Sanlam subsidiary, struck a deal with Anglo American to acquire control of the General Mining and Finance Corporation. This outraged many Afrikaner nationalists, including Verwoerd and other cabinet members – here was Afrikaner capital supping with the devil, doing a deal with 'Hoggenheimer', the symbol of foreign monopoly capitalism (O'Meara 1996: 78, 82, 120).

In spite of these developing tensions in the two decades after 1948, the NP's multi-class alliance held together, but in the late 1960s it started to unravel. The nationalist notion that Afrikanerdom comprised a classless, unified *volk* could no longer be sustained, as internal class conflicts rose to the surface. These conflicts became manifest at the political level with the *verligte-verkrampte* split. The *verligtes* (the enlightened ones) stood for a diluted, redefined nationalism that was more in tune with middle-class interests and culture, and that represented all white South Africans rather than Afrikaners alone. The *verkramptes* (the rigid ones) were led by Albert Hertzog, the racist 'socialist', who saw Afrikaner workers as the mainstay of the nationalist movement, and who was unable to come to terms with the embourgeoisement of large sections of Afrikanerdom. In 1969 they broke away from the NP to form the Herstigte Nasionale Party (HNP), but failed to win any seats in the 1970 white election (O'Meara 1996: 155-64). The split deepened further from the late 1970s as the government became less amenable to white working-class interests, abolishing job reservation in 1979, and ever more supportive of white business interests. This led a growing number of white workers to back the HNP and the Conservative Party, newly established in 1982.

DRAWING THE ANALOGY

Without drawing any unseemly direct comparisons, what parallels can be discerned between the fate of the NP multi-class alliance after 1948 and that of the ANC after 1994? There are similarities in the trajectories of both. The ANC's progressive aspirations and intent before 1994 at least conformed to a more genuine socialism, unlike the racist socialism espoused by elements within the NP before 1948. Notwithstanding these fundamental differences in the two brands of socialism, the ANC, like the NP, soon abandoned any kind of socialist agenda on assuming power.

Critics of the ANC's two-stage theory of revolution had often claimed that once the first stage, the national democratic revolution, had been achieved, the second stage, the achievement of socialism, would be soon be jettisoned as a goal. That this would occur had already become apparent before 1994. Two years after the ANC assumed power this outcome was confirmed when the government dropped its Reconstruction and Development Programme (RDP), which was at least inclined towards the pursuit of social justice, and adopted its Growth, Employment and Redistribution (Gear) policy, which was essentially in line with free-market orthodoxy. Gear was much more about growth, and much less about employment and redistribution. The policy prioritised tariff reduction, financial liberalisation, privatisation, exchange rate stabilisation, and wage restraint – all of which delighted the business sector and soon brought dismay to the ANC's allies, the SACP and Cosatu (Marais 2011: 109-16).

The adoption of Gear in 1996 was a moment that can be likened to the second Ekonomiese Volkskongres (which also occurred two years after the NP assumed power in 1948). Gear was testimony to the rising influence of capitalist-inclined figures within the ANC, as had been the case with the NP. As Hein Marais states: 'Powerful sections in the ANC have developed a reflective sympathy for policies that put the market ahead of society' (2011: 139-40). Some of these figures have become powerful business magnates; men like Cyril Ramaphosa, Tokyo Sexwale, Saki Macozoma and Patrice Motsepe stand out as supreme examples (and as the equivalents of earlier Afrikaner magnates such as Anton Rupert, Jan Marais, and Andries Wassenaar).

Whereas the NP government in the 1950s, as we have seen, expanded state-owned enterprises, the ANC-led government has to a certain extent gone in the opposite direction, stimulating the partial privatisation of parastatals. At the same time, this government, like its NP predecessor, has used the parastatals to further the interests of its middle-class constituents. Executive and managerial posts in the parastatals have been filled largely by members of the newly empowered black elite, often those well-connected politically. Black-owned companies have also benefited from preferential treatment in securing procurement contracts from parastatals. These state-owned enterprises have also facilitated the expansion of black employment. Just as, for instance, the South African Railways (SAR) was once a major employer of 'poor whites' in the apartheid era, so too has the ANC government used SAR's successor, Transnet, to expand black employment. The similarities do not end there. Under the NP government the parastatals gained a poor reputation for inefficiency and corruption. The same scenario is being played out in the post-apartheid era (Southall 2007: 210-14, 222-23).

Since 1994 the main instrument for promoting the growth of a black capitalist class and securing a greater share of the economy has been the policy of Black Economic Empowerment (BEE). After 1948 the emerging Afrikaner business class had had the advantage of building on a foundation laid by the provision of some capital derived from the farming sector and Afrikaner savings. Black entrepreneurs after 1994 did not have that foundation, as the necessary capital was not readily available. So black acquisitions and ownership came to depend upon the provision of capital by banks, financial houses and state financial institutions – and upon the willingness of white-controlled corporations to cooperate in the whole BEE endeavour. The government actively promoted BEE, directing the policy mainly at the mining, energy and financial sectors – for instance, the target for the financial sector was 20 per cent black ownership by 2014 (Southall 2006: 73-78).

The critics of BEE argue that the R300 billion worth of BEE deals since 1994 have benefited only a small, ultra-rich, politically connected elite, have given rise to cronyism and corruption, and have done little to improve the lot of the working class and the poor. BEE has thus created strains within the governing multi-class alliance. We have already seen that such strains developed within the NP's multi-class alliance when it, too, pursued policies deemed by its subordinate components to be too favourable towards capital. The NP government, though, was better able to withstand these strains, more or less because it could bring a fair degree of material comfort to the working-class element in the alliance. Moreover, the size of this component in the NP's alliance was very much smaller than the vast ranks of black workers and unemployed for whom the ANC government has been expected to deliver relief and comfort. Whereas the NP government brought material benefits to each of its main constituencies, albeit unequally, the ANC government has not been able to do so, in part because of the sheer magnitude of the challenge.

In the past decade, the strains within the ANC-led multi-class alliance have become ever more apparent. The governing party has faced growing disaffection from those constituencies from which it would expect to be given electoral support. Vocal popular movements, like the shack-dwellers' grouping, Abahlali BaseMjondolo, have arisen. Service delivery protests have become more widespread. Representatives of the ANC's formal alliance partners, especially those in Cosatu, have spoken out against crony capitalism, excessive elite enrichment and growing inequality, and against the policies, decisions and practices that have made these disagreeable tendencies possible. But as yet, nearly two decades on from 1994, this alliance has held together, albeit under strain. The NP's multi-class alliance only began to fracture twenty or so years after 1948. It remains to be seen how much longer the ANC's multi-class alliance can remain intact in the face of rising internal tensions and conflicts.

PATRONAGE, CRONYISM AND CORRUPTION

Both the NP after 1948 and the ANC after 1994 paid careful attention to the civil service and its composition. Rejecting the notion that the civil service could be neutral, there to do the same job whichever party holds power, the NP and ANC both saw the public sector as an instrument for consolidating power and as a source of patronage.

After 1948, as O'Meara has stated, 'the Malan government sought to extend an iron grip over the bureaucratic apparatus and culture of government. They relied on the Broederbond to patrol senior and middle-class appointments' (1996: 61). This meant ensuring that loyal Afrikaners were appointed to senior civil service positions, and that English speakers, deemed to be imperialist in outlook, were purged, especially from the police and military. The number of Afrikaners employed in the civil service almost doubled between 1946 and 1960. By 1968 there were twice as many Afrikaners in government jobs than there had been before the 1948 election (O'Meara 1996: 61-63; Giliomee 1979: 165).

A similar process of Africanisation in the civil service has occurred since 1994. Whereas an insistence on bilingualism had been one mechanism to drive Afrikanerisation after 1948, the policy of affirmative action and equity was invoked to push Africanisation after 1994. Whereas the Broederbond had been the key agency in the NP era, the ANC's deployment committee has played a similar role in recent years, its decisions, in Marais' words, allowing it 'to extend its (disciplinary) reach into top tiers of the state' (2011: 429, n.22). In both cases ethnic/racial considerations appeared to outweigh concerns about administrative capacity and efficiency. And so, too, public administration in both the post-1948 and post-1994 eras became subjected to critique, and sometimes ridicule, for incompetence and inefficiency.

In both eras, too, the government sector became a major site of corruption. This, though, appears not to have set in immediately. The first two prime ministers after 1948, Malan and Strijdom, appear to have been incorruptible, as was Mandela. The rot started with Verwoerd, who allegedly had dealings with corrupt elements, but the situation worsened significantly from the time of Vorster's premiership in 1966. Under Vorster, NP ministers and MPs commonly acquired shares in companies that stood to benefit from government decisions – for instance, in farm produce companies whose prices were fixed by government. Afrikaner businesses were favoured in the awarding of government contracts. In the 1960s, the Broederbond was able to manipulate the Land Bank so that NP followers were favoured in the granting of loans (Lodge, 2002: 406).

In the late 1970s, Vorster's government became embroiled in the so-called 'information scandal'. In its efforts to win international support for the apartheid regime, the Department of Information became involved in widespread fraud, bribery, plotting and skulduggery, with staff members in the department enjoying lavish lifestyles (Van Vuuren 2006: 24-25, 30-32; O'Meara 1996: 142, 213-14). A key figure in the Vorster era was Nico Diederichs, a cabinet minister from 1958 to 1974, and state president from 1974 to 1978. During his political career he was also involved in business dealings and owned six companies. In 1975 he sold a piece of land at sixty-two times the price he had paid for it only two years before. And there were strong allegations that he had a secret Swiss bank account. There were further rumours linking other government figures to Swiss bank accounts. One such rumour was that an NP election candidate, Robert Smit, was murdered, together with his wife, just before the 1977 whites-only election because he was about to 'spill the beans' about such accounts (Van Vuuren 2006: 32-33).

It has been claimed that President FW de Klerk presided over the most corrupt period of all during the apartheid era. As bureaucrats saw NP rule coming to an end, many are alleged to have plundered the state's resources. The Department of Development Aid and the Department of Education and Training were both found by official inquiries to have been riddled with corruption. Senior members of government and the military were engaged in ivory and drug smuggling. Oil dealing during the sanctions era involved huge payments to the middlemen who secured the purchases, as well as kickbacks to officials (Van Vuuren 2006: 41-45, 49-51, 63-65; Hyslop 2005: 783-84). It was a similar story with arms dealing, where lax accounting and the use of front companies gave rise to corruption (Lodge 2002: 407).

The pattern has been similar under the ANC-led government. Corruption scandals have been regular news items, the notorious arms deal heading the list. Numerous politicians and government officials have had direct associations or close family links with businesses that have benefited from dealings with the government. In 2007-2008 about 40 per cent of ANC MPs were also company directors (Southall 2008: 293). In 2010 almost one-third of the ANC's National Executive Committee sat on the boards of BEE companies. The preferential treatment given to black entrepreneurs in the awarding of government contracts has given rise to cronyism and nepotism. Spouses, relatives and friends of government ministers, politicians and officials have often been the beneficiaries of such contracts. It was reported that over 2 000 government officials in 2008-09 profited from government tenders worth over R600 million (Marais 2011: 140-42).

Even the same names crop up in both the pre-1994 and post-1994 eras. In the late 1960s one Agliotti bought land near the Johannesburg airport for R5 million and sold it to the state for R95 million (O'Meara 1996: 231). Over forty years later another Agliotti has been implicated in drug smuggling and bribing the chief commissioner of police. Marc Rich was one of the key middlemen involved in shady oil deals in the apartheid era; and his company, Glencore, was a participant in the notorious 'oilgate' deal of 2003 (Van Vuuren 2006: 65).

Media coverage of government corruption prompted similar responses in both eras. Following the information scandal, PW Botha's government introduced a Bill to stop the press from publishing details of government corruption without first consulting the advocate general. In the face of a media outcry, the government withdrew the Bill (O'Meara, 1996: 242). The ANC government is intent on forcing its Protection of Information Bill through parliament in the face of widespread popular opposition.

At the same time, there are significant differences between the NP and ANC responses to alleged government corruption. The NP government was more adept at denying and covering up the corruption in its ranks. From 1967 the auditor general usually stopped reporting details of wrongdoing in government ranks (Van Vuuren 2006: 25), whereas the auditor general's reports since 1994 have tended to be more open and forthcoming in this regard. Moreover, some ANC figures, at least, have been more ready to admit to the problem than was ever the case with NP leaders. In 2007 Kgalema Motlanthe, the ANC's secretary general at the time, conceded that corruption within the ANC was 'far worse than anyone imagines', and that the 'rot is across the board' (Southall 2008: 282).

CONCLUSION

This chapter is not putting forward a comparison between the old NP that established one of the world's most abhorrent systems of institutionalised racism and the ANC that led the struggle to overthrow that system. The analysis, rather, points to some similar trajectories in the histories of the two nationalist movements. As is often the case with such movements, they hold together more easily when opposing and challenging an existing ruling order. Both the NP before 1948 and the ANC before 1994 were able to unite their followers, in part by appealing to a common sense of victimhood. This was entirely justified in the case of the ANC, hardly so in the case of the NP. Afrikaner nationalist mobilisers pointed to what they saw as the marginalisation and vulnerability of Afrikaners: the business sector was dominated by imperial capital; and the position of Afrikaner workers in the labour market was threatened by black competition. African nationalists had a straightforward case when they invoked the long history of racial oppression, exclusion and exploitation.

In opposition, each movement was able to devise a programme that appeared to cater for the needs of the different components in its multi-class support base. The Afrikaner nationalist movement would promise to serve the interests of the rising Afrikaner business class, Afrikaner workers and the Afrikaner unemployed. For the African nationalist movement, the Freedom Charter was vague and ambiguous enough for its future implementation in a liberated South Africa to be deemed to meet the needs of all oppressed, excluded classes.

In this way both movements were able to build multi-class alliances. But on attaining power it became much more difficult to hold these alliances together. Whereas the NP government was able, more or less, to meet the expectations of its component classes, it did so unequally, privileging the interests of its growing business class, and this led to a fracturing of its multi-class alliance. By the 1970s the NP had in effect ceased to be an Afrikaner nationalist party but, rather, a party that rested its case on the idea that white supremacy was a prerequisite for white survival – while at the same time openly espousing free market principles.

The ANC, on assuming power, faced a far more daunting challenge in meeting the needs of all its constituent classes. Given the apartheid legacy it inherited and its huge number of followers, it was always going to be nearly impossible to fulfil the expectations and hopes of those who had long been oppressed, marginalised and exploited. Its multi-class alliance held together in the immediate afterglow of liberation, sustained by Mandela's fatherly leadership and the hope of 'a better life for all'. In time, though, the alliance became strained as the ANC-led government, like its NP predecessor, appeared to privilege the interests of its middle-class following over those of its marginalised, impoverished supporters. The state of the alliance now appears to be more precarious than ever, with Cosatu carping at the self-enriching activities of the 'predatory elite', bemoaning the level of corruption, and pointing to deteriorating relations within the tripartite alliance – and there appears to be a growing possibility that Cosatu will walk out of the alliance. The NP's multi-class alliance started to fracture about twenty years after the assumption of power. Over eighteen years into the post-apartheid era it remains to be seen how much longer the ANC's can hold together.

REFERENCES

Adam H (1979) Interests behind Afrikaner power. In Adam H and H Giliomee (Eds) *The Rise and Crisis of Afrikaner Power*. Cape Town: David Philip.
Baskin J (1991) *Striking Back: A History of Cosatu*. Braamfontein: Ravan.
Callinicos L (1999) Oliver Tambo and the politics of class, race and ethnicity in the African National Congress of South Africa. *African Sociological Review* 3 (1): 130-51.

Eley G (2008) Dilemmas and challenges of social history since the 1960s: what comes after the cultural turn. *South African Historical Journal* 60 (3): 310-22.

Giliomee H (1979) The Afrikaner economic advance. In Adam H and H Giliomee (Eds) *The Rise and Crisis of Afrikaner Power*. Cape Town: David Philip.

Glaser D (2001) *Politics and Society in South Africa*. London: Sage.

Hyslop J (2005) Political corruption: before and after apartheid. *Journal of Southern African Studies* 31 (4): 773-89.

Iheduru OC (2004) Black economic power and nation-building in post-apartheid South Africa. *Journal of Modern African Studies* 42 (1): 1-30.

Legassick M (interviewed by A Lichtenstein) (2002) The past and present of Marxist historiography in South Africa. *Radical Historical Review* 82: 111-130.

Lodge T (1994) The African National Congress and its allies. In Reynolds A (Ed.) *Election '94, South Africa*. Cape Town: David Philip.

Lodge T (2002) Political corruption in South Africa: from Apartheid to multiracial state. In Heidenheimer AJ and M Johnston (Eds) *Political Corruption: Concepts and Contexts*. New Brunswick, London: Transaction Publishers.

Marais H (2011) *South Africa Pushed to the Limit: The Political Economy of Change*. Cape Town: UCT Press.

O'Meara D (1983) *Volkskapitalisme: Class, Capital and Ideology in the Development of Afrikaner Nationalism 1934-1948*. Braamfontein: Ravan.

O'Meara D (1996) *Forty Lost Years: The Apartheid State and the Politics of the National Party, 1948-1994*. Randburg: Ravan.

Sampson A (1999) *Mandela: The Authorised Biography*. Johannesburg: Jonathan Ball.

Southall R (1980) African capitalism in contemporary South Africa. *Journal of Southern African Studies* 7 (1): 38-70.

Southall R (2006) Ten propositions about black economic empowerment in South Africa. *Review of African Political Economy* 111: 67-84.

Southall R (2007) The ANC, black economic empowerment and state-owned enterprises: a recycling of history? In Buhlungu S, J Daniel, R Southall and J Lutchman (Eds) *State of the Nation: South Africa 2007*. Cape Town: HSRC Press.

Southall R (2008) The ANC for sale? Money, morality and business in South Africa. *Review of African Political Economy* 116: 281-299.

Van Vuuren H (2006) *Apartheid Grand Corruption*. Pretoria: Institute for Security Studies.

CHAPTER 4

Predicaments of post-apartheid social movement politics: The Anti-Privatisation Forum (AFP) in Johannesburg[1]

Ahmed Veriava and Prishani Naidoo

INTRODUCTION

In May 2012, the authors received an invitation to attend a meeting 'to discuss where do we take the APF?' (McKinley, e-mail communication, 3 May 2012).[2] Subsequently, we met as a small group on the stairs of Museum Africa in Newtown one Sunday morning.[3] Present were about fifteen men and women, including founding members and activists from later struggles. There was, however, no easy path forward, and the discussion turned on whether or not the APF should 'be revived'. For some of us, revival made no sense. The APF belonged to a different time, and what was needed was a new form to bring together communities in struggle. The elected office bearers had also not met in over a year, and were tainted by accusations of corruption. Rather than trying to resurrect a name that we had long outgrown, or trying to clean up the mess left by the office bearers, our task should be to think about ways of bringing back together the existing struggles of the communities in which the APF operated, or those that have been emerging since its departure from the political realm. For others, however, the APF's death could not be accepted (or admitted) as local struggles had depended heavily on its knowledge, skills and other resources. 'The APF had a name' and that meant something: it was too much simply to walk away.

Twelve years earlier, in a precinct close by, the APF held what would later come to be seen as one of its first protests.[4] At that time, there was the idea, and anticipation, that an emerging campaign against privatisation would be transformed into a movement. Activists from Wits University and the city had come together to protest against a conference called Urban Futures that was showcasing the city's and the University's respective restructuring plans. Denouncing the 'neoliberal policies' (APF 2000a; 2000b) of the University and the city, on the last day of the conference (after a week of smaller actions), a group of about a hundred protesters from a range of organisations across the city pushed their way into the Wits Great Hall, taking over the closing session. And so the APF was born.[5]

In the twelve years since then much has happened, yet little seems to have been won. Though the APF undertook many struggles, experimenting with different tactics and strategies, in the end it came up against the limits of its own politics. In this chapter, we make an accounting of a failure, but also of lessons for the necessary work that must follow… This is just one account, a perspective from two of us who came together with many others in what became the making of a movement. It is not, then, an 'objective' outsider piece, but a story that speaks from our experience of being part of a struggle with others, a struggle in which differences (of class, race, gender and political/ideological orientation) were constantly having to be confronted as collective approaches and decisions were made and shaped.

We do not tell the whole story of the APF. This is not a history. It is a reflection on a movement that left a modest mark on political life in the city. We take up the story with the struggle against prepaid water meters in Soweto, for the ways in which it captures something of the predicaments of social movement resistance in post-apartheid South Africa, and helps us to understand some of the forces that have contributed to the decline of movements like the APF.[6]

DENOUEMENT

In 2002, a newly formed Johannesburg Water[7] initiated a pilot project in Orange Farm, a township forty-five kilometres south of the Johannesburg city centre. It was called 'Operation Gcin'amanzi', which in isiZulu means 'Save Water'. With the stated aim of reducing the problem of 'unaccounted-for water', Operation Gcin'amanzi had at its centre plans for infrastructure upgrades and the installation of prepaid water meters for Johannesburg's townships. By its logic, fixing leaking pipes and curbing household and individual consumption were the answers to the problems it faced in sustaining a programme of water delivery that rested on residents paying for consumption over and above the free six kilolitres allocated per household per month by the state. From the very start it provoked resistance.

In Orange Farm, much of this resistance came from the Orange Farm Water Crisis Committee (OWCC), an affiliate of the APF. Although members of the OWCC registered a number of complaints against the new project, the one that increasingly came to stand at the centre of its campaign was the decision to introduce prepaid water meters in the area. For the OWCC, prepaid water meters signalled greater difficulties for the poor, especially those with large households unable to survive on the six kilolitre allocation of free basic water, and they objected to Johannesburg Water's deception of residents, who were told that they could only get access to flush toilets if they bought a prepaid meter. When the project failed to progress beyond a single neighbourhood of the sprawling township, the OWCC declared a victory, believing that the campaign that was mounted – consisting mainly of mass meetings, marches and confrontations with local government and Johannesburg Water officials – had dissuaded Johannesburg Water from extending the project (Coalition Against Water Privatisation et al. 2003; McKinley and Veriava 2005). The opposite turned out to be closer to the truth, and a year later a new iteration of the project started up in Soweto.

The year 2002 was certainly a time of great political optimism for APF activists. Although there were few official victories to which the organisation could point, it had already forced important concessions from state agencies. Just a year earlier, Eskom had announced a moratorium on electricity cut-offs in Soweto, and by May 2003 it had written off the electricity payment arrears of indebted Sowetans.[8] Although the actual write-off agreement had been negotiated with the South African National Civics Organisation (Sanco), it was widely accepted that the pressure placed on Eskom by the Soweto Electricity Crisis Committee's 'Operation Khanyisa' (whose central tactic was the illegal reconnection of residents whose electricity had been cut for non-payment) was the real catalyst in the writing off of arrears (Egan and Wafer 2004; Naidoo and Veriava 2009).[9]

Even beyond Johannesburg and the struggles of these fledgling community movements organised around the APF, the star of 'new social movements' seemed to be rising in the crowded sky of the political realm.[10] The showing of a new crop of social movements and, it should also be said, their representation at the 2001 march at the World Conference against Racism, brought with it the promise of a new political force on the left, potential for a new beginning for a militant politics rooted in community struggles, set apart from the ANC-led Alliance and forged in direct opposition to 'the neoliberal policies adopted by government' (Barchiesi 2006; Desai 2002; Hart 2008; McKinley and Naidoo 2004). This potential seemed to realise itself the following year, when the APF marched with other social movements under the banner of the Social Movements United at the World Summit on Sustainable Development, trumping the official 'civil society march' organised by political forces sympathetic to the ANC (Barchiesi 2006; Hart 2008). When, at the end of the march, John Appolis (then chairperson of the APF) announced 'the arrival of a new movement' in South Africa, he therefore expressed the views of many observers and activists alike (Indymedia video footage, 31 August 2002). Earlier that year, in fact, Ashwin Desai's widely acclaimed book on post-apartheid community struggles had already given a name to the subject of this movement: 'the poors' (Desai 2002).

Like many stories, this one gets more complex the deeper you go, and in years to come understanding its complexity became increasingly urgent for the 'movement' itself.

But in 2002, riding a wave of sympathy and popular support, its activists were able to confront their critics and opponents with a sense of confidence won on the street. For the community groups congregated in the APF, the infectious political optimism of a collective subject discovering its own power translated into militant affirmations of their local struggles, as well as a widening of the organisation's constitutive political claims. If it is clear that this optimism shaped the Orange Farm Water Crisis Committee's perception of its victory, it also characterised the militant energy with which activists attacked Operation Gcin'amanzi a year later. A 2004 essay by Trevor Ngwane and Ahmed Veriava captures something of the mood of the campaign that was starting up in Soweto:

> In a community meeting it was decided that the workers laying pipes would be approached and asked to stop work, and if they refused people would physically block them from moving on. The next day … Phiri erupted. Metro Police, the South African Police Service and private security were called in to ensure the installation of the meters and disperse toyi-toying protests. By the end of the day, five residents had been arrested including … the [Soweto Electricity Crisis Committee] organiser. Later, many residents returned with all manner of tools and digging equipment. People formed their own 'chain gangs' and set about digging up the ground, still loose from the work applied to it earlier that day. At the first skin of the pipe, a flood of excitement and song rushed through the packed streets. People clutched at exposed parts and in mighty collective heaves ripped the pipe from the earth. The whole community came out to witness the orgy of living labour … there was no master strategist or leader, just insurgents with 'destroy the meter' on their lips moving to the next section of pipe (Ngwane and Veriava 2004: 135).

In 2004, nothing was yet certain. Things could still have gone either way. Although it remained unmoved in its determination to roll out prepaid water meters in Soweto, Johannesburg Water had already suffered a number of setbacks as a consequence of the campaign on the streets of Soweto. As resistance to prepaid meters grew, Johannesburg Water would have to readjust its approach to cost recovery, at the level of the kinds of technology and infrastructure it was developing and, with regard to its interventions, at the level of the social relations and everyday practices of Sowetans. However, even by this time it was becoming clear to activists in the APF that although their campaign had made Johannesburg Water's ambitions significantly more difficult to realise it was still far from registering any kind of definitive victory. And though new waves of resistance seemed constantly to emerge, almost in tandem with Johannesburg Water's entry into new areas of Soweto, the project was proving tremendously flexible in making adjustments to 'get around' resistance. Meanwhile, the internal limits of the campaign were beginning to show – divisions among different quarters hardened; repression and its costs were forcing a rethinking of tactics; and levels of mobilisation were proving increasingly difficult to maintain.

What is striking in the Ngwane-Veriava essay, especially when read from a present-day perspective, is the special significance the authors (who present themselves from the start as participants in the events they describe) give to this struggle against prepaid water meters in Soweto for the development of social movement politics in post-apartheid South Africa. In their account, the movements that are the protagonists of the story – the APF, the Soweto Electricity Crisis Committee and the Phiri Concerned Residents – emerge out of the failure of the traditional organs of the liberation movement to act as meaningful vehicles for advancing people's struggles 'today', struggles presented in ways that suggest their continuity with struggles of the 'past' (struggles against the forms of domination that characterised the apartheid era). This sense of potential, of the possibility of rebuilding something of greater political significance than what was immediately at stake in a set of very particular struggles, was often shared by activists working in the new crop of movements that emerged after 2000.[11] From such a perspective, what happened on the streets of Soweto, the success or the pitfalls of the tactics that emerged there, and how it all turned out in the end, take on a meaning and significance for a wider political imaginary.

Confronting some of the limits of the campaign in Soweto, in 2004 Ngwane and Veriava predicted that its future would unfold across two emergent poles: a newly cultivated ability to (illegally) bypass meters, and the possibility of launching a (legal) challenge to the constitutionality of new technology and the city's broader framework for the delivery of water to the poor. The prediction (unsurprisingly)[12] turned out to be correct, but in a way that contradicted the hopeful optimism of the essay. Many people did bypass their meters, and at one point as many as 40 per cent of households were doing so. But this did not shake Johannesburg Water's resolve to use the technology of prepaid water meters – and it is currently searching out and correcting bypassed meters. Bypassing was also often depoliticised – a clandestine and thus 'private' form of resistance. At the second pole, things didn't develop any better. Although a 2006 ruling by the High Court delivered a victory to the campaign when it declared prepaid water meters unconstitutional, this did little more than suspend the further rollout of the project pending Johannesburg Water's and the City's appeal of the judgment. In 2009, when the Constitutional Court finally ruled on the matter, completely overturning the High Court's decision (which had already been significantly whittled down in the Supreme Court), it appeared to announce the end of a decade-long struggle, and with it the failure of resistance to the usage of prepaid water meters in Soweto.

In retrospect, this failure remains deeply ironic and paradoxical. Political resistance failed in Soweto, but without anything like victory for the forces it opposed. At the end, the Johannesburg Water project that first emerged in 2002 in Orange Farm looks very different to what it did then. Prepaid water meters remain, but supported today by a whole series of institutional (and even technological) concessions and adjustments, many of which (in one way or another) owe their place to resistance and to Johannesburg Water's and the City's attempts at responding to it. Even the name of the project – Operation Gcin'amanzi – today seems to have been rendered impossible, a fact that has forced a rebranding of Johannesburg Water's operation (ironically borrowing from the campaign against prepaid water meters in the naming of its own new media operation, 'Water Warriors'). Political resistance forced change, for instance in relation to the City's free basic water allocation and indigent management framework,[13] as well as at the level of Johannesburg Water's practical operations and the ways in which meters are introduced. In some respects such change might be read as working to ensure that poor households have greater security and, at least formally, are afforded more respect with regard to their constitutional rights.

Equally, however, many of the same, seemingly benevolent, measures introduced have also deepened and clarified new forms of subjection and control.

In many ways this story, of the failures and paradoxes of the struggle against prepaid water meters in Soweto, mirrors that of the APF more broadly, as well as of a number of other 'new social movements' in post-apartheid South Africa. For although the appearance of such movements a decade ago was often greeted with 'giddy' (see Marais 2011) expectation, today many have disappeared.[14] And in the case of the APF, though its struggles have fundamentally and irreparably shifted governmental practices, not only have such shifts been double-edged, they have also often been moulded in relation to the rationalities of governmental frameworks, moving towards a politics centred on *making visible* subjects (in need) of governmental intervention, or becoming drawn into depoliti- cising institutional frameworks that often set sections of poor communities against each other. Even if such positions can be shown to be a consequence of the very terrains upon which social movement struggles have unfolded, or even when we recognise that these are but one side of a longer story, it might still be said that the APF was, in a manner (however ambivalent) integrated into the post-apartheid political order – and reflected it. In the end, the subject of this movement seemingly remained a national subject, figured in relation to a historical wrong, and with shifting entitlements that were constantly rene- gotiated within the power relations that characterise post-apartheid governmentality.

Is this the form of our failure?

This story of the APF and resistance to prepaid meters marks out a predicament. Paradoxical outcomes, just like failure, are not uncommon in politics. On the contrary. The paradox outlined in relation to Soweto is merely the form of failure for a wide range of political struggles today. Not even what count as political victories are spared such paradoxes. Even 'the people's victory over apartheid', extolled in countless popular narra- tives and official statements can, *at the end*, be shown to have made its own 'pragmatic pact' with power. Whether in Patrick Bond's estimation that South Africa's transition to democracy finds its limits with our passing from 'race apartheid' to 'class apartheid' (2004), or even the South African Communist Party's (SACP's) perception of a depar- ture from the 'National Democratic Revolution' in the form of 'the 1996 class project' (Nzimande 2006), it is the paradoxical articulations between resistance and power, between the (narrated) political demands and constitutive claims of 'the struggle', and the form of their inscription in the state, around which such narratives and counter-narra- tives revolve. If we refuse the simplistic reductionism of the 'sell-out thesis', as well as the disabling and ideologically thick resignation of 'There Is (was) No Alternative' (TINA), what should we make of such paradoxes? Is it a soft statement of the 'law of revolution', as if every resistance is merely the herald of its eventual recuperation, just as every revolution has already to anticipate its inevitable Thermidor? Even where we cast the problem in less dramatic terms – which, in any case, are those of the ideologists of the right who would have us believe, as Badiou said in the preamble to *The Communist Hypothesis*, that 'to want something better, is to want something worse' – a question still *imposes*: what use is there in resistance apart from power's *own* principle of mutation and development?

In this chapter, we do not as much try to answer this question as make a case for the necessity for going beyond it.

As Alain Badiou (borrowing from Mao) recently reminded us, 'our failures are not the same as theirs … [t]he logic of reactionaries the world over is make trouble, fail, make trouble again', but the logic of the people is 'fight, fail, fail again, fight again, till their victory' (Badiou 2010: 7). At the end then, our question is: how might we begin again? And not in the same way …

BECOMING (INTERRUPTED)

One can say many good things about the APF, and probably just as many bad things. The two points collected in this section are neither good nor bad. They are a confrontation of a political limit and a thinking about how to overcome it.

A limit is clarified in relation to the APF's failure to articulate a politics that could go beyond the interplay between resistance and governmental adjustment and recuperation. As we have argued elsewhere (Naidoo 2010; 2011; Veriava 2012), governmental practices, especially the delivery of basic services, have been profoundly shaped by forms of resistance. In fact, the current configuration of indigent management strategies, lifeline allocations, new technologies and infrastructure, and management principles being deployed in the City of Johannesburg cannot be understood except on the basis of the ways in which policy and practice have responded to the struggles waged by the APF on the streets of Johannesburg.

This is well illustrated in the struggle over prepaid meters, which were themselves introduced to circumvent earlier forms of resistance to cost recovery. Although the installation of prepaid water meters in Phiri angered residents to the extent that they came together in protest, it was also clear, quite soon into the resistance, that Johannesburg Water and the municipality were seriously committed to making Operation Gcin'amanzi work in Phiri, as they had spent vast amounts of money, time and other resources on research, legal expertise and representation, private security, and policy formulation (and reformulation) to this end. With the help of the APF and the Soweto Electricity Crisis Committee, Phiri residents organised themselves as the Phiri Concerned Residents and began to take decisions as a collective. At the other end, Johannesburg Water and the municipality became more heavy-handed in their approach, completely cutting off those refusing to allow prepaid water meters to be installed in their yards from any water supply. As the number of arrests and court cases increased, and the APF's own legal costs mounted, it became necessary to consider different strategic options.

It was agreed that the campaign needed to find a way of expanding its support base and reaching out within civil society. The possibility of launching a more serious legal challenge was also mooted. To these ends, the APF proposed the formation of the Coalition Against Water Privatisation (CAWP), a broad network of civil society groupings that came together in support of the struggle in Phiri (and Johannesburg and Gauteng more generally). It also approached the Centre for Applied Legal Studies at Wits for advice about the law and the potential use of it in the campaign.

The CAWP was a strategy of the APF's for dealing with the challenges in the struggle against prepaid water meters, and it therefore became a central aspect of APF discussions. Though the CAWP proved to be an extremely important formation for the APF in broadening its campaign, its emphasis on the legal strategy in Phiri also shifted the campaign away from more direct action, and tactics such as illegal reconnections and the bypassing of meters.

In 2007, the Centre for Applied Legal Studies and the CAWP began what turned out to be an extremely long court process through which five residents of Phiri brought a class-action suit in the Johannesburg High Court against the installation of prepaid water meters in the township. They demanded that the free allocation of water be increased from six kilolitres per household per month to fifty litres per person per day; that prepaid water meters be declared unconstitutional; and that normal credit meters be reinstalled in homes. When, in 2009, the Constitutional Court passed its final judgement, it argued that the City of Johannesburg was already meeting the demands of the CAWP through Siyasizana ('We are helping'), the name given to its latest indigent management policy, being implemented since July 2009. It did not make prepaid water meters illegal, and left the decision as to what should constitute the amount of free basic water to the local municipalities to determine.

Having submitted themselves to the 'logic' of the courts, APF and CAWP members felt a legitimate sense of defeat. Siyasizana, bringing together prepaid technology with free basic water delivery, debt write-offs and other 'incentives' to 'rehabilitate' consumers within an indigent management framework, was viewed by activists in the APF as further entrenching inequality and the duty to pay for basic services by making increasing levels of service accessible according to ability to pay, as well as by moving towards providing free allocations of water and electricity only to those signed onto the indigent register (Interview, Bricks Mokolo, 21 August 2010; APF 2008). Siyasizana's database of indigents, updated on a six-monthly basis (as each person is required to reapply for indigent status every six months), linked with other national databases such as that registering all social grant recipients, would also serve as a way of monitoring and tracking the habits and behaviour of the poor, becoming a source of knowledge and potential predictive capacity in managing those identified as the poor through the provision of incentives in order to induce particular changes in behaviour in the targeted population. Thus far, we have seen the City of Johannesburg adopt such an approach with regard to the delivery of water, when it began installing prepaid water meters, and with Siyasizana's Jobs Pathways Centre (which provides short-term training and work opportunities for those on the indigent register).[15]

The court case and the road to Siyasizana also forced activists onto a political terrain that reinforced a tendency towards the juridification and technicisation of political engagements. In the end, what the many years of struggle inaugurated was a policy that seems to address all the demands of the APF and CAWP, but through a targeted system of delivery that reproduces inequality by restricting access to higher levels of service to payment. Although some (Everatt 2008, Hart 2007, Von Schnitzler 2008) have argued that Siyasizana marks a move back to more welfare-like and less neoliberal modes of local government, we argue that Siyasizana represents something new, a hybrid form including decommodified access for the targeted, that continues to develop the rationalities of individual responsibility, the duty to pay for services above a certain level considered basic, and the preoccupation of the state with knowing and managing that population group identified as poor.

Although the APF always referred to the court route as only one tactic among others, it came to take centre stage in mobilisations against prepaid water meters. In its own research reports from this period, the CAWP and APF bemoaned the decline of resistance in Phiri and its individualisation, as bypassing the meter needed to be hidden by residents in order to avoid being caught and punished (CAWP 2006). And, as possibilities for change came to be circumscribed by the law, the Constitution and the ability of the state to afford delivery, the imagination of more locally driven, decentralised, and collectivised approaches to service delivery appeared only fleetingly – in rhetorical brushstrokes in speeches given by leaders of APF affiliates such as the Orange Farm Water Crisis Committee and Soweto Electricity Crisis Committee, only to disappear in technical debates of legal proceedings.

Even beyond the struggle in Soweto over prepaid water meters, however, the resistances of the APF tended to become caught in set-piece battles that often served merely to delay the inevitable, or to prepare the terrain for an eventual recuperation.

Ultimately, what the APF lacked was the ability to express a constitutive project. For where the APF always seemed to gravitate towards the building of an alternative, it was pulled in other directions by factionalism, entrepreneurial activism and vanguardist practices. More importantly, it failed to develop its very real potential.

Although the early years of the APF saw a fairly easy coming together of different political traditions and tendencies, with the immediacy of unfolding struggles demanding the formulation of workable tactics and strategies as well as successful actions and demonstrations, as struggle became more institutionalised through the increasingly regular (and regulated) rhythms and routines (of processes, policies and structures) that came to define the APF, political differences became more stark and difficult to reconcile. As it became clear that the APF was a growing force that was having an effect in Gauteng, different political groupings of the APF intensified their attempts to capture space and turn the APF into a vehicle for their own political agendas.[16]

Moreover, although many of us celebrated the resonance of the Zapatistas' slogan, 'walking, we ask questions', in moments of the early life of the APF, embracing our uncertainty and experimentation with what we were becoming and trying to build in common, the conflicts that came to characterise the later APF (and that contributed ultimately to its decline) revolved around who had the right answer. In addition to these problems, rooted in political and ideological approaches, the APF and its affiliates came up against members of communities (and sometimes of the APF itself) who saw participation in the APF as a way of making money for themselves (interviews with John Appolis, 17 March 2010; Teboho Mashota, 15 May 2010; Dale McKinley, 17 February 2010; among many others housed at the South African History Archives).

More decisive (although not unrelated), however, is that the APF's politics never really went beyond the moment of negativity and refusal, beyond acting out an anti-politics: anti-privatisation, anti-neoliberal, anti-ANC. In spite of the empty adoption of socialism as the vision of the organisation,[17] the politics of the APF was in the end stranded on the governmental terrain, and its vitality was drained internally by strife.

Early re-memberings of the Soweto Electricity Crisis Committee and APF (Desai 2002; Naidoo and Veriava 2003, 2005, 2009; Ngwane and Veriava 2004) celebrate the ways in which social movements were built around the illegal act of reconnection as residents and activists came together to claim, publicly, as a collective form of political activism, the once individualised and hidden act of reconnection. In the Soweto Electricity Crisis Committee, reconnection came to be spoken of as a form of 'working-class delivery' (interview with Trevor Ngwane, 22 June 2003), activists imagining themselves as laying claim to those resources due to them immediately, without waiting for some intervention by the state. In the Orange Farm Water Crisis Committee, leaders spoke often about the need for the state to recognise that there were 'community plumbers' (interview with Bricks Mokolo, 21 August 2010) who could very easily participate in decentralised and more localised systems of delivery. Such arrangements, in which community control would be critical, would, however, require a complete rethinking of systems of delivery and processes requiring much research and coordination. What was important about these affirmations was that they spoke to the potential for developing a politics of self-valorisation that went beyond the interplay between resistance and governmental adjustment – or vague references to an alternative socio-political system.

Such possibilities for self-activity and collectivisation of aspects of service delivery did not materialise, or did so only fleetingly. Community control also never emerged as a real and developed demand by the movements. At best, reconnections became a collective refusal to pay for basic services, and the state continued to be imagined as the central provider of services, even in a decommodified system. The implied demand of the APF's resistance was that the state must resume its responsibilities for those of its citizens too poor to pay for the most basic living resources. In the end, then, the collective political act of reconnection could only ever be imagined as a tactic in the broader struggle for the state to assume the provision of decommodified basic services.

CONCLUSION

As APF members come to terms with its death, struggles for basic services continue, sometimes led by formal organisations, and at other times beginning, much as did the Phiri Concerned Residents, in collective refusals to have policies imposed on them. A quick scan of mainstream news verifies this, with statistics from the Incident Registration Information Service providing a more thorough counting of actions, recording a total of 34 610 protests between 2003 and 2008,[18] making South Africa one of the countries with the highest protest rates in the world (Alexander 2010: 26). It is hoped, therefore, that this chapter has provided an entry into the political experiment that was the APF so that analysis of, and engagement with, more recent cycles of struggle might learn from the lessons drawn. It is, however, just one entry point and one point of view. And we hope, too, that this will spark other re-memberings of the APF (as well as of other movements).

It is also important that although the APF emerged in the context of a growing global movement against neoliberalism (in the form of the alter-globalisation movement), its decline takes place at a time when that movement has practically disappeared and new political energies have been expressed in mass protests from Egypt and Tunisia to Spain and Greece, as well as the USA. All over the world, the spirit of resistance seems to be moving again ...

In 2011, *Time* magazine chose 'The Protester' as its person of the year: 'From the Arab Spring to Athens, From Occupy Wall Street to Moscow' (*Time*, 26 December 2011-2 January 2012). What is significant is that a figure (rather than an individual) was chosen as the person of the year. But it is even more interesting that the figure stands in for an emerging collective political subject: 'The Protester' as the face of a new movement that begins with a form of refusal of authoritarian regimes, of the global economic order or government that rules in the interests of what the Occupy movement has called the 'one per cent'. The political importance of *Time*'s choosing what is in effect a multi-headed movement should not be underestimated. It signals that on the streets of Cairo, Athens, New York, and even recently (it is rumoured) Johannesburg, elites are conceding their legitimacy. There is room for optimism. Maybe the world is turning again and if we do not make our history of conditions of our own choosing, we live in a time when there is irrefutable proof that history itself is far from over. More notably, however, there is cause for concern and circumspection. We should always be worried when power invites us in, when our demands become respectable in elite politics.

It is in these moments that we must be sure of what we stand for, of the forms of affirmation in which our politics is grounded, lest the work of resistance is again 'recuperated' on the governmental terrain.

NOTES

1   Sections of this chapter have already appeared in the 2012 PhD thesis of Ahmed Veriava. Overall, this chapter is based on the experiences of the two authors as founding members of the

Anti-Privatisation Forum, in which they were active until around 2006. They both worked in the APF's research subcommittee responsible for the production of three reports on struggles against prepaid water meters in Johannesburg (Orange Farm and Soweto in particular) between 2003 and 2006, with Naidoo coordinating the research subcommittee and Veriava coordinating the legal sub-committee. In addition, much of the information on Soweto and Orange Farm has been gleaned from research projects conducted by the authors in collaboration with others that focused on aspects of the lives of poor communities and their struggles for basic services in Johannesburg.

2   Dale McKinley, former treasurer of the APF, had been asked to pass the invitation on to us by John Appolis and Bricks Mokolo, former chairpersons of the APF. A few months earlier, Appolis and Mokolo had been asked to convene a meeting of any APF activists who were interested in discuss-ing 'a way forward' about struggles that were continuing in spite of the APF's demise. This was meant to include even those of us who had stopped participating in the organisation.

3   Locked out of the previous APF office by Khanya College (caretakers of the building), activists arriving at this scheduled meeting venue decided to reconvene at Museum Africa, where an archive and exhibition of APF materials had been launched a few months earlier.

4   In July 2000, activists gate-crashed a finger lunch in the Market Theatre precinct, at which city officials were present, to condemn their plans for changes in the city that were seen to be working against the interests of its poorer residents.

5   For a more detailed account of this history see Naidoo and Veriava (2003; 2005); Veriava (2012).

6   It is common in the literature about social movements in post-apartheid South Africa for the APF to be grouped with the Concerned Citizens' Forum (CCF – Durban), the Anti-Eviction Campaign (AEC – Cape Town), and the Landless People's Movement (LPM). They emerged around the same time, and they all self-consciously put forward their demands within an overall critique of neolib-eralism. They also came together in 2001 and 2002 in marches against neoliberal policies and their effects under the banner first of the Durban Social Forum (DSF) and then the Social Movements United (SMU). Though the Treatment Action Campaign (TAC) emerged in the same period as these movements, it is often held apart from them as being less antagonistic towards the ANC Alliance (for example, see Ballard et al. 2004).

7   Johannesburg Water is a utility established in 2001 by the CoJ to cater for the delivery of water to its residents. It is owned by the Johannesburg municipality, but its management is outsourced to the private sector, its overall operations being managed according to market principles. Between 2001 and 2006, the management of JW was outsourced to a consortium that included the notori-ous multinational Suez Lyonnaise des Eaux.

8   In December 2001, the then minister of Public Enterprises, Jeff Radebe, attempted to introduce a number of changes in the delivery of electricity in Soweto, including writing off 50 per cent of resi-dents' debts, reforming the billing process, and 'amnesty' for those who reported illegal reconnec-tions. The SECC, however, refused to accept these proposals, repeating its demands and continuing to struggle for access to electricity to be extended to all; the scrapping of all arrears; the implemen-tation of the free basic electricity policy adopted in 2000; and a return to a flat rate for electricity that had become practice under apartheid. (Egan and Wafer 2004; Naidoo and Veriava 2009).

9   The SECC was one of the first community groups to affiliate to the APF in 2000.

10   Between 2002 and 2006, a number of publications were produced that gave the emerging move-ment the name 'new social movements', a name reflecting their emergence post-1994 and outside the fold of the Congress alliance and tradition, often experimenting with new forms of organising and imagining politics. 'New social movements' included the Concerned Citizens' Forum (CCF) formed in Durban in 1999, the Anti-Eviction Campaign (AEC) formed in Cape Town in 2001, the Treatment Action Campaign (TAC) formed in 1998, and the Landless People's Movement (LPM) formed in 2001.

11   This aspect of new social movement subjectivity is precisely what is erased by the simplistic char-acterisation of such movements as 'single issue campaigns'.

12   Ngwane and Veriava helped to shape that direction.

13   For a more detailed account and analysis of this see Naidoo in NSAR 1 (2010).

14   The CCF has not existed for many years now. In Durban, some CCF affiliates have sustained themselves (for example the Bayview Flats Residents Association) but exist in a very different form. The
LPM no longer exists at a national level. The AEC has split several times, and today only a few of its
branches continue to exist. But this has not meant that struggle has ceased. Poor township communities have continued to engage in what are now known as 'service delivery protests', and since 2004
other movements identifying themselves as movements of the poor and making various demands
of the state have continued to emerge.

15   For a fuller discussion of Siyasizana see Naidoo in NSAR 1 (2010).

16   In addition to its community affiliates and independent trade unions, the APF allowed for the
affiliation of small political groups, such as Keep Left and the Socialist Group (SG), both Trotskyist.

17   APF activists across political traditions and tendencies agree that there was no single approach to,
or idea of, socialism. What socialism meant and how it should be attained were always open questions, contested by members of different ideological persuasions.

18   IRIS records 10 437 protests for the period 2005–2006; 9 166 for the period 2006–2007; and 7 003
for 2007–2008.

REFERENCES

Alexander P (2010) Rebellion of the poor: South Africa's service delivery protests – a preliminary analysis. *Review of African Political Economy*, 37: 123: 25-40.

APF (2008) CoJ's Proposed Water Tariff Increases and Shifts in Free Basic Water Allowance Escalates the
War on the Poor. http://apf.org.za/spip.php?article300 [Accessed 1 August 2012].

APF (2000a) Anti-Privatisation Forum Communique No. 1, Johannesburg: APF press release, 15 July.

APF (2000b) Anti-Privatisation Forum Statement on Disruption of Urban Futures 9th Plenary Session,
Johannesburg: APF press release, 15 July.

Badiou A (2010) *The Communist Hypothesis*, transl. D Macey and S Corcoran. London and New York:
Verso.

Ballard R, A Habib and I Valodia (Eds) (2006) *Voices of Protest: Social Movements in Post-apartheid South
Africa*. Scottsville: University of Kwazulu-Natal Press.

Barchiesi F (2006) Classes, multitudes and the politics of community movements in post-apartheid
South Africa. In Gibson N (Ed.) (2006) *Challenging Hegemony: Social Movements and the Quest for
a New Humanism in Post-Apartheid South Africa*. Eritrea: Africa World Press.

Bond P (2004) *Talk Left, Walk Right: South Africa's Frustrated Global Reforms*. Scottsville: UKZN Press.

Coalition Against Water Privatisation et al. (2006) Lessons from the War Against Prepaid Water Meters.
Johannesburg: CAWP.

Coalition Against Water Privatisation et al. (2003) Nothing for Mahala. The Forced Installation of
Prepaid Water Meters in Stretford, Extension 4, Orange Farm, Johannesburg – South Africa.
Washington, DC: Public Citizen; Johannesburg: CAWP.

Coalition Against Water Privatisation et al. (2004) The Struggle against Silent Disconnections. Prepaid
Meters and the Struggle for Life in Phiri, Soweto, Johannesburg. Johannesburg: CAWP.

Desai A (2002). *We are the Poors. Community Struggles in Post-Apartheid South Africa*. New York:
Monthly Review Press.

Egan A and A Wafer (2004) The Soweto Electricity Crisis Committee (SECC). Durban: Civil Society.

Everatt D (2008) The undeserving poor: Poverty and the politics of service delivery in the poorest nodes
of South Africa. *Politikon*, Vol. 35, No. 3: 293-319.

Gibson N (2006) Challenging everything into question: Broken promises, social movements and emergent intellectual currents in post-apartheid South Africa. In Gibson N (Ed.) (2006) *Challenging*

Hegemony: Social Movements and the Quest for a New Humanism in Post-Apartheid South Africa. Eritrea: Africa World Press.

Hart G (2008) The provocations of neoliberalism: Contesting the nation and liberation after apartheid. *Antipode*, Vol. 40: 678-705.

Hart G (2007) The new poor laws and the crisis of local government. *Amandla*, Vol 2.

McKinley D and P Naidoo (2004) New social movements in South Africa: A story in creation. *Development Update* Vol. 5 No. 2: 9-22.

McKinley D and A Veriava (2005) Arresting Dissent: State Repression and Post-apartheid Social Movements. Johannesburg: Centre for the Study of Violence and Reconciliation (CSVR).

Naidoo P and A Veriava (2003) Re-membering Movements: Trade Union Movements & New Social Movements in Neoliberal South Africa & Mauritius, Centre for Civil Society, Durban. http://ccs. ukzn.ac.za/files/Naidoo%20and%20Varieva%202003%20Re-membering%20movements.pdf

Naidoo P and A Veriava (2005) Re-membering movements: Trade unions and new social movements in neoliberal South Africa. In From local processes to global forces, Centre for Civil Society Research Reports Vol.1. Durban: University of KwaZulu-Natal.

Naidoo P and A Veriava (2009). From the local to the global (and back again?): Anti-commodification struggles of the Soweto Electricity Crisis Committee in Johannebsurg and beyond. In MacDonald D (Ed) *Electric Capitalism*. New York and Basingstoke: Palgrave/Macmillan.

Ngwane T and A Veriava (2004) Strategies and tactics: Movements in the neoliberal transition. Development Update Vol. 5 No. 2:129-146.

Nzimande B (2006) The class question as the 'fault-line' in consolidating the NDR. Umsebenzi, Vol. 5. No. 57.

Veriava A (forthcoming). Under the Sign of an Exception: Post-Apartheid Politics and the Struggle for Water, unpublished PhD manuscript.

Von Schnitzler A (2008) Citizenship prepaid: Water, calculability and techno-politics in South Africa. *Journal of Southern African Studies* 34; 4: 899-917.

LIST OF INTERVIEWS

John Appolis, former APF chairperson, 17 March 2010 (interviewed by Dale McKinley; SAHA archive).

Teboho Mashota, former APF administrator and leading member of the SECC, 15 May 2010 (interviewed by Dale McKinley; SAHA archive).

Dale McKinley, former APF treasurer, 17 February 2010 (interviewed by Ahmed Veriava; SAHA archive).

Bricks Mokolo, former APF chairperson, 21 August 2010 (interviewed by Prishani Naidoo for her PhD).

Trevor Ngwane, former APF secretary and organiser and leading member of the SECC, 22 June 2003 (interviewed by Prishani Naidoo for CCS project towards the report 'Remembering Movements').

ECOLOGY, ECONOMY AND LABOUR

2

Ecology, economy and labour

Devan Pillay

———•——

Under Jacob Zuma's leadership, the African National Congress-led government continued along its schizophrenic development trajectory, trying to appease contradictory interests amid modest economic growth and rising social instability. The most powerful of all these interests remain the large corporations, which continue to shape public discourse around issues of ecology, economy and labour.

The chapters in this section speak to these issues. Dick Forslund presents a detailed exposition of the need for a wage-led growth path that tackles, head on, the neoliberal argument that low wages and inequality are necessary for economic growth, with the benefits trickling down to the working class in the long-term (by which time, as Keynes once said, we are all dead). Forslund argues instead that low wages and extreme inequality deprive the country of local markets and jobs. We should support unions in their demand for higher wages, tackle inequality by reducing the profit share of gross domestic product (GDP), abandon export-led growth that is based on wage compression, and move out of excessive reliance on extractive industries in favour of climate jobs that combine sustainable development with employment and decent work.

Martin Nicol continues the discussion on economic policy with a focus on the mining industry and the debate over nationalisation. He argues for nationalisation of a special type, and is sceptical about the feasibility of outright nationalisation (whereby the state takes ownership of mines) as well as bureaucratic state intervention as envisaged by the African National Congress (ANC) task team report. Nicol puts forward a more socially embedded alternative in which workers, citizens and the environment are central actors, ensuring that mineworkers obtain just rewards for their labour through a wage solidarity policy; improved living conditions for workers; a programme of adult education; and a mine veterans policy. He argues that mining with care and efficiency would alleviate unfavourable environmental consequences and provide full economic value, but this, he asserts, can only be achieved through independent union and community organisation, to build a countervailing power against private management and state cronyism, mismanagement and corruption.

William Attwell takes us back to the 'syndicalist' tradition in the Congress of South African Trade Unions (Cosatu) which, he contends, played a major role in shaping a particular, more successful form of black economic empowerment (BEE): Hoskens Consolidated Investments (HCI) started by John Copelyn, former general secretary of the Textile Workers' Industrial Union (which became the South African Clothing and Textile Workers Union (Sactwu)), and Marcel Golding, former assistant general secretary of the National Union of Mineworkers (NUM). These unionists were part of the so-called 'workerist' tradition of unionism, which placed emphasis on independent worker organisation based on shop-floor accountability. Whereas Golding came from a Trotskyist ideological background, and as such initially believed in the formation of an alternative working class party to that of the South African Communist Party (SACP), Copelyn was associated with 'syndicalism', which eschews political parties in favour of trade unions as political actors in their own right. Nevertheless, whatever shades of difference existed between their respective ideological orientations, they were both cautious about the ANC and the SACP, and tried to preserve union independence as much as possible. Ironically, both went on to become ANC MPs, but soon left the political arena for the business world – and became quite wealthy as a result. Attwell, however, argues that, contrary to the critical view of many on the left who feel that Copelyn and Golding betrayed their principles for the lucre of BEE, using the unions as springboards for personal accumulation, their form of BEE, through the HCI, brought real benefits for their respective union memberships – something of which Sactwu and the NUM remain proud. Workers' families have access to education bursaries. Copelyn and Golding have donated funds from their own personal wealth to a range of social development schemes, and both unions have endorsed their activities although it could be argued that by aggressively playing the stock market they have legitimised a system that continues to detract from their initial goal of workers' control. It is still an issue of debate.

Finally, Jacklyn Cock and David Fig take us into the realm of the environment, intimately connected to the economy. Fracking is being put forward as a new route to industrial development that relies less on coal and oil, and depends on hitherto unexplored natural gas that might be embedded beneath the earth in parts of the country – including the Karoo and Eastern Cape. If this exploration is successful, claim companies such as Shell, then South Africa will become energy-rich, and on the cusp of a 'game changer' that would provide untold riches to the country. Fig, however, argues that fracking poses real dangers to the environment in the Karoo, with the distinct possibility of underground water supplies being contaminated, and the formidable amount of water needed to dislodged the gas from the rock.

Fig is particularly worried about the watering-down of public participation in assessing the health and environmental effects of controversial ventures – whether the pebble-bed nuclear reactor, aluminium smelter or the genetic modification of crops. Large companies seem to hold sway, and use the trump card of 'development' to hold back public scrutiny. Hydraulic fracturing for shale gas is the latest example, he asserts, of government failure to allow significant consultation over the social and environmental desirability of such a potentially dangerous new technology. Government should do much more to restore a minimum of public trust in such schemes.

Cock's contribution considers the manner in which the environmental movement mobilised during the Durban climate change conference in 2011. Environmental organisations are divided into two broad camps, which correspond with classical debates around tactics and strategy for social transformation. On the one hand are those (such as Greenpeace) that seek gradual reforms within the current social order, and on the other hand those that mobilise for a fundamental challenge to capitalist power, which is conceived as the root of environmental problems. The first of these have been willing to consider reforms that fall within the green capitalism framework (which critics label greenwashing) whereas the second want to see a transition to a new, ecosocialist paradigm – which critics label maximalist and unachievable in the short-term, given the power of global capitalism, and argue that it is better to tame the beast, which lies within the realm of feasibility, than to seek its immediate removal, which lies within the realm of fantasy.

It seems that the dividing line between such groups may be much more fluid than each of them realises. Any programme of transformation must have short-term objectives, which involve campaigns for reforms within the current system, in order to advance the longer-term objectives. The question is whether these are reformist reforms (with the effect of legitimising and entrenching the current social order) or revolutionary or transformative reforms (with the effect over time of undermining the current order and preparing the way for the new). These calculations cannot always be made in the abstract, and may only be determined in the heat of real struggles. This means that, in the short- to medium-term, the 'reformist' and 'revolutionary' groups will find that they have much common ground, and should combine forces against a common enemy.

Cock contends that the basis of a red-green coalition pivots around the active participation of the most organised sector of civil society: the labour movement, and in particular Cosatu. In recent years, although Cosatu has raised the profile of environmental issues within the federation, the movement remains divided, positions ranging from the accommodative stance of the NUM (which seeks technical solutions within the current system) and the more anti-capitalist stance of the National Union of Metalworkers of South Africa (Numsa), which questions the notion of a 'just transition' from the current system to a green economy if it is not located firmly within a class analysis.

These chapters bring together interweaving economic, ecological and labour issues central to the future of the country. They highlight the power of large companies in shaping public discourse and government decision making – but also the potential power of labour in forging a new counter-hegemony, particularly when working with other civil society actors.

CHAPTER 5

Mass unemployment and the low-wage regime in South Africa

Dick Forslund

———•———

That 'the economy', or 'South Africa', cannot afford wage increases 'way above inflation' is repeated endlessly at the beginning of the annual wage bargaining season. Commenting on the planned strikes in July 2011, Mike Schussler of the think tank 'economists.co.za' insisted that South African unions are living in the 'dark ages', 'stuck in thirty years ago' (Sapa 2011). In July 2012, Daan Groeneveldt, adviser to the National Employers Association of South Africa, supported the minister of public service and administration, Lindiwe Sisulu, against the wage demands of the public sector unions. He added: 'that salary increases for public servants higher than the rate of inflation (6.4 per cent) are not sustainable is also relevant for the private sector' (Groeneveldt 2012). In the 2012 South African Employment Report, which is sponsored by the trade union UASA and which was widely quoted in the media, Schussler maintained that 'South Africa cannot afford South Africans'. He argued: 'Starting and entry level salaries must be lowered in real terms. (That may mean lower increases – below inflation for a decade).' He continued: 'Higher level employees and senior skilled employees could be allowed to have above inflation increases but this would depend on skill levels and responsibility levels' (Schussler 2012). According to Schussler there must be larger wage gaps between skilled and unskilled labour as well as between workers and management in both the public and private sectors.

The annual media onslaught on union demands and industrial action is accompanied by 'expert' surveys and booklets from think tanks such as the Centre for Development and Enterprise (CDE 2011a; 2011b) and, of course, by statements from official business representatives such as the South African Chamber of Commerce and Industry (Sapa 2012b). A list of radio interviews, articles, columns and editorials, in the course of one year, that convey the message that wages are too high, profits too low and labour laws too protective and strict, would be almost endless.

In contrast to the yearly display of the fanaticisation of consensus (Johansson, 2004) around wage compression that 'the economy' allegedly needs, I shall argue for dramatic increases in workers' wages. The South African economy is characterised by a structural demand deficit, and the lack of domestic demand breeds mass unemployment. Higher wages for the majority must start to cut into the excessive profits harvested by the big private corporations within mining, car manufacturing, retail, construction and banking and the food industry – as well as the large farms and the big wineries. Progressive economic reforms in South Africa must be linked to the support of and strengthening of unions. Beyond providing telling examples and official statistics concerning consumption and credits, anecdotal evidence will be offered regarding the importance to employment of domestic demand. The logic of the argument will be to endorse the notion of a wage-led and sustainable growth path (for example, Ghosh 2010) and to refute some of the worst fallacies and incoherence that underpin the dominating anti-union discourse.

The exorbitant remuneration of executives and top managers is challenged internationally as one of the outcomes of neoliberalism, and has already been highlighted in the South African debate (for example, Crotty and Bonorchis 2006; and Southall, this volume). Similarly, another aspect of the neoliberal project has been tax cuts for corporations and the rich, with South Africa having duly followed international examples (SARS 2011: 25f). This chapter relates, however, to a third aspect of the neoliberal offensive, namely the growing international concern that the ever greater minority control over the national income fuels a crisis for economic demand. Wages comprise an ever smaller share of national income when unions everywhere are pushed back by changed legislation, the casualisation of labour and the pressure from growing unemployment. Growing consumer and government debt eventually 'financialises' the economy when credit increasingly underpins mass consumption and state expenditure. The growing indebtedness creates a worldwide situation in which finance (or, rather, the claims of creditors) set the agenda for industrial production, instead of the other way round.

In South Africa, the setting for a wages versus profits debate is different from that in the global North, but this strengthens rather than weakens the argument for higher worker wages. In South Africa, the typical fall of the wage share, which will be discussed and illustrated below, is superimposed on the general low-wage regime of super-exploitation inherited from colonialism and apartheid.

INCOME DISTRIBUTION AND THE CORPORATE VIEW

'Consumption is the sole end and purpose of all production,' wrote Adam Smith in 1776 in *The Wealth of Nations*.[1] It is worth keeping this in mind when following an economic policy debate in South Africa that is dominated by 'the corporate view'. By 'corporate view' I am not referring to pro-capitalist or neoliberal opinions and moral values in general but to a specific point of view in the debate about economic policy and wage levels from which vantage point South Africa's gross domestic product (GDP) is thought of as 'gross domestic profits'. When the economy is viewed through the eye of the corporate beholder, wages and benefits paid to the mass of employees are 'costs to companies', and therefore, through ideological slippage, costs to the nation.

Even a country completely dominated by the capitalist system and corporate hunt for profits is not a privately owned company. In any strand of economics, the new income delivered to society by the capitalist or profit-maximising firm is conceptually divided into two basic parts, wages and profits. The purpose of production for the owners of such firms is of course to maximise profits. But beyond a certain limit, by themselves these private endeavours have no exclusive support in economic theory. On the contrary, even the neoclassical economic school (which theoretically underpins the neoliberal political movement) regards 'profits' as being bad for the economy as a whole: they represent a *loss* to society. Assuming conditions of 'perfect competition' in all markets, this school teaches that the two factors of production, capital and labour, produce two legitimate income streams, one for the owners of labour power and one for the owners of capital. The latter income stream is regarded as 'the cost of capital' and not as profits. 'Profits' is a term that neoclassical economic theory reserves for extra profits illegitimately earned by owners of firms that have monopoly power over the market (cf. Competition Commission 2010 and 2011).

We find the corporate view on the economy and economic policy either explicitly expressed or present in argument as an invisible assumption. In a debate with this author, labour broker Adcorp's chief economist, Loane Sharp, argued that 'the intention behind productivity enhancement is not higher wages for workers, but the increased profitability of the firm' (Sharp, 2011) as if this vested interest should also be the guiding norm for labour market policies. Defending profit levels at the expense of wage levels is to look 'through the prism of the common good', Sharp argues in a later article (Sharp 2012), through which prism and commercial lifestyle statistics he can see that '[t]he idea of the "working poor" in South Africa is a fabrication' invented by Cosatu. For instance, many articles in the media on the crisis-ridden South African textile industry indicate the percentage of minimum wages that employers pay at the different textile factories and whether they are complying with the legislation; whether they say they can afford the legislation, and so on. However, there is an absence of accounts relating to profits levels within the South African textile industry or to how large a share of the profits the owners are investing. In newspaper articles, thought leaders or press statements, quantifications or estimates of the profit part within the textile industry are simply missing.

Indeed, the rationale for supporting existing profit levels, and the *reservation profit* demanded by local and foreign investors in sectors such as mining, retail and construction, are not objects for critical scrutiny, or recognised as the subjects of a legitimate debate that ought to inform economic policy. In the article quoted above, Groeneveldt also argues that 'pay hikes must relate to value' and informs the reader that '[i]n the private sector, jobs will only be created and maintained if the cost of the job is covered by an income stream linked to the value created by the individual performing the job'. However, what appears a commonsensical statement is completely unrelated to the South African reality of super-exploitation, which has become worse since 1998, as will be shown below. Nor has the statement any clear meaning theoretically. Again, from the basic standpoint of different economic schools – with non-Marxist schools trying to take the point of view of 'society' (Myrdal 2007) and Marxist schools trying to take the majority point of view – wages are one of two basic income streams under capitalism. They comprise one part of the value Groeneveldt thinks is the same as profits: wages and profits together make up the total value added by an industry to the economy. In line with this – in South Africa's national accounts as in any national accounts – gross operating surplus ('profits') is one part and 'compensation to employees', or wages in the broad sense, is the other part of GDP. The basic formula is wages + profits = total value added, which becomes GDP at market prices after government intervention with value added tax (VAT) and subsidies, so that the sum of wages and profits roughly equals GDP (StatsSA 2011: P0441, any quarter).

The basic division between wages and profits in the national accounts – and in the capitalist firm – is in its essence a juridical and political division. In a setting of general or common ownership, as in a cooperative enterprise, the balance between profits and wages represents a choice between consumption and investment that ideally is up for debate and decision by the employees and 'all concerned parties'. In a non-capitalist economy, we must discuss the wage issue in terms of what should or must be left over for investments. In the capitalist firm, in the capitalist economy as a whole (and as in mainstream theory), the balance between wages and profits is a matter of class control over different parts of the total value added to the economy. How large a part of the profits is to be reinvested in the ongoing project (the firm) is for the owners of the firm, a minority of all directly affected by such a decision, to decide.

Against this theoretical backdrop, we should make a first reading of what the proponents of the corporate view propose as the remedy for South African mass unemployment. They defend the size of the profit share of GDP and offer new arguments for increasing it further. Seen from a distributional point of view, they are arguing for increased minority control over the national income. It is an interesting paradox that the arguments for increasing profits at the expense of wages, and the anti-unionism this position necessitates, are promoted as a neutral and objective standpoint: the 'scientific' one, so to speak. A distinctly juridical and class political point of view on economic policy and labour market issues assumes the status of common sense based on 'science'. This testifies to the ideological supremacy of the corporate elite in South African economic policy discussions.

THE INCOME DISTRIBUTION APPROACH

In what follows, economic exploitation of labour power and minority economic control will be analysed from the distribution side of the economy. The national accounts of most countries lend themselves well to such a distribution of income approach.

The French economist Michel Husson is one of the anti-capitalist economists whose crucial questions about the global crisis are based on studies of the changes in the division of the national income or GDP (Husson 2008, 2009, 2011 and 2012). He shows, as do many radical critics of capitalism, that international capitalism is more than ever enriching a few, that real investments are in relative decline and that the global destruction of our environment seems unstoppable, despite general agreement on the seriousness of resource depletion and climate change. Defending collective consumption of welfare services and social rights – introduced in Europe after the Second World War, but declared 'unaffordable' in the wake of the so-called sovereign debt crisis – Husson (2012) argues for socialism across national borders in the European Union (EU).

Some readers might object in the belief that when we analyse exploitation of labour we should start from the production side of the capitalist economy, as did Karl Marx (1976: Ch 1). But Marxian economics fits well with the distributional approach. In the last volume of *Capital* we find cautious but positive comments on cooperative firms in England, which were common at that time. His remarks connect to a distributional view on exploitation by implicitly defining it as exclusive minority control over a surplus. Ideally, a cooperative enterprise practises economic democracy. The usual 'antithesis between capital and labour is overcome within them' (Marx 1992: Ch 27). In theory, at least, there is an inclusive control by all members of the cooperative over all new income generated (Satgar and Williams 2011). As suggested above, in such an untypical social setting of economic democracy it becomes obvious that there are practical, political, moral and ethical choices to be made, between individual consumption today (wages) and investments for tomorrow (the part of the surplus left over when the wages are paid, the part called 'profits' in the capitalist firm). This is so whether the choice is about investing to increase production or to improve its quality, to reduce or eradicate environmental pollution, or to improve the work environment. In the model of the democratic firm it is true to say that investment equals the surplus remaining after paying compensation to ourselves.

In the ordinary capitalist company, on the other hand, the minority of owners and their allies at the top of the hierarchy stand against the majority of employees. The wage costs are to be minimised. Consequently, in the propaganda war, when mobilising for industrial action or when sitting at the negotiation table, worker representatives are well prepared if they know how much of the profit was ploughed back into the betterment of the enterprise and how much was transferred as income to owners, and their social and political allies, in the form of top salaries, bribes, remuneration 'packages' or dividends to shareholders. In today's world of globalisation and 'financialisation' it becomes imperative to know how much of the profit is used for financial speculation, hoarded in bank accounts, or simply siphoned off abroad, legally and illegally (Ashman, Fine and Newman 2011).

UNREASONABLE MINEWORKERS?

One part of the wage backlog in South Africa is historical or structural. It is the imprint on wage levels left by colonialism and apartheid. The other part of the wage backlog is conjunctural and created after 1994. Let me first exemplify the conjunctural element.

In July 2011, the National Union of Mineworkers (NUM) had turned down a wage bid of 5 to 5.5 per cent from the employers in the gold mining industry. A press statement called the offer pitiful and infested with racism. With about 300 000 members at that time, the NUM was the biggest union in South Africa (the number is uncertain at the end of 2012, after the massacre in Marikana, and two months of strikes rocking the union). The union demanded wage increases of 14 to 15 per cent. As a comparison, during 2010 wage demands within mining were settled at an average of 8.2 per cent (Naledi 2011: 34), a typical settlement now proved to be insufficient and politically destabilising when repeated every year.

According to Labour Research Services (LRS), the *average* minimum wage agreed within 'low-wage employment' in mining was R3 773 per month in 2010, increasing to R4 243 in 2011. The higher *median* reveals a concentration of lower minimum wages in sections of the industry (Table 1 includes cases of low wages, outside bargaining councils). The actual low wages average around 15 per cent above minimum agreements.[2]

Table 1. Low-Wage Employment in Mining in South Africa 2010/2011

	Minimum Wages 2010	Minimum Wages 2011	Percentage change	Median settlement level in 2011
average	3 773	4 243	12.4	n/a
median	3 919	4 311	10.0	10.0
sample	105	78	n/a	98

(Source: Labour Research Services database)

According to the StatsSA study 'Monthly Earnings of South Africans 2010' (2010: P0211.2), half of about 8.6 million formal employees earned R3 683 or less in 2010. Some 686 000 employers who paid salaries to themselves, 1.2 million generally lower-paid own-account workers, 570 000 agricultural workers and 1.1 million domestic workers (some of whom are also formally employed) are excluded from that R3 683 median.

The built-up frustration and despair over impoverishment and growing inequality (Leibbrandt et al. 2010) is an explosive cocktail, as demonstrated by the strike wave in the mining industry. The mining revolt started in January 2012 after a provocative wage increase of 18 per cent for front-line supervisors ('miners') at Impala Platinum Mining in Rustenburg (Hartford 2012). In a six-week-long and bitter strike, 17 200 workers demanded R9 000 per month after personal income tax (Sapa 2012a). That would more than double the wage for many of them. This was before the demand for R12 500 in net minimum per month was raised in August at Lonmin in Marikana and taken up by tens of thousands of other workers.

Are such wage levels outrageously high for doing one of the most dangerous jobs in the country in a central export industry? Consider what has taken place within South African mining during the 2000s according to the national accounts (Table 2).

Table 2: Profits and Wages in the South African Mining Industry, 2000-2011

R89 billion rand in accumulated wage loss in current prices within mining 2001-2011(Source: StatsSA (P0441, 4th Quarter 2011) and own calculations).[3]

Year	Value added in millions of rands (profits + wages)	Profits in millions of rands	Wages in millions of rands	Wage share of value added	Rm wage loss in relation to year 2000 wage share
2000	66 391	35 133	28 258	42.6 per cent	(n.a.)
2001	77 214	45 932	31 282	40.5 per cent	-1 583
2002	92 730	58 275	34 454	37.2 per cent	-5 015
2003	85 770	50 577	35 193	41.0 per cent	-1 313
2004	91 198	53 293	37 905	41.6 per cent	-912
2005	105 992	65 115	40 877	38.6 per cent	-4 236
2006	132 301	83 970	48 331	36.5 per cent	-7 980
2007	156 970	99 954	57 015	36.3 per cent	-9 796
2008	196 525	128 087	68 438	34.8 per cent	-15 209
2009	196 521	123 002	73 519	37.4 per cent	-10 126
2010	227 117	144 507	82 610	36.4 per cent	-14 058
2011	260 381	168 218	92 163	35.4 per cent	-18 663
				SUM	R -88 891

Over the past decade, the wage share within the entire mining industry fell by seven percentage points, according to StatsSA (Table 2). In the 1990s, the average wage share in mining was above 50 per cent. The political centre of the strike wave has notably been the platinum mines where the wage share of value added hovered, in fact, above 60 per cent during the first half of the 1990s. From 1996 the wage share then fell, reaching below 30 per cent in 2001, and has stayed there ever since.[4]

In 2011, when the unions were allegedly demanding too much but did not get it, the wage share in the mining industry fell one percentage point from the 2010 benchmark. This drop of one percentage point represents over R2.5 billion rands in forfeited wages in one year. With a constant wage share at 42.6 per cent of value added over the whole period (we could say 'at the same relation of strength between capital and labour as in the year 2000'), the employees in the mining sector would have received R89 billion more in wages between 2001 and 2011.

Official inflation was heading towards 6 per cent during the spring of 2011. In demanding 14 to 15 per cent, NUM was roughly asking for real wage increases of 8 to 9 per cent.[5] Would that have been bad for investment?

During the period 1994-2010, about 40 per cent of the profits within mining were, on average, reinvested every year.[6] But let us refer to the year 2009 (for which about 95 per cent of the tax forms from the mining industry had been assessed at the time of writing). This was a year in which real investments in mining as a share of profits reached their highest since 1970: half (52 per cent) of the profits before taxes. To invest about half of the profits made in mining is a new record.

As for corporate income tax (CIT) in 2009, R45.3 billion, or a little more than one third of the R123 billion in profits, was regarded as *taxable* income in the minority of mining companies that reported a positive result to the tax authority. Out of those *taxable* profits of R45.3 billion, R12.8 billion, or 28 per cent, was required to be paid in CIT (SARS 2011: 93) – in effect a tax of a little more than 10 per cent on the R123 billion in profits (gross operating surplus). The tax statistics show that this is a normal state of affairs.

When subtracting R12.8 billion in taxes from R123 billion, R110.2 billion is left at the political disposal of the owners with majority shares.[7] They reinvested R64.1 billion in the mining business during 2009 (SARB 2011: S-114). This leaves R46.1 billion not ploughed back into production in 2009.[8]

We can conclude that an additional R8 billion paid out, on average, in higher wages each and every year between 2001 and 2011 should not have had any *objective* impact on mining investments, and we abstract from this proposition the 'subjective factor' of the business community, in the same manner as the effects on productivity and labour relations are, as a rule, not taken into consideration when proposing wage compression. By means of a sketchy but illustrative calculation, we use the principle of an equal rise for all in rands. This is usually not demanded by the unions although increases in percentages widen the inequality among their members.

An additional R2.604 billion in wages paid in 2011 – wages forfeited relative to the 2010 wage share – would have added an extra R420 per month across the board to the average 8.2 per cent 2010 agreement cited above, or close to 10 per cent extra to the mine worker earning R4 243 per month in 2011. We can repeat this procedure going back to 2001, adding the yearly forfeited compensation to employees from 2001 to the total wage bill for each year (Table 2). We divide the new sum by the average number of employees in mining that year. In 2011, the average monthly compensation to a mining employee would be R17 885 instead of R 14 873, or a R3 000 higher wage level across the board.[9]

Is that 'possible'? There is not anything *intrinsically* impossible about it. Neither is the minimum demand of R12 500 after taxes and deductions for rock drill operators (RDOs), RDO assistants and other underground workers 'objectively too expensive'. The demand has also been expressed as R16 000 to R17 000 before deductions by worker committees. To lift the wage share in mining to 50 per cent of value added at factor prices – 2 to 5 percentage points short of the prevailing wage share within mining in 1998 and earlier in that decade – would in fact increase the average 'compensation of employee' to about R21 000, or by between R6 200 to R7 000 per month across the board, depending on how the average labour cost is calculated (using the average wage reported by StatsSA in the Quarterly Employment Survey (QES) survey, or dividing 'compensation of employees' in the StatsSA GDP reports by the number of employees in mining reported in the QES, or by the Reserve Bank (SARB), which uses seasonally adjusted numbers). This is not to say that top and senior management should take part in this scheme, their wage levels lifting the average. The true labour cost for an RDO in the platinum industry has been mired in confusion, but if in August it was between R9 500 and R10 500 for a permanent employee, all inclusive (Lonmin 2012), the demand for an increase by R6 000 to R7 000 per month is on track.

This is the truth of back-of-the-envelope calculations, assuming an increase in wages at the expense of profits that are not reinvested. The size of wages is a matter of contestation between opposing blocks of interests; a matter of changing multifaceted relations of strength. Persuasion and propaganda are part of these relations. If we could argue for a tidal wave of wage increases for ordinary employees by turning inside out the usual business press discourse on wages and profits, it would, perhaps, read like this in a never-to-be *Business Day* editorial: *The political group behaviour of irrational investors and emotional objections to necessary change – from stockbrokers, decision makers in the multinational corporations, the global business elites and their South African comrades – is an obstacle to economic liberation, but an obstacle that can be moved. It is the absolute duty of a government in South Africa to support this collective endeavour from below. We must counter and temper the narrow economic demands of this wealthy and powerful minority. We must handle its conservatism and inflexibility. We must set limits for what economic blackmail and defiance of labour legislation, decreasing the income from labour, is possible.*

PROFITS AND INVESTMENTS

With some exceptions, the national accounts show the same development in the other branches of industry: the wage shares of the total value they add to GDP also fall within transport, construction, wholesale and so on, as may be ascertained from Tables 5, 6 and 7 in the quarterly GDP reports from StatsSA (P0441).

The extreme development in the 2000s within the monopolised and price-colluding construction industry (Competition Commission 2011) led by the 'top five' JSE-listed companies should be mentioned in this context. According to the Quantec database, the industry employed 691 000 workers in 2011, 423 000 of them formally (StatsSA, QES

Figure 1: The wage share of GDP in South Africa 1993-2010

The falling wage share of South African GDP (at factor prices): For the private business and industrial sector (SIC 1-8), agriculture is included. For 'Whole Economy', the public sector, community, personal services and 'other' (informal) are added

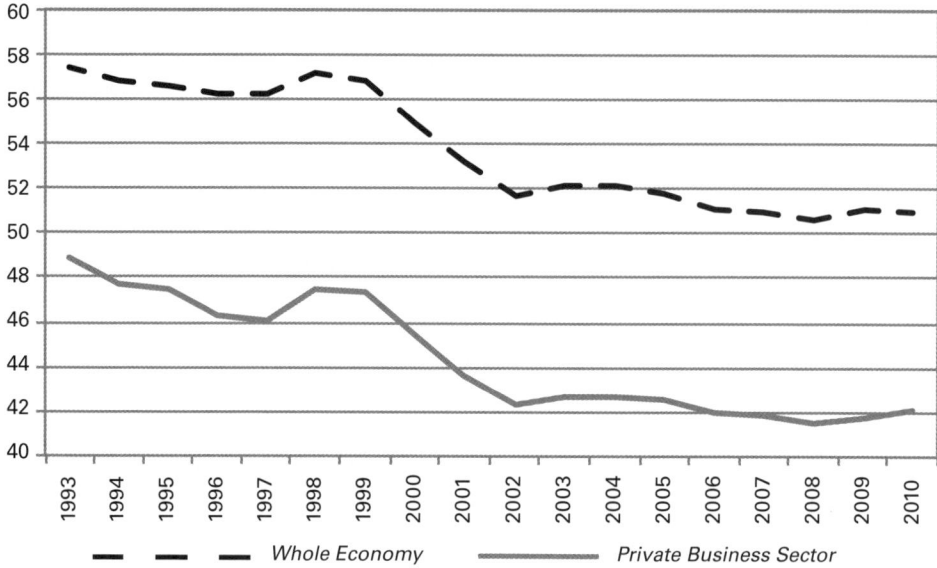

— — — *Whole Economy*   ——— *Private Business Sector*

(Source: StatsSA, 'Detailed GVA data 2010')

Figure 2: Gross Operating Surplus compared with Gross Capital Formation in the South African private construction industry

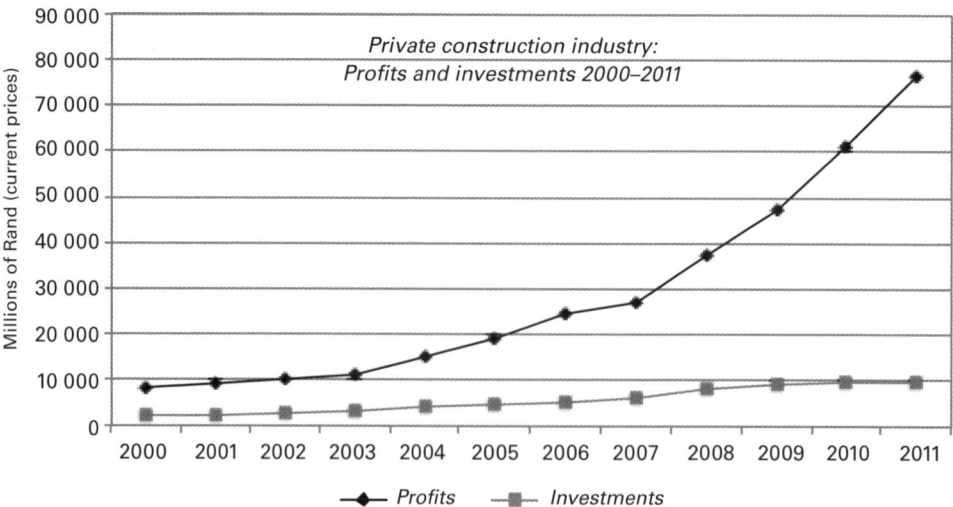

(Source: StatsSA, 2011: P0441 and SARB 2011: S-114)

survey Q42011). During the building decade marked by the 2010 World Cup (Cottle 2012), the wage share of the value the private building industry added to GDP each year fell from 60.6 per cent to 36.6 per cent, a staggering 24 percentage points.

Were the super-profits harvested during the period by the construction industry capitalists 'good for investment'? The category 'construction' (contractors) represents the whole private construction industry, and in Figure 2 the gross operating surplus (profits) in the GDP reports (StatsSA P0441) is compared with gross capital formation (investments) reported by the South African Reserve Bank in the national accounts (SARB 2011). The 2000s saw extreme growth in the profit share of GDP and in profits within the private construction industry. The investment share of profits fell from 24.6 to 12 per cent. Corporate income taxation (CIT) comprised, as usual, around 10 per cent of the gross operating surplus (SARS 2011).

THE COLONIAL-APARTHEID WAGE SHARE GAP

A falling wage share of value added means that real wages are developing at a slower pace than value output per worker, or 'labour productivity' (see explanatory box). This is so whether labour productivity is measured according to the recommendations issued by the Organisation for Economic Cooperation and Development (OECD 2001: 15) – as output per working hour input – or as measured by Statistics SA and the Reserve Bank, as value added (output) per formally employed worker, in the absence of more detailed data.

The logical connection between wage share and labour productivity

In a country with one worker, this worker produces a gross domestic product that is equal to 100 in Year One. She gets 50 in wages. The wage share of GDP is 50 out of 100, that is, 50 per cent.

If she increases production to 105 in Year Two and gets 51 in real wages, the wage share drops to 48.6 per cent (51 out of 105 is 48.6 per cent: 51/105 = 0.486).

Her labour productivity has increased from 100 to 105, that is, by 5 per cent. Her wages have only increased from 50 to 51, or by 2 per cent (1/50 = 0.02). The wage share of GDP must therefore drop.

If her wages had increased from 50 to 52.5, that is, by 2.5 units or 5 per cent, the wage share would have remained constant at 50 per cent: 52.5 is half of 105.

In the wake of the campaign against worker wages and the trade unions, perhaps triggered by some successful wage bargaining in 2009 and 2010, much confusion has been spread about labour productivity data and the very concept of labour productivity. In the 2011 Budget Review (National Treasury 2011: 45), the Treasury contributed to the empirical confusion when arguing for wage restraint, saying that for two decades real wages have been growing at a faster rate than labour productivity. This is a fallacy. Its origin is employment data from StatsSA containing so-called 'structural breaks' in the data series, jumps upwards in the number of employees resulting from previously informally employed workers who have been recorded for the first time (SARB, 2011: S-132f). This time, the data had been used by the International Labour Organisation (ILO) before ending up in the 2011 Budget Review. To make sense of the productivity development from 1990 onwards, the SARB has revised the data. According to the SARB, South Africa places itself comfortably alongside Argentina, Chile or Turkey (see Figure 3): at about a 60 per cent increase in labour productivity from 1990 to 2008, not at about 20 per cent (SARB July 2012).

Figure 3: Quoting data from the ILO, which had used unrevised data from StatsSA, the Treasury goes completely wrong about SA productivity growth in the 2011 Budget Review

To compete in world markets, South African businesses need to increase their productivity. Unit labour costs are an important indicator of competitiveness. Over the past two decades, real wage growth in South Africa has outpaced growth in labour productivity which has been relatively slow.

Figure 3.3: Labour productivity growth 1990-2008

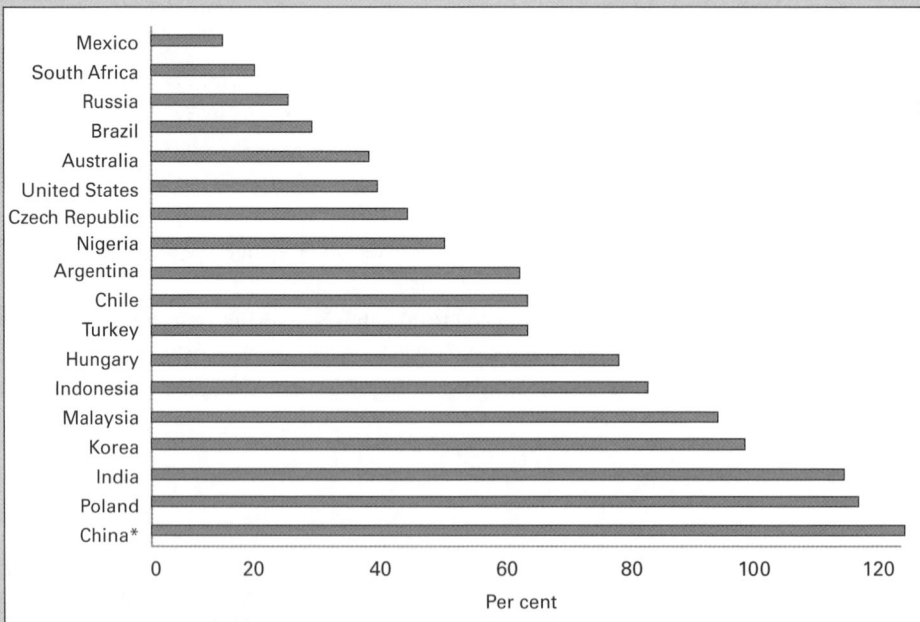

*China's labour productivity growth was 305 per cent over this period
Source: International Labour Organisation

(Source: National Treasury 2011: 45)

Meanwhile, the labour broker Adcorp's research department adds conceptual confusion by regularly publishing reports, quoted in the media, that labour productivity has fallen to the lowest levels in 46 years (Adcorp 2012). The basic idea underpinning Adcorp's analysis is that if we use more machines and tools, labour productivity falls! From the corporate point of view, the tools and machines are the contribution of capitalists to productivity, and it is the capitalists, not the workers, who should be rewarded for such improvements in productivity with a growing profit share of the gross domestic product: the income stream coming from the improved machinery, which we allegedly can separate mathematically from the total income stream, is of their making and rightfully theirs

But at its foundation economic theory on productivity must recognise production as a physical process, not primarily as a juridical or political one. The bottom line in any analysis is that machines are silent without labour. Humans started to use tools tens of thousands of years ago. Machines and tools are invented, produced, used, improved and repaired by human beings. In essence and physically, it is workers who supply the machines to the factories. The basic elements of production are labour, tools and raw material, not the money amassed by a minority – even if the production of commodities and commoditised services in a capitalist system stops without money.

Vertical integration (or the building of new machines, inventions or improvements of some kind by the employees of the factory where they are used) reveals the fallacy of the corporate view of productivity, and that it is in essence political: it is obsessed with dividing society into two classes with separate entitlements. When production per employee increases at one production site – because they are using improved machines, made by workers at another site and designed by engineers on the basis of the research work of scientists – there is always a time lag before there is a general awareness that wealth creation per person has increased. But as democracy and popular pressure for justice and a better life develop, the ownership argument is defeated over time. It is telling that this historical fact also makes sense in theory: it is the increase in output per every *person* ('per capita') in a country that is the basic motive for measuring productivity in the first place.

Historically, growing capital intensity often contributes to a fall in the wage share in the short-term. Such a fall is rooted in a cultural wage lag that reflects the majority's lack of economic control (there is a lag before the mass of employees starts to notice what is happening, as it were). There have been more than 250 years of technological development in the old capitalist countries. If we take the long view, this has not reduced the wage share of the national income in Germany, France or the UK. Despite the fall of the wage share since 1980 that was provoked by the neoliberal offensive in the North, and despite their having much more equipment per employee, the wage share of the national income in the capital-intensive and highly industrialised countries is still 10 to 20 percentage points higher than in South Africa (see Figure 4). This is what democratic development can and should do. A general sense of *ubuntu* wins, in an ever growing economy where new technologies and knowledge are constantly spread and eventually belong to everyone.

Figure 4: The wage share of the national income in the industrialised countries, to be compared with the wage share in South Africa pictured in Figure 1

Wage share in value added
USA + EU + Japan, 1960-2008

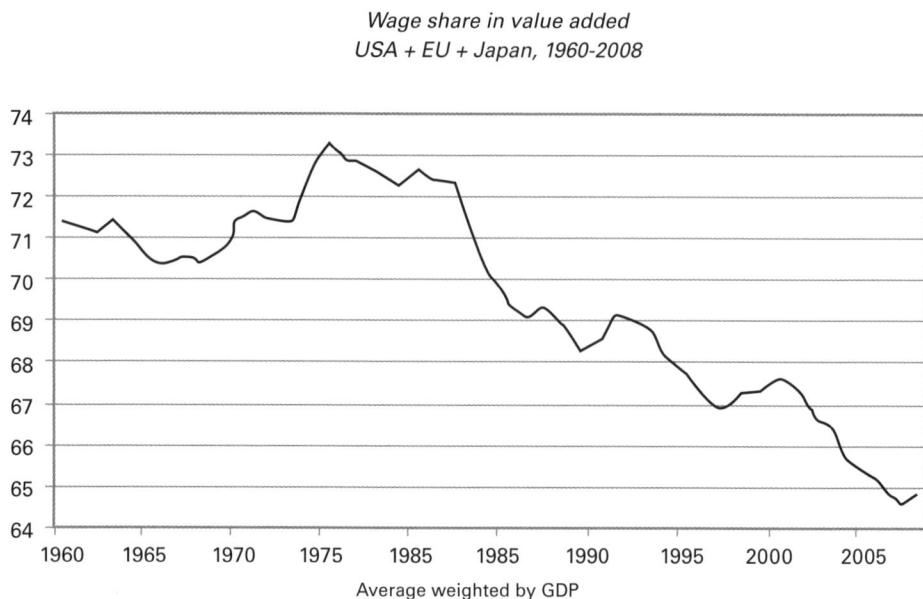

Average weighted by GDP

Source: European Commission, Ameco Database

(Source: Diagram in Husson (2011))

Before the Second World War, the wage share of GDP in countries such as the United States and Britain lay at the same levels as in many industries in South Africa today, hovering on average at under 40 per cent of GDP (Kalecki 2009). After the war came a trade union push in Europe, supported by labour governments – or at least led by large labour parties, as in Italy. Real wages increased more than labour productivity, and the wage share of the national income in the OECD countries increased drastically after the Second World War. The capitalist firms responded to the growth in mass consumer demand with investments in production, and not primarily with price increases (that is, with inflation).

In South Africa, we have, since 1998, instead seen a move in the other direction, to the income and power advantage of capital. On average, real wages have been increasing less than labour productivity, at about 2 per cent per year, with labour productivity averaging about 3 per cent in annual increases since 1994 (SARB July 2012). The wage share of GDP has therefore been falling, further exacerbating the lack of effective domestic demand.

Figure 5: Falling wage share and growing credits

The fall of household consumption and wages as shares of GDP (at market prices) in South Africa. Credit grows in the area between the two curves, stepping in to rescue the system from collapse

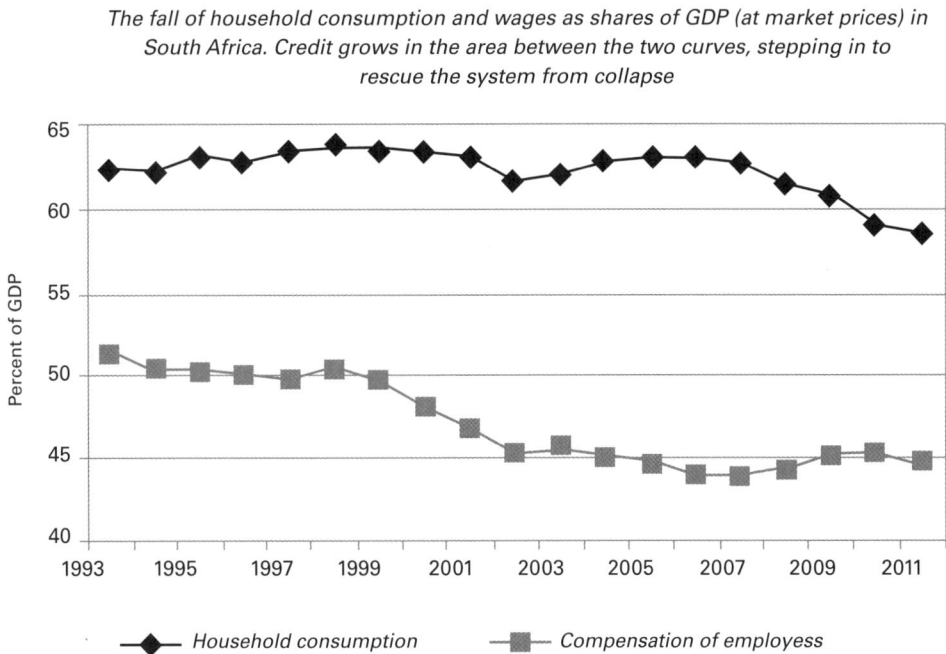

Household consumption   Compensation of employess

(Source: StatsSA (2011: P0441), SARB (2012) and own calculations)

In 1995, the wage share to GDP at market prices was 50.1 per cent.[10] In 2010, it had fallen to 44.5 per cent. It is in the area between the two curves in Figure 5 that we find credit and the space where the finance industry grows, lately including a rapidly expanding market for 'unsecured loans' (*Cape Times*, 26 March 2012). Consequently, the household debt to net disposable income has increased from 59 to 76 per cent from 1995 to 2011 (SARB 2011). In March 2010, the number of consumers with 'impaired credit records' increased year on year by 915 000 to 8 370 000 individuals, comprising 46 per cent of 18 210 000 credit active persons (NCR 2011).

This growth of household debt has not yet stopped household consumption from absorbing less and less of GDP. In 2012, goods and services will be produced in South Africa to an estimated value of about R3 300 billion (National Treasury 2012). Using the same methodology as above for the mining industry, we can conclude that the 5.5 percentage point drop in the wage share of GDP between 1994 and 2011 corresponds to R180 billion not paid out in wages to ordinary employees in 2012 alone – billions of rands that cannot boost demand for everyday goods and services.

THE WAGE HIKE MYTH

A falling wage share of a steadily increasing GDP does not by itself mean that real wages are decreasing. But it does by definition mean that average real wages and salaries are developing more slowly than labour productivity, whether measured as GDP per employee or per hour worked. That this has long been the case in South Africa is confirmed by the SARB (Figure 6). In the language of the OECD, far more labour is supplied than is demanded in South Africa: 'It does not however seem to have been the case that this disequilibrium situation was caused by an economy-wide *rise* in real wages' (OECD 2010: 102).

Figure 6: Labour productivity and real wage development in South Africa (private, public and total) 1989-2012. Year 1989 = Index 100

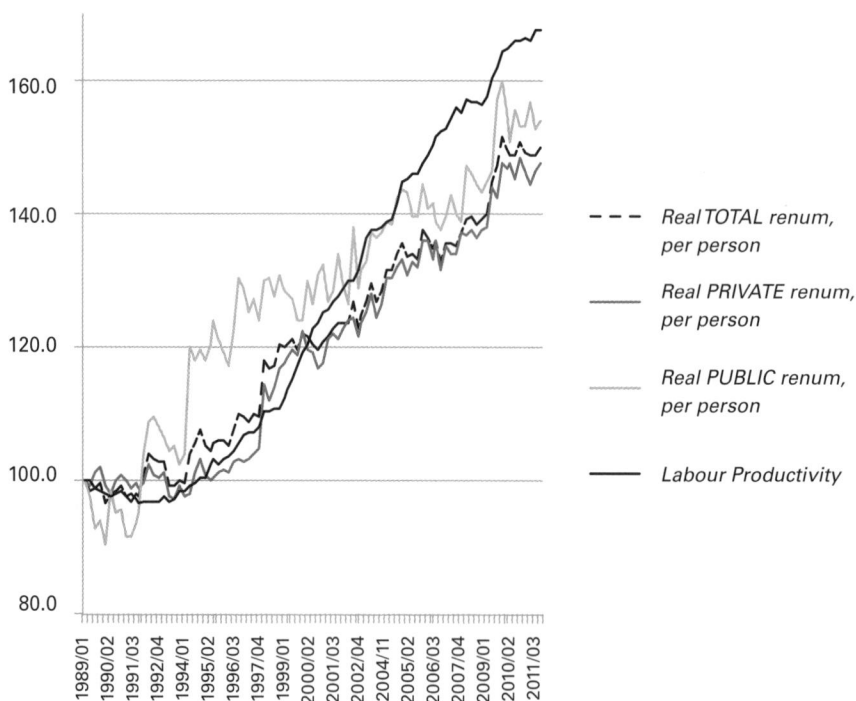

(Source: SARB (July 2012))

There is instead reason to believe that the real wages for the majority of wage earners have been stagnant since 1994 and perhaps even falling since 2005. Half of all employed people earned less than R2 500 per month in 2008 according to the National Planning Commission (NPC 2011: 13). StatsSA now reports (2010: P0211.2) that, of slightly more than 11 million employed persons, half earned R2 800 or less in 2010 (excluding salaried employers who usually have much higher incomes, and so-called 'own account' workers, who usually have very low incomes). This means either that there has been no change in the median real wage for ordinary workers after inflation (over 11 per cent between 2008 and 2010), or that the median real wage has actually fallen, if the true inflation rate affecting the majority of households that spend more of their incomes on food, electricity and transport (households belonging to Quintile 1 to 4 in the monthly Consumer Price Index reports from Stats SA) is taken into account.

Rulof Burger and Derek Yu (2007) have convincingly reconstructed trends from the raw household survey data collected by StatsSA, after cleansing the latter of obvious mistakes. An *average* real wage increase of 2 per cent for *all* employees coincides with the data used and published by the SARB. But this average includes both high and very high wages, including the high levels of remuneration of top managers in the state and the private sectors. Burger and Yu omit all wages above R200 000 per year (in year 2000 prices) from their study.

Figure 7: Wage trends 1995-2005 for employees earning less than R200 000 per year

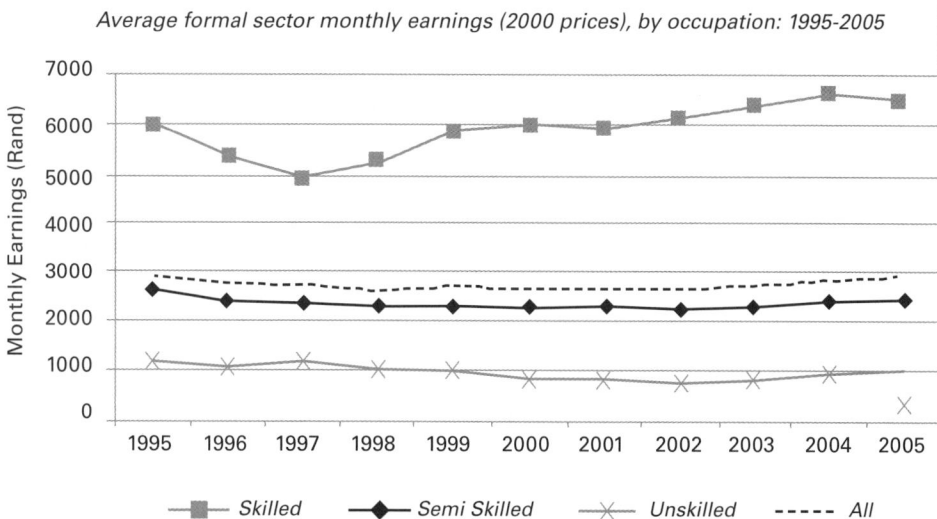

Average formal sector monthly earnings (2000 prices), by occupation: 1995-2005

Legend: Skilled — Semi Skilled — Unskilled — All

(Source: Statistics South Africa and own calculations) (Adapted from Burger and Yu (2007: 17))

For the vast majority of workers, real wages remained stagnant from 1995 to 2005 according to Burger and Yu. The 'skilled' workers reported a slight wage increase. But, again, this is 'on average'. The limit set by the researchers at R200 000 per year, or R16 660 per month (at 2000 prices), lies way above that of ordinary wages. Only 3 to 4 per cent of employees with the highest salaries are excluded (SARS 2011).

An anecdotal indication of what has happened since 2005, because of the growth of temporary employment services or labour broking, is given by the labour broker Adcorp. The corporation's chief economist, Loane Sharp, writes in a CDE booklet (2011b: 28) that 'over the past eight years an entry-level employee in our organisation has earned the same nominal wage. So an eighteen-year-old employed by us today earns the same as an eighteen-year-old with equivalent qualifications did eight years ago.' This is a decrease of at least 35 per cent in the real buying power of that entry wage, due to eight years of inflation.

ABANDONING 'EXPORT-LED GROWTH'

Conservatives argue for the simultaneous reduction of real wages and for casualising jobs, while pointing to the small local markets in South Africa as a problem. These local markets, they indicate, are one of the foundational themes for supporting a deepening of the 'export-led growth path' (CDE 2011a). In other words, too many firms are producing for an oversupplied domestic market! A key reason why overall growth was lagging, suggested a participant in a CDE seminar, 'is that too many firms were not producing goods for export. But the domestic market is too small to support more rapid economic growth, the more so in the absence of pro-cyclical government spending. Therefore, South African firms needed to concentrate on producing goods for export.'

This is simply not true, however, across the board. The growth of the South African security industry is one tragic example of what economic demand can do for employment. The numbers of actively registered security firms grew, from 2010 to 2011, from 7 496 to 8 828. There cannot be too many of them – and they create employment (Figure 8).

Another illustration is provided by a report from the Community Works Programme (CWP), which started in 2009 and which has provided work to 90 000 otherwise unemployed people in seventy towns in 2012. It provides anecdotal evidence for an alternative: useful local and public non-profit projects that create public assets instead of the for-profit struggle for global market shares. More rigorous case studies (Webster et al. 2011) point to the same. 'In Tjakastad, Mpumalanga, community safety patrols, food gardens, clean-ups, school maintenance and the creation of parks and public recreation facilities are among the CWP activities.' The change is evident, says the article (*Financial Mail*, 1 September 2011).

With small-scale public works comes small business. The mantra 'private business is a core driver of jobs and economic growth', repeated in the New Growth Path document (Department of Economic Development 2010: 28), seems either to be refuted or to require appropriate reformulation. The previously absent local market makes an appearance alongside public and non-profit CWP projects.

Figure 8: The growth of employment in the security industry

Numbers of security officers in SA registered as 'active', 1997-2011

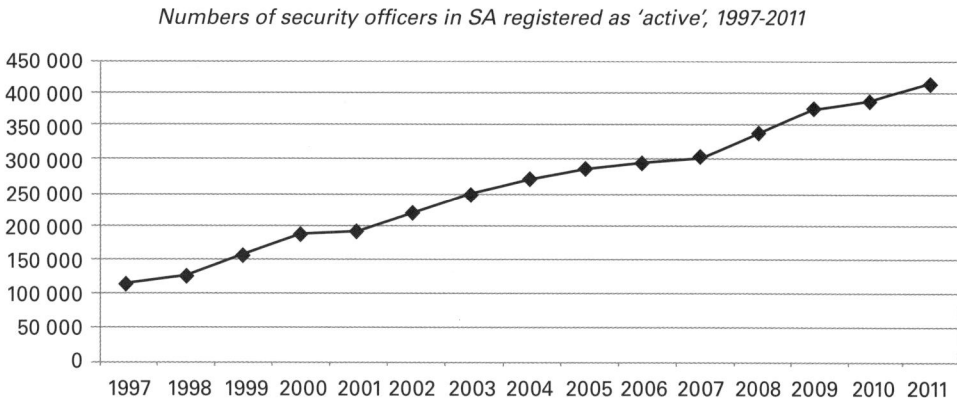

(Sources: (Julie Berg 2007) and Private Security Regulatory Authority (PSIRA) annual reports (www.psira.co.za))

The sense that things are somehow intangibly better in Tjakastad, though everyone remains poor, is perhaps best explained by the cash economy that has come with the arrival of the CWP. When about 2 000 people in the area get a wage, each earning and spending R480 per month on groceries and other consumer goods, nearly R1 million that was not there before flows into the local economy.

For retailers, and for Capitec Bank, business is booming (all CWP participants must have bank accounts and many choose Capitec). In Tjakastad, payday, the last working day of the month, causes a one- or two-day explosion of activity at 'the crossing', the crossroads where the main shops are clustered. 'Mr Jackpot … founded Jackpot Meat Market fifteen years ago,' says his business partner, Ricardo de Gouveia. 'We have a big business community and we are all surviving off this community. There is a lot more money here than there was some years ago.'

Local industry can grow if the buying power of the broad population is drastically increased. Otherwise it cannot. The CWP experience was scaled down by the government in the 2012 budget that combined austerity measures and mega plans centred on expansion of the mining industry and environmentally destructive coal power. Yet the small-scale CWP points to an alternative wage-led growth path that creates useful and sustainable jobs. Much higher wages in an expanded CWP of regulated and useful work in the rural areas would start to challenge wage levels and slave-like labour conditions that persist in many parts of South African agriculture. Competition from such public jobs is currently exerting upward pressure on low rural wages in India (Banerjee 2011). The recipe has been a job guarantee and a minimum wage, as stipulated in the National Rural Employment Guarantee Act.

CONCLUSION

Much has been omitted from this discussion of economic policy, which is limited to arguing that low wages, as well as extreme and growing income inequality, deprives South Africa of local markets and jobs, suggesting a shift to a wage-led growth path that breaks with neoliberalism as one of its preconditions; this is a political break with the corporate elite in South Africa and the advice from organisations such as the World Bank and IMF. It may seem impossible. We know, however, from countries in Latin America, that it is possible.

Such drastic policy shifts, away from neoliberalism, the pressure from speculative finance and the corporate view, are even pointed to by organisations in the United Nations family. Under headlines such as 'Neglected role of domestic demand growth for employment creation', the export-led growth path is today under attack from the United Nations Conference on Trade and Development (UNCTAD 2010, 2011 and 2012), notably in regard to the economic policies pursued in so many developing countries. Everyone is doing the export-led shuffle. This is one of the reasons why it doesn't work.

> A strategy of export-led growth based on wage compression, which makes countries overly dependent on foreign demand growth, may not be sustainable for a large number of countries and over a long period of time. This is because not all countries can successfully pursue this strategy simultaneously, and because there are limits to how far the share of labour in total income can be reduced (UNCTAD 2010: ix).

In South Africa it is increasingly obvious that the rejection of what UNCTAD calls wage compression means support for the struggles of the workers and the poor, for their trade unions and social movements, for efforts to build such organisations where they do not exist (as in the rural areas), as well as the need to confront the labour broking business. It is a necessary policy ingredient when turning from the 'export-led growth path' based on the extraction of minerals.

From the point of view of economic theory, this transforms economics from the 'dismal science' of the anti-union economists into a lifesaving one. The inevitable and intrinsically human thrust towards escaping unbearable living conditions and economic insecurity is not 'bad for the economy'. The immediate fight against the low-wage regime and inequality does not stand in contradiction to the fight against unemployment. The pressure exerted on the system by the workers and the poor – and whatever small successes or bigger victories they can harvest as a result of this pressure – is, instead, a part of the solution. Similarly, a policy shift from 'extractivism' is also necessary to save the environment. The campaign 'One Million Climate Jobs' (www.climatejobs.org.za) is one of the initiatives that combine the fight for the environment with the fight for employment with decent wages.

The history of the welfare states in the global North will not repeat itself. But as a step towards economic democracy, and towards non- and anti-capitalist solutions to the multidimensional crisis we are in, the colonial-apartheid gap in the division of the national income between profits and wages should be drastically narrowed in South Africa. This gap is far too big to be narrowed only through the secondary redistribution of income that taxation provides. Furthermore, it is an income distribution gap between labour and capital that cannot be rationalised with a 'need for investment' argument.

The democratic revolution did not abolish the low-wage regime in South Africa. To abolish it and normalise the present abnormal situation that divides the country between rich and poor and systematically promotes endemic mass unemployment is now the task of an economic revolution.

NOTES

1   The full paragraph in Smith (1776, Book IV, Chapter 8) reads: 'Consumption is the sole end and purpose of all production; and the interest of the producer ought to be attended to only so far as it may be necessary for promoting that of the consumer. The maxim is so perfectly self-evident that it would be absurd to attempt to prove it. But in the mercantile system the interest of the consumer is almost constantly sacrificed to that of the producer; and it seems to consider production, and not consumption, as the ultimate end and object of all industry and commerce.' It is clear from the full quote that the truth of consumption being the ultimate purpose of production is a normative truth for Smith. Marx and Keynes stand out as two economists for whom it is an unfortunate fact that a capitalist firm primarily produces today to achieve more money tomorrow rather than to 'satisfy consumer demand'.

2   In a telephone interview, 8 August 2012, with Trenton Elsley, deputy director at the Labour Research Service (LRS), this was clarified (any mistakes are mine). The *median* minimum wage is the minimum wage in the middle of the minimum wage agreements recorded; that is, it is the typical minimum wage. Half of the minimum wage agreements are lower and half are higher than the *median* minimum wage.

3   In earlier versions of the GDP reports the accumulated wage loss in mining could be calculated to R100 billion, 2001-2010. This table is built on the 2011 fourth-quarter report. StatsSA regularly revises its reports two to three years backwards. Value added is here given in so-called 'basic prices' as in the printed report, also to introduce the reader in sourcing this at the StatsSA website: www. statssa.gov.za. The basic prices measure includes the net of subsidies to, and taxes on, production.

4   According to 'Detailed GVA data 2010' available from StatsSA, all branches of the mining industry except gold mining currently have a wage share of value added (at factor prices) from 40 per cent and lower, down to below 30 per cent. As for gold mining statistics, this author is at the time of writing investigating the accuracy and/or the meaning of the gold mining data on wages and value added. The wage share in gold mining statistics influences the average wage share for all mining (which is 35-38 per cent 2008 to 2010) with 7-8 percentage points upwards.

5   Fifteen percentage points in wage demand minus 6 percentage points in inflation result in a 9 percentage point demand in real wage increase. The problem of the official inflation rate not reflecting how inflation hits ordinary households is not taken into account.

6   Quantec database for the data in this paragraph (courtesy of Productivity SA), using StatsSA and SARB data, plus own calculations for the percentages. Gross Operating Surplus in the national accounts is profits before corporate income tax (CIT) and depreciation of buildings, equipment and the like. In accounting, depreciation due to wear and tear is correctly regarded as an underlying cost to be subtracted from the profits. Worn-out machines must eventually be replaced. Their

ageing must be accounted for long before replacement takes place. Annual reports therefore state what the profits are before and after depreciation of fixed capital. See also endnote 7.

7   Gross Operating Surplus (GOS) 'is the capital available to financial and non-financial corporations which allows them to repay their creditors, to pay taxes and eventually to finance all or part of their investment'. It is *gross* because it makes no allowance for consumption of fixed capital (CFC). By deducting CFC from GOS one calculates net operating surplus (NOS), says Eurostat of the European Commission. In the same vain, gross fixed capital formation includes the replacement of fixed capital bought before and subjective to wear and tear (machines, buildings and other real investments). It is of course possible for the owners of the corporation to decide not to replace worn-out machines, or even to avoid paying creditors, who expect to get their share of the profit as a 'return on investments' (dividends from shares, interest from corporate bonds or interest from other loan agreements).

8   See also endnote 7. All numbers are in current prices. The obvious use of a different deflator for investment than for total value added in the national accounts makes a comparison in real prices cumbersome and problematic. The important thing here is the relationship between real investments and profits.

9   We divide the R2.6 billion in forfeited 'compensation to employees' (total labour cost) by the average number of mining employees in 2011, according to the StatsSA Quarterly Employment Survey (QES), but with the numbers seasonally adjusted by the SA Reserve Bank (SARB), which are provided by the SARB on request. The StatsSA QES reports R13 994 in November 2011 as average earnings in mining, inclusive of bonuses and overtime. When dividing 'compensation of employees' in the GDP reports from StatsSA by the numbers of employees as above we get the higher R14 873 as the monthly average earning in 2011. This is the reason for the span between R6 200 and R7 000 in the text when comparing a wage share of 50 per cent since 2001 with landing on R21 000 as the new average in 2011. The contra-factual account is, of course, not exact or without limitations. It is an argument in principle. The aim is to show what would be possible if it wasn't politically blocked.

10   In order to establish the relation to household consumption, and how large a part of the GDP that wages and salaries can buy without using credit, the wage share of GDP at market prices has been chosen. If compared with GDP at factor prices, the wage share falls from 56.6 to 50.1 per cent during the same period.

REFERENCES

Adcorp (2012) Adcorp Employment Index – July 2012: SA labour productivity at the lowest level in 46 years. Press statement available at www.adcorp.co.za [Accessed 13 August 2012].

Ashman S, B Fine and S Newman (2011) Amnesty International? The nature, scale and impact of capital flight from South Africa. *Journal of Southern African Studies*, 37(1): 7-25.

Banerjee K (2011) The employment guarantee scheme in India. *Amandla*, no.21: 17-19.

Berg J (2007) The accountability of South Africa's private security industry: Mechanisms of control and challenges to effective oversight. Newlands: Open Society Foundation for South Africa. http://osf.org.za/wp/wp-content/uploads/2012/09/The-Accountability-of-South-Africas-Private-Security-Industry1.pdf [Accessed 5 November 2012].

Burger R and D Yu (2007) Wage Trends in Post-Apartheid South Africa: Constructing an Earnings Series from Household Survey Data. DPRU Working Paper 07/117. University of Stellenbosch: Development Policy Research Unit.

Cape Times (26 March 2012) Editorial: Borrowed Time. http://www.iol.co.za/capetimes/borrowed-time-1.1264052 [Accessed 1 April 2012].

Centre for Development and Enterprise (CDE) (2011a) A Fresh Look at Unemployment – a conversation among experts. URL: www.cde.org.za [Accessed 19 March 2012].

Centre for Development and Enterprise (CDE) (2011b) Jobs for Young people. www.cde.org.za [Accessed 19 March 2012].

Competition Commission (2010) Media release: Competition Commission settles with Pioneer Foods. http://www.compcom.co.za/assets/Uploads/AttachedFiles/MyDocuments/Commission-settles-with-Pioneer-Foods2.pdf [Accessed 2 April 2012].

Competition Commission (2011) Invitations to firms in the construction industry to engage in settlements of contraventions of Competitions Act. http://www.compcom.co.za/assets/Files/invitation-to-firms-to-settle.pdf [Accessed 2 April 2012].

Cosatu (2010) A Growth Path Towards Full Employment. www.cosatu.org.za [Accessed 24 January 2012].

Cottle E (Ed.) (2012) *South Africa's World Cup: A legacy for Whom?* Scottsville: University of KwaZulu-Natal Press.

Crotty A and R Bonorchis (2006) *Executive Pay in South Africa: Who Gets What and Why*. Cape Town: Double Storey.

Department of Economic Development (2010) The New Growth Path: The Framework. http://www.info.gov.za/view/DownloadFileAction?id=135748 [Accessed 20 August 2012].

Ghosh J (2010) What does wage-led growth mean in developing countries with large informal employment? Global Labour Column, Number 34, October. http://column.global-labour-university.org/ [Accessed 8 August 2012].

Hartford G (2012) Mining strike analysis and the crisis of leadership. Presentation at the Amandla Colloquium, 16-18 November in Johannesburg. http://www.amandla.org.za/index.php?option=com_phocadownload&view=category&id=14:amandla-colloquium-2012&Itemid=180 [Accessed 20 November 2012].

Husson M (2008) Toxic capitalism. *International Viewpoint* no 406, November. http://www.internationalviewpoint.org/spip.php?article1551 (2012-03-12).

Husson M (2009) Financial Crisis or Crisis of Capitalism? http://hussonet.free.fr/denkeng9.pdf [Accessed 12 March 2012].

Husson M (2011) Growth and Income Distribution: How to Understand the Crisis and Really Get Out of It. Saint-Denis: Presentation at Symposium 9-10 June 2011 CEPN – Groupe AMPK Post-Keynesian analyses and modelling. Power point presentation in possession of the author.

Husson M (2012) Exit or voice? A European strategy of rupture. *Socialist Register*, pp. 298-306.

Kalecki M (2009) *Theory of Economic Dynamics: An Essay on Cyclical and Long-Run Changes in Capitalist Economy.* New York: Monthly Review Press.

Leibbrandt M, I Woolard, A Finn and J Argent (2010) Trends in South African Income Distribution and Poverty since the fall of Apartheid. University of Cape Town: OECD Social, Employment and Migration, Working Papers No. 101.

Lonmin (2012) Lonmin Seeks Sustainable Peace at Marikana. Press statement 24 August. http://lonminmarikanainfo.com/news_article.php?articleID=1317 [Accessed 1 September 2012].

Marx K (1976) *Capital: A Critique of Political Economy* – Volume 1. London and New York: Penguin Classics and New Left Review.

Marx K (1992) *Capital: A Critique of Political Economy* – Volume 3. London and New York: Penguin Books and New Left Review.

Myrdal G (2007) *The Political Element in the Development of Economic Theory*. London: Routledge.

National Labour and Economic Development Institute (Naledi) (2011) Towards a Cosatu Living Wage Conference: A Naledi Research Report. Book 4 before Cosatu's 5th Central Committee Meeting. Johannesburg.

National Credit Regulator (NCR) (2011, 4th quarter) Consumer Credit Market Report. http://www.ncr.org.za/pdfs/Consumerpercent20Creditpercent20Marketpercent20Reportpercent20Q42011percent20FINAL.pdf [Accessed 3 March 2012].

National Planning Commission (NPC) (2011) Diagnostic Overview. Pretoria: The Presidency.

National Treasury (2011) 2011 Budget Review, Pretoria, ISBN 978-0-621-39858-8, www.treasury.gov.za.

National Treasury (2012) 2012 Budget Review, Pretoria, ISBN 978-0-621-40579-8, www.treasury.gov.za.

OECD (2001) Measuring Productivity: Measurement of aggregate and industry-level productivity growth. Paris: Organisation for Economic Cooperation and Development.

OECD (2008) South Africa, Policy Note. Paris: Organisation for Economic Cooperation and Development.

OECD (2010) Economic Surveys: South Africa, Volume 2010/11, July. Paris: Organisation for Economic Cooperation and Development.

Paton, Carol (2011) Works programme a solution to poverty. *Financial Mail*. http://www.fm.co.za/Article.aspx?id=152312 [Accessed 23 January 2012].

Reuters (2012) Swamped by debt, South Africans battle to stay afloat. http://www.moneyweb.co.za/mw/view/mw/en/page295043?oid=565021&sn=2009+Detail&pid=302725 [Accessed 1 March 2012].

SARS, South African Revenue Service and the National Treasury (2011). *2011 Tax Statistics*, Pretoria.

Sapa (2012) 'SA unions in the Dark Ages', *Sunday Independent*, 10 July 2012. http://www.iol.co.za/sundayindependent/sa-unions-in-the-dark-ages-1.1096241#.UAUvrPV0z3A [Accessed 16 July 2012].

Sapa (2012a) We can't live like this say Implats workers. *Mail & Guardian*, 21 February. http://mg.co.za/article/2012-02-21-we-cannot-survive-say-implats-workers [Accessed 15 March 2012].

Sapa (2012b) 'Labour laws will slow job creation – Sacci', *City Press*, 12 April. http://www.citypress.co.za/Business/News/Labour-laws-will-slow-job-creation-Sacci-20120412. [Accessed 16 July 2012].

SARB (2011a), *Quarterly Bulletin,* March 2011, No. 259. http://www.reservebank.co.za/quarterlybulletin [Accessed 20 August 2012].

SARB (2012), *Quarterly Bulletin,* March 2012, No. 263. http://www.reservebank.co.za/quarterlybulletin [Accessed 20 August 2012].

SARB (July 2012), Excel sheets over SA wage and labour productivity development 1989-2012 provided by the SA Reserve Bank's research department. In possession of the author.

Satgar V and M Williams (2011) The worker cooperative alternative in South Africa. In Daniel J, P Naidoo, D Pillay and R Southall (Eds) *New South African Review 2.* Johannesburg: Wits University Press.

Schussler M (2012), The 11th Uasa Employment Report: South Africa can not [sic] afford South Africans' Economist.co.za & Uasa. Power Point presentation in my possession; inactive link on: http://www.uasa.co.za/index.php?option=com_content&view=article&id=215:2012-uasa-south-african-employment-report-can-south-africa-afford-itself&catid=3:latest-news&Itemid=1 [Accessed 4 November 2012].

Smith A (1776) *An Inquiry into the Nature and Causes of the Wealth of Nations*. http://www.econlib.org/library/Smith/smWN18.html [Accessed 18 March 2012].

StatsSA (2010) Monthly earnings of South Africans 2010. Statistical Release P0211.2. www.statssa.gov.za [Accessed July 2012].

StatsSA (2012) Detailed GVA data 2010. Work sheet provided by StatsSA, in possession of the author.

StatsSA (2011) Statistic Release P0441: Gross Domestic Product. www.statssa.gov.za [Accessed July 2012].

UNCTAD (2010) *Trade and Development Report, 2010: Overview*. New York and Geneva: United Nations.

UNCTAD (2011) *Trade and Development Report, 2011: Overview*. New York and Geneva: United Nations.

UNCTAD (2012) *Trade and Development Report, 2012: Policies for Inclusive and Balanced Growth*. New York and Geneva: United Nations.

Webster E, J Cock, K Fakier, T Masondo, M Langa and K Von Holdt (2011) The Socio-Economic Impact of the Community Work Programme as a Potential Employment Guarantee Scheme: Report to the Gauteng Department of Economic Development, Johannesburg. Johannesburg: Society, Work and Development Institute (SWOP), University of the Witwatersrand.

CHAPTER 6

Nationalisation and the mines

Martin Nicol

The arguments against nationalisation are overwhelming. But just because a policy direction is bad does not mean it will not be adopted and pursued.

In recent Cape Town history we have the example of the World Cup stadium being built, at crippling expense and in completely the wrong place, at the insistence of both ANC and Democratic Alliance (DA) politicians.[1] This is a minor example, compared with the Great Leap Forward, the most disastrous policy choice in human history (Dikötter 2010), made by the leaders of the Communist Party of China. The Great Leap Forward came after the lessons of the 'Little Leap Forward' were ignored and before the Cultural Revolution, which even senior party leaders today acknowledge as a huge mistake.[2]

'Nationalisation', whatever that means, is a policy favoured by a majority (or at least a plurality) of South Africans according to opinion polls (TNS Research Surveys 2011). Majority opinion in South Africa probably also favours a return to the death penalty, corporal punishment in schools, a ban on abortion and the abrogation of gay rights. We rely on the Constitution to protect us from the tyranny of public opinion in these areas. Any aggressive policy of nationalisation will face constitutional challenge at an early stage, but it can do a lot of damage before things reach that point. The expulsion of the leader of the Youth League from the ANC in 2012 appeared to some commentators to mark the end of the road for mine nationalisation. Other analysts had previously branded the call for nationalisation as the 'rallying call for a factionalist power play' that had little to do with mining or with the interests of mineworkers (Cronin 2012b). But no popular slogan is ever jettisoned only because it makes no sense.

The ANC tried to manage the stoked-up debate on nationalisation by appointing a research team to report broadly on state intervention in the mining industry.[3] This included international case studies and options for South Africa to consider. In November 2011, after over a year of work, the report was discussed by the ANC's national executive. It was sent back for a rewrite before being released. The researchers were told to 'write us a report that will be read by a member of the ANC, not a professor' (*Business Day*, 29 November 2011). The document was officially released in early 2012 (ANC 2012a; 2012b) and, in a summarised form, was one of the discussion documents considered at the mid-year ANC Policy Conference (ANC 2012c) .

This chapter assesses the merits and demerits of existing proposals related to the South African mining industry (including the *status quo*) and introduces an argument for nationalisation, of a special type.

WHAT ARE THE 'OPTIONS'

'Simple' nationalisation
The ANC Youth League base their call for the nationalisation of the mines on the wording of the Freedom Charter:

> The mineral wealth beneath the soil, the Banks and monopoly industry shall be transferred to the ownership of the people as a whole.

This is given additional weight by historical quotations, such as the 1956 words of Nelson Mandela:

> It is true that in demanding the nationalisation of the banks, the gold mines and the land, the charter strikes a fatal blow at the financial and gold-mining monopolies and farming interests that have for centuries plundered the country and condemned its people to servitude. But such a step is absolutely imperative and necessary because the realisation of the charter is inconceivable, in fact impossible, unless and until these monopolies are first smashed up and the national wealth of the country turned over to the people.

For the Youth League of 2011, the debate on nationalisation was no longer a policy question. They saw the policy as being quite decided. The then League president, Julius Malema, said: 'Nationalisation is concluded. I don't understand the ANC process to be saying we are investigating nationalisation of mines. I understand the ANC process to be saying we are looking to get the best model for nationalisation.'[4]

This interpretation was contested. Joel Netshitenzhe (2010) acknowledged that the ANC Youth League was factually correct 'in its interpretation of the interpretation of the Freedom Charter in years gone by'. After 1955, and before the document 'Ready to Govern' in 1992, the nationalisation of the mines was accepted ANC policy. Netshitenzhe presented evidence that since 1992 'there has been a shift from an *a priori* determination to nationalise the mines, the banks and all monopoly industry and to view monopoly capital as an enemy of the National Democratic Revolution'. This shift, he emphasised, was not simply a tactical compromise – the ANC changed its position because of the lessons learned from the collapse of the socialist system in Europe.

For Netshitenzhe, this did not mean that the debate was closed, but he insisted that there must be a proper debate. The question was whether nationalisation is the best mechanism for the mining industry to 'play a larger role in improving the country's fiscal capacity; in creating more jobs and in improving working conditions; in enhancing South Africa's sovereignty; and in transforming the country's accumulation path' (Netshitenzhe 2010). These objectives were set out by the Youth League. Netshitenzhe argued that 'the call for *holus bolus* "nationalisation of the mines" is not supported by strong enough evidence'.

But the Youth League was not listening to any debating points about the policy of nationalisation. They proposed nationalisation to be implemented through three actions:

a)   establish a state mining company to bring all mining operations that are currently under public ownership under a single authority;

b)   change laws as needed for the state to acquire at least 50 per cent controlling share in all existing mines '(with and without compensation)'; and

c)   amend legislation so that new mines will be at least 60 per cent state owned and there will be greater state participation in the downstream activities related to mineral resources. At least 30 per cent of the non-state share in mining activities should, in addition, be in the control of historically disadvantaged individuals.[5]

Several principles were put forward to indicate how the restructured mining sector would operate. The most interesting is that 'it will not be run like a private business corporation whose extent of progress is solely measured through the amount of profit generated'. The state-owned mining company would be held to account for its success in creating jobs, maximising the country's gain from mineral resources, contributing to socio-economic development and assisting mining communities.

The weak performance of other state enterprises to date (for example, Eskom, Transnet, SAA, SABC and Denel) was not seen as a warning, but as a resource for useful lessons on what should not be done.

The Youth League was never clear on the compensation issue. Mines that are not profitable can be expropriated without compensation (but how could the state justify taking over such operations 'who are laying off huge numbers of workers and are in financial crisis'?). There is no intention to 'bail out indebted capitalists'. Compensation in other instances would be decided on the merits of the case. The Youth League has a bias towards not paying compensation: when someone steals your car, you should not have to buy it back.[6] But issues are complex because mining shares are owned by a wide variety of stakeholders – workers' pension funds (of which the Government Employees Pension Fund is the largest), foreign investors (who may be shielded by bilateral investment protection agreements), in addition to black economic empowerment (BEE) beneficiaries (from Employee Share Ownership Plan (ESOP) participants to empowered millionaires) and traditional white mine owners.

Most critics of nationalisation assume that the Constitution will require the state to pay 'market price' for mining shares. The cost would be enormous – R2 000 billion is one figure that has been mentioned[7] (perhaps on the high side, but even half of this is a staggering sum).

And the spending cannot end with the purchase of shares. Many years would be needed to recoup the compensation costs, during which time funds would still be needed to develop the mines and expand their reserves to open up more areas that can potentially be mined. The state could buy all the mines, but it would still need to raise additional funds – substantial funds – to invest in the mining operations. The costs of providing proper benefits to workers and of improving environmental and safety standards would also be high. All of the income from mineral sales may not be enough to cover these requirements. So the problem is not even solved if the state 'refuses' to pay compensation – and abrogates the Constitution.

There are three financial arguments against nationalisation:
- It is not affordable.
- It makes no sense to spend huge amounts of state resources on mines to give expression to a principle (even one in the Freedom Charter) when these resources have better alternative uses, in health, education or infrastructure.
- Once the state has bought out all the mines, it still has to raise additional investment money to pay for mine development.

It is also relevant that the state has, even since 1994, shown itself to be a poor superintendent of productive assets. The Youth League itself drew attention to SAA, Eskom, SABC and Denel, which have been crippled, as it said, by 'criminality, mismanagement and patronage, coupled with weak accountability systems'. The only state-run mine is also a cautionary tale. South Africa nationalised the diamond diggings in Namaqualand in the 1930s and the benefits of these diggings were diverted to white voters in the area. When the Alexkor mine was taken over by the new government in 1994, it was thoroughly mismanaged (and continues to be to this day).[8]

Letting things develop – the effective view of the mining industry

In the 2011 documentary film 'Mining for Change', Julius Malema, then the leader of the Youth League, said that the country's mines must be nationalised to return to the black majority the mineral wealth that was stolen by white colonists (Reuters, 8 June 2011).

The mining industry understandably sees different problems. The main problem the industry acknowledges is the failure of the sector in South Africa to grow and prosper in tandem with other mining industries across the world, particularly in the light of the boom in mineral commodity prices since about 2000.[9]

The second problem is the wide use of the 'N' word. This issue is raised by the Chamber of Mines,[10] traditional mining company leaders such as former AngloGold Ashanti CEO Mark Cutifani (now head of Anglo American plc), and newer recruits such as Nchaka Moloi, a former official of the Department of Minerals and Energy, who became the CEO of Motjoli Resources (*Business Day*, 10 October 2011).

New black mine owners and partners in mining ventures have an uncomfortable fence to straddle. On the one hand they represent the involvement of black people as new business leaders in mining (allowing black people to share in the wealth beneath the soil as promised in the Freedom Charter). On the other hand they cannot but be critical of the tardiness of the industry as a whole in assisting black people to acquire high-level skills in mining, and the lack of progress in uplifting mining communities. They point to this as a lack of transformation. As Cyril Ramaphosa said: 'It should therefore be a matter of great concern to all of us that transformation in mining appears to have faltered. This is a risk both to the industry and the country' (*Sunday Times*, 7 August 2011). This is an ironic statement because the one industry in South Africa that has transformed itself – beyond all recognition – since the early 1990s is the mining industry. The old mining houses, which invented themselves to exploit the mineral wealth of South Africa under colonial and white rule, have gone. South African mining capital skillfully used the opportunities of the democratic transition to internationalise itself – and its international expansion has been prodigious. Annual reports of Anglo American, BHP Billiton and Xstrata are less and less about South Africa. They are still very concerned about South Africa – not only because they have large investments here already, but also because of the vast mineral wealth that remains – but they are developing options for their managers and shareholders in other parts of the world as they wait for things in South Africa to develop.

The tardiness of the mining industry in addressing 'real' transformation is due to two factors: poor government policy and an almost inexplicable lack of effective pressure from below – from mineworkers and their unions.

In fairness to the mining industry, it has tried to work with government. The industry agreed to the fundamental change in the mineral rights regime (which ended the private ownership of mineral rights) without launching a constitutional challenge. It has negotiated at great length on transformation issues and it has responded to the incentives that government has put in place. The black economic empowerment (BEE) models in the industry, assembled in the 2004 Mining Charter, were framed under the guidance of the complex BEE formulas generated by government. A huge amount of effort was put into developing targets and measuring 'performance'. The industry accepted subsequent amendments to the Charter, which were introduced because the incentives and guidelines in the original Charter were not having the intended effect. A very few, politically well-connected, people came to benefit hugely from the partnership incentives indicated by government after 1994, while the growth of the industry slackened and work on the mines continued pretty much as before, at least for the workers who escaped the continuing great retrenchments that affected one-third of those who voted for the ANC and the Reconstruction and Development Programme (RDP) mining policy in 1994 (all mineworkers, whatever their nationality, were allowed to vote in 1994).

In the face of demands for the 'nationalisation' of the mines, the leaders of the mining industry (both black and white) have condemned the idea.[11] Leaders are concerned by or about the inability of the mining industry to share in the international commodities boom.[12] The Chamber of Mines believes that 100 000 additional jobs in mining could be created by 2020 if there were 'security of tenure and a predictable business environment' (Mining Weekly, 10 October 2011). In general, the way forward presented by the mining industry proposes doing better in implementing the new Mining Charter and continuing with other industry initiatives such as the Mining Industry Growth, Development and Employment Task Team established in December 2008 with all stakeholders 'to position the industry for long-term growth and transformation'.

The idea that all that is needed to scotch the nationalisation debate is a determined implementation of the undertakings in the Mining Charter has fairly wide currency: Sandile Nogxina, the outgoing director general of the Department of Mineral Resources, told *Business Day* in June 2011 that the industry had itself to blame for the current situation. 'If there had been compliance, nobody would now be complaining,' he said. 'The industry has brought this debate on themselves ... because if they had done all those things they could have averted it and given ammunition to those opposed to nationalisation.'[13]

Cyril Ramaphosa, in a talk at the Gordon Institute of Business Science, 'laid much of the blame for the "ferment" around mine nationalisation at the door of the industry, which he said had failed to live up to its transformation promises ... "young people, who are unemployed ... many of them have never worked ... see these big corporations raking in a lot of money, and they also see that these corporations have not transformed in the way that was agreed"'.[14]

Although not commenting directly on the Charter, James Motlatsi, then deputy chairperson of AngloGold Ashanti, said that 'if South African business fails to act decisively, it may present political opportunity to those on the lunatic fringe, particularly within a scenario of faltering economic growth and high unemployment.'[15]

Government wanted the Mining Charter implemented and black directors wanted mining companies to take strong action towards transformation, but the industry did not do so. Who is to blame? The easy answer is to point fingers at the untransformed white management. But just because a golf ball will fit into a hole does not mean it will get there. And this is where the role of the union needs some scrutiny.

Could the *status quo* make sense if the union movement put pressure on the mine owners and the government for 'full implementation'? The National Union of Mineworkers (NUM) is not supportive of the Youth League's call for the simple nationalisation of the mines – although it does support the wording of the Freedom Charter and participated in the ANC research project into state intervention in the minerals sector.[16] In its initial response to the Youth League, the NUM in effect came out in support of the *status quo* – with implementation by government. The NUM (2011) said that the social and economic goals of the Freedom Charter could be secured within the framework of the laws passed since 1994 and that, without taking ownership of the mines, the state could:

- appropriate some of the surplus from mining (via royalties and taxes), which can then be used for state development initiatives;
- enforce laws to improve the working conditions of miners (health and safety, minimum wages, early retirement);
- encourage 'downstream' industries that use the output of the mines (making pots and pans, railway lines, roofing material, cement, bricks, cables and so on);
- encourage 'upstream' industries that supply the mines – electricity, IT systems, vehicles, piping, cables, mining capital equipment);
- limit foreign ownership to ensure a South African share in all mines;
- use the mining sector as a basis for subsidising and encouraging new industries that grow because of their human resource quality and not because of access to raw materials; and
- ensure that mines in rural areas benefit local communities and that infrastructure is put in place to allow all communities to benefit from mining the resources in their local environs.

The NUM argument is that good laws, sound regulations and adequate enforcement by government are what is needed to make the mining industry contribute properly to development. The framework for all of this already exists. It can easily include a state-owned mining company and nationalisation (with compensation) on a case-by-case basis.

Reading the NUM documents, one is struck by the confidence that results can be achieved by negotiations, policies and the power of the government. The NUM views are underpinned by a belief that because political change and the defeat of apartheid was achieved through negotiation, the same can be true of economic justice for mineworkers and mining communities. The union has somehow forgotten the tremendous organisational impetus it contributed to in the 1980s and 1990s to hasten the negotiations for political freedom and to shape their form. Now that the ANC is in power, a lot of the effort of the union appears to go into appearing before parliamentary subcommittees and lobbying.

The power of worker organisation in the mining sector is frequently seen,[17] but in the form of strikes and marches that respond to local wage issues or national mobilisation calls, not as strategic campaigns towards meeting a series of progressive objectives.

ANC: We have already nationalised, we must just tax and regulate better
Since 2002, the South African government has taken ownership of all the mineral rights in the country. The riches beneath the soil belong to the state. They have been nationalised.

The ANC government addressed the mineral wealth issue in the Freedom Charter directly. South Africa used to be one of the very few countries where mineral rights could be owned. It was a property right that could be severed from land ownership and passed on by right of succession. This was an anomaly – greatly favoured by the mining houses (and by the Bafokeng to whom in the nineteenth century Paul Kruger gave the mineral rights along with the platinum-rich land he allocated to the tribe near Rustenburg). Everywhere else in the world, the tradition is that the state owns the mineral rights and makes commercial arrangements with mining companies to mine and market the minerals in return for royalty payments – which go to the state according to the amount that is mined – and mining companies also pay tax on their profits.

The *mines* (the operations put in place to extract the minerals) have not been nationalised. The ANC-led government followed the Freedom Charter to the letter in passing the Mineral and Petroleum Resources Development Act, No. 28 of 2002 (MPRDA). They had to defend this Act from the mining industry, which first said they could not pass it because of the property clause in the Constitution (the Bafokeng also objected!). The result was a negotiation and a compromise. The state owns all the mineral wealth beneath the soil and the mining companies have the right to mine them. They retain this right as long as they actually mine minerals and as long as they comply with the law of the country. This includes adherence to the Mining Charter (which sets a minimum target of 26 per cent ownership by historically disadvantaged South Africans by 2014).

In his response to the initial Youth League paper, Paul Jourdan (ANC 2010) acknowledged that 'we failed to maximise the beneficial developmental impacts for our people, when we concessioned [mineral rights]' in terms of the MPRDA after 2002. He proposed a raft of measures to 'undo the wholesale handing out of twenty-five year renewable mineral concessions/licences with minimal developmental conditions'. Future concessions, he suggested, should be allocated by auction – and bidders would have to accept tailored developmental undertakings. Existing concessionaires would be closely monitored, and if they did not use their rights, these could be taken away. But for the most part, the state would have to use tax laws and revised BEE regulations to improve the spread of benefits from mining. This should be combined with direct interventions through the Industrial Development Corporation (holding and beneficiating strategic mineral assets itself.)

Jourdan is one of the ANC research team into state intervention in the minerals sector (SIMS). Most of the measures he mentioned in 2010 and in subsequent and earlier writings (Jourdan 2011) form the backbone of the SIMS recommendations released publicly in 2012. According to *The Economist* of 3 December 2011, the initial draft of the recommendations said that 'the nationalisation of mines in South Africa is a costly, high-risk proposition that should be adopted only as a last resort'. The ANC leadership was not happy with the academic phrasing of the SIMS report and its clear, negative judgement on nationalisation, which was reached after a year-long study of the policy in fourteen countries. It sent the report back to the panel for redrafting, saying it wanted 'more options'. The main options offered in 2012 related to a more aggressive approach to mining taxation so that state coffers would be swelled by a greater share of the economic rents from successful mining ventures. This is not a controversial principle – even for mining companies – although there are obviously very different views of how it should best be realised (Collier 2011:85-95).

Government's New Growth Path (2010) envisages, as one of its 'core strategies', 'setting up a state-owned mining company that would co-exist with a strong private mining sector and that promotes beneficiation, as well as greater utilisation of the mineral resource base of the country for developmental purposes …'. The use of the state-owned mining company, which has existed as a shell since 2010, is also a prominent feature in the proposals of the Youth League (and is explicitly supported by the NUM).

The SIMS report was discussed at the mid-2012 ANC policy conference, but it did not lay the basis for consensus within the factionally stressed ANC. Some reports said there was agreement that taxes on mines should be used to tap into resource wealth and encourage its local beneficiation, and as an acceptance of 'strategic nationalisation' as an abiding developmental tool in the right circumstances. Others said that six provincial delegations had favoured 'nationalisation' (*Business Day*, 6 July 2012) and that a physical fight had broken out in the final commission session when it became clear that its report would indicate no change in the longstanding position that nationalisation simply remains one of many policy options.

Presenting a new mining tax regime and an active state minerals company as a credible response to the popular demand for 'nationalisation of the mines' has tested both the unity and the communication powers of the ANC. The SIMS report, for all its 600 pages, is disappointing in its neglect of the social and environmental aspects of mining.

NATIONALISATION, OF A SPECIAL TYPE

South Africa is probably the most mining-intensive country in the world today. Its industrial economy was built from mining; it still employs a huge number of mineworkers (close to half a million) and still has vast unmined resources. A great deal of its mining estate is deep underground. Extraction processes – to separate the ore from the rock – are often extremely complex. Above all, mining has created particular patterns of human interaction and human settlement, cultures of mining that are deeply embedded after over a century of intensive mining activity and that will continue into the future.

Mining ought to be a much more prominent part of South Africa's industrial strategy. For many years it was characterised by the Department of Trade and Industry as a low-wage, low-skill sector – a sunset industry and a relic of our past. It did not fit the vision for a high-wage, high-skill economy producing manufactured exports. In reality, mining is a highly technical sector demanding great skills. Mining companies that operate in South Africa rely on this indigenous capability, which is highly marketable internationally. The industry is labour intensive because of the nature of many ore deposits, particularly gold and platinum, where deep-level hard-rock mining cannot be mechanised to the extent it can in open-cast mining. Despite the lower level of qualification required for many jobs, mining ought not to be a low-wage sector. Dangerous and demanding work should be well rewarded.

The mining industry is not just about mines. The infrastructure needed to transport minerals to ports and processing facilities has additional uses that can open up opportunities in corridor areas along road and rail routes and at the ports themselves. South Africa

Table 1: South Africa – still the world's most mining economy

	Country	Population 2009	Number of mineworkers	Total employment	mining % of total employment
1	South Africa	49 320 150	491 222	13 061 000	3.76%
2	Botswana	1 981 576	13 099	449 235	2.92%
3	Namibia	2 242 078	7 600	385 300	1.97%
4	Norway	4 828 726	45 000	2 508 000	1.79%
5	Zambia	12 723 746	65 500	4 360 700	1.50%
6	Australia	21 951 700	135 000	10 740 500	1.26%
7	Chile	16 955 737	62 102	5 085 885	1.22%
8	Venezuela	28 384 000	106 800	11 863 100	0.90%
9	China	1 331 380 000	5 300 000	706 666 667	0.75%
10	Malaysia	27 949 395	54 500	10 659 600	0.51%
11	Brazil	193 246 610	379 000	90 786 000	0.42%
12	Sweden	9 298 515	9 000	4 593 000	0.20%
13	Finland	5 338 871	5 000	2 553 000	0.20%

(Sources: ILO, US Geological Service, DMR, World Bank, CIA World Factbook)

could get many advantages from establishing itself (as it has done to a degree already) as a reliable supplier of quality raw materials. In many mineral products (including gold, but most notably in platinum group metals, manganese and chromium), South Africa has reserves that rank it in first place in the world (Baxter 2011).

The demand for mineral commodities is only growing, as China and India develop. Figure 1 shows how increasing mineral consumption (here copper) is correlated with rising gross domestic product (GDP) per capita.

There are indications that the role of mining is being accorded more attention in the New Growth Path. It points to the potential for the mining value chain to 'add 140 000 additional jobs by 2020, and 200 000 by 2030, not counting the downstream and side-stream effects'. But private sector mining companies are not falling over themselves to expand mining operations in South Africa in the present climate of policy uncertainty and labour unrest and the state minerals company has yet to take on a clear form.

In his survey of development efforts in post-colonial Africa, Richard Dowden describes how many countries 'mortgaged their countries' wealth to fund … huge state companies such as national mining houses and marketing boards, called "parastatals" … In the mid-1990s it is estimated that capitalist Nigeria had more than 600 state companies. Kenya had 360. In Zimbabwe before the economy collapsed about 35 per cent of it was under the control of state-run companies.' He continues:

The stated aim of nationalisation was to bring the whole economy in line with a national development plan and prevent capital being exported. The effect was to give leaders total control of the money. Nationalisation gave them a vast barrel of patronage, allowing them to reward political allies and pay off enemies … While para-statal jobs and contracts went to cronies, the state companies were run for explicitly political ends, such as keeping politically important sectors of society happy … The parastatals bled Africa to death (Dowden 2008: 271).

This may be a journalistic take, but it rings many bells for surveyors of South Africa's record with state-owned companies since 1994 – SABC, Denel, Eskom, Coega Development Corporation. There is a strong likelihood that the state minerals company will work like existing mining companies and existing parastatal enterprises. They all pay lip service to social goals and environmental responsibility, but they are driven by money and politics.

Despite all the summits, initiatives, task teams, laws and regulations, very little has changed since 1994 on the mines and in the way they operate. Blacks still do all the hard, back-breaking manual work. Workers still feel that there is racism in the way the mines operate. Wages paid by mining companies have gone up – but they do not reflect the danger and effort of most mining work – and there are many subcontractors who are not subject to negotiated wages (the unions turn a blind eye.) Some three-quarters of mine-workers remain illiterate. Fatal accidents have gone down, but there are signs that disease

Figure 1. The world needs metals (copper consumption per capita)

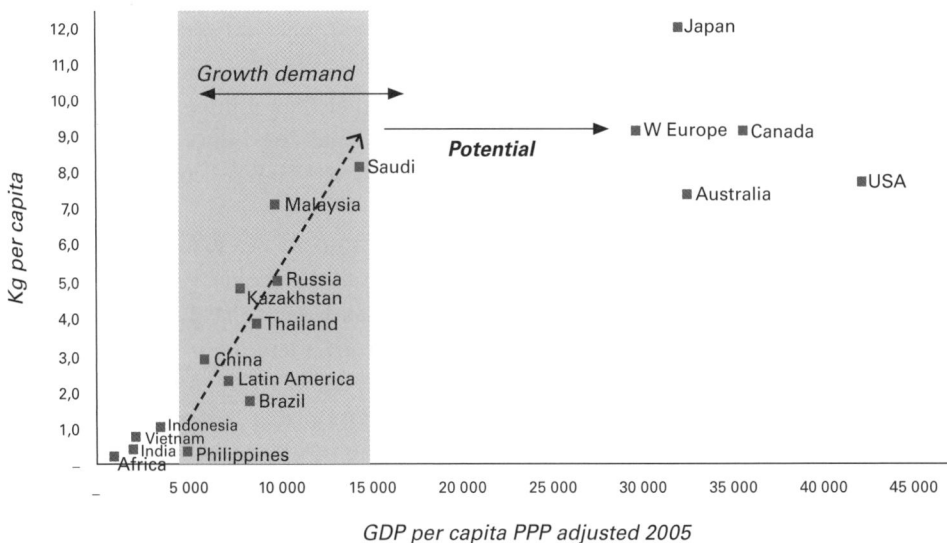

GDP per capita PPP adjusted 2005

(Source: Lindvall 2010)

and sickness have increased. Single-sex hostels have, in some cases, been converted into family accommodation, but many workers and former mineworkers live in shacks with limited rights and poor conditions. Mineworkers have their life and spirit drawn out of them by the mines and then are tossed as empty shells back into the rural areas and informal settlements. The old story continues.

Despite the slick, beautifully illustrated and carefully written 'sustainability reports' that major mining companies now all produce, the environmental harm that flows from mining continues apace. The pressures to intensify mineral extraction and to downplay environmental consequences grow stronger by the year, as China and India, with their huge populations, accelerate their development.

In their chapter on South Africa's mineral-energy complex in *New South African Review 2*, Khadija Sharife and Patrick Bond (2011) imply that shifting to an economy without mining is desirable and ought to be possible. They write of the 'need to leave minerals in the soil' as South Africa moves to a 'genuinely sustainable economy'. One registers the strong arguments they, and David Fig (2011), make about the impact of acid mine drainage from mines and the need for 'ecological reparations'. But human society needs and demands metals and minerals, and there is no end in sight for coal-fuelled electricity in South Africa. Mining will continue and the question is not whether to stop it but how to make a place for it in a 'green economy', whatever that popular phrase actually means. Nationalisation is not the obvious place to start on either account.

The most dangerous mines in the world are in China. They kill and injure more mine-workers every year than any other mining industry and are responsible for extensive environmental degradation. Workers have no rights to organise freely. These are nation-alised mines.

The coal mines in Britain were nationalised after the Second World War by the new Labour government. Health and safety improved once the government took over, but the government did not invest in the industry and coal mine employment fell steadily – from 700 000 after the War to only 7 000 in 1995. (Britain still has huge coal deposits, but government policy was to move to natural gas rather than mining them. Margaret Thatcher's Conservative government privatised the remaining mines and went on a political campaign to destroy the British National Union of Mineworkers and the culture and traditions of mining communities.)

The nationalisation of mines does not guarantee a positive result. Nationalisation could have predominantly negative consequences – for all stakeholders.

Argument around the nationalisation of mines in South Africa has emphasised ques-tions of ownership. The ANC response has been to divert attention to what the proper role of the state may be in the minerals sector. These are issues of importance, but if we are seeking an approach to mining and nationalisation that is 'popularly credible' (Ford 2012) we need a human, environmental and economic strategy so that the country benefits fully from its still incredible mining riches and so that mineworkers have safe jobs that are well remunerated. Instead of emphasising ownership and the role of the state, we should look towards outcomes that ensure that mines are operated for the full benefit of those who work them; that ensure that the environmental consequences of mining are mitigated; and that ensure that the full economic value is gained from mineral deposits by mining them with care and efficiency. These have been summarised as the three Ps: people, planet and prosperity. (This is the slogan of government's 2008 National Framework for Sustainable Development – and is also used by several international companies in their new-found enthusiasm for 'sustainability'.)

The aim is to create a just mining industry, a capable industry that is able to provide the metal, raw materials and power from natural resources that we need to improve our standard of living as a country. The aim is to build a revived industry that is efficient and responsible and that promotes recycling and the wiser use of the world's scarce natural resources. The aim is to foster an industry that cares for the people who work in it and the communities that live alongside its operations.

Mining should be a temporary use of the land, after which it should be restored to being available for other uses. Mining should not be synonymous with ecological devastation – as it is in many parts of South Africa, with acid mine drainage, the collapse of poorly maintained slimes dams, the dispersal of cancer-inducing asbestos dust and the poisoning of ground water with arsenic. Underground mining should not be a death sentence for so many workers. Mining is dangerous – but it can be done more safely.

Popular credibility is not the only requirement. As noble as the three outcomes cited above may be, the question is whether they can also meet the test of economic viability, and the way things are at present, they probably cannot. Minerals have to be sold at internationally determined prices – and these prices do not include the 'external' costs of mining. An externality is an activity that imposes uncompensated costs on other people (Nordhaus 2011). Externalities from mining include the toxic water that drains from mines and waste dumps (as well as the waste dumps themselves), the dust that blows off abandoned workings, the damage to national roads from huge mining trucks, the limits on ecotourism in mining areas and, particularly, the greenhouse gas emissions. These come from some mining operations directly and from all indirectly, through the carbon dioxide that comes from burning coal to create the electricity they need to run the mines. A 2010 study by the US National Research Council estimated that the external costs of electricity generated from coal were as much as 70 per cent of the market price.[18] 'The tradition in economics is to treat occupational injuries and deaths as job characteristics that are traded in labour markets rather than to treat them as externalities.' In a well-functioning market workers are imagined to receive 'compensating wage differentials for the higher risks that they face on the job' (NRC 2010 citing Viscusi 1993). This is not an argument that is credible in South Africa.

Until 1980, the mining industry actively resisted the unionisation of black workers. White unionisation was institutionalised as part of the racist pact formed in the 1920s but black worker unionisation was anathema to all the mining houses. The buying power of wages for black workers in 1968 was lower than it had been before the First World War (Wilson 1972)! Until 1990, more than one worker died for every ton of gold that was extracted from mines in South Africa; that meant 675 deaths in 1980 alone. Today, most mining wages for less-qualified workers are above the median wage for similar job levels in manufacturing industry – but they are not at levels that compensate for the extra danger of working underground.

There is a third type of external cost to mining in addition to the environmental and human impacts on sustainability. This relates to a particular characteristic of mining: that it deals with a *non-renewable* resource, whereas in the case of our other great raw material resources – agriculture, forestry and fishing – the natural resource is renewable. With proper care, you can grow crops again, with proper management you can sustain fisheries and forests and protect biodiversity. When you sell the wool from your sheep, you still have the sheep. With mining, however, your natural resources are progressively run down. Mines are a 'wasting asset'. For this reason, humankind needs to make sure that ore deposits are mined responsibly and that mining companies do not just pick out the richest parts of a deposit but mine to the lowest average grade that is economical. This ensures that the maximum amount of minerals is extracted before a mine is closed. It may not be possible to go back to mine lower grade deposits at another time, and it will often not make economic sense to do so. One way around this issue, for the world, is to pay more attention to recycling. Much metal dumped or thrown away as trash could be recovered and used in new production. This, however, is expensive and it could be cheaper, in the short term, to mine more bauxite and coal and to transform them into aluminium than to recycle used cans or auto components made from the metal.

There is also the national interest to consider. South Africa possesses huge mineral wealth, far more than we can use ourselves. This is the reason we export millions of tons of coal, of iron and manganese ore and partly processed chrome. We sell it at prices that do not reflect the real costs for people or planet and that create attractive income flows that are appropriated by tiny interest groups (including the richly rewarded executives and government-appointed board members of Transnet – which transports the export ore and coal at huge profit – and Eskom, which beneficiates coal to make electricity).

A mining industry that does justice both to the environment and to the people who work in it cannot be a capitalist industry driven only by the profit motive. The plans for the state minerals company mention the need for social and environmental responsibility, but there is no mechanism evident to ensure such behaviour.

This is not to say that nothing can be done. The three outcomes related to nationalising the mines can each be pursued:

To ensure that mines are operated for the full benefit of those who work them
- a wage solidarity policy – so that workers' wages are determined by the *work* they do, not by whether they are employed to mine a rich or a marginal deposit (this implies minimum standards for contract workers as well; underground miners should be paid a substantial premium to recognise the effort and danger associated with this work);
- a real choice in living conditions for workers so that compounds are relegated to history and mineworkers do not have to live in informal settlements;

- a programme of adult education for mineworkers that encourages them to use their experience and knowledge to improve the quality of their work (this should be linked to changes in the workplace that, while respecting disciplinary and safety rules, allow worker participation in improving operations – a real effort to educate and build the capacity of mineworkers at all levels is the only way to break out of the vicious cycle that imprisons black mineworkers across the generations); and
- a 'mine veterans' policy – a separate policy approach is needed to deal with the historical claims of workers for proper compensation if they now have health problems related to their previous mining employment, whether from injury or disease.

To ensure that the environmental consequences of mining are mitigated
- legislation and regulations designed to correct externalities are in place in many instances, but they are not effectively enforced;
- community education and broad social activism in support of sound laws and sensible administration should be welcomed and supported by government, not resisted as is often the case at present;
- there needs to be a tight framework around the sale of mines to prevent mining companies from withdrawing from operations before their environmental obligations have been met; and
- a separate policy approach is needed to deal with the historical legacies of environmental irresponsibility by mining operations, where the original operators have disappeared. This may include the legal pursuit of past directors of companies.

To ensure that the full economic value is gained from mineral deposits by mining them with care and efficiency
- an appropriately skilled workforce, backed up by mining research and development, wise incentives for managers and real investment in the training of black mineworkers and young people; and
- productivity bargaining – including arrangements for continuous operations, which will require mineworkers, and unions, to adopt a stance that welcomes workplace changes that enhance productivity (an employment guarantee for mineworkers is one element that will be needed to support such an approach).

Nationalisation, in the narrow sense of assuming ownership, is not what is called for. As we have discovered with BEE, changing ownership is rarely linked to broad-based transformation, even when a 'worker trust' owns 26 per cent of the shares and a trusted struggle leader is the executive chairperson.

But more is required than a tax policy that catches economic rents from mining and ploughs them into a development model that simply fills in gaps within the South African minerals complex. Organised struggle – proper union organisation with a strategic transformation plan – is the missing additional ingredient. Strong union and community organisation was mobilised for the struggle against apartheid. What led the democratic movement to the present conclusion that the struggle against capitalism can be left to laws and negotiations that are not backed up by organisation? The proposals for the mining sector currently under debate, whether they are narrow or wide, all lack the idea of a countervailing force within the industry to guard against the abuses of the management of private mining companies on the one side and, on the other, the danger that state involvement in the mining sector will take on the traditional forms of cronyism, corruption, mismanagement and theft. Independent worker and community organisations around social and environmental issues in the mining sector need to get access to state support for their work – and resources for playing a watchdog role as well.

I call this nationalisation of a special type.

Mining companies cannot object – because the proposal involves using the Constitution to enforce and develop the rights it confers on people and their organisations.

There is a distant echo here of some of the interventions of the South African Communist Party (SACP) concerning the nationalisation of the mines. Jeremy Cronin, the deputy general secretary, writes that 'socialisation' of all key resources and means of production (including socialisation of the state) is a better concept and a better objective. The idea of 'socialisation' emphasises the need for popular/working-class power and activism in and outside the state, versus an obsession with bureaucratic power (and bureaucratic ownership) (Cronin 2012a). But there has been no programme of education or intervention around real organisation on the mines or in mining communities.

And echoes fade away. Cronin welcomed the ANC's task team report on state intervention in the mineral sector – which is firmly founded in notions of bureaucratic power. He described it as 'an extremely well researched document that will lay the basis, finally, for a comprehensive policy and programme of action to transform this critical sector of our economy' (Cronin 2012b).

NOTES

1   Towards 2010: White elephant looms at Green Point. *Cape Argus* 18 September 2007.
2   Such as Mr Ai Ping, vice-minister of the International Department of the Communist Party of China Central Committee.
3   The research team comprised Dr Paul Jourdan, former CEO of Mintek and long-time ANC advisor on mineral issues; Dr Pundy Pillay, economist and University of the Witwatersrand researcher; and Professor Margaret Chitiga-Mabugu of the Human Sciences Research Council.
4   Nationalisation scary, so drop the word – Cutifani. *Business Day*, 10 October 2011.
5   The Youth League's views are mainly taken from ANC Youth League 2010.
6   Julius Malema in the film 'Mining for Change: A Story of South African Mining': ANC youth leader targets mines in new film. Reuters 8 June 2011.
7   Cyril Ramaphosa in South African mining movie rekindles nationalisation debate. *Mining Weekly*, 24 June 2011. Two-thirds of GDP, or twice the national budget, are also cited as measures of the costs of buying the mines: Mining Industry: SA plans to dig deep on mine overhaul study. *Mining Weekly*, 24 August 2011.

8   From our vault: So how is SA's only nationalised mine doing? Badly, very. Tim Cohen, *Daily Maverick*, 3 February 2010.

9   Commodity price boom did not lead to higher SA mining output. *Mining Weekly*, 25 October 2011; Baxter 2011.

10   Get nationalisation issue out of way, says migrating chamber strategist *Mining Weekly*, 10 October 2011.

11   Patrice Motsepe, the richest of the new black mine owners, said in a radio interview in 2010 that he was willing to accept nationalisation (Nationalisation's okay if people say so, says ARM's Motsepe. *Mining Weekly*, 5 March 2010). Some cynical observers have said that participants in black empowerment mining deals that have gone sour see nationalisation as a way of exiting the industry with generous compensation. Motsepe expressed a view against nationalisation in the 2011 Harmony Annual Report.

12   The mining sector's local concern is tempered by its successful international participation in the boom. Minerals that are not mined today will, for that reason, be available tomorrow, and the rapid development of China and India guarantee that demand will be strong. Capital can wait for the right moment.

13   South African nationalisation: business speaks out. *Financial Times*, 30 June 2011.

14   Industry failures sow 'terrible' nationalisation seeds – Ramaphosa. *Mining Weekly*, 13 July 2011.

15   Mine nationalisation without compensation will spark revolution – Motlatsi. *Mining Weekly*, 1 April 2011.

16   Mine nationalisation absurd – union boss. *Mining Weekly*, 13 May 2011.

17   In a bizarre case, the NUM won a strike against Xstrata on the terms of an ESOP voluntarily introduced by the company. The NUM insisted that the benefits be equal between management and worker participants alike. *Mining Weekly* 2 November 2011.

18   Nordhaus 2011. The 70 per cent figure is not simply translatable to South African conditions.

REFERENCES

ANC (2010) Debate: Nationalisation of the mines. *Umrabulo* 33(2).

ANC (2012a) Maximising the Developmental Impact of the People's Mineral Assets: State Intervention in the Minerals Sector (SIMS): Summary. http://www.anc.org.za/docs/reps/2012/simssummaryz. pdf [Accessed 19 February 2012].

ANC (2012b) Maximising the Developmental Impact of the People's Mineral Assets: State Intervention in the Minerals Sector (SIMS): Report prepared for the ANC Policy Institute. http://www.anc.org. za/docs/reps/2012/simsreport.pdf [Accessed 19 February 2012].

ANC (2012c) National Policy Conference 2012: Policy Discussion Documents. *Umrabulo Special Edition*.

ANC Youth League (2010) Towards the transfer of mineral wealth to the ownership of the people as a whole. A discussion paper of the ANC Youth League, February 2010. *Umrabulo* 33 (2).

Baxter R (2011) The Vision towards Competitive Growth and Meaningful Transformation of South Africa's Mining Sector. Presentation to the South Africa's Mining Industry Day, Chamber of Mines of South Africa. 7 March 2011.

BUSA (2011) ANC research project on state intervention in the mining sector: a Draft Submission by Business Unity South Africa (Busa).

Collier P (2011) *The Plundered Planet: How to Reconcile Prosperity with Nature.* London: Penguin.

Council for Geoscience (2010) Mine water management in the Witwatersrand Gold Fields with special emphasis on acid mine drainage. Report to the Inter-Ministerial Committee (IMC) on acid mine drainage, prepared by the Expert Team of the IMC under the Coordination of the Council for Geoscience, December 2010. http://www.dwaf.gov.za/Documents/ACIDReport.pdf [Accessed 12 December 2011].

Cronin J (2012a) Civil society ... or democratic popular power? *Umsebenzi* 11 (2) 26 January.

Cronin J (2012b) The mines, the media, the judiciary… an epidemic of misguided debates. *Umsebenzi* 11 (4) 9 February.

Department of Environmental Affairs and Tourism (2008) People – Planet – Prosperity: A National Framework for Sustainable Development in South Africa July 2008. http://www.environment.gov.za/ [Accessed 28 August, 2008].

Department of Mineral Resources (2010) <The Mining Charter > - Amendment of the Broad-Based Socio-Economic Empowerment Charter for the South African Mining and Minerals Industry, September 2010. http://www.bullion.org.za/MediaReleases/Downloads/Miningpercent20Charter.pdf [Accessed 17 February 2011].

----- (2011) South African Minerals Industry (SAMI) 2009-2010.

Dikötter F (2010) *Mao's Great Famine: The History of China's Most Devastating Catastrophe, 1958-62.* London: Bloomsbury.

Dowden R (2008) *Africa: Altered states, Ordinary Miracles.* London: Portabello.

Du Plessis S (2011) Nationalising South African mines: Back to a prosperous future, or down a rabbit hole? Presidential address to the biennial conference of the Economic Society of South Africa 5-7 September 2011.

Fig D (2011) Corrosion and externalities: The socio-economic impacts of acid mine drainage on the Witwatersrand. In Daniel J, P Naidoo, D Pillay and R Southall (Eds) *New South African Review 2: New Paths, Old Compromises?* Johannesburg: Wits University Press.

Ford J (2012) South Africa's 'Nationalisation' Debate. Oxford Analytica. http://africanarguments.org [Accessed 6 January 2012].

ILO Labour Statistics website: http://laborsta.ilo.org/STP/guest.

Jourdan P (2010a) Towards a refined ANC minerals policy and strategy. *Umrabulo* 33 (2).

Jourdan P (2010b) A seminar on African mining and its development potential. Raw Materials Group (RMG) Stockholm.

----- (2011) Africa's Mineral Resources: What Must be Done to Make Them Drivers of Development? In Mbeki M (Ed.) *Advocates for Change: How to Overcome Africa's Challenges.* Johannesburg: Picador Africa.

Khumalo L (2011) The ANC Youth League: Slogans are not enough. *New Agenda* 41:53-55.

Lindvall P-E (2010) Welcome address to the Bergforsk Conference. Mineral supply – a grand challenge and opportunity. May 4th 2010. http://bergforsk.se/wp-content/uploads/2011/08/pe_lindvall.pdf [Accessed 10 December 2011].

Mandela N (1956) In our Lifetime. *Liberation* June.

Matshiqi A (2011) Road to Nowhere? *Optima* 57 (2) November.

McCarthy T (2010) The decanting of acid mine water in the Gauteng City-Region. Johannesburg: Gauteng City-Region Observatory.

National Research Council (U.S.) (2010) *Hidden costs of energy : unpriced consequences of energy production and use.* Washington, DC : National Academies Press www.nap.edu [Accessed 29 December 2011].

National Union of Mineworkers (NUM) (1996) New Times, New Challenges: Lessons for the NUM from a visit to Britain and France. Mimeo.

----- (2011) Perspective on nationalization of mines – NUM. *Umrabulo* 35.

Netshitenzhe J (2010) State ownership and the National Democratic Revolution: debating the issue of nationalization. *Umrabulo* Number 33 (2).

Nicol M and J-P Leger (2011) Reflections on South Africa's gold mining crisis: challenges for restructuring. *Transformation* 75:173-184.

Nordhaus WD (2011) Energy: Friend or Enemy? *New York Review of Books* 27 October.

RSA, Economic Cluster (2010) The New Growth Path: Executive Summary.

Sharife K and P Bond (2011) Above and beyond South Africa's minerals-energy complex. In Daniel J, P Naidoo, D Pillay and R Southall (Eds) *New South African Review 2: New Paths, Old Compromises?* Johannesburg: Wits University Press.

TNS Research Surveys (2011) Just over a third of metro adults feel that SA's mines should be nationalized. Press Release 7 April 2011.

US Geological Survey (2011) Mineral commodity summaries 2011 http://minerals.usgs.gov/minerals/pubs/mcs/ [Accessed 15 December 2011].

Viscusi WK (1993) The value of risks to life and health. *J. Econ. Lit.* 31(4):1912-1946.

Wilson F (1972) *Labour in the South African gold mines 1911-1969.* Cambridge: Cambridge University Press.

Xstrata South Africa (2010) *Sustainability Report 2010.* http://www.xstrataalloys.com [Accessed 5 December 2011].

Yager TR (2011) The Mineral Industry of South Africa, in 2009 US Geological Survey 2011.

CHAPTER 7

Broad-based BEE?
HCI's empowerment model and the syndicalist tradition

William Attwell

INTRODUCTION

Black economic empowerment (BEE) has become a highly contested concept in South Africa's post-apartheid economic policy discourse. Its critics have argued that the set of policies and programmes that constitute BEE amount to little more than elite enrichment and elite 'co-option' (Mbeki 2011). Some point to the opportunistic, rent-seeking behaviour of many BEE investors (Cargill 2010: 16), whereas others suggest that it has become a self-reinforcing institution in need of urgent reform (Lindsay 2011: 236). This chapter engages with the BEE debate in a rather different way by placing the question of post-apartheid black empowerment within a broader historical and intellectual context. Using Hosken Consolidated Investment (HCI), a BEE company that grew out of the investment wing of the South African Clothing and Textile Workers Union (Sactwu) as a case study, it makes the argument that an approach to broad-based empowerment existed before 1994, and in fact *preceded* official attempts to legislate for it through the 2004 Broad Based Black Economic Empowerment Act (South Africa 2004).

The chapter begins by outlining the establishment and subsequent development of HCI, and how its founders, John Copelyn and Marcel Golding, sought to capitalise on some of the earliest, and most lucrative, empowerment deals in the post-1994 period.

It explains how, by channelling funds to union members as well as to a comprehensive welfare programme under the aegis of the HCI Foundation, the two businessmen constructed a holistic empowerment 'ecosystem' for union members and their families. The chapter then locates HCI's idiosyncratic approach within a historical tradition in the independent trade union movement that has its intellectual roots in the worker-oriented syndicalist movement of the early twentieth century. It concludes by juxtaposing the HCI story with the underlying ideology, and subsequent critiques, of mainstream BEE, and makes the case that scholars and policy makers alike would do well to consider the diverse historical precedents, and subsequent manifestations, of broad-based empowerment when considering reforms to the current policy framework.

LAYING THE FOUNDATIONS

After attending the University of the Witwatersrand, where he graduated with a BA Honours degree in 1974, John Copelyn worked as a union organiser and activist until 1976 when he was banned by South Africa's apartheid government. Three and a half years later Copelyn's ban was lifted and he took up the position of general secretary of what would become Sactwu. It was in this capacity that Copelyn started to actively leverage the discourse and vocabulary of 'syndicalist' or 'workerist' trade unionism in a highly publicised debate with a prominent South African Communist Party (SACP) member, Jeremy Cronin, now deputy transport minister and deputy general secretary of the SACP, in the *South African Labour Bulletin*.

'The two hats debate', as it was later known, centered on the appropriateness of formal institutional links between trade unions and the national liberation movement, led by the African National Congress (ANC). Whereas Cronin viewed the Tripartite Alliance – a political alliance including the ANC, the SACP and the Congress of South African Trade Unions (Cosatu) – as adequate representation of workers' interests in a future democratic dispensation, Copelyn warned of the dangers of surrendering union independence to a future ANC-led government (Copelyn 1991: 59). At stake, he continued, was the union movement's future capacity to criticise the government of the day should the latter's policies conflict with the interests of union members in particular, and the working class in general. Moreover, in order to present a vision that was both cohesive and independent-minded, Copelyn maintained that: 'It is not enough to simply adopt an ideology of independence. We will also have to map out an alternative vision of a just society in which unions play an important role which is fundamentally independent of the state' (1991: 31). With reference to the agency of trade unions in effecting social change, he continued: 'The union movement will have to identify areas of activity that will provide it with an independent institutional base to constructively influence society' (1991:31).

Underlying Copelyn's concerns was an essential scepticism that a post-apartheid state would uphold the interests of workers rather than those of political elites. Unions, he argued, needed independent resources and capabilities with which to effect change.

Copelyn practised what he preached, and in 1993 he took the first step towards developing an independent base by establishing an investment trust company on behalf of his union, Sactwu, which at the time had approximately 150 000 members (Skinner 2002: 28). The idea was to build up a considerable capital base (initially funded through workers' subscriptions) that would operate separately from the union itself but be managed by the union's leadership for the purposes of financing the education and welfare needs of its members (*Business in Africa*, 26 June 2006). As the first union-backed investment company in South Africa, Copelyn's concept set a precedent that would be later emulated by most Cosatu-affiliated trade unions, and indeed predated official attempts to create a legislative framework for broad-based black economic empowerment (*Financial Mail*, 27 September 2007).

Marcel Golding's early career similarly featured a high level of involvement in the trade union movement. After completing a BA honours degree at the University of Cape Town, Golding continued to work at the university as a lecturer and tutor. He boasts a long history of involvement in the trade union movement, having served on the central executive committee of Cosatu, the SA Miners Federation executive committee and the Miners' international executive committee (*Bloomberg*, 19 March 2012). However, it was during his time as deputy general secretary of the National Union of Mineworkers (NUM) that he too became involved in the establishment of an investment trust company.

Like the Sactwu Investment Group, the Mineworkers Investment Company (MIC) was born out of concern for the future material welfare of mineworkers and their dependents in the post-1994 era. Fearful that funding for the Mineworkers Development Agency (MDA), the social development arm of the NUM, would not be forthcoming in the post-transition period, Golding, among others, set about actively pursuing profitable investment opportunities in order to build up a stable capital base that could meet the financial needs of the MDA (*Financial Mail*, 27 September 2007).

THE POST-1994 PERIOD

The historic elections of April 1994 heralded a new era in South African politics. When members of the country's first democratically elected National Assembly took their seats in Parliament in Cape Town, Copelyn and Golding were among the 252 members of parliament (MPs) representing the ANC. While giving the appearance of ideological acquiescence to the positions of the largest party in Parliament – perhaps surprising given his strong antipolitical arguments in the 'two hats debate' – Copelyn, with Golding, focused efforts on consolidating their respective investment projects during this period.

Both gained reputations as talented investors and entrepreneurs as they moved swiftly to secure many of the country's earliest, and most lucrative, empowerment deals (Cargill 2010: 139). By capitalising on the willingness of corporate South Africa to grant preferential share options to black-owned entities in the years immediately following the transition, by 1996 the investment company had channelled more than R100 million into projects that would directly benefit its parent union, Sactwu (*Financial Mail*, 28 September 2007). Copelyn vigorously pursued empowerment opportunities in the growing media and telecommunications industries, including a 5 per cent stake in Vodacom (one of South Africa's first cellular telephone networks) as well as Highveld Stereo, a popular radio station (*Financial Mail*, 28 September 2007).

It was during this period that Copelyn and Golding began to discuss seriously the possibility of a joint venture. Their discussions came to fruition in 1997 when the two men reverse-listed R481.6 million worth of shares from both SIG and MIC into Hosken Consolidated Investments (HCI), an investment holdings company, in return for 63.5 per cent of HCI equity (*Business Times*, 12 October 1997). The transaction proved pivotal to Copelyn's and Golding's careers. Not only did it transfer the locus of both their business interests to HCI, it also prompted their request to leave Parliament, a move that was greeted with mixed enthusiasm by trade unionists and politicians alike (*Business Times*, 12 October 1997).

Under the banner of HCI, Copelyn and Golding continued in their spirited mission to expand the range and depth of their business interests. One of the most highly publicised of these early acquisitions occured in 1998 when HCI bought up a 25 per cent shareholding in Midi Television, the parent company of e.tv, South Africa's first free-to-air television station (*Business in Africa*, 26 June 2006). The deal would prove to be a steep learning curve. Although it was initially conceived as a 'cash cow', it took six years, and millions of rands in additional capital investments, before Midi Television finally turned a profit in 2004. In an interview with *Business in* Africa on 26 June 2006, Copelyn recounted that: 'A television licence was initially perceived as a licence to print money, but it's not. It's a tough business, television; people lose money as well as make it. It took all of six years of HCI's focus to make it come right. It took all of our resources and more.'

He noted that the perceived instability of the South African market in the 1990s caused their international investment partner, Warner Brothers, to disinvest from Midi (*Business in Africa*, 26 June 2006). Those were not easy times. The credit crunch after the 1997 Asian financial crisis and subsequent global economic downturn meant that many of HCI's minority partners were unable to deliver on their contributions to the television station's capital costs (*Business Times*, 30 September 1999). Rather than admit defeat – and to the consternation of their institutional backers – HCI successively bought out its competitors to the extent that, by 2006, it held a substantial controlling stake in Midi Television.

During their first three to four years in the private sector, Copelyn's and Golding's business opportunities were still funded almost exclusively through debt, an approach that – though storing up for the future the greater benefits associated with larger, long-term investments – did not provide much in the way of a cash flow for the unions. In order to get around this problem and deliver some tangible value to the union's trust funds, Copelyn resolved to unbundle further shareholdings in the company. This he did in May 1999. The result was that R750 million was transferred to the unions and their members.

Copelyn noted that, up until this point, this was 'probably the single largest delivery of benefit to black shareholders in South African history' (*Business Times*, 30 September 1999). Although perhaps not one of HCI's most immediately profitable deals, the Midi case is interesting because it illustrates Copelyn's and Golding's idiosyncratic business style, their firm commitment to delivering value to their union partners both in the long- and short-term and, on a more patriotic note, their confidence in the South African economy's potential to transcend the economic crisis of the late 1990s.

A HOLISTIC APPROACH TO EMPOWERMENT

The development and delivery of value to their trade union constituency was just one side of Copelyn's and Golding's empowerment model. The other, more practical, element concerns the functioning of the HCI Foundation. When HCI acquired Golden Arrow Bus Services in 2005, it also took charge of the company's outreach arm, the Golden Arrow Foundation (GAF). Established in 1994, the Foundation sought to promote social development and self-reliance through the provision of bursaries for tertiary education and various youth leadership programmes. GAF's reincarnation as the HCI Foundation brought with it a massive injection of assets, notably half the purchase price paid to Golden Arrow as well as a personal donation of R200 million from Copelyn and Golding (*Mail & Guardian*, 26 August 2006).

The Foundation functions as an independent trust with its own board of trustees, drawn from a wide spectrum of human experience including 'members of the HCI board of directors, employees from subsidiary companies and independent experts who are able to add value to the specific foci of the Foundation's work' (HCI Foundation 2006: 2). These focus areas – the principal beneficiaries of the Foundation's funding – encompass a variety of sectors including education, healthcare, women's empowerment, and youth activities as well as the cultural legacy of public transport in Cape Town (a throwback to the Foundation's roots, its support for the Cape Town Public Transport Museum Project can also be interpreted as a form of recognition of the 'lived lives' of working-class people in Cape Town) (HCI Foundation 2006: 11).

The central pillar of the HCI Foundation's social development programme is its education segment, and in particular its generous bursary scheme. Citing a commitment to 'human capital development' as well as emphasising the benefits of tertiary education for the personal development of individuals and the economy as a whole, in 2006 the Foundation awarded a total of 692 bursaries, to the value of R3 882 684, to underprivileged tertiary applicants. In 2007, this was increased to R6.1 million, a figure that translated into 162 new bursaries (HCI Foundation 2007: 20).

In addition to its size and scope, another notable feature of the HCI Foundation is its underlying ethos of 'community-orientedness'. Through partnerships with HCI's dominant union shareholder, Sactwu, and by engaging in joint projects with the social development arms of HCI's subsidiary companies, the Foundation has sought to implement an 'inclusive' vision of civic responsibility. This has involved promoting awareness of social issues among the HCI workforce (for instance, through a programme that encourages Golden Arrow bus drivers to give of their time to take underprivileged children on outings); contributing to various education enhancement projects that specifically target the dependents of HCI-affiliated workers (for instance, Sactwu's 'Edu-peg' programme that teaches essential language, literacy and numeracy skills to young children); and the promotion of schemes that encourage communities to take charge of their own socio-economic development (HCI Foundation 2006: 13). HCI's relationship to Clover Industries Limited (a producer of dairy products) as its pre-eminent BEE partner opened opportunities for the Foundation to invest in Clover's community-based caring and entrepreneurial programme, Mama Afrika/Ukwakha Isizwe, launched in 2004 (HCI Foundation 2006: 13). Roughly translated as 'building and nurturing our nation', Mama Afrika/Ukwakha Isizwe builds on the roles traditionally played by mothers as caregivers in many African communities by supporting the development of self-sustaining care centres for orphaned and abandoned children and the elderly (HCI Foundation 2006: 13). The project works to identify and assist women in these communities to extend and improve their facilities and to provide 'training in cooking, sewing, food gardening, creative courses, baking and administration to help these institutions become self-sustainable' (HCI Foundation 2006: 13). This 'self-help' approach has proved highly successful and has subsequently received numerous awards including the Proudly South African Homegrown Award and the Bridge Builder of the Year Award (HCI Foundation 2006: 13).

Although this emphasis on an independent approach to proactive self-help concurs neatly with the ethos of the HCI Foundation as a whole, it also points to a particular continuity of values that pervades and informs the functioning of the entire Copelyn-Golding empire. On the one hand, Copelyn was concerned to establish an independent institutional base from which to influence society constructively. Having transformed a relatively small amount of Sactwu capital into a multibillion-rand investment holdings company (of which the union's 40 per cent stake is collectively owned), with twenty-two subsidiaries spread across a range of sectors, it can be confidently asserted that this institutional base has been achieved (*Business in Africa*, 26 June 2006).

On the other hand, the HCI Foundation's emphasis on promoting a sense of communally shared social responsibility, and its practical programmes to empower individual workers to themselves become productive members of society, suggests that the foundation functions as the principle vehicle for delivering their 'alternative vision of a just society'. The Copelyn-Golding approach refers to the symbiotic agency of both these elements: while the investment holdings company, HCI, works to establish and expand an independent institutional base, the Foundation and its affiliates work to effect social transformation through practical programmes and partnerships. Underscoring this vision is an ethos that stresses collective interest and concern, the material well-being of workers and the independence of the movement from party politics and the state.

SYNDICALIST THOUGHT AND THE TWO HATS DEBATE

The language and discourse used by Copelyn in the 'two hats debate' to express his scepticism about a future ANC-led state upholding the interests of workers draws on an intellectual tradition within the trade union movement that has hitherto received little attention from labour historians: revolutionary syndicalism. Described as 'an attempt to combine socialism and trade-unionism in a higher synthesis in which the labour unions should become the basis of socialism and socialism the ideal expression of the unions', historically, syndicalist thought dovetailed with the aims of nineteenth-century anarchism by being simultaneously anti-capitalist *and* anti-state. Its aspiration was a form of 'stateless socialism' in which workers would seize direct control of the means of production and replace the 'political' state and capitalism with a form of socialism based on workers' 'self-management' through union structures (Levine 1912: 10; Van der Walt 1999: 8).

This chapter argues that Copelyn's aim of mapping out an 'alternative vision of a just society' that utilises 'an independent institutional base', owned by unions for the benefit of union members, finds a compelling intellectual precedent with this earlier worker-oriented tradition. The relative lack of attention paid to syndicalism by labour historians can to some extent be explained by the dominance of writers associated with the SACP (such as Jeremy Cronin) in recording the history of the early left in South Africa. Van der Walt argues that these writers constituted a 'communist school' of socialist historiography, noting that they tended to paper over the central role played by syndicalist ideas in the early labour movement by claiming its key institutions and protagonists, such as the weekly newspaper *The Voice of Labour* and the early political group the International Socialist League (ISL), as part of a longer-running Marxist heritage (2004: 68).

Van der Walt takes issue with the communist school interpretation, arguing that 'the early South African left were heirs of Mikhail Bakunin (1814-76), the Russian anarchist who formulated the core ideas of revolutionary syndicalism, rather than scions of Karl Marx' (2004: 68). He stresses that it was revolutionary syndicalism, and not classical Marxism, that was the animating ideology of the early trade union movement during South Africa's 'industrial revolution' of the late nineteenth and early twentieth centuries. In fact, the country's first majority black African trade union – the Industrial Workers of Africa – grew out of the first wave of international syndicalist organising in the 1910s (it was initially called the Industrial Workers of the World or IWW, after the American organisation of the same name), and was ultimately founded on the basis of syndicalist aims and principles (Van der Walt 1999: 22).

It was the ISL, however, that constituted the dominant syndicalist voice during this period. Though it was founded by white British, European and American immigrants, many of whom were literate, highly skilled workers, the ISL came to distance itself from the white labour movement, led by the South African Labour Party, which it saw as racist and conservative and, as a consequence, ultimately divisive of the working class. In contrast to the Labour Party, anti-racism and the political liberation of black South Africans were cornerstones of ISL policy at this time. Van der Walt notes that this support for black political rights, and its call to workers to organise across racial lines, had the effect of alienating white workers, many of whom supported the colour bar as a way to protect their relatively privileged position and higher wages from being undermined by black competition (1999:21). This would ultimately undermine the ISL's prospects in the long-run.

Interestingly, and perhaps counterintuitively, the ISL's commitment to independent trade unions as the fundamental building blocks of workers' self-management in an ideal nonpolitical state meant that it openly criticised the (now) most famous advocate of political rights for black people, the South African Native National Congress (SANNC), later the African National Congress (ANC). In the ISL's view, the SANNC was a nationalist organisation that, because of its explicit focus on black political rights rather than workers' interests in general, undermined working-class unity across racial lines. Its interest and outlook was that of an emergent African petit bourgeoisie of mission-educated lawyers and clergymen that appealed to the liberal – and capitalist – values of the British Empire as a defence against the racism of the Afrikaner-dominated South Africa Party (SAP) government of Louis Botha (Van der Walt 2004: 80). In short, the SANNC bought into the very system that the ISL opposed.

Despite its considerable influence during the early development of trade unionism in South Africa, and its pioneering antiracism, revolutionary syndicalism began to lose its distinctive character and independent voice by the early 1920s. There are two main reasons for this. First, the period following the Russian Revolution in 1917 saw the rise of classical Marxism, as espoused by the Bolshevik Party led by Vladimir Lenin, as the preeminent ideology of the left. Responding to this global shift, the ISL subsequently joined forces with the Social Democratic Federation (SDF) and the International Socialist League (ISL), as well as a number of smaller left-leaning organisations, to form, in 1921, the Communist Party of South Africa (CPSA), which based its platform on that of the Communist International (Johns 1976: 371). Although syndicalist ideas and vocabulary influenced CPSA discourse well into the 1920s, it no longer had a dedicated champion or an independent *raison d'être*.

Second, the lack of an organisational centre, or support from a substantial international movement or organisation (Marxism had the Bolshevik Party in Russia, later the USSR), meant that syndicalist thought remained open to a variety of interpretations and manifestations, its core tenets available for appropriation by those sympathetic to its practical, worker-oriented values (but not necessarily its radical revolutionary nonpolitical and anti-state ideals) to its detriment as an independent movement. Although the syndicalists' emphasis on anti-racism and working-class unity has, over time, been absorbed by the nonracial trade union movement, their distinctive contribution to the intellectual and organisational development of the left, together with the legacy of syndicalist newspapers and institutions has, over time, been quietly appropriated and subsumed by the mainstream Marxist tradition.

The strategic ideological question of how trade unions should engage with national political movements gained new prominence in the 1970s and early 1980s when the ground-breaking Wiehahn reforms of 1979 deracialised South Africa's collective bargaining system and paved the way for the legal recognition of black trade unions (Wood 2001: 135). The reforms ushered in a period of intense union organising, and saw the establishment of a series of new trade unions, which proceeded to merge, align and realign in response to the politics of the day. The end result was two principal union federations, the nonracial Congress of South African Trade Unions (Cosatu), and the smaller black consciousness-oriented National Council of Trade Unions (Nactu) (Wood 2001: 135). The 1980s were a tumultuous time in South African politics, featuring multiple states of emergency; heightened political violence; the rise of mass-based civic organisations; and attempts at limited reform by the apartheid government in order to shore up its position.

This demanded a coordinated response from the trade union movement. Within the largest trade union federation, Cosatu, two distinct groupings emerged. The first, the 'populists', advocated close alliances with the mass-based political and civic organisations, whereas the second pushed for a narrower emphasis on workers' interests by focusing on shop-floor organisation. This grouping was variously caricatured as 'workerist', 'syndi-calist' and 'economistic' (Waterman 1993: 274; Wood 2001: 135). For the workerist/syndicalist grouping, the danger of aligning wholeheartedly with the mass liberation movement risked prioritising political liberation at the expense of economic justice for the working class. This position strongly resonated with Bakunin's own observations of European political upheavals in the 1860s, when he stated that:

> Every exclusively political revolution – be it in defence of national independence or for internal change – that does not aim at the immediate and real political and economic emancipation of the people will be a false revolution. Its objectives will be unattainable and its consequences reactionary (cited in Van der Walt 2001: 14).

Copelyn's own union, Sactwu, took a leading role in the independent trade union movement at this time. Resonating with the political precedent set by the Industrial Workers of Africa and the ISL in the 1910s, it advocated for a separate workers' charter to be drawn that would accompany the more general Freedom Charter adopted in 1955 by the Congress Alliance (which included representation from the ANC, the South African Indian Congress, the South African Congress of Democrats and the Coloured People's Congress, among others) that outlined key political and socio-economic rights for all South Africans. Underlying Sactwu's call was a desire to guarantee the prioritisation of workers' economic interests in a future democratic dispensation and, more specifically, their insistence that unions should be able to work independently of the state to secure the interests of their members (Plaut 1992: 399).

These issues came to a head during the 'two hats debate' between Copelyn and the SACP's Jeremy Cronin. Central to the debate was the issue of dual leadership positions within the Tripartite Alliance: the tendency of leading members of Cosatu to hold positions on the SACP's internal leadership group at alliance policy-making forums simultaneously (Copelyn 1991: 55). Whereas Cronin viewed these developments as functional to the internal cohesion and strength of the liberation movement, Copelyn argued that dual leadership would result in an elite form of consensus politics that could potentially undermine the economic interests of workers in the long run (1991:55).

UNDERSTANDING THE HCI APPROACH

As noted earlier, Copelyn's scepticism of the future ruling alliance's capacity and commitment to effecting economic justice for the working class finds a compelling intellectual precedent in the South African syndicalist movement of the late nineteenth and early twentieth centuries, particularly its scepticism of the 'political' state, which its adherents maintained would inevitably bend to serve elite interests, and its emphasis on workers' independent organisation through unions. This intellectual precedent reveals an independent tradition within the trade union movement that links the earliest union activity on the Rand to the concerns of the independent trade unions during the tumultuous 1980s, ultimately shaping an alternative vision of empowerment in post-1994 South Africa. For their part, it must be emphasised that neither Copelyn nor Golding was consciously adhering to a syndicalist framework, and their joint project to build an independent institutional base certainly did not preclude support for, or engagement with, the 'political state'. This is clearly illustrated by their presence in Parliament, however brief, as ANC MPs representing Cosatu. Their personal outlook was far too eclectic, and their strategies too pragmatic, for me to label them modern-day 'heirs of Bakunin', although their commitment to independent union organising, and their worker-oriented approach, has remained a consistent feature of the HCI model.

This eclecticism is illustrated, for example, by the approach of the HCI Foundation, which, with its emphasis on communal responsibility and human capital development, underlined by the shared ownership of assets, suggests that Copelyn's alternative vision also features strong discursive synergies with the kibbutz movement in Israel, which Helman has described as an attempt to 'translate socialist principles into everyday practice', and which has at its core an ethos of self-help and mutual aid (1992: 170). Interestingly, the founders of Israel's kibbutzim sought to establish a new kind of society that eschewed *both* the principle of private property ownership, which underpins capitalist economics, *and* the communist model of vesting property and the means of production with the state. Similar to the aims of the early syndicalists, the kibbutz movement sought an independent, nonpolitical path (Helman 1992: 170). Copelyn and Golding did not, of course, take issue with the principle of private capital accumulation, or indeed with the capitalist system itself. Like many protagonists from the anti-apartheid left, they adopted a pragmatic position, and learned to adapt to the market realities of the post-Cold War world order and, more immediately, the opportunities presented by the post-1994 South African economy.

John Copelyn's highly personal involvement in every aspect of HCI, its subsidiaries (he and Marcel Golding chair the boards of a number of HCI-affiliated companies) and its Foundation, to which he personally donated R144 million in 2006, points to an equally idiosyncratic, almost paternalistic, attitude towards his and Golding's shared project (HCI Foundation 2007: 57). This paternalism extends to the staffing at HCI itself where he has employed a number of fellow former Sactwu colleagues including Virginia Engel as executive chairperson of the HCI Foundation; Yunis Shaik as a non-executive director of HCI; and Velaphi Elias Mphande as chairman of Golden Arrow Bus Services (HCI Foundation 2007: 7). Copelyn therefore behaves as something akin to a father figure to an extended family of one-time trade unionists and current union members in a highly personal, even patrimonial, set-up that could be described as 'looking after your own'.

The Copelyn and Golding story therefore represents something of an intellectual anomaly in the discourse of economic empowerment in post-apartheid South Africa. Although their early investments suggest a pragmatic response to the economic uncertainties (and opportunities) of the political transition in South Africa in the early 1990s that resonates with the early syndicalist tradition, the communitarian 'self-help' values of the HCI Foundation, coupled with Copelyn and Golding's deep-seated personal involvement in every aspect of the project points to an eclectic mix of kibbutz-style mutual aid values and old-fashioned paternalism. In the section that follows, the HCI empowerment model is considered in light of the ideological development, and subsequent criticism, levelled at South Africa's dominant transformation discourse: BEE.

AN 'ALTERNATIVE VISION' TO MAINSTREAM BEE?

The ANC's accession to power as the lead partner in the Government of National Unity (GNU) following South Africa's landmark elections in 1994 heralded a new, democratic era in South African politics that brought with it the promise of a more equitable distribution of wealth and opportunity. The extension of basic services and social security to poor communities that had been denied them in the past was one important component in addressing the socio-economic legacy of apartheid. The other – aimed at addressing the racially skewed patterns of ownership in the economy – was black economic empowerment (BEE). An eclectic collection of policies and programmes that today include broad-based black economic empowerment (BBBEE), employment equity, land reform, initiatives focused on the minerals and energy sectors, and state-sponsored programmes to assist black-owned businesses, BEE has, in recent years, become a highly contested issue in South African policy discourse (Lindsay 2011:238).

Part of the reason for this is that it lacks a single, dedicated government ministry, agency or programme and consequently the meaning and core aims of BEE shift according to the goals and objectives of the particular initiative or government entity concerned. Another, less acknowledged but no less influential, factor informing contemporary debates about the meaning of BEE stems from the diverse influences and interest groups that shaped the ANC-led government's initial approach. The corps of black business leaders that emerged following the limited reforms introduced during the late apartheid period, represented by organisations such as the National African Federated Chamber of Commerce (Nafcoc), the Foundation for African Business and Consumer Service (Fabcos) and the Black Management Forum (BMF), constituted one such interest group that pushed for the economic advancement of black people through progressive policy changes (Lindsay 2011: 240).

On the other hand, established white business, which saw its position potentially threatened in the unpredictable political climate of the late 1980s and early 1990s, sought to protect its interests by coming to an accommodation with the ANC, threshed out during a series of high-level meetings in Geneva, Dakar and elsewhere, in which the liberation movement would refrain from the radical redistributionist policies it espoused in exile (although these were in any case becoming increasingly discredited by the end of the Cold War). In return, established business would actively seek to recruit blacks into the senior ranks of corporate South Africa while 'facilitating the rapid expansion of ANC-related black-owned business' (Southall 2006: 70). The vehicle for this was BEE. For the ANC, this accommodation with business necessitated a reframing of its initial position that the transition to democracy – the national democratic revolution, or NDR in party parlance – would be a stepping stone towards socialism.

The key quandary was how the party could square its acceptance of capitalism, and its settlement with the established business community, with its identity as a liberation movement. After all, the recruitment of black executives into the public and private sectors, and the promotion of black business, would inevitably result in the development of a distinctive black middle class with its own set of interests, distinct from that of the poor and working class, which would in turn underpin rising inequality *among* black South Africans. Southall suggests that this problem was not as intractable as it might at first appear, at least at the level of ideology. ANC thinking had always had a strong nationalist element that viewed the economic advancement of individual black people as part of a necessary and desirable process of 'internal decolonisation' that sought to correct the country's historical legacy of dispossession and exploitation (2006: 69).

Consistent with the radical, albeit pragmatically reimagined, liberationist discourse of the NDR, this black middle class would form the core of a 'patriotic bourgeoisie' whose capital accumulation was justified to the extent that it adhered to certain values and modes of behaviour laid down by the party, and whose collaboration with white business interests may eventually lead to their incorporation into a middle class supportive of the revolution (Southall 2004: 315). For many, however, the argument that it was consistent with revolutionary values for a small group of people to become, in the words of former Deputy President Phumzile Mlambo-Ngcuka, 'filthy rich' (cited in Alexander 2006:7) did not hold ground. Rather than further the aims of economic justice for the working poor, the accommodation between the ANC and big business appears as an 'elite pact' designed to co-opt the ANC into the capitalist fold. Moeletsi Mbeki, brother of former president Thabo Mbeki, suggests that:

> The first purpose of BEE was to create a buffer group among the black political class
> that would become an ally of big business in South Africa. This buffer group would
> use its newfound power as controllers of the government to protect the assets of big
> business. The buffer group would also protect the *modus operandi* of big business and
> thereby maintain the *status quo* in which South African business operates. That was
> the design of the big conglomerates (*Business Day*, 10 February 2011).

It seems that Copelyn's doubts about the commitment of a post-apartheid government
to uphold the interests of the working class, rather than those of political elites, proved
to be prophetic even as he and Golding, perhaps paradoxically, moved to secure some
of the earliest BEE deals in the post-1994 period. Though some critics, such as Mbeki,
have argued that BEE has been a strategy to align the interests of post-1994 political
elites with those of big business, further criticism has pointed to the insufficient breadth
and depth of black equity ownership. This is clearly illustrated by a recent analysis by
the Johannesburg Stock Exchange (JSE) that showed that black South Africans owned
only 17 per cent of the country's largest listed companies (*Engineering News*, 4 October,
2011). Others have pointed to the failure of many BEE beneficiaries to launch productive businesses of their own as a consequence of 'fronting', and the phenomenon of black
individuals being appointed to 'token' positions on company boards, with little or no
decision-making power (Southall 2004: 316).

In recognition of the limitations of early BEE initiatives to deliver genuine broad-
based empowerment, the Black Economic Empowerment Commission recommended in
a report to then-president Mbeki in 2001 that the state should play a more interventionist
role to promote a 'meaningful transfer of ownership to the black majority' (Southall
2004: 321). Subsequently, the government moved to tackle some of the problems associated with early approaches to BEE by passing the Broad Based Black Empowerment Act
in 2004. Key aspects of the Act include the need for a more rigorous regulatory system;
the urgent need to expand the breadth and scale of black-owned equity; and recognition
that the definition of 'empowerment' itself should be expanded to include provisions
that emphasise small and medium enterprise growth and human capital development
through employment equity and training (South Africa 2004).

It is important to note that many of the provisions laid down in the BEE Act correlate
with ideas expressed by Copelyn back in 1991: namely that genuine economic empowerment entails provision for the ownership of assets by broad social groups; and equally
that in order for social transformation to be truly effective, strategies for the transfer of
capital ownership should be accompanied by programmes that stress the human capital
development of individuals and communities through educational projects and social
entrepreneurship. Copelyn's and Golding's approach *pre-empted* the shift to broad-based
black economic empowerment through its idiosyncratic, worker-oriented ownership
model and its integrated 'ecosystem' approach to empowerment through its affiliated
foundation. It also circumvents many of the standard criticisms levelled at mainstream
BEE in the early period following the transition to democracy in 1994.

First, the pattern of BEE firms sinking under the dual pressures of heavy debts and volatile markets does not hold true for HCI. Although suffering the scepticism of its institutional investors following the 1997 recession, HCI rebounded through a series of highly successful acquisitions to attain a market capitalisation of around R5 billion in 2006 (*Business in Africa*, 26 June 2006).

Second, rather than siphon off easy profits through rentier business practices or 'fronting', HCI has unambiguously added value to subsidiary businesses. In addition to its highly effective turnaround strategy for the loss-making Midi Television, HCI similarly set out to develop Golden Arrow Bus Services following its acquisition in 2005. After a series of considerable capital investments, including the addition of 150 new buses to the Golden Arrow fleet, HCI helped the latter company to achieve an after-tax profit of R84 million in 2006, an increase of 56.7 per cent from the previous year (*The Citizen*, 27 June 2006).

Third, the criticism that affirmative action appointments have tended to occupy 'figurehead' or 'token' positions that either do not require or develop specialised skills or that lack executive authority, is inappropriate in the HCI case. On the contrary, three of its five executive directors are persons of colour, including the company's director, Marcel Golding, and the executive chairperson of the HCI Foundation, Virginia Engel (HCI Foundation 2007: 3). Each one of them plays a vital role in the effective functioning of the Copelyn and Golding business empire.

CRITICISM OF COPELYN AND GOLDING'S BUSINESS

As with many businesspeople who have made money out of BEE deals in the post-apartheid period, Copelyn's and Golding's personal fortunes have become the focus of recurrent scrutiny in the financial media. Copelyn's massive R525 million shareholding in HCI, as well as the often stated fact that he is one of only a handful of white entrepreneurs to have benefited from post-apartheid empowerment legislation has, in particular, singled him out for criticism (*Mail & Guardian*, 29 August 2007). Writers have typically emphasised the discrepancy between the value of his shareholding and the equivalent shareholding per Sactwu member (which, when divided among the union's 110 000 members, comes to approximately R14 500) (*Mail & Guardian*, 14 August 2007).

Similarly, it has been pointed out that, because their shares are listed shares, Copelyn and Golding are free to sell at any time whereas ordinary Sactwu members – whose 40 per cent stake is collectively owned – can only access the benefits of HCI's success through the Foundation's educational and social development projects. These critics fail to note that Copelyn and Golding did not, in the first instance, set out to reap personal fortunes from their political connections. During the first few years of both union investment companies, their personal stakes remained minimal. It was only later, in 2002, when HCI offered to buy back shares from their institutional investors (which had, since the 1998 purchase of Midi Television, exhibited a marked lack of confidence in the company) at R2.37 per share, that 280 of the 380 million shares were handed in, despite predictions that they would rise to over R7 (*Business in Africa*, 26 June 2006). Ironically, it was this lack of public confidence in the company that enabled Copelyn and Golding to concentrate their personal shareholdings and position themselves to reap massive returns when the HCI share price skyrocketed to over R40 per share in 2006.

Additionally, criticism that Sactwu's collective ownership model does not amount to 'real empowerment' offers a very narrow interpretation of what empowerment means. As earlier approaches to BEE have amply demonstrated, the individual ownership of shares is by no means a guarantee of effective empowerment. Instead, successful empowerment models should adopt a broader, more holistic approach and seek to equip previously disadvantaged individuals and communities with the skills and material circumstances necessary to participate as successful economic agents in South Africa.

CONCLUSION

Copelyn's and Golding's story provides compelling evidence of an alternative approach to empowerment that draws on a long-standing independent tradition within the South African trade union movement, one that scholars and policy makers alike would do well to consider in light of the sustained criticism, and relatively limited success, of mainstream BEE. At the core of this alternative approach is a sophisticated critique of elite interests and behaviour, and a firmly held belief that to secure working-class interests in post-1994 South Africa workers would themselves need to 'map out an alternative vision of a just society in which unions play an important role which is fundamentally independent of the state' (Copelyn 1991: 31). Although, in practice, Copelyn and Golding's business model was shaped by pragmatic considerations and opportunities – at times evincing an ambiguous relationship *vis-à-vis* the state and business – there is no doubt that in HCI Copelyn has built the 'independent institutional base to constructively influence society' that he called for in 1991 (1991: 31). This chapter has explained how this was achieved by capitalising on some of the earliest, and most lucrative, empowerment deals in the post-1994 period, and how, by channelling funds to union members as well as into a comprehensive welfare programme under the aegis of the HCI Foundation, Copelyn and Golding constructed a holistic empowerment 'ecosystem' for union members and their families. Given that HCI grew out of the respective investment arms of unions Sactwu and NUM, the chapter has furthermore argued that the HCI model of broad-based empowerment traces its origins to the pre-1994 period, and thus *preceded* official attempts to legislate for BBBEE through the 2004 BBBEE Act.

REFERENCES

Cargill J (2010) *Trick or Treat: Rethinking Black Economic Empowerment* (2010). Johannesburg: Jacana.
Copelyn J (1991) Preparing ourselves for permanent independence. *South African Labour Bulletin* 15 (8).

Copelyn J (1991) Collective bargaining: a base for transforming industry. *South African Labour Bulletin* 15 (6).

Davenport R and C Saunders (2000) *South Africa: A Modern History.* Basingstoke: Macmillan.

Hellman A (1992) The Israeli kibbutz as a socialist model. *Journal of Institutional and Theoretical Economics* 148 (1).

Johns S (1976) The birth of the Communist Party of South Africa. *The International Journal of African Historical Studies* 9 (3).

Levine L (1912) Syndicalism. *The North American Review*, 196 (680).

Lindsay D (2012) BEE reform: The case for an institutional perspective. In Daniel J, P Naidoo, D Pillay and R Southall (Eds) *New South African Review 2: New Paths, Old Compromises?* Johannesburg: Wits University Press.

MacShane D, M Plaut and D Ward (1984) *Power! Black Workers, Their Unions and Their Struggle for Freedom in South Africa.* Cambridge: South End Press.

Plaut M (1992) Debates in a shark tank: The politics of South Africa's non-racial trade unions. *African Affairs* 91 (364).

Skinner C (2002) Understanding formal and informal labour market dynamics: A conceptual and statistical review with reference to South Africa. Research report No. 50. School of Development Studies, University of Natal, Durban.

Southall R (2004) The ANC and black capitalism in South Africa. *Review of African Political Economy* 31(100).

Southall R (2006) Ten propositions about black economic empowerment in South Africa. *Review of African Political Economy* 111.

Van der Walt L (1999) The Industrial Union is the embryo of the socialist commonwealth: The International Socialist League and revolutionary syndicalism in South Africa, 1915-1920. *Comparative Studies of South Asia, Africa, and the Middle East* 19 (1).

Van der Walt L (no date) Race, capitalism and revolutionary socialism in South Africa: Marxism, revolutionary syndicalism and the national question in South African socialism, 1910-1933. In *The Burden of Race? Whiteness and Blackness in Modern South Africa* (Pamphlet for History Workshop at the Witwatersrand Institute for Social and Economic Research).

Van der Walt L (2004) Bakunin's heirs in South Africa: Race and revolutionary syndicalism from the IWW to the International Socialist League, 1910-1921. *Politikon* 31 (1).

Waterman P (1993) Social Movement Unionism: A New Union Model for a New World Order? *Ferdinand Braudel Centre Review* 16 (3).

Wood G (2001) Trade Unions in a Time of Adjustment. *Labour* 47.

CHAPTER 8

'Ask for a camel when you expect to get a goat': Contentious politics and the climate justice movement[1]

Jacklyn Cock[2]

INTRODUCTION

The climate crisis is deepening. Despite seventeen years of multinational negotiations there is no binding global agreement on the reduction of carbon emissions. In fact, carbon emissions are rising, which means that climate change will intensify and have devastating effects – particularly on the working class – in the form of rising food prices, water shortages, crop failures and so on. Shifting to a new energy regime will be particu-larly challenging for South Africa, given the carbon-intensive nature of our economy and the continued dominance of the 'minerals-energy complex'.

The failure of the multinational has generated an emphasis on the mobilisation of civil society. As environmental justice analyst David Hallowes states, 'the "theatre of engage-ment" needs to shift away from the international negotiations'.[3] Civil society, however, contains deep differences and serious power imbalances, as the 2011 Global Day of Action march demonstrated.

Theatrical elements were in evidence in this march of 15 000 people from all over the world to the site of the COP17 negotiations in Durban. It was a very colourful event, with different movements marching in their battalions, singing and chanting 'A people united will never be defeated'. There were the 400 members of the Rural Women's Assembly in their green T-shirts proclaiming 'WOMEN – THE GUARDIANS OF SEED, LIFE AND EARTH'; 500 Democratic Left Front and Climate Jobs campaigners in red with the slogan 'LISTEN TO THE PEOPLE. END CAPITALISM NOT NATURE'; SA Transport and Allied Workers' Union (Satawu) members in orange; giant banners bearing differing messages; puppets; a balloon proclaiming 'RIGHTS FOR MOTHER EARTH NOW'; an inflated octopus wearing an 'Uncle Sam' hat; some of Via Campesina's 200 million world-wide members; a funeral procession following a coffin to mark the end of 'King Coal'; loud chants such as 'Away with the capitalist agenda, away!' (as well as 'Phantsi COP17 that does not represent the people, phantsi!'); and three topless women carrying an anti-nuclear banner. At first glance it seemed a powerful illustration of the World Social Forum slogan of 'Unity in Diversity' with many different traditions and forms of struggle all heading in the same direction and converging at the International Convention Centre.

The unity of direction was, however, geographic rather than political. Early in the march, violence was provoked by some 300 people labelled 'Host City Monitors' who turned out to be paid members of the African National Congress Youth League (ANCYL) claiming to be angered by 'these anti-Zuma people behind us'. Despite an exception-ally heavy police presence , they threw stones and water bottles, tore up banners and posters, made physical threats, sang ANC songs and flourished placards such as 'ZUMA UNTIL JESUS COMES'. On another occasion in the Durban City Hall the same contin-gent attacked silent protesters holding placards appealing for Zuma to 'LISTEN TO THE PEOPLE OF AFRICA'. Overall, COP17 demonstrated a number of tensions and an ideo-logical faultline that divided mobilisation around climate change into two broad group-ings: those who adhere to a 'green' reform agenda that implies a form of 'green capitalism' stressing market-based solutions, and those committed to a 'red-green' agenda centered on transformative change.

Many climate change activists are eager to overcome these divisions and mobilise a unified movement. This chapter asserts that, as a 'master frame', climate justice has the potential to connect particular local struggles, generalise them and link them to a global project of transformation. It could generate a form of solidarity, larger and deeper than anything we have yet seen. But this global potential may not be realised because of the way climate change has become embedded in 'contentious politics' involving competing claims and interests.

'Contentious politics' is a terrain 'where people make discontinuous, public, collective claims on each other' (Tilly 2001:26). The scale of the contention reflects the significance of the central issue. Climate change is having massive social and economic effects. It signi-fies increases in the temperature of the earth's atmosphere, less predictable rainfall, rising sea levels, and more extreme weather events such as droughts and floods that will result in major social and geographical displacement, crop failures and increased food insecurity.

It is a deeply political issue in the sense that it reflects relations of inequality, power and injustice. It is the over-consumption and waste of the powerful elites in the rich industri-alised countries of the North who are mainly responsible for the carbon emissions that cause climate change, but it is the people of the South – particularly in southern Africa

– who will suffer the most. Africa only contributes 4 per cent of global greenhouse gas emissions but is the most vulnerable to their adverse effects.

THE SITES OF CONTENTIOUS POLITICS

There are two sites of contentious politics around climate change, involving different actors and interests, both marked by extreme power imbalances:

    (i) inside the United Nations Framework Convention on Climate Change (UNFCCC) negotiations, as demonstrated at the multinational Conference of the Parties (COP) at Kyoto, Copenhagen, Cancun and Durban; and

    (ii) outside the negotiations but inside the civil society groupings mobilising around the issue.

In both sites the central ground of contention is competing notions of 'justice'. The concept of climate justice fuses a variety of survivalist issues, such as rising food prices and access to adequate water, as well as international trade, development rights, technology, migration and biodiversity. In this sense it is possible that the climate justice movement is not only a source of radicalisation but is also promoting a more holistic, ecological understanding. In the past, environmental justice struggles have too often been scattered and narrowly focused on single issues – the destruction of a wetland here or water pollution there. The global nature of climate change generates a broader, more integrated perspective.

INSIDER CONTENTIOUS POLITICS

Negotiations within the UNFCCC reflect 'interactions in which actors make claims bearing on someone else's interests, in which governments appear either as targets, initiators of such claims or third parties' (Tilly 2008:5). Disagreements reflect the main fault line within the UNFCCC, which has geographical, political and economic dimensions: differences between the powerful, industrialised, developed countries of the North and those of the 'developing' countries of the South. The two main issues of contention are, firstly, the future of the Kyoto Protocol, which promotes carbon trading; and, secondly, the operation and funding of the Green Climate Fund. The developing countries want a second commitment period of the Kyoto Protocol, with stronger targets and with finance and technology to help with 'mitigation' of and 'adaptation' to the effects of climate change.[4]

These issues are embedded in competing notions of justice. Developing countries maintain that the rich countries must agree on reparations in the form of financial support – as well as far deeper cuts in carbon emissions – because they are largely responsible for the problem. The notion of 'climate justice' is emphasised to mean that developed countries have a historical responsibility, as a wide range of activities in addition to carbon emissions contribute to the ecological debt owed to countries in the global South:

the extraction of natural resources, unequal terms of trade, degradation of land and soil for export crops, loss of biodiversity, and so on.

Contention reflects the dominance of narrow, national and corporate interests on the part of those with power. All the major national governments are commited to economic growth, and none seems willing to consider any emission reduction policy that would undermine it. The result is that to date not only have the global elites failed to achieve a binding reduction of carbon emissions through the UNFCCC framework but, on the contrary, carbon emissions are rising. This failure is largely due to a 'corporate capture' of the UNFCCC process (Fernandes and Girard 2011), which has involved the promotion of 'false solutions' such as carbon trading including offset schemes that allow multinational corporations to profit while continuing to pollute.[5]

These 'false solutions' are retained in the COP17 package of decisions known as the 'Durban Platform for Enhanced Action' that was reached by the 195 countries participating. In terms of this, delegates agreed to start work early in 2012 on formulating a new, universal (including both developed and developing countries), legally binding treaty to cut greenhouse gases, to be decided by 2015 and to come into force by 2020.

The contentious nature of climate politics is dramatically evident in the different responses to this agreement. Several positive responses focus on the continuation of the carbon market as the instrument to encourage private investment to address climate change. For instance, National Business Initiative CEO Joanne Yawitch welcomed the agreement for this reason.[6] In his State of the Nation speech of February 2012, President Zuma described the agreement as a 'huge success'.

The commitment to this new agreement (driven by the European Union and supported by South Africa and some of the big international environmental NGOs in the Climate Action Network) is, however, widely viewed by climate justice activists as an excuse for inaction, as a delaying tactic that obscures the real agenda of rich, developed countries: to escape their responsibility to reduce emissions. Bobby Peek of groundWork said: 'It is clear what is driving this agenda. More and more countries are coming to the international climate talks with one objective in mind: to defend and advance the economic interests of their polluting industries and multinational corporations and resist the global effort for a strong and fair agreement to tackle climate change.'[7]

According to Climate Justice Now (CJN), because of the devastating impact climate change will have on hundreds of millions of people, especially in Africa, the agreement 'is creating a climate apartheid where the richest 1 per cent of the world have decided that it is acceptable to sacrifice the 99 per cent … It constitutes "a crime against humanity"'.[8] Scientists maintain that the delay until 2020 will be too late, as the world would have surpassed the scientific cut-off point of halting a temperature rise of more than 2 degrees Celsius. 'Delaying real action until 2020 is a crime of global proportions. Increase in global temperatures of 4 degrees Celsius, permitted under this plan, is a death sentence for Africa, the Small Island States and the poor and vulnerable worldwide,' said Nimmo Bassey, chair of the Friends of the Earth International.[9] Other climate justice activists describe it as 'a demonstration of the palpable failure of our current economic system to address economic, social or environmental crises'.[10] The enormous power and influence of corporate polluters is the main reason for this disastrous outcome. As Kumi Naidoo expressed it: 'Polluters won, people lost'.[11] Overall it means not only the continuation of 'green capitalism' but, as Esther Vivas writing in ZNet on 24 December 2011 argued, COP17 also means 'an increase in green capitalism'.

GREEN CAPITALISM

Capital's response to the ecological crisis generally, and climate change specifically, is that the system can continue to expand by creating a new 'green capitalism', bringing the efficiency of the market to bear on nature and its reproduction. The climate crisis has been appropriated by capitalism as another site of accumulation: what Patrick Bond calls 'climate-crisis capitalism', namely, 'turning a medium/long-term system-threatening prospect into a short-term source of commodification, speculation and profit' (Bond 2011:2).

The two pillars on which green capitalism rests are technological innovation and expanding markets, and the existing institutions of capitalism are kept intact.

More specifically green capitalism involves:

- the carbon trading regime, which is enshrined in the Kyoto Protocols, and involves measures such as the Clean Development Mechanism (CDM) and Reducing Emissions from Deforestation and Forest Degradation (REDD), which allow developed countries to profit while avoiding the reduction of their own carbon emissions;
- considering nature (and even the crisis) as a marketing tool;
- developing new, largely untested, technologies such as 'climate-smart agriculture' and clean coal technology; and carbon capture and storage, which involves installing equipment that captures carbon dioxide and other greenhouse gases and then pumps the gas underground;
- the development of new sources of energy such as solar, nuclear and wind, thereby creating new markets; and
- the massive development of biofuels, which involves diverting land from food production – the ideological basis is the notion of 'sustainability'(Cock 2011).

Underlying all these strategies is the broad process of commodification: the transformation of nature and all social relations into economic relations, subordinated to the logic of the market and the imperatives of profit. This is at the centre of the notion of a 'green economy', the foundational concept at the 'Rio+20' conference in June 2012. Here, the 'Davos class', the global elite created by corporate globalisation, is promoting the further commodification of nature by claiming that the 'services' provided by nature (clean air, pure water) should be given an economic value that would allow them to be bought, traded or offset.

The process is disguised by a heavy reliance on manipulative advertising – 'greenwash' – to persuade us of the efficacy of these strategies. But the main concern of the corporates remains profitability and the awareness that shrinking natural resources could damage it, as well as how 'green' measures such as energy efficiency could reduce costs, lessen risks and enhance public images. For this reason the notion of the green economy has been dismissed as a 'wolf in sheep's clothing' – the wolf being green capitalism and its drive for the further commodification of nature (Lander 2011). Lander views it as 'a sophisticated effort to demonstrate that it is possible to resolve the problems of the planet's environmental crises without altering the existing power structures' (Lander 2011:14).

This notion of green or sustainable capitalism is being subjected to growing criticism rooted in the understanding that it is capital's logic of accumulation that is destroying the ecological conditions that sustain life (Harris-White, in Panitch and Leys 2006; Kovel 2001; Foster 2000, 2009; Shiva 2008; Angus 2009). One outcome is an emphasis on popular mobilisation.

OUTSIDER CONTENTIOUS POLITICS

Many now look to civil society if there is to be any hope of achieving meaningful emissions reductions. The most powerful actor is Climate Justice Now (CJN), a 'network of organisations and movements from across the globe committed to the fight for social, ecological and gender justice' (http://www.climate- justice-now.org).

The global climate justice movement
The global climate justice movement has been steadily growing since CJN was formed in 2007 from different strands in the women's, environmental and democratic popular movements from the global South such as Via Campesina and Jubilee South.

The CJN movement emphasises four themes. First, there is the focus on 'climate justice', which is stressed in global and local terms. Globally, it is highlighted that a wide range of activities contribute to an ecological debt owed to countries in the global South. Locally, it is demonstrated that it is the poor and the powerless who are most negatively affected by pollution and resource depletion and who will bear the brunt of climate change.

Second, it is recognised that it is the expansionist logic of the capitalist system of production and consumption, driven by large multinational corporations, financial markets and captive governments, that are the cause of climate change, with loss of biodiversity, water scarcity, the acidification of the oceans, and so on. CJN is marked by an anti-capitalist discourse.

Third, CJN is calling not only for rethinking the commitment to economic growth, but also for an altered relationship to nature. It is spreading the insights that the commodification of nature involves the deepening of both social and environmental justice; that the concepts of 'green' or 'sustainable' capitalism are oxymorons; that the notion of 'sustainable development' is vacuous and has been appropriated by neoliberal capitalism; and that capitalism cannot accommodate the ecological changes necessary for human survival.

Lastly, CJN is driven by the recognition that global elites have so far failed to solve the climate crisis through the UNFCCC process because they have relied on 'false solutions', particularly carbon trading.

This failure underlies the potential of this moment for global civil society to build solidarity around climate justice. The balance of forces means that doing so in South Africa is particularly difficult.

THE SOUTH AFRICAN GOVERNMENT RESPONSE TO CLIMATE CHANGE

Agreement on reducing carbon emissions is particularly challenging to South Africa because of the centrality of the 'minerals-energy complex', which revolves around a dependence on fossil fuel-based energy. In his 2012 State of the Nation address, President Jacob Zuma painted a picture of a resource-intensive industrial development policy to promote economic growth. There was no reference to the National Planning Commission's recommendation that 'South Africa needs to move away from the unsustainable use of natural resources' (National Planning Commision 2011:4). The government's climate change policy favours carbon trading and is rooted in a 'green capitalism' that includes technological innovation in expensive schemes such as nuclear energy, developing 'climate smart crops', untested carbon capture and storage underground, and expanding markets – while keeping the existing institutions of capitalism intact.

Currently, South Africa has no legislation requiring a reduction in carbon emissions, but the government seems aware of the seriousness of the threat of climate change.[12] Like the earlier Green Paper, the 2011 National Climate Change Response White Paper warns that 'potential impacts on South Africa in the medium to long term are significant and potentially catastrophic', for 'after 2050 warming is projected to reach around 3-4 degrees C along the coast and 6-7 degrees C in the interior. With these kinds of temperature increases, life as we know it will change completely'(Government of the Republic of South Africa 2011:9).

The White Paper, however, fails to engage with the full impact of climate change on the working class – especially in relation to rising food prices, water shortages and crop failures. Although there is reference to a 'long-term just transition to a climate-resilient and lower carbon economy and society' (op cit: 5) the notion of 'justice' is not developed. There is a vague reference to the potential of 'green jobs'(op cit: 15) and the 'new, green economy'(op cit: 32) but these are not defined.

Other official policy documents demonstrate an incoherence, and aspirations towards reducing carbon emissions are contradicted by government practices that involve massively expanded coal-fired and nuclear energy (Trollop and Tyler 2011). Overall, policy and practice display the continued power of the corporations at the centre of the minerals-energy complex to shape development to their own profit-driven interests.

MOBILISING CIVIL SOCIETY IN SOUTH AFRICA

This is the context in which some of the organisations involved in popular mobilisation are trying to create a unified voice on climate justice. Several analysts have stressed the unifying potential of the CJN SA movement formed in 2009. According to Bond, 'the CJ organisations and networks offer great potential to fuse issue-specific progressive environmental and social activists, many of which have strong roots in oppressed communities' (Bond 2010:3).

The director of Greenpeace International has also emphasised the importance of unity. According to Kumi Naidoo, 'as the host of COP17 the government of South Africa has a great opportunity to represent Africa which will be hardest hit by climate change. We must come together and speak with one voice … Having different marches at the World Summit on Sustainable Development meant we let South Africa down.'[13] Tristan Taylor of Earthlife Africa, Johannesburg, believes that there is potential for unity if there is tolerance for political differences and the campaign focuses around one simple idea: 'Stop climate change now. Then the different organisations can take the idea in different political directions.'[14]

The organisations participating in the COP17 process – whether 'inside' or 'outside' the negotiations – demonstrate different shades of 'green' (meaning minimally some level of commitment to more sustainable society-nature relations). Overall, the main fault line runs along ideological lines between those organisations with a 'green' reform agenda and those with a 'red-green' transformative agenda. To some extent this reflects the divison between those organisations that are part of the Climate Action Network (CAN) and those of CJN but these divisions are not absolute. All the organisations are working on the mobilisation of civil society, and most appeal to the notion of 'climate justice' to do so. All emphasise the need for change towards the goal of a low-carbon economy but differ on the scale of change involved, and the ways of reaching it. There is also no agreement on what a 'low-carbon economy' would look like.

At the same time, some of the 'green' reform organisations engage in radical actions such as Greenpeace Africa's occupation of a crane on the construction site of Kusile, one of the world's largest coal-fired power plants. Similarly, the energetic promotion of renewable energy by Richard Worthington of the World Wildlife Fund (WWF) appears 'radical' to supporters of the *status quo* dependence on coal. However, there are sharp lines of contention that focus on five wedge issues: the role of technology; the value of the UNFCCC process; market mechanisms, particularly carbon trading; the expansionist logic of neoliberal capitalism as the cause of the climate crisis; and how our relationship to nature should change.

The main issue of contention is the reliance on market mechanisms enshrined in the Kyoto Protocol, which is viewed with a level of scepticism among CJN activists. Generally, those organisations with a reform agenda accept market-based solutions such as carbon trading, place a heavy reliance on technologies such as carbon capture and storage, and view positively the UNFCCC process and the South African government's negotiating position. The reform agenda is the object of intense criticism by organisations with a transformative agenda which stress that market-based solutions such as carbon trading are one way in which capital is attempting to appropriate the crisis and make climate change a site of capital accumulation. They are particularly critical of CDM and REDD as 'unsustainable' and 'unjust'. REDD is particularly controversial; it is supported by some environmental groups, which maintain that it contributes to forest preservation, whereas others claim that it involves the further commodificiation of nature and will benefit corporate investors while damaging the livelihoods and cultures of forest-dependent communities. They are sceptical of expensive and untested technologies such as the 'climate smart agriculture' promoted by the World Bank and the Food and Agriculture Organisation, and of carbon capture and storage; and they strongly emphasise the cause of the climate crisis as the expansionist logic of the capitalist system. Some organisations prioritise a class analysis, whereas many of the Northern NGOs are 'class blind', for example following the influential Mary Robinson Foundation for Climate Justice in framing climate change within the liberal discourse of human rights.[15] Others understand the issue as a stark choice between 'green capitalism' or 'eco-socialism'.

Differing understandings of nature are another source of contention that undermine unified action. It is generally recognised that we are living in a period when our relationship to nature is being dramatically transformed in the process of commodification. More and more of nature is being framed in terms of exchange value and mediated through the market. According to Burawoy (2006) this commodification of nature is the 'central feature' of the contemporary period of what he calls 'third wave marketisation'.

Consequently, some have called for a 'new, civilisational paradigm, one grounded not in dominance over nature but in respect for natural cycles of renewal – and acutely sensitive to natural limits' (Klein 2011:5). Contention is clearest in how the idea of protecting the Rights of Mother Earth counterposes directly to the commodification of nature, particularly through carbon markets.[16] According to Joel Kovel (2011), the understanding of 'humankind as part of nature is central to eco-socialism', whereas other socialists view nature in instrumental terms as a store of natural resources for economic activities.

Provisional mapping of the climate change terrain would indicate a loose grouping around a few key nodes such as groundWork, the South Durban Environmental Alliance and Earthlife Africa Johannesburg, now the lead organisation in South Africa of the international alliance Climate Justice Now, which supports a transformative agenda. A key node in an alternative approach centres on the WWF, an international NGO that supports both carbon trading and offsets such as REDD, and the role of the World Bank in mitigation funding in a reform agenda. The thrust is on reforming or greening the present form of 'suicide capitalism'. At COP17, the CEO of WWFSA appealed to business to 'take the lead and show that a low-carbon economy is feasible'.[17]

The organisations groundWork and Earthlife Africa Johannesburg build on an earlier tradition of environmental justice struggles, some of which involved grassroots communities, such as the Vaal Environmental Justice Alliance, which emerged from struggles against the pollution of the ground water in the Vaal (Cock 2006). Both organisations are not only key nodes with transformative agendas in this movement, but are also both locally grounded and globally connected, and thus transcend the primary emphasis on localism, which Albo has identified as a common weakness in ecology movements (Albo, in Panitch and Leys 2007: 359). A specific Earthlife Africa Johannesburg project, the Sustainable Energy and Climate Change Project (SECCP), illustrates this exceptional 'reach' stretching up into global campaigns as well as down into grassroots communities. For example, in partnership with groundWork and others in 2009, the SECCP played an important part in making connections between organisations in the global North and South to mobilise opposition to the World Bank loan to South Africa to build more coal-fired power stations. It demonstrated that the $3.75 billion loan to Eskom would increase the price of electricity for poor people and worsen South Africa's contribution to carbon emissions and climate change. An Earthlife/groundWork briefing document was produced, and within three months more than 200 organisations across the world were mobilised to endorse a critique of that loan.

Earthlife SECCP and groundWork assisted the World Bank inspection panel in a tour of areas surrounding the Medupi power station, and helped to bring together a coalition of residents, traditional leaders and farmers to oppose the development. SECCP argued that 'this loan is not about poor people or jobs or even the climate' but is benefiting vested interests (Adam et al. 2010:12). They were accused by the public enterprises minister, Barbara Hogan, of being 'unpatriotic'.[18] Although the campaign failed to block the loan, it 'showed that environmental groups in South Africa have the international and domestic reach to seriously interfere with government plans'.[19]

This example demonstrates both organisations' capacity to globalise local resistance. Doing so frequently involves linking four repertoires of action: capacity-building work-shops with grassroots communities, targeted protest actions, policy interventions, and research. All four repertoires were illustrated when, in 2010, Earthlife, in partnership with groundWork, launched a research report on a major polluter (in global terms), Sasol. The report was simultaneously released in both Johannesburg and COP16 at Cancun, thus connecting the local and the global.

Earthlife Africa Johannesburg was a powerful presence in Durban at COP17. The organisation coordinated the COP17 mobilisation process in Gauteng with monthly meetings and has organised numerous protest actions involving grassroots communities with which it has strong links. For example, at a demonstration at Sasol's headquarters in Johannesburg in October 2011 against Sasol's presence (along with Eskom) on the South African official negotiating team for COP17, the majority of the participants (on a boiling hot day) were older women from the Soweto Concerned Residents Association. Earthlife emphasises a feminist perspective. The organisation brought about 1 500 people to Durban for the march.

But although there are divisions between those organisations with a reform agenda and those with a transformative agenda, the climate justice movement has also been a site of cooperation and shared logistical planning. Both Earthlife and the WWF were present at the foundational meeting in January 2011 when more than eighty organisations representing a broad spectrum of civil society came together at a COP17 planning conference in Durban. A coordinating committee of seventeen mandated persons, representing a wide range of civil society organisations, was formed as a facilitatory body and tasked with promoting and coordinating civil society engagement in COP17. Its tasks included coordinating the Global Day of Action (a traditional event at the UNFCCC COPs, which includes a mass march), coordinating the autonomous Civil Society Space, organising a climate refugee camp and supporting mobilisation across South Africa. It included a diverse range of environmental organisations including the WWF, Greenpeace, Earthlife, SAFCEI (South African Faith Communties Environmental Initiative), SDCEA (South Durban Community Environmental Alliance), EMG (Environmental Monitoring Group), PACJA (Pan African Climate Justice Alliance), Climate Justice Now SA, Timberwatch, the Global Climate Change Alliance, groundWork, Oxfam SA, Amnesty International and grassroots organisations such as Abahlali baseMjondolo. The only union represented was Samu (South African Medical Union), and Sibusiso Gumede was the only person from Cosatu.

The grouping includes many different shades of green and the participating organisations stated different objectives. The meeting has been described as 'fraught', with a major source of division being the issue of market-based solutions such as carbon trading. Then there were disagreements on the goal of civil society mobilisation, whether the focus should be a specific event – COP17 – or the process of building a movement. Though some focused on COP17, others argued for moving beyond it to Rio+20 or to building the environmental movement globally. An Earthlife official stated: 'COP17 is not the end goal – it is a means of creating a stronger environmental movement' (Ferial Adam, Earthlife meeting, Johannesburg, 20 February 2011).

This goal was achieved at COP17 when a massive amount of energy was demonstrated in the 225 registered events held in the People's Space at the University of KwaZulu-Natal. Almost 5 000 people converged from all across the country to attend seminars, demonstrations, cultural events and vigils, generally marked by a spirit of shared learning, deep concern and tolerance. A particularly moving event involved a 'climate justice hearing' at which grassroots representatives from across the globe presented their experiential testimony on the impact of climate change on their livelihoods to a panel of representatives from Tibet, Brazil, Bolivia and South Africa to a packed auditorium. Numerous demonstrations and protest actions took place outside the International Convention Centre (ICC), especially in a designated 'speakers' corner' during the two weeks, including an occupation by over 100 activists of the hallowed corridors of the ICC one afternoon.

There was, however, a degree of tension between grassroots formations and some of the larger well-resourced international environmental NGOs, some of which have 'insider status' at UNFCCC negotiations.[20] It has been pointed out that: 'many of those big green groups have avoided, with phobic precision, any serious debate on the blindingly obvious roots of the climate crisis: globalisation, deregulation and contemporary capitalism's quest for perpetual growth' (Klein 2011:15). The absence of any shared agreement on strategy and tactics was clearly a serious organisational weakness.

One expression of these differences that emerged at COP17 concerned some complaints about the different food and sleeping arrangements for the 2 000 grassroots activists staying in the climate refugee camp and a minority of NGO activists staying in expensive hotels, as well as those who had travelled in the 'climate change bus' (a twenty-seven-hour journey from Cape Town) and those who had a two-hour flight. Ironically, a similar criticism has been made from the 'right' about 'rich politicians and film stars from the West and the privileged activists from Greenpeace and WWF, flying in on jet aircraft to Durban …' (*Business Day*, 28 November 2011).

All of these COP17 actions could be criticised as ephemeral and limited to creating what has been called 'carnival bonds' (Bauman 2006). However, the discourse of justice and the emphasis in these actions on how the worst-affected by climate change are (and will be) the poor and the powerless could have a more enduring force. Sidney Tarrow has emphasised the mobilising power of the justice frame. In *Power in Movement* he argues that injustice and emotionality are central to framing contention. 'Collective emotions are triggered by an injustice frame, which highlights and morally condemns human suffering, contending that such suffering is not inevitable, not "written in the stars"' (Tarrow 1998:111). This justice frame is prominent in two new political developments in South Africa – the emergence of the Democratic Left Front and the labour movement's engagement with the climate change issue. Though it is too early to speak of an emerging 'red-green' alliance, there are grounds for a potentially powerful network of environmental and labour activists, a linkage that could foreground climate justice in an anti-capitalist agenda.

NEW POLITICAL DEVELOPMENTS

New left initiatives

A concern with climate justice was strong in the declaration that came out of the founding conference of the Democratic Left Front (DLF) in January 2011. The declaration states: 'We believe that our anti-capitalism must be green as well as red. Global capitalism threatens our world with disaster. If it is left to plunder the natural resources of our planet and pollute the atmosphere, the oceans and the soil, life itself will be under grave threat' (Declaration of the Democratic Left Front adopted by the First National Conference, 20-23 January 2011). Many DLF activists are committed to a new form of ethical, democratic and ecological socialism. This is not encoded in any blueprint but is to be built 'from the bottom up'.

The unifying potential of the climate crisis suggests that the DLF need not necessarily go the way of earlier attempts at convergences in the form of the Social Movements Indaba and Social Movements United. A DLF resolution was passed 'to work closely with the Climate Justice Now network and other organisations towards making COP17 a focal point to expose the alignment of the South African government to green neoliberal capitalism' (DLF press statement, 20 February 2011). The organisation was committed to 'mapping out a concrete and alternative agenda for the transition to a post-carbon economy', and with this in mind it invited 'forces linked to the Cochabamba People's Summit', which means the Bolivian government, Bolivian social movements, forces linked to the leading eco-socialist networks, anti-capitalist and climate justice groups, to a strategic conversation in Durban in September 2011. The period between September and December 2011 involved much grassroots awareness work on climate change, and the DLF was a powerful presence at COP17. The conference on eco-socialism organised in the People's Space emphasised how the climate crisis is embedded in a more general social crisis characterised by poverty, inequality, violence and the destruction of community.

This ideological thrust could promote the inclusion of the labour movement. As Bond has argued, the linkage of red and green struggles under the climate justice banner 'will require society moving from a fossil fuel dependent capitalism to eco-socialism', and this depends on 'a stronger labour input' (Bond 2011:195).

The mobilisation of labour

In many countries there is a gulf between the trade union and the environmental movements. The labour movement in South Africa has traditionally neglected environmental issues in favour of jobs, as illustrated by the 'steel valley struggle' (Cock 2007). However, this is changing. Several unions participated in the mobilisation of civil society for COP17 and were represented by Cosatu on the organising committee. The climate justice movement could revitalise trade unions both globally and locally, as it is increasingly recognised that workers and their organisations are an indispensable force for a just transition to a low-carbon economy.

The 'million climate jobs campaign' is modelled on a British trade union campaign and is taking hold in the South African labour movement. It is structured on the argument that if we are to move in a 'just transition' to a low-carbon economy using renewable energy instead of coal, it will be workers who will have to build wind, wave/tidal and solar power. It is workers who will have to renovate and insulate our homes and buildings and build new forms of public transport. It is stressed that the lives of working people could improve in the process. Research findings were launched at COP17 that demonstrated that 3.7 million climate jobs (jobs that reduce carbon emissions) could be created to address both the unemployment crisis and the climate crisis in South Africa. It is also stressed that climate jobs must be 'decent', largely publically driven jobs that promote equality and justice.

The trade union federation Cosatu is starting to recognise climate change as a developmental and social issue that constitutes 'one of the greatest threats to our planet and our people' (2010 National Congress resolution). Following discussion at a workshop in Durban in July 2011 on climate change attended by national office bearers, representatives of the twenty affiliated unions and nine provincial structures, a climate change policy framework was adopted. Fifteen principles were agreed, of which the most controversial were:

- Capitalist accumulation has been the underlying cause of excessive greenhouse gas emissions and, therefore, global warming and climate change.

- A new low-carbon development path is needed that addresses the need for decent jobs and the elimination of unemployment.
- We reject market mechanisms to reduce carbon emissions.
- Developed countries must pay their climate debt and the Green Climate Fund must be accountable.
- A just transition towards a low-carbon and climate resilient society is required.

Whereas capital's discourse of a transition to a new energy regime or a low-carbon economy emphasises growth, competitiveness and efficiency, the labour movement is committed to this notion of a 'just transition'. There are, however, very different understandings of the scale and nature of the changes involved in a just transition. To some, the just transition involves shallow change focused on protecting the most vulnerable sectors of the workforce, and to others it requires deep, transformative change to ensure both sustainability and justice in the move to a low carbon economy. In this sense the ecological crisis is understood to represent an opportunity: an opportunity not only to address the unemployment crisis in our society, but also to demand the redistribution of power and resources; to challenge the conventional understanding of economic growth; and to mobilise for an alternative development path .

In the final Cosatu policy framework on climate change endorsed by the central executive committee in August 2011, the explanation of a just transition reads: 'The evidence suggests that the transition to a low-carbon economy will potentially create more jobs than it will lose. But we have to campaign for protection and support for workers whose jobs or livelihoods might be threatened by the transition. If we do not do that, then these workers will resist the transition. We also have to ensure that the development of new, green industries does not become an excuse for lowering wages and social benefits ...'

The question is: Are these necessary but sufficient conditions for a just transition?

Whereas the International Trade Union Confederation (ITUC) speaks of a 'paradigm shift', some activists of the Cosatu affiliate the South African Municipal Workers' Union (Samwu) speak of 'regime change'. Samwu's response to the National Climate Change Response Green Paper of February 2011 states: 'Tackling greenhouse gas emissions is not just a technical or technological problem. It requires a fundamental economic and social transformation to substantially change current patterns of production and consumption.'

The Cosatu president, Sdumo Dlamini, addressing a COP17 public meeting in Durban on 7 December 2011, stressed that: 'We need a just transition which will not lead to job losses. We need a transition that will create jobs.' The National Labour and Economic Development Institute (Naledi) researcher Fundi Nzimande has said that Cosatu wants 'just transition strategies to a green economy in which there are as few job losses as possible'. She has referred to building 'alliances with civil society' and emphasises a class analysis: 'We want to view climate change from a working-class perspective. We want to counter the big business point of view' (interview, Durban, 15 July 2011).

The National Union of Mineworkers (NUM), representing some 500 000 mineworkers, is obviously particularly sensitive to job losses and some shop stewards have expressed faith in new technology to reduce carbon emissions. By contrast, another Cosatu affiliate, the National Union of Metalworkers (Numsa), one of the biggest unions representing almost 300 000 workers in energy-intensive industries, is sceptical of the 'just transition' approach and warns that the shift to a low-carbon economy, and particularly the development of renewable energy, is being dominated by green capitalism (interview with Numsa official, Johannesburg, 7 February 2012). According to the Numsa president, 'the language of "just transition" needs a class analysis. We believe that a "just transition" can become a disarming term for the working class if we are not careful. It must always be clear that capitalism has caused the crisis of climate change that we see today. There is an urgent need to situate the question of climate change in a class struggle perspective' (opening address by the Numsa president, Cedric Gina, to the Numsa International Seminar on Climate Change and Class Struggle, 4 December 2011).

Numsa believes that 'a just transition must be based on worker controlled democratic social ownership of key means of production and means of subsistence …Without this struggle over ownership and the struggle for a socially owned renewable energy sector, just transition will become a capitalist concept, building up a capitalist "green economy"' (statement from the Numsa Central Committee issued on 14 December 2011). In 2011, Numsa established two worker-led research and development groups, one on energy efficiency and the other on renewable energy (interview with Dinga Sikwebu, Numsa official, 7 February 2012), which will investigate the carbon emissions of various products and then work with groups in the community that use them. The aim is to build into their negotiating strategy an evaluation of these products in relation to carbon emissions.

Overall, there are differences within the labour movement in the responses to the climate crisis. Contention is emerging over five issues:
* the substantive content of a 'just' transition;
* the use of market mechanisms to reduce carbon emissions;
* the efficacy of technologies such as clean coal and carbon capture and storage;
* whether it is possible to delink economic growth from carbon emissions; and
* the scale of change necessary to address the climate crisis.

A transformative understanding of a 'just transition to a low-carbon economy' could be a precursor to an alternative social order. It could take labour beyond the 'real world historical options' of green capitalism 'where economic growth is de-linked from emissions and environmental destruction generally', or a 'suicide capitalism scenario where fossil-fuel corporations and major industry, agriculture, transport and retail interests are successful in maintaining business as usual' (Sweeney 2011:9).

For example, it could involve:
* the collective, democratic control of production;
* the mass rollout of socially owned renewable energy, which could mean decentralised energy with much greater potential for community control;
* the localisation of food production in the shift from carbon-intensive industrial agriculture to agro-ecology, which could promote food security, cooperatives and more communal living, and also a more direct sense of connection to nature;
* the reduction of consumption, which could mean the simplification of

middle-class lifestyles, with reduced waste, extravagance and ostentation;
- the shift to public transport, which could reduce the reliance on private motor cars as symbols of power and freedom;
- more sharing of resources in more collective social forms, which could erode the individualism marking neoliberal capitalism;
- the shift towards a more appreciative use of natural resources, which could reduce the alienation from nature of many urban inhabitants; and
- the spreading of the values of sharing, simplicity, solidarity and more mindful living.

A vision of an alternative social order could demonstrate how climate justice can only be realised in a social order that changes the present patterns of production and consumption that are based on waste, competition and pollution, and focuses on the provision of basic human needs such as clean air, unpolluted water, safe food, adequate sanitation, public transport, universal healthcare, quality education, useful work and renewable energy. Mapping such an alternative vision would challenge the 'deepest shadow that hangs over us which is neither terror, nor environmental collapse or global recession. It is the internalised fatalism that holds that there is no possible alternative to capital's world order' (Kovel, cited in Kelly and Malone 2006:116).

CONCLUSION: CREATING TRANSNATIONAL SOLIDARITY

At present there is no coherent, militant climate justice movement in South Africa. There were militant elements in the Global Day of Action march but it did not present any kind of political challenge to the negotiators inside the ICC. The messages presented to Christiana Figueres and Maite Nkoana-Mashabane, the minister of International Relations, at the end of the march were politely *asking* to be heard: 'listen to the voices of rural women' and 'listen to the youth'. Only the message from Zwelinzima Vavi struck a stronger note.

One crucial lesson from COP17 is to shift from 'asking' (whether for camels or goats or simply to be heard) to 'demanding'. The crucial question is whether different civil society actors can form a common ground for militant action.

The problem is that civil society includes serious power imbalances. The UNFCCC welcomes civil society engagement as a democratising force, but 'this sector includes everything from grassroots peoples' movements to business and industry organisations representing the world's largest corporations …' As a consequence of this infiltration the UN's climate change solutions 'are largely driven by market mechanisms with the private sector as a leading player' (Fernandes and Girard 2011:10).[21]

At the same time, there are strategic weaknesses in anti-capitalist global civil society. Satgar maintains that at the 2011 World Social Forum meeting in Dakar 'hard lessons were drawn from the recent Copenhagen and Cancun climate negotiations. NGO technocrats, donor-driven agendas, big egos, celebrity intellectuals and hard line social movement agendas prevented a common voice and united agenda to prevail outside the negotiations in the streets'.

The political reality is that although there has been mass mobilisation of climate justice activists, the multilateral climate negotiations remain dominated by green capitalism. Anti-capitalist civil society is a splintered movement. There is no master 'frame' of climate justice encoded in any blueprint, and no single, collective actor with a clear and singular identity mobilising around climate change. The issue is attracting deeply committed and energetic activists, but there is no coherent centre and no tidy margins; it is an inchoate, fragmented sum of multiple, diverse struggles and organisations.

But, most clearly in its warnings of the threat to human survival, this could change. Building a powerful climate justice movement, a movement grounded in a coherent, strong, restitutive concept of justice, a movement that can make its demands heard at both the national and global levels, is clearly necessary but difficult. To achieve it and to shift from being a site of carnival bonds and contentious politics, the climate justice movement must do more to:

- **promote the recognition that capitalism is both unjust and unsustainable**
  The climate crisis is due to the expansionist logic of the capitalist system and this system has to be changed if human survival is to be secured.
- **draw on the energy of grassroots struggles**
  There are many strong grassroots formations in existence, particularly the Rural Women's Assembly, and numerous faith-based organisations that are engaging with climate change. Numerous civil society formations organised grassroots educational workshops in the run-up to COP17, and a 'climate train' visited seventeen towns in a month-long educational campaign. All reported extensive calls for education and information about climate change, especially when framed in terms of issues such as access to adequate water, crop failures, flood damage and rising food prices.
- **persuade the labour movement to bring its organisational capacity to the climate justice question**
- **connect with the current anger about deepening social injustice, expressed by the 'Occupy movement', which has involved protest actions in 900 cities around the world**
  This has to demonstrate that injustice is intrinsic to capitalism. As David Harvey has written, '… an ethical, non-exploitative and socially just capitalism that rebounds to the benefit of all is impossible. It contradicts the very nature of what capital is about' (Harvey 2010:239).

It is clear that the post-apartheid state is driven by vested interests. It perpetuates market-led economic growth models that benefit large corporations at the expense of job creation and the social needs of the majority. It will not drive ecological transformation and solve the problem of climate change, which threatens us all. Neither will capitalism.

If these understandings were linked to a vision of an alternative social order, and could draw on the organisational strength of the trade unions and the energy of grassroots struggles, an alliance of labour and environmental activists in a climate justice movement could generate a transnational solidarity that is larger, deeper and more powerful than anything we have yet seen.

NOTES

1   'Ask for a camel when you expect to get a goat' is a Somali saying meaning aim high but settle for less. It has been used to illustrate the strategy of developing nations in the United Nations negotiations on climate change.
2   This paper is based on the analysis of relevant primary and secondary sources, participant observation and numerous discussions and interviews with key activists.
3   Interview, Durban, 2 December 2011.
4   A contentious issue is the source of the funds, with the majority of climate justice activists arguing for public finance.
5   Carbon trading involves the buying and selling of an artificial commodity, the right to emit greenhouse gases, and comes in two main forms, 'cap and trade' and 'offsetting'. The largest offset scheme is the Clean Development Mechanism (CDM) established under the framework of the Kyoto Protocol, which allows rich countries 'flexibility' in their emissions reductions by allowing them to buy those reductions from developing countries instead.
6   Cited in *Business Day*, 15 December 2011.
7   groundWork press release, Durban, 7 December 2011.
8   CJN press release, Durban, 10 December 2011.
9   *Africa Focus Bulletin*, 7 December 2011.
10 Janet Redman of the Washington-based Institute for Policy Studies (Climate Justice Now press release, 11 December 2011).
11 *Business Day*, 12 December 2011.
12 At the UNFCCC negotiations in 2009 in Copenhagen, South Africa said it would reduce emissions by 34 per cent by 2020 and 42 per cent by 2025 below a business-as-usual baseline structured on a fanciful 'growth without constraint' scenario.
13 Kumi Naidoo, Uppsala interview, 13 April 2011.
14 Interview, Johannesburg, 12 March 2011.
15 Mary Robinson, from the Mary Robinson Foundation for Climate Justice, asserts that 'climate change represents the greatest threat to human rights that we will ever face' (Johannesburg seminar, March 2011).
16 In response to the failure of COP15 at Copenhagen, the Bolivian government organised the People's Conference on Climate Change and the Rights of Mother Earth in Cochabamba. Many climate justice activists maintain that the Cochabamba Agreement is the best roadmap around.
17 Cited in *Business Day*, 7 December 2011.
18 Tristan Taylor, policy officer at Earthlife. Interview, Johannesburg, 7 October 2010.
19 Ibid.
20 It is important not to homogenise these groups. For example, Friends of the Earth International is the world's largest grassroots environmental network. It has a transformative agenda, and opposes carbon trading, whereas the World Wildlife Fund supports it.
21 For this reason Standing asserts that a transformative capacity lies within the 'precariat' (the millions who are unemployed or in insecure employment), whom he describes as naturally the green class in arguing for a more egalitarian society in which sharing and reproductive, resource-conserving activities are prioritised (Standing 2011:179).

REFERENCES

Bond P (2011a) *Climate Justice. Paralysis Above, Movement Below*. Scottsville: UKZN Press.

Bond P (2011b) SA reps at climate talks 'are letting us all down', *The Sunday Independent*, 6 February 2011).

Bond P (2011c) A dirty deal coming down in Durban, *The Mercury*, 6 December 2011.

Cock J (2006) The environmental justice movement. In Ballard R et al., *Voices of Protest. Social Movements in Post-apartheid South Africa*. Scottsville: UKZN Press.

Cock J (2011) Green capitalism or environmental justice. *Focus*, No 63.

Cock J (2007) Sustainable development or environmental justice: questions for the South African labour movement from the Steel Valley struggle. *Labour, Capital and Society*, Vol 40, nos 1 and 2.

Clark P (2011) Towards a standstill, *Financial Times* 28 September 2011.

Fernandes S and R Girard (2011) *Corporations, Climate and the United Nations*. Ottowa: Polaris Institute.

Friends of the Earth International (2011) *Climate Justice and Energy*. Amsterdam: FO.

Government of the Republic of South Africa (2011) *National Climate Change Response White Paper*. Pretoria: Government Printer.

Hallowes D SDCEA (2011) *Feeling the Heat in Durban, People's Struggles and Climate Change*. Durban: Oxfam.

Harvey D (2010) *The Enigma of Capital and the Crises of Capitalism*. New York: Oxford University Press.

Kelly J and S Malone (2006) *Ecosocialism or Barbarism*. London: Socialist Resistance.

Kovel J (2002) *The Enemy of Nature. The End of Capitalism or the End of the World*. London: Zed.

Klein N (2011) Capitalism versus the climate. *The Nation*, November 28 edition.

Kovel J (2011) Presentation to the Seminar on Ecosocialism. The People's Space, Durban, 3 December.

Lander E (2011) The green economy: the wolf in sheep's clothing. Paper presented at the Transnational Institute conference, Durban, December.

Panitch L and C Leys (2006) *Coming to Terms with Nature*. Socialist Register. Toronto: Palgrave.

Standing G (2011) *The Precariat. The New Dangerous Class*. London: Bloomsbury.

Tarrow S (1998) *Power in Movement: Social Movements and Contentious Politics*. Cambridge: Cambridge University Press.

Tilly C (2003) *The Politics of Collective Violence*. Basingstoke: Macmillan.

Sweeney S (2011) How unions can help secure a binding global climate agreement in 2011. http://www. sustainlabor [Accessed 4 March 2011].

Trollop H and Tyler E (2011) Is South Africa's Economic Policy aligned with our National Mitigation Policy Direction and a low carbon future?. Paper presented to the National Planning Commission Second Low Carbon Economy Workshop, July.

Wallis V (2010) Beyond green capitalism. *Monthly Review*. February: 32-47.

CHAPTER 9

Hydraulic fracturing in South Africa:
Correcting the democratic deficits[1]

David Fig

Land grabbing is clearly not confined to examples of appropriation for agricultural use, but can also apply to the acquisition of extractive resources. In the case of South Africa, the advent of shale gas exploration has made over 20 per cent of the country's land area vulnerable to acquisition by transnational oil companies. Though the surface of the land may be owned by existing local landowners, mineral and petroleum legislation allows for the allocation of exploration rights under the surface by the state to be granted to transnational as well as to domestic corporations.

This chapter will examine the potential impacts of the shale gas industry in South Africa on people and the environment. The lifting, on 7 September 2012, of a government moratorium on the mining of shale gas, brings exploitation of the resource much closer to realisation.

Despite having experienced almost two decades of constitutional democracy, South Africans still have no transparent and participatory mechanisms for deciding democratically on the uptake of new technologies or development projects, particularly those that affect millions of lives and livelihoods. There are limited opportunities for intervention in very circumscribed public participation processes linked to narrow administrative decisions rather than to broad policy questions. The processes of sharing any sovereignty with citizens in the name of producing better public policy are often derisory. When citizens are left out of debates confined to government and the business community, the only ways of influencing policy are to petition, protest, or litigate, usually after the horse has already bolted.

Examples of this abound, especially in relation to controversial technologies. Government took little trouble to consult the public on questions of building the now defunct pebble bed modular nuclear reactor; of allowing aluminium smelters to consume massive amounts of the country's once cheap electricity; or of the introduction of genetic modification of our food crops (Fig 2007; Fig 2010a; Hallowes 2011). The mining industry has almost free range in operating in fragile buffer areas around world heritage sites or in the face of opposition from local communities (Capel 2012). Adjudication of these kinds of conflicts is usually through government fiat, not through any fair, transparent, democratic consultation process.

There has been a steady watering down of public participation in environmental and health effects, as these are seen as a brake on development. The protocols associated with environmental impact assessments have been streamlined, often resulting in insufficient time for well-informed public consultation. Often, government resorts (as did its predecessor regime) to the publication of opportunities for public comment in the *Government Gazette*, allowing only a thirty-day public response time. No efforts have been made, nor have any resources been set aside, to facilitate or promote effective public participation. The National Environmental Advisory Forum, which was a consultative body of civil society representatives established under the National Environmental Management Act No 107 of 1998, was subsequently abolished in later amendments to the Act.

Fracking, a shorthand term for hydraulic fracturing, is the latest example of a new technology that is likely to be introduced without any significant consultation of the public or affected parties.

This will happen as soon as one of the oil companies receives an exploration right from the oil and gas regulator, the Petroleum Agency of South Africa (PASA). This body has, simultaneously, the legal role of promoting and of regulating the oil and gas industry – a strong internal conflict of interests. Applicants for the exploration right have to lodge an environmental management plan, and have 120 days in which to publish it (see Table 1). Only then is the public, in the form of registered interested and affected parties, given a short time in which to comment.

The environmental management report process has been a controversial one. Normally in South Africa all new developments have to undergo some form of prior environmental impact assessment. The one exception has been the mining industry, which, to date, has been exempt from environmental authorisations issued by the Department of Environmental Affairs. Instead it has been subjected to less rigorous processes overseen by the Department of Mineral Resources, which has little expertise, interest in, or incentive to undertake environmental management. This anomaly has long been recognised, and a process instituted to change it.

In 2008, the then minister of Environmental Affairs and Tourism and the then minister of Minerals and Energy came to an agreement transferring the right to make

Table 1: Timeline and procedures for oil and gas exploitation

	Period	Exclusivity	Activities	Reporting
Reconnaisance Permit	12 months	Non-exclusive		When permit issued, applicant has 30 days in which to present an Environmental Management Report (EMR)
Technical Cooperation Permit	12 months	Exclusive	Desktop study, right to apply for exclusive exploration right	
Exploration Right	3 years, renewable for a maximum of three 2-year periods	Exclusive Transferable	Exploration must commence within 90 days of receiving the right	When right issued, applicant has 120 days in which to present an EMR
Production Right	30 years, renewable for 30 years	Exclusive Transferable		When right issued, applicant has 180 days in which to present an EMR

Source: Minerals and Petroleum Resources Development Act, no. 28 of 2002, Chapter 6.

environmental authorisations about minerals and petroleum to the environment func-tion at national and provincial level. For the transfer to occur, it became necessary to amend both environmental and mining legislation, and the idea was that eighteen months after both amendments came into effect the functions would be transferred. The necessary amendments were made to the environmental law, reflected in section 14(2) of the National Environmental Management Amendment Act, No 62 of 2008 promulgated on 5 January 2009 and came into effect on 1 May 2009. Although amendments to the Minerals Act were promulgated on 19 April 2009, the minister has not yet brought them into effect. The environmental authorisations of mining, oil and gas projects, therefore, continue to remain, at the time of writing, under the Department of Mineral Resources. It is not clear whether this lapse is due to administrative incompetence or strategic foot-dragging but it means that the potential fracking industry will not, at the outset, have to comply with more rigorous environmental authorisation processes.

The threat of litigation resulting from the imperfections of the environmental manage-ment report content and process, especially with the absolute lack of any impartial scientific investigation into the technology and its impacts, resulted in the minister of Mineral Resources, Susan Shabangu, declaring a moratorium on the issuing of exploration licences (*Government Gazette*, 30 August 2010 and 11 February 2011). Further development was frozen until the lifting of the moratorium after a Cabinet meeting held in September 2012 (Department of Mineral Resources 2012).

The minister created a task team to undertake research into fracking to enable a decision on the lifting of the moratorium. Certain key government departments were excluded, namely Economic Development, Rural Development, Trade and Industry, Tourism, Agriculture and Health. Without transparency, suspicions mounted that the task team was obliged to consult the very oil companies that are seeking licences to frack. Litigation was initiated to put pressure on the minister to reveal the membership, qualifications, terms of reference, minutes, research undertaken, and experts consulted by members of the task team.

Further conflicts may have to be resolved in the courts of the land, since there is no other social space in which they can be fairly adjudicated.

To understand the conflicts over fracking, this chapter will first examine the growing demand for energy in South Africa. It will then look at fracking technology, the applicants that plan to introduce it, and its potential spatial reach. It will assess some of the dangers and challenges posed by the technology to water, waste management, climate, livelihoods, governance and monitoring. After a discussion of the ways in which opposition to fracking has built up, it will turn to a brief examination of the state of poverty and inequality in the Karoo, and raise some final questions with respect to fracking, including the question of trust.

SOUTH AFRICA'S THIRST FOR ENERGY

By the time of the national power outages dating from January 2008, South Africa was generating over 39 000 megawatts (MW) of electricity. Although full demand was never exceeded at that time, Eskom struggled with problems such as closure of power stations for routine maintenance, insufficient coal availability, and coal that was delivered too wet to incinerate in the power stations. Over 90 per cent of South Africa's electricity is supplied by burning coal, with around 5 per cent generated from nuclear energy and the rest supplied by hydro, diesel and other minor sources. Eskom's first consultation was with the most energy-intensive industries – mining, synfuels, steelmaking and smelting companies. They were urged to close down temporarily to avoid the grid being destroyed. Later they were asked to use 20 per cent less electricity in production, with a similar request to households (17 per cent of consumption) to drop by 10 per cent. Random outages were followed by planned outages circulating between different areas and scheduled for specific times. These outages lasted until March 2008 (Fig 2010b).

The shortage of electricity came as a deep blow to government's attempts to attract new foreign investment to the country. The crisis reflected longstanding neglect of warnings that had been issued by the state-owned electricity utility Eskom and industry since the late 1990s to the effect that demand was fast outpacing electricity supply. Government neglect was partially due to unrealised plans to privatise Eskom. It was believed that new infrastructural investment could be left to the new private owners but political objections to selling off the utility mounted and the sale never materialised. However, the urgent need to extend supply remained unmet. Government also abandoned plans to develop small modular nuclear reactors, after sinking R9 billion into the project, without its attracting any customers or other investors. An announced tender for new large-scale reactors also had to be abandoned owing to Eskom's facing recessionary conditions and difficulties in securing sufficient finance (Thomas 2012).

Under pressure from intensive user companies, which formed a strong lobby – the Electricity Intensive User Group – government became convinced that instead of investing heavily in renewable energy and energy efficiency it should continue to make major investments in coal and nuclear, arguing that these were the only reliable sources for provision of base-load electricity. No attempt was made to reassess the heavy dependence on fossil fuels and uranium, both of which have excessively polluted the South African environment. Trapped in an industrial paradigm that allotted primacy to the 'minerals-energy complex' (Fine and Rustomjee 1996), the country's planners failed to use the opportunity to set South Africa on a more resource-efficient development path. Instead, older mothballed coal-fired power stations have been brought back into production. The country has embarked on building some of the largest new coal-fired power stations on earth (Medupi ranks third and Kusile fourth in terms of output, around 4 800MW each). And, despite extensive public misgivings and objections, the Integrated Resource Plan for Electricity, produced in 2010, allows for an additional 9 600MW of new nuclear power by 2030. The horizon of new renewables was set at about one-third of this level (Department of Energy 2010).

Elsewhere, the argument has been put that, as a developing country, South Africa's greenhouse gas emissions should peak at some point between 2020 and 2025, followed by a plateau for a decade, and only later a decline. Pledges on the decline were simultaneously made by President Jacob Zuma in the run-up to the fifteenth Conference of the Parties of the UN Framework Convention on Climate Change at Copenhagen. The reductions were set at 32 per cent by 2020 relative to a 'business as usual' scenario, followed by 42 per cent in 2025. The pledge depends on the extent to which industrialised countries provide financial, capacity building and technology transfer support to South Africa (Molewa 2011).

Chairing the seventeenth Conference of the Parties in Durban in November-December 2011, South Africa continually emphasised its commitment to a low-carbon future in the long run. However, this undertaking has to be seen within a context of continued multiform global crisis in the fields of finance, energy and ecology (Hallowes 2011). Like other emerging economies, South Africa claims that it has the right to 'develop', as currently industrialised countries of the global North were able to do in the past, and that climate concerns should not become a brake on development in the short term. Hence, although South Africa argued for a second commitment period for the Kyoto Protocol, it did not regard itself as being bound by it. In any case, its chairing skills in Durban were unable to bring about a global acceptance of such a second commitment period, which has been deferred to the future.

The ambiguities of South Africa's climate commitments have helped to shape a context in which fracking is being encouraged. Instead of emulating the many juris-dictions that have ruled out fracking; to date these include France, Bulgaria, Quebec, British Columbia, New York state, New Jersey, New South Wales and others (for coun-tries involved in fracking see Franco et al. 2012), South Africa has permitted a series of transnational oil companies to apply for exploration rights. Instead of discouraging the further extraction of fossil fuel, the state is buying into the oil companies' claim that shale gas will be a 'game changer', a chance for the country to develop greater energy inde-pendence. Shell has commissioned studies by a local economist whose modelling vastly exaggerates potential job possibilities, tax revenues, gross value added, and the economic viability of the resource (Twine 2012; Njobeni 2012).

Table 2: Current (2010) and future (2030) share of energy mix in South Africa

Source	Share in 2010	Added Gigawatts	Share in 2030	Notes
Coal	90%	6.3	65%	
Nuclear	5%	9.6	20%	
Hydro	5%	2.6	5%	Imported
Gas CCGT*	0%	2.4	1%	
Peak OCGT**	<0.01%	3.9	<0.01%	
Renewables	0%	17.8	9%	8.4GW wind, 8.4GW solar PV and 1GW Concentrated Solar Power

(Source: Department of Energy (2011) *Integrated Resource Plan 2010, Final Report*: 7. Reproduced with permission.)
*CCGT = Closed Cycle Gas Turbine; **OGCT = Open Cycle Gas Turbine.

Plans for fracking

In the past decade, technology has emerged for the extraction of shale gas, or methane, from deep under the surface of the earth. Although research and exploration remain to be done, estimates have been made that South Africa could be a rich source of shale gas. Its extraction requires drilling deeply for between four and six kilometres, through underground freshwater supplies. When the drilling reaches the level where the gas is found, it changes direction from vertical to horizontal. Enormous quantities of water, combined with sand and a cocktail of toxic chemicals, are pumped at high pressure into the rocks. The injection of sand particles causes the rocks to fracture and release the gas, which is captured and piped back to the surface by means of the same equipment. This process is known as hydraulic fracturing, or fracking for short.

Figure 1: The fracking process

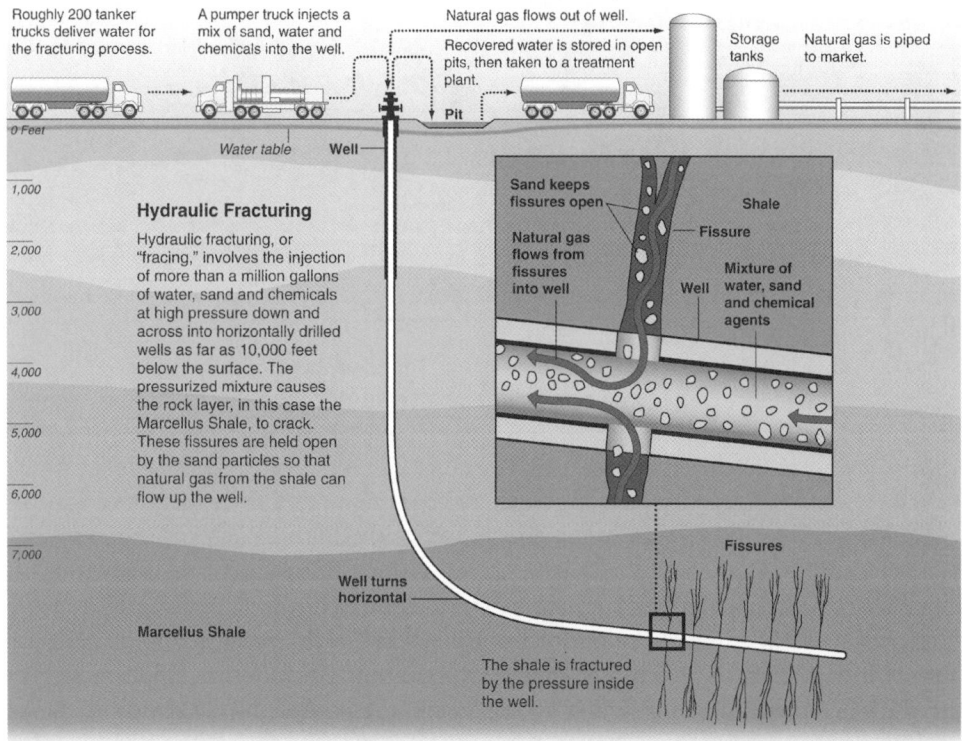

Roughly 200 tanker trucks deliver water for the fracturing process.

A pumper truck injects a mix of sand, water and chemicals into the well.

Natural gas flows out of well.

Recovered water is stored in open pits, then taken to a treatment plant.

Storage tanks

Natural gas is piped to market.

Pit

Water table   **Well**

0 Feet

1,000

Hydraulic Fracturing

Hydraulic fracturing, or "fracing," involves the injection of more than a million gallons of water, sand and chemicals at high pressure down and across into horizontally drilled wells as far as 10,000 feet below the surface. The pressurized mixture causes the rock layer, in this case the Marcellus Shale, to crack. These fissures are held open by the sand particles so that natural gas from the shale can flow up the well.

2,000

3,000

4,000

5,000

6,000

7,000

Sand keeps fissures open

Shale

Natural gas flows from fissures into well

Fissure

Mixture of water, sand and chemical agents

Well

Well turns horizontal

Fissures

Marcellus Shale

The shale is fractured by the pressure inside the well.

Graphic by Al Granberg

(Source: Al Granberg/ProPublica.)

A number of companies have lined up to explore shale gas locally, and have been granted permission by the regulator, the Petroleum Agency of South Africa, to undertake preliminary technical studies in different parts of the country. Four bids cover a total area of 223 000 km², which amounts to 18.3 per cent of the territorial surface of South Africa. Three bids are for parts of the Karoo, and the fourth covers parts of the Free State, Northern and Cape, and KwaZulu-Natal. A fifth bid, about which little is known, is located in the Northern Cape just south of Botswana.

Map 1: Areas allocated for fracking in South Africa, 2012

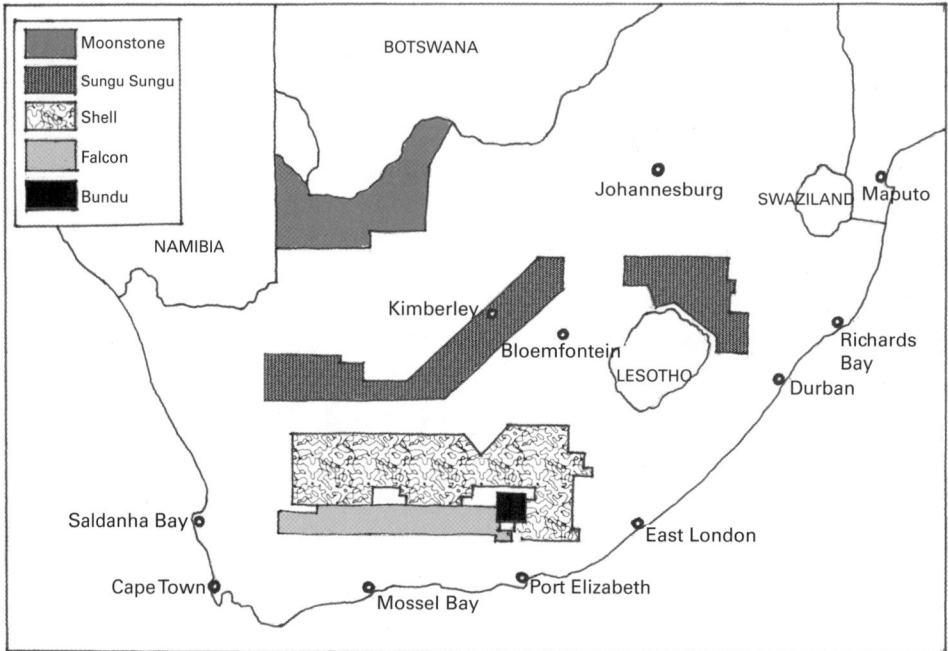

Source: Petroleum Agency of South Africa.

Under the law, the Mineral and Petroleum Resources Development Act 28 of 2002, the regulator first allocates a technical cooperation permit. This gives the applicant a year in which to conduct desktop studies on the feasibility of extracting the shale gas, and an exclusive right to apply for an exploration right. If successful, the applicant may undertake exploration for three years, renewable for another six years. During that time, if the deposits of gas are found to be economically viable, the company can apply for an exclusive production right lasting thirty years, which is also renewable.

The regulator does not hold open hearings in granting these rights. The only way in which the public can intervene is when the company applies for an exploration right. To do so, the company must hire consultants to produce an environmental management report (EMR). It needs to release the EMR to those registered as interested and affected parties, hold public meetings, and allow time for the public to make comments on the report. As the exploration rights are often, in South African practice, converted almost automatically to production rights, this is one of the very few occasions in which the public has any voice in the process.

Table 2: Applicants for exclusive exploration rights for shale gas in South Africa, 2011-12

Company	Nationality	Area of exploration	Surface area granted (km²)
Royal Dutch Shell	UK/Netherlands	Karoo (W & E Cape)	90 000
Bundu	Australia	Karoo (E Cape)	3 100
Falcon	US	Karoo (E Cape)	30 350
Sungu Sungu	South Africa	Free State , E Cape & KZN	100 000
Moonstone Investments 90	South Africa	Northern Cape	n/a

Sources: Petroleum Agency of South Africa, www.petroleumagency.com (downloaded 11 October 2011 and 25 September 2012); Falcon, www.falconoilandgas.com (downloaded 11 January 2012, equivalent to 7.5 million acres); Bundu is now owned by Challenger, www.challengerenergy.com.au/projects/south-africa-project/cranemere (downloaded 11 October 2010); (Sungu Sungu, http://sungusungugroup.com (downloaded 24 January 2013). Cranemere is the very farm made famous by Eve Palmer in her *Plains of Camdeboo* (1966). Sasol and associates, Norway's Statoil and US-based Chesapeake Oil, announced in late November 2011 that they would no longer pursue their right to explore, leaving their territory open to Sungu Sungu (Njobeni 2011).

Fracking is a controversial new technology, for which almost no research has been undertaken in South Africa. In order for companies to find out how large the resource is, and whether it is worth exploiting, fracking has to be undertaken during the exploration phase. Therefore, giving permission to explore means that government would be allowing fracking to take place immediately. It is unlikely that the effects of fracking could ever be reversed once it has started taking place.

Things were moving at such speed that many of the large questions about water contamination, waste management, climate change, employment and social effects had not even begun to be discussed. Instead of the government creating a space for the transparent public policy discussion about whether the technology is appropriate for South Africa's development needs, it was left to obscure administrative processes in which the public has no say.

The oil companies have argued that the technology is safe, proven and reliable and that the shale gas is plentiful (485 trillion cubic feet, although these estimates have to be confirmed scientifically). They claim that the energy from shale oil is more climate-friendly than coal, and that therefore its production would make a contribution towards reducing carbon emissions. Shell, in particular, has offered assurances that the huge amount of water needed for fracking would not be drawn from the Karoo. It has also undertaken to consult communities and to reveal in confidence the list of toxic chemicals it will be using to a small committee drawn from selected interested parties. The oil companies say the finds of shale gas will be a 'game changer', allowing South Africa to become more self-sufficient in energy sources.

The government sees the mining of shale gas as a way of substituting for imported fuels, providing South Africa with increased energy security. A recent policy process to determine South Africa's energy mix, the Integrated Resource Plan 2010 (IRP2010) did not take the exploitation of shale gas into account in its calculations of local electricity production to 2030 (Department of Energy 2011).

As opposition pressure built up, Mineral Resources Minister Susan Shabangu declared a moratorium on the granting of exploration licences. This was due to run out in February 2012, but was renewed for an indefinite period until the task team established by the minister had time to investigate fracking properly in order to report back. Water and Environment Affairs Minister Edna Molewa has stated in Parliament that the water legislation needs to be made more robust in order to 'ensure adequate control' to prevent contamination from fracking (Pressley 2011). The final lifting of the moratorium occurred on 7 September 2012, and the report of the task team was made available in the public domain (Department of Mineral Resources 2012).

The National Planning Commission stated in its 2011 report that 'shale gas has the potential to contribute a very large proportion of South Africa's energy needs … South Africa will seek to develop these resources provided the overall environmental costs and benefits will outweigh the costs and benefits associated with South Africa's dependence on coal [and] nuclear' (National Planning Commission 2011: 143). This enthusiasm was not the product of any intense debate on fracking within the NPC, and pre-empted any scientific examination of the issue. Subsequently in the National Development Plan, the Commission has come up with the following formulation of shale gas:

> South Africa should seek to develop these resources, provided the overall economic and environmental costs and benefits outweigh those associated with South Africa's dependence on coal, or with the alternative of nuclear power. The national value of this resource needs to be maximised (National Planning Commission 2012: 167-8).

Some commissioners have stigmatised the opposition to fracking as emanating from rich white landowners outside the Karoo and bankrolled by billionaire industrialists. This prejudice militates against more sober and scientific reflection on the social, economic and environmental concerns about shale gas exploitation.

Dangers and challenges
In examining the costs and benefits of fracking, a number of dangers and challenges have come to light.

Water
In many of the fracking areas of the United States, such as the Marcellus Shale area of Pennsylvania, water is plentiful. Not so in the shale fields of the Karoo, one of South Africa's most arid areas. Life in the Karoo depends on access to groundwater from

underground aquifers or chambers containing fresh water that is replenished by the infrequent rains. The Water Research Commission has determined that 94 per cent of Karoo towns are totally dependent on groundwater (Greef 2012: 8-9). The Karoo is char- acterised by its extensive sheep, ostrich and, increasingly, game farming, with steel wind pumps drawing up the groundwater for animal and human consumption. Surface dams or reservoirs provide the rest of the area's water requirements, but these can be unreliable. For example, in recent years the dams supplying drinking water in the Beaufort West area dried up, causing a water crisis in the town. Travellers passing through Beaufort West were asked to donate bottled water to help to alleviate the problem.

Most of South Africa's surface fresh water (98 per cent) has already been allocated to existing users. This raises the question of how the fracking industry will source the millions of litres it will need to undertake its operations. It has been calculated that beween 2 000 and 18 000 cubic metres of water may be needed to frack a single well, amounting to up to 216 000 m^3 for the first twenty-four exploratory wells (Hartnady 2012: 10). This would require transportation of water by at least 1 667 trucks per well and possibly the building of expensive pipelines and desalination plants. Shell and other companies have failed to announce from where this large quantity of water will be drawn. Shell has, however, undertaken not to draw it from the Karoo, but some hydrologists have recommended that it be sourced from the already overstretched Gariep (formerly Orange) catchment. A hydrological study commissioned from Shell by SRK, a firm of consulting engineers, has, according to Shell exploration head Jan Eggink, discovered that there are plentiful underground sources of brackish water in the Karoo (Williams 2012).

Between less than 30 per cent to over 70 per cent of the water used in the process will be unrecoverable and will remain underground. This subtracts it from the water that might be recycled. The water that flows back to the surface may contain radioactive mate- rials and toxic chemicals such as benzene (NaturalGas.org, Sink or Swim: Water Disposal Issues, accessed 23 October 2012).

The use of toxic chemicals in the drilling process has also raised questions about whether any damage to the drill casing will release toxic fracking liquid into underground freshwater sources and contaminate them. These kinds of accidents are not common in the United States, but there have nevertheless been records of at least eight instances of large-scale pollution resulting from drilling and fracking and such instances are increasingly coming to light in new studies being undertaken by the US Environmental Protection Agency (EPA). For example, a three-year research paper found that test wells proved that fracking had caused contamination of groundwater and high methane levels at Pavilion, Wyoming (Johnson 2011).

Zoback et al. (2010) have pointed to the dangers and adverse effects of blowouts and seismic events resulting from fracking. The risk of contamination is such that 'the fracking liquid *will* contaminate the groundwater. There is no doubt at all,' according to the University of the Free State's professor of groundwater studies, Gerrit van Tonder (Du Toit 2012).

Waste management

As we have seen, fracking entails the pumping at high pressure of toxic chemicals, with water and sand, into underground shale rock formations. Although forming only 1 per cent of the mix, the toxic chemicals used vary between wells, depending on their geology. Most of the fracking liquid returns to the surface after use, and has to be disposed of without causing harm to the environment. Onsite there must be lined ponds or tanks to receive the toxic sludge initially. Questions arise about how this is handled and what arrangements are made for the final disposal of the wastes. In the US, home to about a million wells, 25 per cent of wells transgress the rules of safe management, and the regulatory agencies find this very difficult to enforce (Vermeulen 2011).

The management of hazardous waste in South Africa falls under provincial jurisdiction. The Eastern Cape is likely to be the site of most of the fracking, and remains South Africa's 'poorest, least resourced and most administratively weak' province (Ruiters, Ed. 2011: 8). Capacity to deal with the extensive management of hazardous waste arising from the fracking industry does not yet exist, and will have to be funded and planned into the system. Most municipalities in the province are not even coping, in terms of budgets and the necessary human capital, with the management of ordinary household and industrial waste.

Aside from liquid and solid wastes, there will be enormous dust pollution arising from the large-scale transportation of water, sand and chemicals on mostly gravel-surfaced roads.

Climate

Shale gas consists mostly of methane (CH_4), a fossil fuel whose combustion contributes to global warming. Although carbon dioxide emissions are less than coal or conventional gas, we need to remember that methane is recognised as a greenhouse gas under the Kyoto Protocol and is far more deadly for our climate than carbon dioxide. Recent research from Cornell University shows that shale gas has a larger greenhouse gas footprint than coal, 20 per cent more, rising to 40 per cent more over twenty years and only becoming lower than coal after 100 years (Howarth et al. 2011). This and other studies in the US have shown that up to 8 per cent of the mined methane is directly released into the atmosphere during the fracking process (see the review of this research at Hughes 2011).

The oil industry nevertheless claims that fracking is less harmful to the environment than coal mining. It advocates that although shale gas is indeed a fossil fuel, it is a sensible 'transition' fuel to use while South Africa tries to move towards more climate-friendly energy options. What it does not calculate is that the requirement for the government to invest in infrastructure for the industry (improved roads, waste disposal, regulatory functions) will take investment away from support for the emerging renewable energy industry.

In December 2011, South Africa hosted the seventeenth annual conference of the parties signatory to the UN Framework Convention on Climate Change in Durban, making commitments to a plan to lower greenhouse emissions and to develop a greener economy. Support for a shale gas industry would compromise such commitments.

Livelihoods

If the industry is introduced, will this not lead to an expansion of employment and of the local economy?

During the exploration phase, which would last up to nine years, very few jobs (about 100) will be created onsite. Running the wells and doing the drilling requires a small number of very skilled operatives. The oil companies admit that they do not do the fracking themselves, but outsource these functions to experienced subcontractors. This implies that the tenders will be awarded to foreign companies, which will use their own labour and will not draw from unskilled Karoo residents. Figures from the Pennsylvania area in the US indicate that only 13.3 direct jobs are generated per well (Food and Water Watch 2011). Jobs will expand in the areas of truck driving, security, road construction, service provision and so on, but each well can only be fracked around eighteen times, and the drilling will move from place to place as wells are closed. This means that there is a cycle of local 'boom and bust' as the fracking moves to new areas.

With the increased risks of water contamination and severe air pollution, the fate of local agriculture is at stake. In the Eastern Cape, agriculture employs over 60 000, and provides livelihoods for many thousands of emerging farmers (StatsSA 2010). Julienne du Toit, a Karoo-based journalist, believes that farming and fracking will not be compatible. In her view, farmers will not be able to continue under conditions of air and water contamination. The Karoo would lose its reputation for clean air, soil and farm produce. Those trying to sell up would experience difficulty in finding willing buyers, and property prices would plummet. Many farm workers would be displaced, adding to the epidemic of unemployment (interview, Cradock, 17 October 2011).

With the anticipated air and water pollution, niche industries such as astronomy, palaeontology and ecotourism will also be adversely affected in the Karoo. South Africa's successful bid in conjunction with Australia to host the Square Kilometre Array (SKA) of new-generation radio telescopes was announced in April 2012. However, measures must be enforced to ensure that pollution from fracking does not compromise the ability of the project's radio telescopes to operate effectively. The manager of SKA's site bid, Adrian Tiplady, served on the working group of the government task team, and believes his presence helped to secure the project's interests. It is further protected by legislation in the form of the Astronomy Geographic Advantage Act 21 of 2007, which gives the minister of Science and Technology the power to declare astronomy advantage areas in order to ensure that large-scale and globally important astronomy facilities are protected from developments that might interfere with their research activities (SKA and DST 2009). Although Tiplady is convinced that this Act will protect the integrity of the project, which will be of global importance, its robustness has not yet been tested, and might have to be tested in areas of overlap between the SKA project around Carnarvon in the Northern Cape and the area granted to oil companies for exploration, should the oil companies fail to cooperate (interview, 2 March 2012).

Map 2. SKA Astronomy Geographical Advantage Area

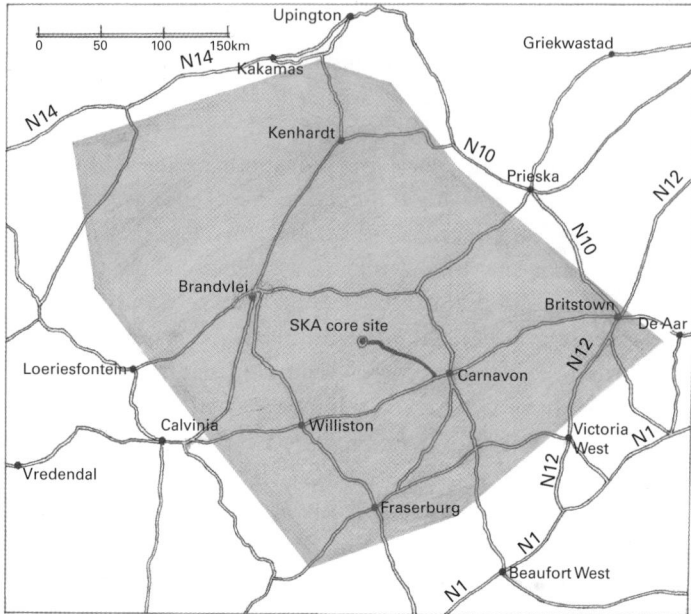

(Source: Square Kilometre Array)

The central astronomy advantage area in the Karoo region of South Africa's Northern Cape province is protected by legislation. It should be noted that Williston and Fraserburg fall within the Western Precinct of Royal Dutch Shell's application for exploration rights to establish the extent of shale gas in the region.

Governance
The decision to allow fracking to go ahead should have been based on wide consultation with interested and affected parties, and should be part of a transparent, rule-based process that is independent of vested interests.

Part of the difficulty is that the 'designated agency' under the Minerals and Petroleum Resources Development Act, the Petroleum Association of South Africa, is responsible for both the promotion of the oil and gas industry and its regulation. The Act should be amended to separate these powers. A clearer mandate covering the regulatory functions should be outlined in the legislation.

There were clearly flaws in the composition of the ministerial task team charged with looking into fracking. Its terms of reference were not transparent, and it failed to include representation from relevant departments and affected provinces. The team presented its report to the minister, and was considered by Cabinet in August 2012. Having lifted the moratorium on 7 September at the behest of the applicant oil companies, government should now effect substantial changes in the law in order to accommodate fair regulation of the industry in future. The task team stopped short of a fully credible scientific appraisal of the effects of fracking and the moratorium was ended before assessments conducted into fracking by the United States Environmental Protection Agency were published in their entirety.

One of the key limiting factors in relation to fracking is the sourcing of fresh water. As South Africa's current fresh water resources are currently almost entirely allocated, there should be a much more transparent public discourse on how the considerable new amounts of fresh water will be sourced. The National Water Act must be amended to take into account not only the sourcing of the fracking water, but also its management and final disposal, as well as the protection of aquifers and other underground water sources from industrial contamination. The question of whether fracking operations should pay into pollution indemnification funds has to be debated.

Management of hazardous waste is a function designated to the provinces. It will be important to do an assessment of whether the Eastern Cape and other affected provinces have the means and expertise to manage and safely dispose of the considerable volumes of hazardous waste arising from the fracking operations. It is uncertain whether the Eastern Cape can devote sufficient public resources to this function.

The regulatory agency, the Petroleum Agency of South Africa, currently also has responsibility for the promotion of oil and gas. These functions should be separated to prevent a broad conflict of interest.

Government has set aside a period of six to twelve months in order to strengthen the regulatory apparatus necessary for fracking, but most experience of legislative change in South Africa shows that this requires considerably more time.

Monitoring

In order to regulate the industry and protect the environment from some of the potential dangers, South Africa must put in place a system of robust and independent monitoring. To date the country has no independent expertise on fracking or its effects. There is insufficient hydrological or geohydrological research. There is no ability to test whether fracking chemicals are polluting subsurface water or affecting public health. Professor Maarten de Wit (2011: 6), writing in the *South African Journal of Science*, emphasises this lack of local expertise:

> There is no national instrument pool to monitor seismic pulses related to fracking, and a severe lack of academic training of geophysicists to use such instruments and interpret the data; we cannot undertake rare gas analyses to monitor leakage; and we barely have a minimum laboratory capacity in the way of isotopic fingerprinting of methane or radiogenic isotopes. Add to that the fact that our academic and research institutions do no work at the cutting edge of this rapidly evolving science and technology: we lack the capacity to gather the empirical data and to evaluate the potential for techniques like hydraulic fracturing to effect contamination of underground sources of drinking water from injection of hydraulic fracturing fluids into gas shale

wells, or its potential effects on astronomical observatories. This requires a new phase of Science and Technology investment.

It is ironic that one of the factors used to justify extraction of shale gas, the development of energy security (that is, independence), is likely to make the country even more dependent on foreign investment, science research and expertise. No thought has been given in official circles to technology transfer or the localisation of such skills.

OPPOSITION BUILDS

Propelled by the applications for exploration rights, a new opposition movement quickly arose during 2011. It includes a number of campaigns, principal of which is the Treasure the Karoo Action Group (TKAG). It has placed resources in public outreach, research, and legal interventions. It has gained an extensive following through the use of traditional and social media, and its membership consists of residents of both the Karoo and the large cities. It has made links with other sympathetic campaigns and NGOs, but remains the main civil society organisation speaking out against fracking. Other campaigns include the Knysna-based Fractual (www.fractual.co.za) and the Karoo Anti Hydraulic Fracturing Action Network (www.kahfan.blogspot.com).

Public meetings have attracted a great deal of interest, and have seen interventions opposing fracking from personalities such as entrepreneur Johann Rupert, polar swimmer Lewis Pugh, entertainer David Kramer and Hollywood actor Mark Ruffalo. Marches in Cape Town have been well attended, and the movement has generated a plethora of posters, T-shirts, leaflets and considerable media attention (interview with TKAG coordinator Jonathan Deal and researcher Jeanie le Roux, Cape Town, 7 November 2011). TKAG has formed an alliance with the US campaign Water Defense, led by Ruffalo, and locally with the Wilderness Foundation and the Endangered Wildlife Trust.

TKAG has a backup team of legal and communications professionals that put together a comprehensive response document to the Environmental Management Report issued by Shell (Golder 2011; Havemann et al. 2011). The team also challenged claims in advertisements placed in the country's major newspapers by Shell in April 2011 by appealing to the Advertising Standards Authority (ASA). The Authority ruled in July that the claims were 'unsubstantiated and misleading' and ordered Shell to withdraw the advertisements (*The Media Online*, 2011). The legal team also initiated litigation under the Promotion of Access to Information Act to challenge mining minister Shabangu, who had failed to reveal information about the government task team she had established to research fracking. The minister had appointed officials from the Petroleum Agency and the Council for Geosciences, as well as the departments of Mineral Resources, Science and Technology, Energy, Water and Environmental Affairs to serve on the team; however, she had neglected to include representatives from the departments of Tourism, Health, Economic Development, Rural Development, Trade and Industry, or Agriculture. There was no transparency about whom the team had consulted or what research it was reviewing, and no clarity on the team's terms of reference. The former TKAG lawyer Dr Luke Havemann stated that 'unfortunately any report that the task team may eventually produce will be tainted by their failure to play open cards' (*Cape Times*, 5 August 2011). The North Gauteng High Court ordered the minister to respond to TKAG's request for information by 31 January 2012 (Samodien 2012).

Opposition has also developed within commercial agriculture. Dougie Stern farms in the Murraysburg district, in the area Shell plans to frack. With fellow farmer Lukie Strydom, Steyn was sponsored by BKB (a former farmers' cooperative that markets wool and livestock) to investigate fracking in the United States. The two of them returned as convinced opponents, and have been mobilising other members of the farming community. Steyn is an office bearer of Agri-Eastern Cape and has been organising anti-fracking resolutions to be passed at provincial and Agri-SA conferences. Steyn rejects the claim that shale gas could be a bridging fuel and believes that government should speed up its support for renewables rather than letting oil and gas companies exploit fossil fuels (interview, Rietpoort farm, Murraysburg, 18 October 2011).

The Southern Cape Land Committee has been working to sensitise farm workers to the likely effects of fracking. Organisers Amos Dyasi and Nettly Maarman report that farm workers have opposed fracking because most of the jobs will not go to local people, and because fracking could destroy existing jobs on farms (interview, Graaff-Reinet, 20 October 2011).

The Centre for Environmental Rights and the Western Cape branch of the Wildlife and Environment Society of South Africa conducted workshops with seventeen Karoo communities on the question of fracking during June 2011 (telephonic interview, Andy Gubb, 18 September 2011). Numerous campaigns demonstrated on 22 September 2012 outside Parliament in Cape Town to mark Global Anti Fracking Day. In Prince Albert, in the Karoo, businesses and homes displayed wreaths with black ribbons, and residents wrapped bands of black material around the trees in Church Street 'to mourn the destruction of the Karoo habitat' (*Prince Albert Friend*, 2012).

Poverty and social inequity

The Karoo, and the Eastern Cape in general, demonstrate all the contradictions of South Africa with its legacies of segregation, social inequality, racial privilege and dispossession (see Atkinson 2007 on farm labour; Ruiters 2011). On the one hand, fracking may give rise to alliance formation across the social divides, where common resistence to the violation of the Karoo's sense of place and traditional livelihoods might occur. This would require that those in the Karoo who oppose fracking learn to form political partnerships that defy traditional loyalties. Is it possible, despite past divisions, for campaigners to learn new ways to coalesce in a united campaign?

On the other hand, fracking may serve to deepen social and racial divisions. It is argued in some quarters, notably by influential members of the National Planning Commission, that most of the opposition to fracking is being articulated by the privileged 'white' community

(Müller 2012), which has traditionally not shown a great interest in the advancement of others. Opposition to fracking places a demand on solidarity from the black community, and could potentially divide communities further, with oil companies taking advantage of the situation to claim that opposition to fracking means depriving people of livelihoods, opportunities and resources. Already there are attempts to form a pro-fracking forum across the Karoo, bankrolled in part by beneficiaries of black economic empowerment legislation such as former dominee, United Democratic Front (UDF) activist and Western Cape politician Chris Nissen, who has connections with Graaff-Reinet. Forum coordinator Vuyisa Jantjies has been active in lobbying PASA to grant 5 per cent of the revenues from fracking to communities, and a further 5 per cent to Petrosa, the state-owned petroleum corporation (interview, Graaff-Reinet, 19 October 2011).

Shell has also been active in approaching local black communities in the Karoo to obtain their support and reassure them about job prospects. It has encouraged local politicians to back its position, and this has seen the acceptance of fracking in resolutions passed by some local structures of the ruling African National Congress. As a result, some critical local politicians have in effect been silenced because opposition to fracking is regarded as disloyalty. However, at a briefing by Shell exploration head Jan Eggink, the executive mayor of the Cacadu district municipality, Khunjuzwa Eunice Kekana, rapped the oil company representative over the knuckles because of perceived exclusion of the leadership of the Karoo municipalities from its decisions. 'Nothing about us without us', she averred, and got Eggink to admit that local job opportunities would be scarce during the initial three-year exploration phase, once the moratorium has been lifted. In response, Kekana was reported to have said: 'The Karoo is not just about jobs. It is the site of important agro-industries like sheep, ostriches and angora goats, all of which are 100 per cent dependent on outstanding water resources' (Janeke 2012). More recent anti-fracking rallies in Nieu-Bethesda in the Karoo have seen a convergence of black and white opposition, with black emerging farmers, farmworkers and schoolchildren joining the anti-fracking chorus. Daniel Vywers of the Sneeuberg Emerging Farmers' Association was quoted as saying: 'Fracking could ruin our future as farmers. We say no to fracking.' Phumi Booysen of the Southern Cape Land Committee said: 'We must ensure this campaign is not seen as one of white people who say "no" to fracking. Black people say "no" also' (Marina Louw, report quoted in Yeld 2012).

Clearly the question of jobs is very contentious. Shell's commissioned study (Twine 2012) claimed that, in the most optimistic scenario, 700 000 sustainable jobs would result from the shale gas industry. Given the evidence in the US and elsewhere, this seems extremely unlikely. Currently the entire coal mining industry in South Africa employs around 50 000 people, and the Econometrix estimate is higher than all those employed in the entire mining sector (Piet du Plooy of Trade and Industrial Policy Strategies, quoted in Njobeni 2012). What is needed is a full livelihood impact assessment that measures job creation and offsets it against job losses that the industry might create in other sectors of the economy.

The question of trust

How do South Africans decide on the most appropriate energy future for their development needs? As yet, democratic spaces for decision making on the adoption of new, controversial technologies have not been fully created. There are no robust regulatory or administrative institutions that could guarantee the public interest and rights to clean energy, a safe and healthy environment, and decent livelihoods. The fracking controversy has shown up this deficit in the democratic order. Will South Africans continue to resolve these issues through administrative procedures and litigation? Instead, there is an urgent need for a more institutionalised space to house a broad, lively, transparent national debate that should occur independently of vested corporate interests.

Meanwhile, the question of trust looms large. Will citizens rely on government to defend the public interest? This seems unlikely, when government is making decisions to favour the technology in the absence of real scientific enquiry. Can the multinational oil companies be trusted? Shell's record in Nigeria has revealed its complicity in the violation of human rights and it has already been caught transgressing South African advertising standards. Chesapeake, originally a co-applicant with Sasol, has had its reputation roundly censured in an article in the American popular press (Goodell 2012). If the country's leaders are serious about the creation of 'green' jobs in a low-carbon economy (*BuaNews*, 2012), why is there such a strong continued state interest in inviting large new investment in fossil fuels?

Sztompka argues that in order to theorise better the array of complex social relationships, there should be a turn towards the 'soft variables' such as trust (1999: 1-17). He regards democratic regimes as embodying greater public trust than autocratic regimes, citing the Polish transition as a case in point. However, he neglects to theorise about the imperfections in democratic regimes, particularly in those where there is a growing gap between citizens and ruling elites. His support for democracy blinds him to some of the predatory behaviour of large corporations relative to the state, particularly in the wake of deregulation, privatisation of former state assets, trade liberalisation and corporate capture of the policy-making process.

If fracking goes ahead in South Africa, a number of measures will need to be taken to restore a minimum of public trust: the establishment of a wholly independent regulator; the passage of a new law dedicated to hydraulic fracturing; strengthening of the environmental assessment provisions attached to the industry; strengthening of the Water Act with respect to the enhanced protection of groundwater resources; the costs of hazardous waste management and the building of access roads to be borne by the fracking companies; full disclosure of the chemicals used by the fracking companies; transparency with respect to the sourcing of water for drilling; no automatic transfer of exploration into production rights; job preferences, skills and royalties need to be localised; full compensation needs to be paid for any damage to human health and the environment, and for the loss of any livelihoods (Fig, 2012). Without such a social contract of rights and responsibilities, chartered before the onset of fracking, there will be no chance for the industry to develop any public trust.

NOTE

1   Thanks to the Taco Kuiper Fund for Investigative Journalism for sponsoring this research.

REFERENCES

Atkinson D (2007) *Going for Broke: The Fate of Farm Workers in Arid South Africa*. Cape Town: HSRC Press.
BuaNews (2012) Rio+20: Zuma Challenges World Leaders, 22 June. http://www.southafrica.info/news/international/rio-220612.htm [Accessed 6 August 2012].
Capel J (2012) Are Mining Profits Ethically Earned?, *Business Report*, 8 February.
Department of Energy (2011) *Integrated Resource Plan for Electricity 2010-2030: Final Report*. Pretoria: Department of Energy, 25 March.
De Wit MJ (2011) The Great Shale Debate, *South African Journal of Science 107* (7/8): 1-9.
Department of Mineral Resources (2012) Report on Investigation of Hydraulic Fracturing in the Karoo Basin of South Africa. Pretoria: Department of Mineral Resources.
Du Toit J (2012) Confessions of a Fracking Defector, *Daily Maverick*, 15 June. http://dailymaverick.co.za/article/2012-06-15-confessions-of-a-fracking-defector [Accessed18 July 2012].
Fig D (2007) Technological Choices in South Africa: Ecology, Democracy and Development. In Buhlungu S, J Daniel, R Southall and J Lutchman (Eds) *State of the Nation: South Africa 2007*. Cape Town: HSRC Press.
Fig D (2010a) *Nuclear Energy Rethink? The Rise and Demise of South Africa's Pebble Bed Modular Reactor*. Pretoria: Institute for Security Studies.
Fig D (2010b) Darkness and light: Assessing the South African energy crisis. In Freund B and H Witt (Eds) *Development Dilemmas in Post-Apartheid South Africa*, Scottsville: University of KwaZulu-Natal Press.
Fig D (2012) Fracking Issues Require New Laws. *Mail & Guardian*, Johannesburg, 10-16 August.
Fine B and Z Rustomjee (1996) *The Political Economy of South Africa: From Minerals-Energy Complex to Industrialisation*. Boulder: Westview.
Food and Water Watch (2011) *Exposing the Oil and Gas Industry's False Jobs Promise for Shale Gas Development: How Methodological Flaws Grossly Exaggerate Jobs Projections*. Washington DC: Food and Water Watch.
Franco J, AM Rey Martinez and T Feodoroff (2012) *Old Story, New Threat: Preliminary Report on Fracking*. Amsterdam: Transnational Institute.
Golder Associates (2011) Environmental Management Plan: South Western Karoo Basin Exploration Application Proposed by Shell Exploration BV: Draft Summary Report for Public Comment from 7 March to 5 April 2011. Johannesburg: Golder Associates.
Goodell J (2012) The Fracking Bubble. *Rolling Stone* 1152 (15 March): 48-55.
Government Gazette (2010) Moratorium under Section 49 of the Minerals and Petroleum Resources Development Act Number 28 of 2002 on Receiving New Applications for Prospecting Rights in Terms of Section 16 of the Act for a Period of Six Months from 1 September 2010 until 28 February 2011. R.768. 33511. Pretoria, 31 August.
Government Gazette (2011) Moratorium under Section 49 (1) of the Minerals and Petroleum Resources Development Act Number 28 of 2002 on Receiving New Applications for Reconnaissance Permit, Technical Co-operation Permit, Exploration Right, Production Right in Terms of Sections 74,76, 79 and 83 of the Act. R. 54. 33988. Pretoria, 1 February.
Greef L (2012) *You Can't Have Your Gas and Drink Your Water: Hydraulic Fracturing in the Context of South Africa's Looming Water Crisis*. Cape Town: Environmental Monitoring Group.
Hallowes (2011) *Toxic Futures: South Africa in the Crises of Energy, Environment and Capital*. Scottsville: University of KwaZulu-Natal Press.

Hartnady C (2012) Environmental Impacts and Geophysical Risks of Shale-Gas Development: Address to the Shale Southern Africa Conference, Cape Town, 26 March. www.issuu.com/erinbosendesign/docs/hartnady_2012_shalesaconference-v120314 [Accessed 23 October 2012].

Havemann L, J Glazewski and S Brownlie (2011) A Critical Review of the Application for a Karoo Gas Exploration Right by Shell Exploration Company BV. Cape Town: Havemann Inc.

Howarth RW, R Santoro and A Ingraffea (2011) Methane and Greenhouse Gas Footprint of Natural Gas from Shale Formations. *Climatic Change* 106: 679-690.

Hughes J (2011) *Life Cycle Greenhouse Gas Emissions from Shale Gas Compared to Coal: An Analysis of Two Conflicting Studies*. Santa Rosa CA: Post-Carbon Institute.

Janeke A (2012) Skaliegas: Shell Skarrel met Antwoorde. *Landbouweekblad*, 8 March.

Johnson K (2011) EPA Links Tainted Water in Wyoming to Hydraulic Fracturing for Natural Gas. *New York Times*, 8 December.

Molewa E (2011) Economic Growth and Climate Change. In Ebersohn W (Ed.) *Climate Change: The Global Commitment*. Johannesburg: Succeed Magazine.

Müller M (2012) Verbal Intervention in Response to Author's Presentation on 'Fracking in South Africa: The Deficit in Democratic Policy Making', Society Work and Development Institute, University of the Witwatersrand, Johannesburg, 18 May.

National Planning Commission (2011) National Development Plan: Vision for 2030, Pretoria: The Presidency, 11 November.

National Planning Commission (2012) National Development Plan 2030: Our Future, Make It Work. Pretoria: The Presidency, August.

NaturalGas.org (2012) Sink or Swim: Water Disposal Issues. www.naturalgas.org/shale/waterdisposal.asp [Accessed 23 October 2012].

Njobeni S (2011) Sasol Decides against Karoo Exploration. *Business Day*, 1 December.

Njobeni S (2012) Scepticism over Shell's Karoo Gas Report. *Business Day*, 7 March.

Palmer E (1966) *The Plains of Camdeboo: A Classic Book of the Karoo*. London: Collins.

Petroleum Agency of South Africa (2011) Petroleum Exploration and Production Activities in South Africa. www.petroleumagencysa.com/Files/Hubmap0911.pdf [Accessed 28 October 2011].

Petroleum Agency of South Africa (2012) Petroleum Exploration and Production Activities in South Africa. www.petroleumagencysa.com/Files/Hubmap09a12.pdf [Accessed 25 September 2012].

Pressley D (2011) Fracking May Test Water Law. *Business Report*, 21 December.

Prince Albert Friend (2012) Prince Albert Protests Against Fracking, September/October: 43.

Ruiters G (Ed.) (2011) *The Fate of the Eastern Cape: History, Politics and Social Policy*. Scottsville: University of KwaZulu-Natal Press.

Samodien L (2012) Minister Ordered to Provide Fracking Affidavits. *The Star*, 10 January.

Square Kilometre Array and Department of Science and Technology (2009) The SKA and the Protection of the Astronomy Site in the Northern Cape. Johannesburg: SKA.

Statistics South Africa (StatsSA) (2010) *Quarterly Labour Force Survey: First Quarter 2010*. Statistical Release P0211, May. Pretoria: Stats SA.

Sztompka P (1999) *Trust: A Sociological Theory*. Cambridge: Cambridge University Press.

The Media Online (2011) Shell Fracking Ad Unsubstantiated and Misleading, 7 July. www.themediaonline.co.za [Accessed 2 December 2011].

Thomas S (2012) The Economics of Nuclear Energy. *Focus* 64, February: 49-54.

Twine T Ed. (2012) Karoo Shale Gas Report: A Special Report on Economic Considerations Surrounding Potential Shale Gas Resources in the Southern Karoo of South Africa. Johannesburg: Econometrix.

Vermeulen D (2011) Views on Hydraulic Fracturing of the Marcellus Shale, Pennsylvania and the Karoo Basin: Presentation to the Geological Society of South Africa, Origins Centre, University of the Witwatersrand, Johannesburg, 23 November.

Williams F (2012) Karoo Hidrobreking: Taakspan Sê Gou. *Die Burger*, 8 March.

Williams R and S Mills (1986) *Public Acceptance of New Technologies: An International Review*. London: Croom Helm.

INTERVIEWS

During 2011 and 2012, interviews were conducted with Prof Doreen Atkinson, Judy Chalmers, Gaby Cheminais, Jonathan Deal, Heather Dugmore, Lynn Dugmore, Julienne du Toit, Amos Dyasi, Liz Fish, Cllr Nyameka Goniwe, Prof Jan Glazewski, Dr Luke Havemann, Vuyisa Jantjies, Derek Light, Jeanie le Roux, Bonang Mohale, Marina Louw, Nettly Maarman, Chantal Marais, Prof Bruce Rubidge, Dini Sobukwe, Dougie Steyn, and Adrian Tiplady. Where cited, dates are given in the text.

PUBLIC POLICY AND SOCIAL PRACTICE

3

Public policy and social practice

Prishani Naidoo

———•———

Although it is not uncommon to hear the view expressed that the South African government has good policies on paper but has failed many times in their implementation, it is less often that we examine the possibilities that such policies might be flawed in their very approaches (that is, before their implementation even begins). The chapters in this section allow us to consider such a possibility in relation to a set of diverse topics, offering detailed accounts and assessments of the evolution of policy (and its relation to concrete practice and lived experience). As we read the accounts of skills development, the state of education and health sector transformation, the politicisation of senior appointments in the public service, and male circumcision, we are able to develop a deeper understanding of the crises being faced in each of these areas of experience and engagement, allowing us to move beyond merely repeating the observation that the state lacks the capacity to implement policy (which it admittedly often does). These chapters draw our attention to some of the major blind spots, points of mismatch with lived reality, and areas of neglect that characterise policies that guide contemporary efforts to address persistent problems and needs.

Stephanie Allais kicks off this section with a close analysis of skills policy, identifying key problem areas, and relating developments in the sphere to international debates with the aim of 'building a conceptual language as well as an empirical base' from which to evaluate South African skills policy. She offers a brief history of skills development in the country, emphasising clear failures of the key strategies adopted in the post-apartheid period, including the National Qualifications Framework (NQF) and the system inaugurated by the national skills levy (levy-grant system), followed by a survey of international approaches (in the 'developed' world) to the question of expanding and improving the vocational skills of national populations. She suggests that at least four major factors contribute to the persistence of low levels of skills in South Africa: economic inequality and job insecurity; a poor school system; 'the tendency of the NQF towards low-level fragmented skill' with 'cumbersome' related requirements; and 'a contractualised provision model which does not provide a framework for building public provision', worsened by difficulties of implementation.

Allais also suggests that certain moves towards greater state intervention in the interest of centralising its different approaches to skills development (noted since 2009) could reflect a shift 'away from the neoliberal notions of a regulatory state, and towards a "developmental state"'. Though she puts forward some evidence of concrete shifts at policy level that emphasise the importance of greater centralisation, a more hands-on role for the state, and the prioritisation of public provision of training (vocational and adult education provided by colleges), she points to ongoing difficulties with the development of curricula and qualifications in the NQF, and admits that the overarching systems and policies governing the colleges remain unchanged. If one considers that much of the recent work of the Department of Higher Education and Training may be viewed as existing within the broader logic of the state with regard to the funding of education more generally, and that the Department continues to support the improvement of skills development in the interests of making a person employable (as opposed to securing a person an occupation, as Allais concedes) when full-time, permanent employment is on the decline, it becomes less easy to think of recent changes in policy as reflecting of a fundamental shift away from a neoliberal approach.

In a related chapter on the state of primary and secondary education, Shireen Motala draws attention to matriculation pass rates 'too low to meet the skills-intensive growth requirements of the economy', and shows that a decreasing number of students actually sit the National Senior Certificate examination. Motala argues that the problem in the sphere of education policy emanates from 'the relationship between poverty, inequality in education and the resultant labour market outcomes which mirror differentials based on race and class in South African society'. Her chapter offers a broad-sweep survey of developments in education, highlighting changes in policy as well as the persistent problems that policy has failed to address.

Motala argues that although policy has been successfully implemented through increasing access to schooling, it has not guaranteed access to a good quality of education for all scholars, with poor (mainly black) scholars often receiving inferior schooling, and high drop-out rates becoming the norm. Hunger, the inability to pay for transport, uniforms, books, stationery and other indirect costs, are some of the difficulties that make the school life of a poor child difficult and challenging. In addition, many of the schools to which poor scholars have access are poorly resourced, resulting in a very low-quality educational experience that often deters scholars from continuing past a particular point. Motala offers a strong critique of the policy that expects some public schools to generate their own income by charging fees whereas some have been declared 'no-fees' schools, arguing that it has resulted in the entrenchment of inequality of access to quality education. Those with money are able to pay for access to better schools and those without money have little choice over where, and how, to learn.

Laetitia Rispel's and Julia Moorman's chapter on health sector transformation is useful not only for its overview and summary of recent policy developments, but also for providing a historical basis from which to think about why it might be that South Africa's health policy landscape has been characterised by so much repetition in spite of the experience of failure. Reading through their chapter, one gets the feeling of déjà vu as many of the so-called reforms seem to repeat much of what came before them. Rispel and Moorman examine and analyse the content of the Negotiated Service Delivery Agreement for the Health Sector, signed by the minister of Health in October 2010, in recognition of continuing problems in the sector, and recommitting government to the four strategic outputs of 'increasing life expectancy; decreasing maternal and child mortality; combating HIV and AIDS and decreasing the burden of disease from tuberculosis; and strengthening health system effectiveness'. Since 2010, then, several policy initiatives have emerged to improve the South African health sector, including 'the re-engineering of primary health care, improving human resources for health', in particular the nursing profession, the compulsory accreditation of health facilities, and the National Health Insurance.

Drawing on data from in-depth interviews with ten key informants, the chapter provides an assessment of these policies, arguing that their effectiveness 'depends on: managing the tension between political priorities and funding realities; addressing existing health inequalities, and the social determinants of health; greater involvement of provincial health departments; and improving the performance of the public health system'. It should be added that the choice by government to adopt a selective approach to primary health care (as opposed to a comprehensive approach) has played a fundamental role in determining the nature and pace of change in the sector by restricting access to resources as well as the kinds of changes that could be imagined. But this is a subject for a chapter on its own.

In any discussion of the success of public policy, the role of political parties and their influence in processes comes to the fore. In trying to ensure that its particular approaches to public policy are upheld, the ANC has sought to exert its own influence and control in the appointment of senior officials in the public service. Vinothan Naidoo offers an analysis of the practice of cadre deployment by the ANC and the widely held belief that such a practice has politicised the public service to the detriment of its capacity to perform effectively and efficiently. Showing first how the ANC's post-1994 appointment policies were driven by notions of correcting the past, Naidoo proceeds to examine different phases of ANC deployment, suggesting a post-1997 shift to more overtly political appointments.

He identifies a tendency towards widening politicisation in the upper echelons of the public service (with resulting 'domain wars' between different institutions of government), and confirms popular perceptions of the negative impact cadre deployment has had, particularly at the level of local government. In turn, politicisation has seriously compromised attempts to improve the quality of the public service (through managerial tools such as 'performance management'), seriously undermining its capacities. Nonetheless, Naidoo warns of the dangers of our becoming fixated on the need for short-term measures to stem the harmful effects of party political abuse at the expense of the longer-term question of how to incorporate the real need for elected leaders to hold the bureaucracy accountable. He welcomes the recent recommendations of the National Planning Commission, which seek to combine a sophisticated understanding of what constitutes a 'political appointment' with recognition of the need for regulation of appointments according to administrative criteria.

In the final chapter of this section Louise Vincent presents an account of traditional male initiation in the Eastern Cape as 'a window into a much wider debate concerning the relationship between culture and rights, between traditional and democratic authority, and between customary and formal law'. With initiation continuing to be one of the most important rites of passage for South African amaXhosa boys to mark their transition into manhood, this chapter raises important and timely questions for a tradition that continues to result in unacceptably high numbers of injuries and deaths in the Eastern Cape (in particular), and that continues to be practised in conditions very different from those of the past. Vincent explains that 'the reproduction of the custom has become fragile and uncertain'. Although the social prescription for boys to be initiated continues, together with forms of punishment for those who do not conform, 'the social networks and foundations upon which that imperative once securely rested, and which served to support it, are no longer in place in many communities', leading to 'a crisis the dimensions of which are multiple including bogus fly-by-night surgeons and lodge operators, widespread reports of alcoholism and drug abuse by initiates along with those practising as traditional surgeons and nurses, under-age boys being abducted into circumcision lodges or taking it upon themselves to be circumcised without the knowledge of their families'.

Attempts by the state to regulate circumcision, as Vincent argues, come up against the claim that anything to do with tradition and culture, such as circumcision and virginity testing, remain under the authority of the traditional leader. Honing in on the contention that the rite of initiation teaches boys 'how to be men', that is, how to take on and meet the responsibilities of adulthood as a man, Vincent shows how the changed social context in which initiation happens can also mean that it is practised without these important life lessons being passed on: the example of the rape of a twenty-seven-year old woman by eight initiates is presented as evidence for this. The chapter provides some analysis of the views of various traditional leaders as well as relevant legislation and the Constitution, grounding these views in an account of other lived experiences of initiates; demonstrating that policy and law related to the practice of male initiation have to take account of the place of tradition and culture in African society; acknowledging its influence and power; and ensuring that all interests are served without the reproduction of inequality of any kind.

Though each chapter in this section sheds new light on an old area of enquiry, together they offer a set of explorations that encourage us to look more deeply into the now old mantra that, although policies and laws might be good, the state fails when it comes to the process of their implementation, to acknowledge that much about many of these policies requires serious rethinking and reworking as the approaches guiding them are not reaping great success. The chapters also, on their own and together, illustrate the need for integrated and interdisciplinary approaches to the study, development and implementation of policy that recognises the important place of culture and tradition, as well as poverty and inequality of access, in determining the nature of problems and their solutions.

CHAPTER 10

Understanding the persistence of low levels of skills in South Africa

Stephanie Allais[1]

A shortage of skills is widely believed to be a major factor inhibiting economic growth in South Africa. Extremely high levels of unemployment are frequently attributed to our poor education system (Bloch 2009) and to the weaknesses of our 'skills development' system (National Planning Commission 2011). Standards of training for artisans and other mid-level skills are low (Mukora 2009), as are the numbers enrolled in vocational and occupational education programmes. The quality of provision is erratic, and throughput rates of the colleges are at a low level (Taylor 2011). The institutions set up through the levy-grant system, the sectoral education and training authorities (Setas) and the National Skills Fund (NSF), have been much criticised. Many employers simply treat the skills levy as an additional tax: although 65 per cent of employers who should pay the levy are doing so, by 2004 only 10 per cent of levy-paying employers were participating effectively in the system (Kraak 2004a). Some blame overly bureaucratic and incompetent Setas, and others argue that employers do not want to train their staff. Setas are also criticised for their ineffectiveness in mediating between training and economic and social requirements, with one weakness seen as the fact that their labour market analysis is based on reports from workplaces and not on research (Erasmus 2009). Public perception, as reported in the media, suggests concern with the large amounts of money in the system, particularly where this has remained unspent, as in the NSF. Corruption and poor governance in the Setas have received copious media coverage.

Has anything been achieved through the skills levy? André Kraak (2011: 98-99) provides one of the few pieces of research arguing that there have been positive achievements:

> The Learnerships system has survived its bad publicity rather well over the past ten years as some of the HSRC 2008 survey results show. Completion rates were 65 per cent, and 57 per cent of completed learners found employment (HSRC 2008a). In a difficult youth labour market, these are extraordinarily good outcomes and they should be embraced and built upon.

His research, an evaluation conducted under the auspices of the Human Sciences Research Council (HSRC) commissioned by the Department of Labour, does not evaluate the substance of the learning programmes or the nature of the jobs found; it argues that in terms of its own targets the system has not been a failure. Another evaluation commissioned by government (Singizi Consulting 2007) suggests that in general the Setas have received better audits than most government departments. Although this is an important corrective to popular perceptions of poor governance, it says nothing about whether the Setas are actually making a useful contribution to increasing levels of training.

With the new Cabinet announced in 2009, a new ministry of Higher Education and Training was created, headed by the general secretary of the Communist Party, Blade Nzimande. Skills development moved from the ministry of labour to the minister of Higher Education and Training, and now, for the first time in South African history, the entire post-school education and training system is in a single ministry, including the institutions surrounding the levy-grant system.

As a powerful political player, Nzimande is much in the national spotlight, and there are inevitably many criticisms of the new Department of Higher Education and Training (DHET). However, with regard to the skills system, initial signals from the DHET have indicated its willingness to grasp the bull by the horns and deal with the problems in the system. Substantial changes, for example, have been introduced to the governance of the Setas. Are the changes addressing the underlying problems? It is difficult to enter this fray because of the paucity of research and empirical data in this area – and also, and perhaps more importantly, paucity of conceptual analysis – which makes it difficult to critique current developments and leads to a focus either on policy minutiae or on corruption, which is inevitably present, and personal politics. This chapter explores South African skills policy in relation to international debates in order to contribute to building a conceptual language and an empirical base from which to evaluate it, and provides some preliminary analysis of recent developments.

SKILLS DEVELOPMENT IN SOUTH AFRICA: A BRIEF HISTORY

In pre-apartheid colonial South Africa, education for the workplace was associated with low-achieving learners and the control of 'social deviancy' (Badroodien 2004). Apartheid vocational education was racialised, low status, fragmented, and separated from the rest of the education system (Gamble 2003). The strongest part of it was the artisan training system, aimed at white men and conducted through state-owned enterprises and the technical colleges (McGrath 1996; Gamble 2004; McGrath et al. 2004). Like the current South African government, the late apartheid state engaged in reform of vocational education as part of a response to increasing economic difficulties. The reforms introduced industry training boards that were given control over administration and certification of training (Gamble 2003; Kraak 2004b). The time-based apprenticeship system was converted into a competency-based one (similar to the reform that was later to be reintroduced by the democratic government, as I will discuss below).

In the 1990s, racially based admissions ended in the college system, resulting in a dramatic shift in the student population in a ten-year period, from 60 per cent white and 18 per cent African students in 1990, to 12 per cent white and 75 per cent African by 2000 (DHET 2009). Many of these students had a matric, and a declining number of them had work placement through an apprenticeship. One reason for this was that the privatisation or corporatisation of state-owned enterprises had led to a focus on the bottom line and a consequent decline in training positions, although Kraak (2004b) points to various other problems with the apprenticeship system. Nonetheless, since the 1980s the colleges had provided a way of obtaining a qualification for those who did not complete their secondary education, and the certificates learners obtained could, with the addition of language courses, give them a matric certificate, albeit at what was then known as 'standard grade'.

After the first democratic elections, a Ministry of Education was put in charge of schools, adult education, colleges and universities, and a Ministry of Labour in charge of 'skills development'. The Department of Labour introduced a levy-grant system through which employers were taxed 1 per cent of their payroll. This enabled the creation of the Setas to replace the old industry training boards. The Setas were set up in different areas of the economy, with two broad areas of work. The first, which was intended to create an incentive for employers to train and also to develop a picture of the training needs of each sector, was the distribution of grants back to employers upon receipt of training plans and reports (Department of Labour 1997). The payroll levy is collected by the South African Revenue Service (SARS), which pays 80 per cent of the money to the Setas.[2] Setas can use up to a tenth of it for their operations; they then pay up to 50 per cent back to employers – subject to the submission of various reports – and the rest is spent on discretionary projects.

The Setas' second area of work was the quality assurance of educational provision in their respective economic sectors, although they did not automatically gain this authority but had to apply for it from the South African Qualifications Authority (SAQA) as is discussed further below. The remaining 20 per cent of the skills levy goes to the NSF, which was intended to fund training for disadvantaged groups, particularly the unemployed.

Because the term 'skills' is frequently used to refer to the training that happens under the Setas and the NSF, these institutions are sometimes seen as a sector of educational provision separate from the other sectors: schools, colleges and universities. This is misleading. The Setas are not *providers* of any kind of education or training. The education they support and fund includes programmes in different sectors of the system, through colleges, universities, workplace-based providers, and private (for-profit and not-for-profit) providers. The logic behind the arrangement was that all education providers, both public and private, could offer courses as part of the skills development strategy, under the overarching National Qualifications Framework (NQF).

Introduced in 1995, the NQF was intended to replace all existing qualifications with a set of new outcomes-based qualifications and part qualifications (unit standards) designed by new stakeholder-based structures (Republic of South Africa 1995; SAQA 2000a; 2000b). The new qualifications and unit standards would be registered by the SAQA on the NQF. This was intended to change *all* learning programmes and curricula, at all levels, in all sectors.

Together the NQF and the skills development strategy were supposed to lead to 'a demand-led enterprise training policy ... underpinned by appropriate supply-side measures'. The NQF and the skills development strategy were seen as policies that would enable and support educational institutions to develop new relevant qualifications. They were also intended to make it easier for new educational institutions to be created, and to enable people to get qualifications based on their existing knowledge and skills. Employers and union representatives would be involved in defining the learning outcomes required in their respective industries to ensure that the programmes provided by education institutions were appropriate. The learning outcomes would be captured in qualifications and unit standards and registered on the NQF. There would be no prescribed curricula. All educational providers would apply to quality assurance bodies to be accredited to offer or to assess specific qualifications and unit standards; they would then develop their own curricula and assessments. Quality assurance bodies would be accredited by SAQA. Assessors would be 'registered' by quality assurance bodies, to assess specific unit standards and qualifications.

The Department of Labour announced that the apprenticeship system would be entirely replaced by a new system of 'learnerships', using newly developed outcomes-based national qualifications registered on the NQF. This signalled the end of the main courses the colleges had historically taught, known as the 'N' courses. For the colleges, this meant that for the first time they would teach courses other than the theory component of the apprenticeships and, for the first time, they would develop their own curriculum and assessment for these new courses. Some started attempting to be accredited by Setas. The Department of Education then introduced a new qualification for the colleges to offer, known as the National Certificate (Vocational).

The NQF, the subject of extensive criticism, has offered very little evidence of success (Allais 2011a). Through the NQF, many new qualifications have been developed – over 787 – and over 10 000 unit standards have been created. There has, however, been very little corresponding provision: by 2007, 172 unit standards-based qualifications and 2 211 unit standards had awards made against them, to a total of 37 841 and 562 174 learners respectively (Allais 2011a). In 2009, following a long and protracted review process, the NQF and the quality assurance institutions and systems linked to it were substantially changed (Republic of South Africa 2008) and, as mentioned above, the Department of Higher Education and Training was created, bringing the whole post-school education and training system under one roof.

So far, the whole suite of policies introduced in the late 1990s to raise the levels of skills in South Africa seems not to have delivered clear successes. In order to provide some systematic insights into the policies so far, as well as changes that are currently being implemented, I consider below some analysis of skills formation systems internationally.

TYPOLOGIES OF SKILLS FORMATION SYSTEMS[3]

Christopher Winch (2011: 94) argues that in informal labour markets skills are usually not formally recognised, and workers tend not to be classified as belonging to an acknowledged category of skilled labour, 'even when the know-how required to carry out the work requires a high degree of manipulative and coordinative ability that is difficult to acquire, and the task concerned necessitates a low degree of tolerance for error'. 'Skill' is clearly a contested notion:

> As a historical concept, skill is a thundercloud: solid and clearly bounded when seen from a distance, vaporous and full of shocks close up. The commonsense notion – that 'skill' denotes a hierarchy of objective individual traits – will not stand up to historical scrutiny; skill is a social product, a negotiated identity. Although knowledge, experience, and cleverness all contribute to skill, ultimately skill lies not in characteristics of individual workers, but in relations between workers and employers; a skilled worker is one who is hard to replace or do without, an unskilled worker one who is easily substitutable or dispensable.[4]

Notions of skill, as well as skill formation systems, are deeply embedded in different ways of organising economies and societies. This is why:

> … developments in vocational training cannot be understood solely by examining the inner dynamics of education and training systems. They do not acquire their societal significance and their value for companies and trainees until they are embedded in the labour market. In particular, differences in industrial relations, welfare states, income distribution and product markets are the main reasons for the persistently high level of diversity in vocational training systems.[5]

Eliot Freidson (2001) distinguishes between three ideal types of labour markets: those which are 'free', those that are organised bureaucratically, and occupational labour markets,[6] proposing that differences among the three have major implications for successful training programmes. Literature in the developed world suggests that there are two main types of skill formation systems, which correspond with differently organised labour markets (Brockmann 2011, drawing on Rauner 2007). The first type is vocational education and training focused on education for an occupation, as is exemplified by the German dual system. Here, vocational education and training aims to develop vocational competence and identity for labour markets that have characteristics that correspond to Freidson's notions of occupational and bureaucratic labour markets. An occupation is a formally recognised social category, with regulations for qualifications, promotion, and the range of knowledge (theoretical and practical) required. The employment relationship is a long-term one, which makes it possible for it to be founded on broad abilities: an understanding of the entire work process and of the wider industry and an integration of manual and intellectual tasks, in order to be able to plan, execute, and evaluate, and not merely carry out narrowly specified tasks. Vocational education 'is provided through comprehensive programmes that are part of the national education system and thus constitute the continuation of 'education' (commonly based on a curriculum, with a broad content) rather than 'training' as more narrowly focused on the labour market and the job' (Clarke 2011: 108).

The second type of skill formation system is aimed at 'employability' in a labour market that corresponds more closely with Freidson's notion of a 'free labour market', especially at lower levels, although of course it is not completely free (for example, the countries that have this type of skill formation systems have immigration controls[7]). This model relies on a 'market of qualifications' that is supposed to support 'individuals to enhance their employability through continuing vocational education or certification of sets of competencies acquired either through work experience or modularised courses' (Brockmann 2011: 120-121). Typical of this model are weak relationships between vocational education, regulated through the 'market of qualifications', and the workplace, because work is not organised through regulated occupations; instead, 'modularised systems of certification function as regulatory frameworks for the recognition and accumulation of skills that are largely independent from each other and disconnected from genuine work contexts' (Rauner 2007: 118).

These two models can be mapped onto the two main types of capitalist systems described by the 'varieties of capitalism' literature: coordinated market economies and liberal market economies (Hall and Soskice 2001). In this literature, coordinated market economies (for example, Germany, France and Scandinavian countries) are described as resting on multiple mechanisms of institutional coordination, including tight coupling between the financial and industrial wings of big business, collective wage determination, and strong and well-supported systems of general and vocational education, buttressed by the state. Liberal market economies (such as the United States, the United Kingdom, Australia, and Canada) are closer to the textbook model of the unfettered 'free market'.

The former set of economies has changed since this body of literature emerged, and the differences between the two types may be diminishing. Nonetheless, the literature usefully highlights the *relationships* between distinct modes of capitalist production and different systems of social protection, on the one hand, and education and training on the other. The relationships are not coincidental; they are *intrinsic* to the way the different systems are structured. For example, high levels of social protection in the coordinated market economies encouraged individuals to acquire specific skills, supporting a training system that enabled firms to specialise in lucrative international niche markets. Strong provision of vocational education and apprenticeships provided the motivation – for those at the lower end of the achievement distribution – to work hard in high school, thus raising skills at the low end and supporting a more compressed wage structure (Iverson and Stephens 2008). Torben Iverson and John Stephens further argue that in the Scandinavian countries, which they describe as coordinated market economies dominated by centre-left coalitions, redistribution of wealth, heavy investment in public education (including high-quality public day care and preschool), and industry-specific and occupation-specific vocational training lead to high levels of both general skills and industry-specific skills. Spending on retraining allows flexibility in the labour market. The result of this combination of policies is that workers at the bottom end of the skills distribution have specific skills that the workers at the bottom in liberal market economies do not have; they also have better general skills, making it easier for them to acquire additional technical skills. These countries also have high levels of specific skills that support high value-added production in international niche markets; high levels of general skills also support services. By contrast, in liberal market economies, where redistribution of wealth to public schooling and social welfare is much lower, the middle and upper middle classes self-insure by attaining high levels of general education, often through private institutions. Students who expect to go to higher education have strong incentives to work hard. Because vocational education is weak, learners in the bottom third of the achievement distribution have few incentives to do well in school, and few opportunities to acquire skills. Low skills at the bottom end are used in poorly paying jobs with little prospect for advancement. It is difficult for unions to gain bargaining leverage, as workers are easily replaced. This in turn weakens unions, as the incentive to join them is low. Wages for labourers are based on outputs, generally at variable rates (Clarke 2011). The labour process is fragmented into discrete work processes, and employers are interested in skills for the immediate job at hand. Intellectual functions (planning, coordinating, evaluating, controlling) are sharply separated from execution. Training is aimed more at 'jobs' than at 'occupations'.[8] In short, the structure of the economy and the labour market leads to weak vocational education. Subcontracting and outsourcing are a serious problem for work-based learning and the acquisition of qualifications (Brockmann et al. 2011). As Freidson (2001: 87) points out, a free labour market, as opposed to an occupational labour market or even a bureaucratically coordinated one, works against skills development because demand is so fluid that it is 'difficult to imagine many workers investing in training for specialised skills before entering the market'. Guy Standing (2011: 40) similarly asks: 'Why invest in an occupational skill if I have no control over how I can use and develop it?'

The 'market of qualifications' approach is associated with qualification reform and qualifications frameworks (except in the US). It started in England, Northern Ireland and Wales in the 1980s through a framework of National Vocational Qualifications, 'the first national attempt to base vocational qualifications on the idea of competences' (Young 2009: 6). These qualifications introduced a new concept of 'standards', in the form of learning outcomes derived from an analysis of work functions, as an alternative to 'knowledge-based' curricula (Young 2009). The outcomes/competency approach was intended to replace the time-bound apprenticeship system and the syllabus-based curriculum system (Young 2009); the former was perceived by the government of the day as leaving too much control to the trade unions (Wolf 1995; Raggat and Williams 1999), and the latter as giving too much control to teachers, colleges and awarding bodies (Young 2009). The new standards were intended to specify the expectations and requirements of employers expressed as outcomes (Stewart and Sambrook 1995: 98). This was explicitly linked to an attempt by the Thatcher government to marketise vocational education: providers were described as having a 'monopoly' on education, which needed to be broken. Learning outcomes were to be used to ensure that any provider could compete; the learning outcome would be the mechanism for contracting and evaluating their service.

What lessons can be derived from these international studies, focused on wealthy industrialised nations, when considering the developing world? Aid money for vocational education in developing countries has increased in recent years, as has technical assistance from a range of international organisations. The World Bank, long-time critic, has started advocating the building of vocational education systems. With this shift has come a move from traditional notions of building technical skills to a focus on skills as the basis for entrepreneurship. Qualifications frameworks, which are intended to regulate a 'market of qualifications' and give employers more power over vocational education, are being created in many countries around the world. The idea is that government leads the creation of a framework of qualifications, using employers (and other stakeholders) to define 'competences' or 'learning outcomes' that are the basis of the qualifications. Individuals can then choose learning outcomes from this framework, to enhance their 'employability'. The state regulates both private and public providers against the outcomes captured in the qualifications. In developing and middle-income countries this is happening with assistance from UK-based agencies and organisations, and from international organisations.

It is not surprising that policy models in developing countries have been derived largely from the liberal market economies. Developing countries are typically dominated by informal economies, and lack the regulated occupational labour markets and the capacity to implement social welfare that form the foundations of skill formation in the coordinated market economies. Outcomes-based qualifications frameworks and quality assurance systems have immense appeal because they are focused on the regulation of provision, rather than on trying to build and improve the providing institutions, because they lead to 'employability', rather than employment, in a context in which education systems and particularly vocational education are weak and the state has no viable policy to ensure employment for all citizens.

This is also part of the neoliberal policy consensus that has driven development aid over the past decades, positing education as the solution to economic problems, and unemployment as a learning problem to be solved by individuals (Brown, Lauder and Ashton 2011). Government interventions must, according to this consensus, be aimed at supporting and encouraging entrepreneurship: individuals must become entrepreneurs, and institutions must behave entrepreneurially (Marais 2011). Thus, public sector reform such as 'new public management' has forced state institutions to operate 'as if' they were in a market, or to compete in markets, by attempting to focus on 'results' (Hood 1995; Pollit 1998). This leads, not to a 'small' state, but to a state focused on regulation and contractualisation (Hudson 2010), which explains why vocational education systems like those of the UK, which aim to regulate a market of provision through a qualifications framework, lead to a model dominated by a complex array of 'arms-length' state institutions (Keep 2007) – and similarly (as I discuss below) it explains the complexity of regulatory and other arm's-length state institutions in South Africa, with very little actual provision to show for it.

Later versions of neoliberalism (what Ben Fine (2001) calls the post-Washington consensus) admit that markets do not always work, but they still emphasise that the role of government is to improve their functioning (and this logic seems, in many countries, to have prevailed after the recent crises of neoliberalism). Information asymmetries are seen to be a key reason for market failure; the role of government is then seen as improving information flows, to help individuals to make rational choices in the market. Qualifications frameworks operate in this logic: the outcomes specified in qualifications are intended to provide information about what specific training programmes will lead to for 'investors in skills' (people acquiring qualifications). These outcomes are also intended to provide information about what skills potential employees have to buyers of labour (Allais 2011b).

Turning to South Africa, with its fair share of arms-length institutions and of complexity, I suggest three fundamental problems that have worked against raising skills levels.

SKILLS AS SALVATION

Franco Barchiesi (2011:134) points out that the policy view of the poor is '… a Janus-faced creature, constantly lured into laziness and sloth, but also in possession of a natural economic ambition that the state has a duty to nurture and guide'. The first problem with 'skills development' in South Africa is that 'skill' is seen as salvation for poor people, posited as a 'bridge' into a world of formal employment or an enabling factor for self-employment. The problem is that the world of formal employment is tiny, and where employment does exist it often does not lift people out of poverty. This is particularly so for self-employment.

Economic inequality in South Africa is well documented. Lack of industrial policy, and macroeconomic policy focused on attracting foreign investment, has led to deindustrialisation and a shrinking manufacturing sector (Mohamed 2010). The historic and current built-in dependence on cheap labour and on the exploitation of primary resources, and a bias towards importing technology solutions (Marais 2011) are also detrimental to the broad-based development of skills. Economic policy as a whole has not been developmental; as Giovanni Arrighi et al. argue (2010: 435), by 'betting' on capital, the South African government 'forfeited the kind of investments in the welfare of the population (housing, public transport, health and, above all, mass lower and higher education) that would have been key developmental objectives in themselves and may well be the most essential, though by no means sufficient, condition of renewed economic expansion.'

Job insecurity is on the rise, in the context of extremely high unemployment. In 2008, out of the entire workforce of 13 million, 2.7 million did not have employment contracts, and 4.1 million did not have paid leave entitlements. The numbers of working poor have increased dramatically: 'vast numbers of workers earn low wages and do so on such insecure terms and so often without attendant benefits that their jobs do not shield them against poverty. Even formal sector employment is increasingly insecure, wages and benefits poor and less easily distinguishable from informal-sector employment' (Marais 2011: 181). Hein Marais documents how low-skilled workers' real wages dropped by 19 per cent from 1995 to 2003, and those of self-employed people by 62 per cent. In 2005, a substantial portion of workers in the agricultural, service and domestic sectors in the formal economy were being paid an average of R1 012 a month. Almost half of domestic workers earned less than R500 a month in the mid-2000s, as did one third of other workers in the informal sector. And in the formal sector, nearly a fifth of workers earned less than R1 000 a month. Within sectors, gaps between the top and bottom have grown. The average real wage is propped up by small numbers of highly skilled high-salaried workers, and even then the median wage in 2009 was R2 500 per month (Marais 2011).

Debates in the media focus on the alleged inflexibilities of the South African labour market, but Marais (2011: 180) points out that, 'if labour laws were a major underlying cause of unemployment, job growth should be most vigorous in those sectors where the laws have the least impact, such as agriculture, domestic and formal work. The opposite seems to be true.' He also points out that there are so many exemptions to wage agreements that in many cases they are empty shells. Expanding low-wage work would simply put additional strain on already burdened livelihood networks, without adding to net well-being, because wage earners in the middle and lower sections of the income distribution depend, in addition to their wages, on broad networks of support including government grants, top-down subsides from other households, and the bottom-up subsidies provided by unpaid reproductive work within their own household and from other households.

South Africa's social welfare system is the largest in Africa, and considerable by the standards of any developing country. It has done more to provide relief from poverty than any other policy (Marais 2011). But it consists of grants that are targeted and means-tested. Able-bodied people capable of work are given nothing, although they cannot work because there are no jobs. A basic income grant, even at extremely low levels, has been rejected as encouraging a state of dependency.

All these factors, and a school system in which the majority of schools are dysfunctional (Fleisch 2008), are diametrically opposed to the factors described in the literature above which have, in some developed countries, led to high levels of both general and vocational education, with considerable economic and social benefits. It is almost impossible to build 'successful' vocational education in a context of extreme job insecurity and casualisation. It is also almost impossible to develop strong vocational education where learners have very weak general education. Further, a policy focused on self-help and responsibilisation, by presenting unemployment as an individual failure, enables policy makers to avoid addressing structural problems in the economy. Substituting 'skills' policies for social welfare is not only failing to combat unemployment; it is making it more and more difficult to raise levels of skills. This does not mean that there are not specific problems with skills policies or educational institutions – there are many. I analyse two underlying problems below.

LOW-LEVEL COMPETENCES THROUGH THE NQF

Our NQF has entrenched a narrow notion of skills that are really descriptions of task-related activities. This is despite the good intentions of policy makers because the outcomes-based qualification framework model (as well as competency-based training) are located in, and reinforce, a narrow notion of skills. Christopher Winch (2011) argues that the notion 'skill' partly derives from fragmentation of the labour process through casualised, precarious work and short-term work, which is why countries with broader occupational categories tend to use it less often.

The original qualifications framework model, the National Vocational Qualifications in England, Northern Ireland and Wales, attempted to make constantly shifting, job-type specifications, easier to accredit (Winch 2011), which is one reason why it emphasises separate 'units of competence', or 'unit standards' in the South African terminology. The notion of knowledge and competence that underpins this model is very different to the skill and knowledge associated with crafts, regulated occupations and professions. Employer-specified competencies in a liberal labour market tend to be narrow and aimed at the short-term. As King (2012) points out in relation to Indian skills policy, 'demand-driven training' can be driven by 'a massive demand for using cheap, unskilled labour, and training on the job'. The irony is that employer-led, demand-driven vocational education frequently has low labour market currency – in both the United Kingdom and Australia, competence-based and outcomes-based vocational qualifications have weak links with the labour market, and are dominated by low-level qualifications (Winch 2011; Cooney and Long 2010).

This tendency to low-level qualifications and fragmented, atomised skills is aggravated by one of the explicit aims of outcomes-based qualifications frameworks: separating learning outcomes from particular learning programmes or institutions. The combination of low-level fragmented skills and the separation of learning outcomes from particular learning programmes or institutions lead to learning outcomes that are very narrow and over-specified. Perhaps the most extreme example in South Africa is a unit standard containing fifteen assessment criteria for washing your hands! The problem is not one of incompetent people developing unit standards. It is inherent to the model. When the goal is for statements of learning outcomes to provide sufficient clarity to the range of possible users, and when policy requires that learning outcomes must be specified in such a way that these possible users will all interpret them similarly enough, over-specification becomes inevitable (Wolf 1995; Allais 2007; 2010). The result is qualifications documents that are cumbersome and difficult to work with.

As I mentioned above, citing André Kraak (2004b) the late apartheid state attempted to introduce industry-led modular competence-based training into the apprenticeship system. The tragedy is that the logic of the NQF, introduced to overcome the atomised and low-level skills produced by the apartheid system, was in fact the same as that of the apartheid system: reliance on employer-specified competencies and the breaking up of learning programmes into smaller pieces. This is not unusual; as I have pointed out elsewhere (2012) the apparent logic behind employer-specified competences holds so much sway that the assumption of policy makers frequently seems to be that the previous methods for specification of competences, and not the underlying idea, were wrong. Thus, the same policy is introduced to replace itself.[9] There were, of course, many significant differences between the policies of the democratic government and those of the apartheid state – one being that the NQF attempted to apply the qualifications model described above (learning outcomes specified outside of learning institutions as the basis for qualifications against which learning programmes should be developed) to the *whole* education and training system.

The original model of the NQF has been a key underlying problem for the work done by the Setas and for other organisations attempting to offer vocational and workplace-based education in South Africa. Most of the formal education and training system, providers (such as universities, and the school and college system), and the two largest quality assurance bodies (the Higher Education Quality Council and Umalusi, the Quality Council for General and Further Education and Training), did not comply with the learning outcomes and unit-standards model of the NQF, and ultimately, as mentioned above, the NQF was changed. The Setas, which did not inherit a strong and organised system of providers, with built-in traditions of qualification and quality assurance policy, and which relied on accreditation from SAQA for their authority to conduct quality assurance, largely complied with the model of the NQF. Exceptions have largely been Setas that deal with substantial numbers of higher education qualifications. Thus, workplace-based providers, providers attempting to offer learnerships, and as community-based organisations offering any kind of educational programme, have been forced to comply with the new qualifications developed through the NQF, adapting their courses to unit standards. The formal education and training system continued to use their own qualifications. This may be partly why the Setas have come to be seen as a sector of provision: the provision that has happened under them has operated in a particular model that has frequently alienated formal education institutions.

A CONTRACTUALISED STATE THROUGH THE NQF

The quality assurance system introduced through the NQF and implemented by the Setas was based on the idea of provider accreditation and decentralised assessment conducted by 'registered assessors'. The focus was on regulatory systems, rather than on building and developing educational institutions. All institutions, public and private, were to be treated the same: they were to apply for accreditation to offer specific qualifications and unit standards, and to obtain funding based on the number of learners who enrolled for their programmes. Setas, in turn, applied to SAQA for accreditation to be quality assurers. This arrangement cannot but remind us that a regulatory state is not a smaller state, as neoliberal orthodoxy suggests it should be.

The rise of quality assurance has affected all education and training institutions in South Africa. However, it is predominantly providers of vocational, occupational, or adult education programmes that have been forced to comply with the specific logic of Seta accreditation systems, including layers of moderators and verifiers 'quality assuring' the work of individual assessors. In some instances this has applied to providers that were not even applying for Seta funding – donors and even government departments have expected providers to comply with the accreditation system, thereby forcing community-based organisations and non-governmental organisations to offer unit standards-based qualifications in order to be in line with official policy (the irony is that the formal education and training system on the whole has not complied with this policy framework). The upshot is a policy framework that weakens the weakest sectors of provision, with a large and complex regulatory system for a small and weak system of provision.

The main part of the formal education and training system that attempted to engage with the qualifications and quality assurance systems of the NQF and the Setas was the college system. Positioned as the best hope for skills development, colleges were weak institutions placed in a difficult situation. They were expected to participate in the Department of Labour's skills development strategy, and be accredited and funded by Setas to offer qualifications and unit standards. Many tried to participate in this system – no mean feat given that it meant interacting with a range of Setas, all with different bureaucratic requirements. However, this never became a major part of colleges' work, in part because of restrictive regulations under the Department of Education, which was the colleges' primary line of authority (DHET 2012). The Department of Education's policy thrust was at odds with the NQF model. Though institutional reform through the FET Colleges Act of 2006 gave councils substantially increased power (intended to enable them to become autonomous and responsive), the national qualifications, curriculum and assessment system of their main courses remained in place. As mentioned above, when the Department of Labour announced the abolition of the apprenticeship system, the Department of Education developed a new curriculum, and a new national qualification for the colleges to offer, the National Certificate (Vocational), which had a prescribed curriculum and external examinations. Colleges did not have to be *accredited* to offer this qualification but, rather, were *mandated* to offer it.

In other words, colleges have been subjected to two different kinds of logic. On the one hand, college lecturers were supposed to be entrepreneurially minded, selling qualifications, designing curricula and assessment, and navigating a complex accreditation, qualifications and quality assurance system. On the other hand, they were supposed to teach a prescribed curriculum, preparing learners for a national examination, through a state-funded system, managed by the national Department of Education. To complicate matters further, colleges were under the direct authority of provincial governments, due to the semi-federalisation agreed to through the negotiated settlement.

In sum, when attempting to understand the persistence of low levels of skills in South Africa, I suggest at least four major contributory factors. First is the economic inequality and job insecurity that counteract the possibility of long-term and sustained skills development; second are the weaknesses in our school system; third is the tendency of the NQF towards low-level fragmented skills specified in great detail through cumbersome qualification documentation; and fourth is a contractualised provision model that does not provide a framework for building public provision. Exacerbating these underlying problems are implementation difficulties, notably how the very small and weak public college sector has been pulled in different directions by government departments.

IS POLICY CHANGING?

Has the government that came to power in 2009, claiming a shift away from the neoliberal notions of a regulatory state and towards a 'developmental state', been able to address skills policy – which is, after all, centrally located in a neoliberal policy agenda?

Easiest to tackle is the problem of conflicting agendas of different government departments, now that the skills-levy institutions are no longer under the Department of Labour but situated in the Department of Higher Education and Training. This move, of course, does not in itself change the policies and systems that govern the colleges, particularly the funding systems, but the Department has signalled strongly that it intends to change the way funds are allocated to colleges. The first Green Paper released by the Department, which deals with the entire post-school system including universities, colleges, adult education, private provision, vocational education and the levy-grant institutions, signals a vision for bringing the system together into a coherent whole (DHET 2012). In this and other policy documents, the Department has emphasised its intention to direct Seta funding to formal public institutions (DHET 2011a).

Prior to the release of this Green Paper, the Department had already communicated its intent to bring the Setas under greater central control, changing their constitutions to enable the minister to appoint two members of the board, including the chairperson. Amendments to the Skills Development Act, together with the new Skills Development Strategy (DHET 2011a), introduce a substantial step towards a more centralised state, opening the possibility for a more developmental approach, as opposed to the previous arm's-length regulatory arrangements. A ministerial task team on Seta performance was, at the time of writing this chapter, investigating the entire levy-grant system and may introduce substantial changes, but the specifics of the changes were not publically available at the time of writing.

Continuing with the trend towards centralisation, the role of provinces in relation to colleges is in the process of being phased out. The FET Colleges Act gave colleges the power to hire lecturers (although they were still on the state payroll) and proposed amendments to existing legislation will transfer college lecturers back to being state employees (DHET 2012). The apprenticeship system, together with the 'N' courses, has been officially reinstated, and state-owned enterprises have committed themselves to taking on apprentices again (DHET 2011b).

The Green Paper (DHET 2012) discusses ongoing problems with the NQF, and signals the possibility of some substantial changes to it. The difficulty, of course, for this new department is that a whole host of institutions have been created that are now powerful stakeholders – including the Setas and the SAQA. Nonetheless, so far the minister has demonstrated determination to deal with these organisations when necessary, and has faced down one of the most powerful Seta chief executive officers. Although the minister lost a court case challenging his powers to change Setas' constitutions, the changes he wanted were made anyway, after stakeholders agreed to them, and the Seta officials who had challenged him resigned.

Another area in which there seems to be a shift is the model of contractualised provision through the accreditation system. The new skills development strategy emphasises that levy-grant money should be spent on substantial training programmes for artisans, technicians and middle-skilled areas of work, through public providers where possible, instead of the current system dominated by short courses through private providers (DHET 2011a). Setas have lost their authority to accredit providers, and quality assurance is far more centralised, through three quality councils (Republic of South Africa 2008). There is a sense, at least at the level of policy rhetoric, of the need to build a system and to support educational institutions (DHET 2012); an important shift away from the previous model in which public and private providers were all located within the same market of provision. In particular, the focus of the Green Paper is on the expansion and strengthening of public provision that is not part of the school or university – in other words, vocational and adult education offered through colleges. This is currently the weakest part of the system and strengthening it will increase access for poor people. The problem, though, is how it is actually going to happen, and it remains to be seen whether this is merely the politics of desire, offering a long 'wish list' with no institutional capacity to deliver.

There is as yet no concrete *plan* for the massive expansion of the colleges, nor for the creation of new community education and training centres, whereas expansion seems essential, particularly in light of the dire lack of educational provision for people who have passed matric but do not qualify for university, or for people who have not finished school. But even if enough buildings can be procured or built, the reality is that the current system is extremely weak, with very poor throughput rates. What will ensure that the expanded system offers something better? The biggest challenge will be the staffing of new institutions. The Green Paper suggests that universities will be engaged in a massive programme to train college lecturers (DHET 2012), but one of the problems with this is that in many instances universities do not teach the subjects that colleges teach so there is no corresponding disciplinary expertise. Another drawback is that universities have not historically played this role and, with a few exceptions, know very little about the colleges or about vocational education. Further, over the past fifteen years universities have provided massive programmes for teacher upgrading – most of which have had very little effect on the performance of schools (Taylor 2011) for reasons relating to the depth of the crisis in our schools and the inadequacy of short-term training programmes. Although some of the problems in schools may not pertain in the colleges, the inef-fectiveness of these initiatives provides a salutary warning about the role of short-term 'upgrading' programmes. It is conceivable that universities could start to build capacity in this area, and that colleges could also start playing a role in staff development, but this would be a long-term project. Another challenge is that the Department itself will require dramatically increased capacity to manage any kind of meaningful expansion.

Many of the substantive changes introduced thus far predate the creation of the Department of Higher Education and Training, in particular changes to the NQF and the removal of the quality assurance role from the Setas.[10] The apprenticeship system was never formally abolished, and despite the weaknesses of these old courses, it seems that many employers still have more faith in the old pre-1994 apprenticeship system (Marock 2011).

Many policy problems remain. One key problem is lack of qualifications and curricula for artisan training, despite the proliferation of new qualifications through the NQF. The new NQF consists of three 'sub-frameworks', for the three separate educational sectors: higher education and training; general and further education and training, and occupa-tional and trade qualifications. The qualifications framework for the last sector, devel-oped by the newly created Quality Council for Trades and Occupations, has yet to be tested. Current documents emanating from this body suggest a highly contractualised model of operation, with almost every function to be provided by appointed and accred-ited 'partners' (QCTO 2011b; QCTO 2011a). This is contrary to the spirit of the rest of policy coming out of the Department of Higher Education and Training, and may yet change, as this body is very new, with hardly any permanent staff.

If the Department manages to address these problems there will still be limitations on what can be achieved in building a successful vocational education and skills develop-ment system in the absence of a stronger economy and a more regulated labour market. Education policy cannot change economic policy. Doing away with the NQF or, at least, its worst features, will help to some extent, as will streamlining the mandate of the Setas, and improving their functioning. But the attraction of the NQF as policy was precisely the lack of an occupational labour market. It is the structure of the labour market, the nature of industrialisation, and the extent of social welfare that will create the conditions for an extensive and long-term skill formation system. Are these changing? Anthony Butler (2010: 175) suggests that if there is a change at all it is to the right, with a 'reassertion of economic orthodoxy accompanied by a fitful shift towards social authoritarianism'. Government seems absolutely determined not to move away from stigmatised and limited welfare provision, and there have even been signals that current policies are 'unsustainable'.

Perhaps the best the DHET can do in this context is to focus on its core mandate – building and providing education and training, strengthening teachers, and developing curricula that provide general as well as specific skills to learners. All of this requires a long-term view. It also requires considerable support from researchers to build our understanding of the relationship between the state, the economy, and social policy; and our insights into the possibilities for particular types of vocational education and training and skills formation, conceptualising vocational and professional knowledge and improving curricula, and strengthening education institutions.

NOTES

1   I am very grateful to Jeanne Gamble for comments on earlier drafts, and to Carmel Marock for invaluable information and insights.
2   Different rules apply to the public service.
3   This section draws on an analysis that is provided in more detail in Allais (2012).
4   Tilly 1988: 452-3
5   Bosch and Charest 2010, p. 22
6   These are ideal types, which, though not representing the exact detail of actual cases, recognise 'the importance and empirical existence of three mutually exclusive circumstances … One in which a labour market operates without organised constraints and is controlled by the individual decisions of participants, a second organised hierarchically and controlled by administrative authority, and a third organised and controlled by those offering their specialised labour' (Freidson 2001: 63).
7   Indeed, Freidson (2001) suggests that, of the three types of labour markets, the 'free labour market' has the weakest link with empirical reality.
8   The word 'occupation' itself is used in different ways across different contexts. Winch (2011) distinguishes between a restricted sense, usually used in Anglophone contexts, in which an occupation is considered to be occupational standards and series of skills (in other words, a set of related tasks bundled together) and the broader German notion of *Beruf*. The concept of a *Beruf* in Germany structures the labour market, mainly at the level of intermediate qualifications (setting demarcations between unqualified/skilled workers and academically qualified workers), and the vocational education system (Hanf 2011). This organises and reduces competition in the labour market, and protects those who have a *Beruf*. To pursue a *Beruf*, an individual needs a systematic combination of formal knowledge, skills, and experience-based competence, and their deployment is not linked to a specific workplace. *Berufe* are strongly linked to the collective bargaining system as well as the welfare system. It is also part of a broader concept of 'cultivated and qualified' labour, and the idea of dignity in work, as opposed to humiliating forms of work (Hanf 2011: 55).

9   My research into qualifications frameworks in sixteen countries around the world suggests that this
     is a common pattern (Allais 2010).

10   This could be seen of an echo of broader economic policy: Marais (2011) argues that shifts in
     economic policy predate the change of government in 2009: in the 2000s, fiscal parsimony started
     to be replaced by infrastructure rehabilitation and expansion, redrawn industrial policy, and more
     generous social protection.

REFERENCES

Allais S (2007) The Rise and Fall of the NQF: A Critical Analysis of the South African National
     Qualifications Framework. Doctoral thesis, University of the Witwatersrand.
———— (2010) The Implementation and Impact of Qualifications Frameworks: Report of a Study in
     Sixteen Countries. Geneva: International Labour Office.
———— (2011a) The changing faces of the South African National Qualifications Framework. *Journal of
     Education and Work* 24 (3-4): 343-358.
———— (2011b) 'Economics imperialism', education policy and educational theory. *Journal of Education
     Policy*: 1-22.
———— (2012) Will skills save us? Rethinking the relationships between vocational education, skills
     development policies, and social policy in South Africa. *International Journal for Educational
     Development* 32 (5): 632-642.
Arrighi G, N Aschoff and B Scully (2010) Accumulation by dispossession and its limits: The Southern
     Africa paradigm revisited. *Studies in Comparative International Development* 45 (4): 410-438.
Badroodien A (2004) Technical and vocational education provision in South Africa from 1920 to 1970.
     In McGrath S, A Badroodien, A Kraak and L Unwin (Eds) *Shifting Understandings of Skills in South
     Africa. Overcoming the Historical Imprint of a Low Skills Regime.* Cape Town: HSRC Press.
Barchiesi F (2011) *Precarious Liberation. Workers, the State, and Contested Social Citizenship in Post-
     apartheid South Africa.* Albany and Scottsville: Suny and UKZN Press.
Bloch G (2009) *The Toxic Mix: What's Wrong with South Africa's Schools and How to Fix It.* Cape Town:
     Tafelberg.
Bosch G and J Charest (Eds) (2010) *Vocational Training. International Perspectives.* London and New
     York: Routledge.
Brockmann M (2011) Higher education qualifications: Convergence and divergence in software
     engineering and nursing. In Brockmann M, L Clarke and C Winch (Eds) *Knowledge, Skills and
     Competence in the European Labour Market. What's in a Vocational Qualification?.* Abingdon and
     New York: Routledge.
Brockmann M, L Clarke, C Winch, G Hanf, P Méhaut and A Westerhuis (2011) Introduction: Cross-
     national equivalence of skills and qualifications across Europe? In Brockmann M, L Clarke and
     C Winch (Eds) *Knowledge, Skills and Competence in the European Labour Market. What's in a
     Vocational Qualification?.* Abingdon and New York: Routledge.
Brown P, H Lauder and D Ashton (2011). *The Global Auction. The Broken Promises of Education, Jobs,
     and Incomes.* Oxford and New York: Oxford University Press.
Butler A (2010) The African National Congress under Jacob Zuma. In Daniel J, P Naidoo, D Pillay
     and R Southall (Eds) *New South African Review 2. Development or Decline?.* Johannesburg: Wits
     University Press.
Clarke L (2011) Trade? Job? Or occupation? The development of occupational labour markets for brick-
     laying and lorry driving. In Brockmann M, L Clarke and C Winch (Eds) *Knowledge, Skills and
     Competence in the European Labour Market. What's in a Vocational Qualification?.* Abingdon and
     New York: Routledge.
Cooney R and M Long (2010) Vocational education and training in Australia: The evolution of a

segmented training system. In Bosch G and J Charest (Eds) *Vocational Training: International Perspectives*. Abingdon and New York: Routledge.

Department of Higher Education and Training (2009) The Draft National Policy Framework for Lecturer Qualifications and Development in FET Colleges in South Africa. *Government Gazette*, Notice 1194 of 2009. Pretoria: DHET.

——— (2011a) National Skills Development Strategy 3. Pretoria: DHET.

——— (2011b) National Skills Accord. Pretoria: DHET.

——— (2012) Green Paper for the Post-school System. Pretoria: DHET.

Erasmus J (2009) The identification of scarce and critical skills in the South African labour market. In Erasmus J and M Breier (Eds) *Skills Shortages in South Africa. Case Studies of Key Professions*. Cape Town: HSRC Press.

Fine B(2001) *Social Capital Versus Social Theory: Political Economy and Social Science at the Turn of the Millennium*. London and New York: Routledge.

Fleisch B (2008) *Primary Education in Crisis*. Cape Town: Juta.

Freidson E (2001) *Professionalism, the Third Logic*. Oxford: Polity Press.

Gamble J (2003) *Curriculum Responsiveness in FET Colleges*. Cape Town: HSRC Press.

——— (2004) Tacit Knowledge in Craft Pedagogy: a Sociological Analysis. Doctoral thesis, University of Cape Town.

Hall PA and D Soskice (2001) (Eds) *Varieties of Capitalism: The Institutional Foundations of Comparative Advantage*. Oxford: Oxford University Press.

Hanf G (2011) The Changing Relevance of the Beruf. In Brockmann M, L Clarke and C Winch (Eds) *Knowledge, Skills and Competence in the European Labour Market. What's in a Vocational Qualification?*. Abingdon and New York: Routledge.

Hood C (1995) The 'New Public Management' in the 1980s: Variations on a theme. *Accounting, Organizations and Society* 20 (2/3): 93-109.

Hudson C (2010) Transforming the educative state in the Nordic countries. In Jakobi AA, K Martens and KD Wolf (Eds) *Education in Political Science. Discovering a Neglected Field*. Routledge/ECPR Studies in European Political Science.

Iverson T and JD Stephens (2008) Partisan politics, the welfare state, and three worlds of human capital formation. *Comparative Political Studies* 45 (4/5): 600-637.

Keep E (2007) The multiple paradoxes of state power in the English education and training system. In Clarke L and C Winch (Eds) *Vocational Education: International Approaches, Developments and Systems*. Oxford: Routledge.

King K (2012) The geopolitics and meanings of India's massive skills development ambitions. *International Journal for Educational Development*.

Kraak A (2004a) The National Skills Development Strategy: a new institutional regime for skills formation in post-apartheid South Africa. In McGrath S, A Badroodien, A Kraak and L Unwin (Eds) *Shifting Understandings of Skills in South Africa. Overcoming the Historical Imprint of a Low Skills Regime*. Cape Town: HSRC Press.

——— (2004b) Training policies under late apartheid: The historical imprint of a low skills regime. In McGrath S, A Badroodien, A Kraak and L Unwin (Eds) *Shifting Understandings of Skills in South Africa. Overcoming the Historical Imprint of a Low Skills Regime*. Cape Town: HSRC Press.

——— (2011) The Post-school System and Its Contribution to Human Resources Development and Vision 2025. Research Report commissioned by the National Planning Commission.

Marais H (2011) *South Africa Pushed to the Limit. The Political Economy of Change*. Cape Town: UCT Press.

Marock C (2011) Considering Key Themes Relating to the Objectives of the NQF and the Post-school Objectives. Johannesburg: Centre for Education Policy Development.

McGrath S (1996) Learning to Work? Changing Discourses on Education and Training in South Africa, 1976-96. Doctoral thesis, University of Edinburgh.

McGrath S, A Badroodien, A Kraak and L Unwin (Eds) (2004) *Shifting Understandings of Skills in South Africa. Overcoming the Historical Imprint of a Low Skills Regime.* Cape Town: HSRC Press.

Mohamed S (2010) The State of the South African Economy. In Daniel J, D Pillay, P Naidoo and R Southall (Eds) *New South African Review 1. Development or Decline?.* Johannesburg: Wits University Press.

Mukora J (2009) Artisans. In Erasmus J and M Breier (Eds) *Skills Shortages in South Africa. Case Studies of Key Professions.* Cape Town: HSRC Press.

National Planning Commission (2011) National Development Plan. Vision for 2030. Pretoria: Presidency.

Pollit C (1998) Managerialism revisited. In Peters BG and D Savoie (Eds) *Taking Stock: Assessing Public Sector Reforms.* Montreal: Canadian Centre for Management Development.

Quality Council for Trades and Occupations (2011a) A Step-by-Step User Guide Towards Signing a Service Level Agreement for the Development of an Occupational Qualification. Pretoria: QCTO.

———— (2011b) Policy on Delegation to DQPs and AQPs. Pretoria: QCTO.

Raggat P and S Williams (1999) *Government, Markets and Vocational Qualifications. An Anatomy of Policy.* London and New York: Routledge.

Rauner F(2007) Vocational education and training: A European perspective. In Brown A, S Kirpal and F Rauner (Eds) *Identities at Work.* Dordrecht: Springer.

Republic of South Africa (1995) South African Qualifications Authority Act. Pretoria: *Government Gazette.*

———— (2006) Act No. 16 of 2006: Further Education and Training Colleges Act, 2006.

———— (2008) National Qualifications Framework Act. Vol. 524. Pretoria: *Government Gazette.*

Republic of South Africa, Department of Labour (1997) Green Paper on a Skills Development Strategy for Economic and Employment Growth in South Africa. Pretoria: Department of Labour.

South African Qualifications Authority (2000a) The NQF: An Overview. Pretoria: SAQA.

———— (2000b) The National Qualifications Framework and Standards Setting. Pretoria: SAQA.

Singizi Consulting (2007) Seta Review. Pretoria: Employment Promotion Programme, Presidency.

Standing G (2011) *The Precariat. The New Dangerous Class.* New York: Bloomsbury.

Stewart J and S Sambrook (1995) The role of functional analysis in national vocational qualifications: a critical appraisal. *Journal of Education and Work* 8 (2): 93-106.

Taylor N (2011) Priorities for Addressing South Africa's Education and Training Crisis. A review commissioned by the National Planning Commission. Johannesburg: JET Education Services.

Tilly C (1988) Solidary Logics: Conclusions. *Theory and Society* 17 (3, Special Issue on Solidary Logics): 451-458.

Winch C (2011) Skill – a concept manufactured in England? In Brockmann M, L Clarke and C Winch (Eds) *Knowledge, Skills and Competence in the European Labour Market. What's in a Vocational Qualification?* Abingdon and New York: Routledge.

Wolf A (1995) In Torrance H (Ed.) *Competence-based Assessment.* Buckingham: Open University Press.

Young M (2009) NVQs in the UK: Their origins and legacy. In Allais S, D Raffe, R Strathdee, M Young and L Wheelahan (Eds) Learning from the Early Starters. Employment Sector Working Paper no. 45:5-29. Geneva: ILO.

CHAPTER 11

Equity, quality and access in South African education:
A work still very much in progress

Shireen Motala

————•••————

INTRODUCTION

Central to South Africa's transformation from the inequitable system of apartheid into a democratic society that aims to equalise opportunities for its citizens is the establishment of a quality, equitable and democratic education. If schooling under apartheid was deliberately inequitable, and the first decade of democracy was characterised by a dogged if somewhat inflexible drive for equity, then current developments can be said to be searching for more efficient ways of improving the quality of the schooling system, particularly for poor children. Such improvement has been given priority by the post-apartheid governments in an attempt to address the high levels of social inequality and the low skills base. The intractableness of inequality in South Africa is well documented (Taylor 2011; Leibrandt et al. 2009; NPC 2011). The Gini coefficient of 0.67 continues to be high by international standards. Inequalities in schooling show up in labour market outcomes, perpetuating current patterns of income inequality (Van der Bergh et al. 2010).

Access to education is a central pillar in development strategies linked to the Millennium Development Goals and the Dakar Framework for Action associated with Education for All (Unesco 2008). The achievement of universal primary education and the attainment of gender equity in enrolments in low-income countries are seen as essential components of efforts to reduce poverty, to increase equity and to transform people's developmental prospects. These goals are supported by studies highlighting the social rates of return on primary schooling (Psacharopoulous and Ng 1994; Hanushek 2005) and the improved income distribution, economic growth, political stability and better governance that would follow from raising the average educational level of the poor.

South Africa's commitment to the Millennium Development Goals is premised on the right to basic education enshrined in Section 29(1) of its Constitution. Unlike a number of other developing countries, South Africa provides near universal access to formal public schooling up to the end of the compulsory phase (Perry and Arends 2003; StatsSA 2006; Chisholm 2011). Estimates of a gross enrolment ratio of 99 per cent in primary grades and 87 per cent in secondary grades place South Africa above what are seen to be feasible targets for middle-income countries (Lewin 2011). This chapter argues, however, that although South Africans enjoy substantial physical and structural access to schooling, this does not guarantee that learners have equal experience of, or access to, quality education. The specific policy challenge for meaningful access in South Africa is less one of enrolment in formal public schooling and more one of retention, attendance, achievement and completion on schedule for age, all of which will contribute to quality outcomes.

A review of the literature suggests that most learners in South Africa enrol in and complete primary education, despite numerous barriers to success, and even though substantial early childhood education and pre-schooling provision have not yet been achieved. Only a negligible percentage of children of schoolgoing age have never been to school at all, approximately 4 per cent drop out before completing primary school (Grade 7), and 92 per cent finish basic education (Grade 9) (DoE 2008). Girls persist longer than boys through the higher grades, which is not common in some other developing countries. Despite these impressive rates of participation, the actual age of entry is often higher than the official age (DoE 2007), and this appears to reduce the chance of completion and to retard progression through the grades (Anderson 2005; Hallmann and Grant 2004). Certainly, net enrolment rates drop significantly after Grade 3, suggesting that many learners fall behind age-grade norms. In addition, although repetition rates are declining, significant numbers of children take more than nine years to get as far as Grade 9 (Deacon and Dieltiens 2007).

Distinctive features in South Africa are 'school delays' (Hallman and Grant 2004), slow progression (Anderson 2005) and differential and inequitable access to public schooling (Motala 2006). Learning achievement levels, measured through national and international benchmarking tests, are also low (Unesco 2000; DoE 2005; ANA 2010), confirming that many learners with structural access to schools do not have access to the content, knowledge and skills necessary to reach required levels of achievement and competency (DoE 2005; Motala et al. 2007).

The main argument in this chapter is that although there is a high rate of participation in schooling throughout basic education, meaningful access, equity and quality are yet to be achieved, and inequalities in learning outcomes continue to entrench marginalisation and the exclusion of poor communities. Deeper insight into these factors is critical to inform policy making if South Africa is to achieve equitable access to quality schooling within the next decade.

THE POLICY CONTEXT

Despite seventeen years of substantial education policy shifts in post-apartheid South Africa, efforts at improving quality and redressing past inequities have not been achieved and endemic racial and class differentiation still persists (Chisholm, Motala and Vally 2003; Fleisch 2008; Jansen 2009; Tikly 2011).

South Africa has a quasi-federal system with nine provinces, and legislative responsibility for schooling resides with the provincial governments. Of the population of 47.9 million, 79.6 per cent are black African. Just over 15 million children are of schoolgoing age and 12 million learners between the ages of five and nineteen (of whom 49.8 per cent are girls) are at school. School age for compulsory education is from seven to sixteen or up to the end of Grade 9. The schooling system is divided into primary (Grades 1 to 7), junior secondary (Grades 8 and 9) and senior secondary (Grades 10 to 12). Education is the largest category of government spending, at around R61 billion for 2009/2010 (National Treasury 2010: 3), although growing inflation diminishes the real growth of investment in education (Wildeman 2003; Kraak 2007). Moreover, government expenditure on schooling declined from 4.9 per cent to 4.1 per cent as a percentage of GDP in 2009 (DBE 2011a) and the auditor general has noted significant underspending in some provinces (PMG 2011), which shows that the availability of resources is not the only problem. Decentralised governance and poor service delivery also affect equitable access to quality education.

In 2008 there were 26 065 ordinary schools (including 1 086 independent schools) in South Africa, containing 12 048 821 learners in public ordinary schools, 352 396 learners in independent ordinary schools, and 394 225 teachers altogether (DoE 2009: 3). Of these 12 401 217 learners, 30.4 per cent were in the foundation phase (Grades R-3), 25.2 per cent in the intermediate phase (Grades 4-6), 22.4 per cent in the senior phase (Grades 7-9) and 21.5 per cent in the FET band (Grades 10-12) (DoE 2009: 11). Between 2002 and 2006, the attendance of children aged five increased from 40 per cent to 62 per cent, and the attendance of children aged six from 70 per cent to 84 per cent (*Government Gazette* 2010). The government aims to achieve the full participation of five-year-olds in pre-school Grade R education by 2014. The independent or private schooling system occupies about 2.8 per cent of the overall schooling system. Its coverage is now extending to poorer learners in areas where there is insufficient state provision (CDE 2010).

Endemic poverty, however, directly affects the affordability of access to the potential benefits of education (Van der Bergh 2010). Significant income inequality mirrors the race and class divides in South African society (Kraak 2007: 2), with high rates of unemployment, poor conditions of living and poor access to basic services such as electricity, water and sanitation, particularly on the urban fringes and in rural areas (StatsSA

Development Indicators 2010). One indicator of the extent of poverty is that, in 2010, 64 per cent of children aged up to six received a child support grant, with 1.6 per cent also receiving a care dependence grant and 0.2 per cent a foster care grant. Poverty does not necessarily result in exclusion in the basic education phase because, despite the fact that the majority of learners can be classified as poor, the gross enrolment ratio (GER) remains high throughout this phase. But poverty induces hunger, and hunger affects school attendance and academic performance. In 2003, children in 24 per cent of house-holds were always, often or sometimes hungry (DoE 2006b: 21). Poverty and exclusion are also highlighted by the indirect costs of education: uniforms, transport, books, statio-nery and examination costs (Motala et al. 2007; Sayed and Motala 2009).

Successive education ministers have committed themselves to ambitious plans aimed at addressing access, equity and quality, and one of the best-known was the much discussed Tirisano action plan by Minister Kader Asmal in 2000. The current minister, Angie Motshekga, has developed another strategic plan, Schooling 2025, as part of the priori-tisation of education under President Jacob Zuma. Schooling 2025 focuses on ensuring greater throughput for learners in specific grades and with specific competencies, and on early childhood development (DoE Notice 752 of 2010). The plan speaks directly to the need for equitable access to quality education by aiming to improve physical infrastruc-ture, facilitate grade promotion and promote inclusive education and greater parent and community participation. Goal 12, for instance, aims to 'improve grade promotion of learners through the Grades 1 to 9 phases of school', and Goal 24 promises to 'ensure that the physical infrastructure and environment of every school inspires learners to want to come to school and learn, and teachers to teach'. A number of the output goals affirm that quality involves improved literacy and numeracy, and identify corrective measures to achieve them, measures that are similar to those outlined by the Global Monitoring Report of Unesco (2008), and thereby highlighting that South Africa is in line with inter-national developmental priorities in education. At the same time, this 'back to basics' approach, with its increased attention to literacy and numeracy and 'drilling learners in fundamentals' (DoE 2010), is cognisant of local realities and acknowledges that a primary problem has been many innovations that have destabilised the system, coupled with the introduction of policies not appropriate for marginalised groups (Sayed and Kanjee, forthcoming).

South Africans now enjoy near universal physical access to formal public schooling up to and including Grade 9 (Meny-Gibert and Russell 2009; Child Gauge 2008; DoE 2010). Although schooling is compulsory only until the end of Grade 9, the government is constitutionally obliged to make the next three years (Grades 10-12) progressively available as well. In 2003, 92 per cent of fifteen-year-olds completed Grade 9, compared with 78 per cent in 1997. In 2008, the gross enrolment ratio (GER) was 114 per cent and the net enrolment ratio (NER) was 87 per cent. In 2006, over 90 per cent of children aged seven to sixteen and about 80 per cent of children aged seventeen and eighteen were attending an educational institution (StatsSA 2007). Overall gender parity was achieved in 2004, and from Grades 6 to 12 there are more girls than boys at school (Unesco 2008).

However, spot checks (Dieltiens 2008) suggest that real enrolment rates may be 5 per cent to 10 per cent lower. Late entry is not uncommon and significant numbers of learners are overage. Repetition persists, although the age-grade norm progression policy, which permits a learner to repeat only one grade in each phase of schooling (foundation, inter-mediate and senior), has reduced it. Access to post-basic education is severely hindered by high levels of repetition and dropout after Grade 9. Meny-Gibert and Russell (2009), concurring with the findings of the Ministerial Review on Retention (2008), note that the biggest dropout in South Africa is from Grade 10 to Grade 12. Of particular concern is the poor progression rate across all years of schooling, with only 46 per cent of learners who started Grade 1 in 1997 getting to Grade 12 in 2009 (Soobrayan 2010). Related to, though distinct from, these problems of enrolment, repetition and dropout is learners' persistently poor performance in both local and international learning assessments.

Near universal access to largely low quality and poorly managed schools is hardly access at all, and is certainly not meaningful access, which would entail regular atten-dance, appropriate achievement, progress on schedule and successful completion (Lewin 2007). Thus, despite undoubted and substantial improvements in both policy and prac-tice, it can be said that most learners lack access to quality education. Educational access in South Africa is characterised by irregular attendance patterns because of starting school late, repetition overagedness is increasing, and schooling continues to be poor in quality and inefficient in learning outcomes. Put differently, many children are still excluded, or at risk of being excluded, from basic education.

MEANINGFUL ACCESS TO EDUCATION

The fact that most learners of schoolgoing age are at school, but are not learning much, calls for a more nuanced understanding of 'access to education'. It suggests that access must be coupled to additional indicators such as overagedness, repetition and gender if current patterns of participation, inclusion and exclusion are to be properly understood and adequately addressed.

Overagedness is a problem throughout the system, but especially in the higher grades. Overage entry is being addressed by the age-grade norm policy, but an unintended conse-quence is that many learners who should repeat are in fact being allowed to progress, and thus actual repetition is being deferred to higher levels of schooling (Motala, Dieltiens and Sayed 2009). The more children repeat, the more overage they become, and ever more likely to drop out (Meny-Gibert and Russell 2009) and figures from the commu-nity survey of 2007 indicate that there are about 386 000 children who are out of school (Shindler, forthcoming). Overagedness is also related to academic underperformance, exacerbated by difficulties associated with being older than one's classmates (such as feel-ings of embarrassment or being humiliated by a teacher). Another persistent age-related feature of the system is the enrolment of underage learners in Grade 1; indeed, in the absence of specialised early childhood facilities, this might be considered to be a form of pre-school provision.

Gender parity has been achieved and is maintained in enrolments and attendance, but more boys repeat, and fewer girls excel academically – however, these gender patterns mask substantial differentiation in the schooling system, which has a gender bias in terms of boys retention into the FET phase, of curriculum choices, and in the broader social context where girls could face sexual harassment in the absence of safe spaces (ComSS 2008; Dieltiens and Ngwenya 2009). Taylor et al. (2010), investigating Grade 4 learners in a longitudinal study, found distinct socio-economic and gender patterns in repetition; and age appropriateness also has a clear gender bias – more girls are age appropriate than boys by Grade 9 (Motala, Dieltiens and Sayed 2009).

The quantity and quality of the education to which learners have access continue to be a function of demography, race and class. For the majority of parents, who are also poor, school choice does not depend on a school's track record, but is instead based primarily on proximity (although proximity is less persuasive, and perceived school quality much more so, for those parents who can afford higher fees or higher transport costs (Motala and Ngwenya 2009)), and to a lesser extent on social, historical or customary factors such as parents or siblings having attended the same school, or that certain schools serve certain areas, or feed specific secondary schools, or even that a school by (apartheid) tradition has always served a certain ethnic or language group. School choice is further restricted by competition for places in secondary schools, which are fewer in number than primary schools, and especially for places in former Model C whites-only schools, and this shortage and skewed demand also restricts parents' ability to transfer their children to another school at a later stage. Middle-class parents often have valuable skills in school governance, but these skills are lost to township schools when such parents choose to move their children to former Model C schools. A school's official language of learning and teaching also limits school choice, forcing some learners to travel long distances to other schools. Inadequate mastery of the language of learning and teaching is also a major factor in the abysmally low levels of learner achievement; yet many parents prefer (with their children's concurrence) for their children to be taught in the second language of English by teachers who are themselves second-language speakers of English (ComSS 2008; Lafon 2009; Alexander 2010).

Decentralised school governance with greater community participation has been highlighted as one possible way to improve access and quality. Research suggests that parents' voices are not sufficiently heard at school level. Nevertheless, for all parents, discipline, the quality of teaching and care are high on the list of educational priorities. Schoolgoing is highly valued, to the extent of making the best of what one has, or keeping one's child in a school one does not like but which is better than no school at all; but why many parents appear to acquiesce tamely to the poor quality of education received by their children has not been adequately explained (Ngwenya 2008). Evidence from Create, a five-year research programme on education access, suggests that many parents and learners appear to be satisfied with their school and with the overall quality of education

(Luxomo 2011). What is not clear, however, are the reasons, and whether satisfaction is genuine or an expression of parents' resigned acceptance of the limited choice of schools and the few alternatives that poverty permits, or of their own lack of knowledge and of relevant comparative information, or of their unwillingness to contest the real or reputational power of school authorities.

There is increasing debate on how participation is conceptualised and the shift from vigorous civil society participation in the 1990s to the current managerial discourse on participation evident in education (Tikly and Barrett 2009; Stenvol-Wells and Sayed 2011). Parental participation in school governance is 'fairly good' (DoE 2010: 31) but the laudable policy intention of local school governance has not achieved its aim of capacitating and empowering local communities so that they can play an effective role at the school level, particularly in relation to teaching and learning.

EQUITY, FEES AND PRO-POOR POLICIES IN EDUCATION

Although discrimination in social spending has been considerably reduced since the 1980s (Fedderke, De Kadt and Luis 2000), spending inequalities remain because of the high costs required to achieve fiscal parity in education. In the immediate post-apartheid period, there was a strong emphasis on distributing resources through policy and legislation based on equity and redress, but by 1999 the education system was still characterised by 'rampant inequality' (DoE 1999). Under particular scrutiny was whether the gap between rich and poor schools in the public schooling system was closing or growing wider. In particular, a key policy change which has led to much debate is that of fee charging and what is referred to as the 'privatisation of public schooling' (ERP 2002; Department of Education 2003; Motala 2003; Woolman and Fleisch 2006, Sayed 2005; Motala and Sayed 2009). This resonates with international debates on making more explicit the relationships between the state and non-state actors in the education arena (Rose 2006).

The post-apartheid government made an explicit decision to encourage public schools to supplement public funds with compulsory school fees and other private contributions. It was a decision that has elicited considerable comment ever since (ERP 2002; DoE 2003; Motala 2003; Woolman and Fleisch 2006; Roithmayr 2002). Significantly, South Africa's decision to allow fees and encourage a market-driven approach was made in an international context of increasing opposition to such fees, which emphasised that all children should have access to completely free compulsory and quality education (Rose 2003; Daniel 2004).

The argument in favour of fees points out that private contributions to schooling in developing countries are an important financing source for quality inputs; the practical realities of financial constraints require some contribution from households and communities. User fees also release resources for redistribution from wealthy to poorer schools (Fleisch and Woolman (2004) argue that if fees were eliminated it would remove R3.5 billion from the public schooling system – more recent estimates suggest that the sum is closer to R5 billion). Then, the school fee exemption policy ensures the cross-subsidisation of a small number of learners, children of poor parents, who gain access to schools serving wealthy communities.

Opponents of user fees have argued that they are also a source of education inequity (Tsang and Taoklam 1992; Bray 1996). When school fees are added to expenditure per pupil, they result in enormous inequities between schools (Motala 2006; Motala and Sayed 2011). Learners in the wealthiest quintile of schools are likely to receive a per capita combined public and private expenditure that is 50 per cent higher than the per capita combined public and private expenditure in the poorest quintile. Internationally, fees are a major cause of non-enrolment among the poor. In South Africa fees have not limited access to schooling, particularly at the primary level, but although enrolment numbers have not been affected by fees, the pattern of enrolment has. Because fees constitute a benchmark, parents tend to sort themselves according to their willingness to pay. There is a clear recognition, within and outside the state, that there is essentially a two-tier education system in South Africa, one catering for the wealthy (the partly deracialised middle class) and one catering for the poor (which remains mainly black).

To deal with these disparities, the Department of Education made amendments to the South African Schools Act (DoE 2004). Specifically, legislation was passed in 2006 declaring all schools in Quintiles 1 and 2 (the poorest schools) as 'no fee schools'. Do these amendments to the National Norms and Standards for School Funding, which became effective on 1 January 2007, and the no-fee schools policy more generally, signal a more interventionist state policy and a significant attempt at addressing existing inequities?

Previously, all schools were permitted to complement the state school allocation by collecting school fees. Policy changes in 2007 provided that any fee-charging school can now apply to the provincial education department to be declared a no-fee school and by 2009 all Quintile 1 to 3 schools were declared no-fee schools. Resource allocations also differ for different provinces, and nationally determined poverty tables are used to guide school allocations (see Table 1 below). For example, the Eastern Cape is identified as the poorest province, with 34.8 per cent of its learners falling in Quintile 1, whereas the Western Cape is the least poor, with only 6.5 per cent of its learners falling in Quintile 1. The provincial education department targets for each province therefore differ: 34.8 per cent for the Eastern Cape and 6.5 per cent for the Western Cape.

In poor provinces the majority of learners are in the poorest quintile. The Eastern Cape and Limpopo have just over 56 per cent of their learners in the first two quintiles whereas KwaZulu-Natal has 43 per cent of its learners in the two poorest quintiles. Gauteng and the Western Cape have relatively small percentages of their learners in the poorest quintiles, as the average income in these provinces is much higher than the national average.

Much discussion has taken place over whether this policy is in fact pro-poor. Primary interventions, and the greater school allocations for the poorest pupils, are clearly pro-poor. More importantly, the differential allocation is a significant departure from previous policies that focused on equalising state per capita expenditure. It acknowledges that the poor need stronger support.

Table1: Annual determination of no-fee schools for 2007 (DoE 2006)

	1	2	3	4	5	Total
Eastern Cape	34.8 per cent	21.6 per cent	21.0 per cent	11.6 per cent	10.9 per cent	100 per cent
Free State	30.8 per cent	14.9 per cent	20.1 per cent	18.8 per cent	15.4 per cent	100 per cent
Gauteng	10.5 per cent	11.4 per cent	27.4 per cent	27.2 per cent	23.6 per cent	100 per cent
KwaZulu-Natal	24.2 per cent	18.8 per cent	25.5 per cent	17.3 per cent	14.1 per cent	100 per cent
Limpopo	34.0 per cent	22.3 per cent	24.9 per cent	11.6 per cent	7.2 per cent	100 per cent
Mpumalanga	26.7 per cent	20.2 per cent	29.8 per cent	19.9 per cent	13.5 per cent	100 per cent
Northern Cape	26.3 per cent	26.3 per cent	21.6 per cent	14.8 per cent	19.6 per cent	100 per cent
North West	22.7 per cent	15.2 per cent	30.5 per cent	20.5 per cent	11.0 per cent	11.0 per cent
Western Cape	6.5 per cent	23.1 per cent	23.1 per cent	34.6 per cent	34.6 per cent	100 per cent
South Africa	20.0 per cent	20.0 per cent	20.0 per cent	20.0 per cent	20.0 per cent	100 per cent

The introduction of the no-fee schools policy, however, has not been accompanied by adjustments in the provincial equitable shares nor led to the introduction of a national conditional grant. Increases in school funding must be covered by ordinary changes to the baseline allocations of provincial governments. These resources have not been made available as a conditional grant. More attention should be given to the levels of responsibility between national and provincial governments and to the notion of provincial autonomy.

Poor provinces feel much greater pressure on their budgets as they have the larger share of poor learners in the national poverty quintiles where schools may no longer charge fees. The increasing provision of social grants, historical underfunding and backlogs all place increased pressure on an overextended fiscus. To affirm a point made by Dieltiens and Meny-Gibert (2008), one effect of the revised quintile proposal is that it differentiates between poor and less poor and thus introduces the notion of relative poverty. Poorer provinces are limited in their ability to deal with the less poor quintiles.

The South African discourse on the financing of education is not at a stage at which adequacy can be benchmarked (Amsterdam 2006), but questions can be raised about whether the costing per learner is adequate and correctly channelled. A body of evidence emanating from the Education Law Project of the Centre for Applied Legal Studies at the University of the Witwatersrand has consistently shown how the current costing per learner unit is underestimated. Technically, 'no fees' do not amount to no costs for the poor, as costs such as transport and uniforms are not part of school fees and form a significant part of poor households' expenditure (Roux 2003; Wilson 2004; Veriava

2005; Ahmad and Sayed 2008). The Department's own estimates, in its Plan of Action for improving access to free and quality basic education for all, place per learner costs at between R600 and R1 000 annually, but R500 was chosen owing to budgetary constraints (DoE 2010).

Equity and redress, understandably, have been the major drivers for education transformation in South Africa. The extent to which the no-fee school policy can achieve greater equity is an open question, and the challenge is to tackle the deep-seated and endemic inequities in society in general and in education in particular. Unless the overall costing of education, including subventions for no-fee schools, is addressed, the no-fee policy, no matter how forward looking, will not achieve its aim. In particular, the absence of conditional grants and dedicated fiscal decisions to ensure sufficient resources in poor schools may dilute the effects of these pro-poor efforts. Although current research (Gustafsson, 2011) has shown that there has been a reduction of inequality, particularly among poorer quintiles (Quintiles 1 to 3), a new form of differentiation between the poor and the less poor has been introduced. Poor children in Quintiles 1 to 3 may receive additional attention through school nutrition and learner support material, but children in Quintile 4, who may be equally poor, are falling off the pro-poor agenda.

Concerns about adequacy, particularly about the need to ensure that minimum learning resources are available for all children, and about the relation between providing more resources for poorer children and obtaining better educational outcomes, are being eclipsed in education discourse by discussions of the notion of 'no fees'. There are also continuing implementation and monitoring problems, including evidence that allocations through the school funding norms are not reaching schools timeously (Dieltiens and Motala 2011) and questions about changes in school status as a result of municipal demarcations.

It is not clear who safeguards the constitutionality of basic rights in terms of provincial delivery on national mandates. Although recent policy and legislative developments have paved the way for a more detailed plan for new school financing arrangements, much more work needs to be done at the systemic and implementation levels, including the mechanisms of decentralised governance, to ensure the success of this policy.

Describing pro-poor reforms to the education system as 'appearing to be largely ineffective', Van der Berg (2010) points out that personnel spending continues to represent 80 per cent of the education budget, which limits the extent to which education spending can be redistributive. Despite the finance equity reforms that have come to target poor children more accurately, their effect on the quality of education is disappointing. A related issue, then, is that a substantial reduction in income inequality will only be achieved if pre-labour market inequalities, specifically inequalities in the quality of education, are reduced. This has important consequences for social mobility and, as Van der Bergh notes, for addressing the 'socially embedded exclusion' that so aptly characterises South African society.

WHITHER QUALITY IN EDUCATION?

The massification of education in South Africa, with increased access and high enrolments from the late 1990s, has been paralleled by low levels of achievement (Taylor et al. 2010; Motala et al. 2011; Gilmour et al. 2009). International and local assessments of children's literacy and numeracy skills from the early 2000s have provided rich evidence and analysis of the problems of poor quality and underperformance (Reddy 2006; Howie 2007; Fleisch 2008; Bloch 2009). Most recently, the diagnostic report of the National Planning Commission has noted that the quality of education for poor black South Africans is substandard, and suggests that 'the efforts to raise the quality of education have largely failed' (NPC 2011).

Although much of the understanding of quality rests on performance and outcomes, there is broader discussion that locates quality within a social justice approach to education that moves beyond an emphasis on human rights to include other human capabilities such as participation, recognition and redistribution (Sayed and Ahmed 2011; Alexander 2008). Such an approach is critical of and opposed to the dominant World Bank view, which adopts an input-output conceptualisation of quality, focusing narrowly on single factors such as textbooks or teacher qualifications without understanding their complex interrelationships and their contextualised settings, and gives insufficient attention to processes within which learning takes place (Torres 2003).

While cognisance is taken of the above debates, it is important to set the stage in South Africa by establishing the current profile of learning outcomes, and the absence of improvement over time. In the national systemic evaluation of Grade 6 in 2005, learners obtained a national mean score of 38 per cent in the language of learning and teaching, 27 per cent in mathematics and 41 per cent in natural science (DoE 2005). South Africans often score lower than learners internationally, including learners in other African countries such as Botswana, Swaziland and Tanzania (Strauss and Burger 2000; HSRC 2004). Van der Berg (2005) also notes that among these countries South Africa has the highest levels of differentiation between schools in performance in mathematics and reading. More recent data from SACMEQ, the Southern and Eastern African Consortium for Monitoring Education Quality, found no change in reading scores and a little improvement in the mathematics scores in South Africa among Grade 6 learners. Moreover, the learners performed below the SACMEQ mean in both reading and numeracy in comparison to other countries in the SADC region (SACMEQ 2011).

In the attempt to establish its own benchmark, the Department of Education undertook annual national assessments (ANAs), in 2009 and 2011 of all Grade 1-6 classes across the country. The ANAs illustrate and confirm the alarmingly low levels of cognitive performance, how unequal the scores are between schools located in different socioeconomic contexts, and the progressive deterioration in results from Grades 1 to 6. In the ANA numeracy tests, children were unable to perform basic numeracy operations such as subtraction, multiplication and division involving whole numbers, and mathematical misconceptions seem to be shared by teachers and students (Carnoy, Chisholm and Chilisa forthcoming; Taylor 2011). Separately, Pereira (2010) tested a thousand Grade 5 and Grade 7 learners on Grade 4 and Grade 6 mathematics, and found that they performed way below expected levels. Overage and underage learners were the worst. Prior learning for most of the learners was poor.

For those children who do get to matric, the National Senior Certificate (NSC) is still the gateway to either the labour market or meaningful opportunities in tertiary education. The employment and earnings prospects for those with a matric are higher than for those without, and are higher still for those with some form of tertiary education – and even better for those with a matric and proficiency in English (Casale and Posel 2010). In 2011, 70.2 per cent of Grade 12s passed the NSC examination, an increase of 2.8 per cent over 2010, with 51 per cent (or 262 351 matriculants) achieving admission to either Bachelor's or Diploma studies – a positive development.

Concerns remain, however, including the declining numbers of learners sitting the examination, the lower pass requirements for those who achieve a higher education certificate, and especially the low level of pass rates in mathematics and science (only 30 per cent of mathematics learners and 33.8 per cent of science learners achieved a mark of 40 per cent or above in 2011). Such a poor pass rate is considered too low to meet the skills-intensive growth requirements of the economy, especially in science and technology. Poorer provinces continued to underperform in 2011 (Mpumalanga's pass rate was 64 per cent, Limpopo's was 63 per cent, and the Eastern Cape achieved only 58 per cent, whereas the wealthier provinces of Gauteng and the Western Cape achieved pass rates of around 80 per cent), confirming that the education system is producing outcomes that reinforce current patterns of poverty and privilege instead of challenging them. As Van der Berg (2010) notes, these inequalities in schooling outcomes, via labour market outcomes, perpetuate current patterns of income inequality. The dropout or 'push out' factor from Grades 10 to 12 means that large numbers of learners do not get to matric and add to the growing pool of unemployed youth, currently estimated at about 40 per cent. Research on the South African labour market shows that the rate of return to education is higher for matric and beyond (Bhorat and Leibrandt 2001; Keswell and Poswell 2004). The reality, however, is that many of our learners leave school without the requisite skills and knowledge, which will contribute to their further marginalisation and exclusion in a society that values high-level skills and knowledge, creativity and innovation.

The quality of teaching has also come under particular scrutiny in recent research. Many foundation phase (Grades 1-3) educators are unable to adequately teach learners how to read and write (Taylor et al. 2010). Many educators come late to school, leave too early and spend only some 46 per cent of their time teaching during a thirty-five hour week, with most of the rest of their time at school spent on administrative tasks (HSRC 2005; Taylor et al. 2010). The national Department of Education has noted that the poor conceptual and content knowledge of the majority of teachers, along with their low productivity and indifferent teaching practices, are direct contributors to the low levels of learner achievement (DoE 2006a: 6; DoE 2003: 10). Researchers undertaking the Create research in Gauteng and Eastern Cape provinces found very little actual teaching and learning taking place: lessons often start late, much time is spent maintaining order, teachers do most of the talking, and learners are passive and contribute little. The absence of writing and of written work in classrooms was striking, rote learning and the chorusing of lessons were common, and coverage of the curriculum was very uneven (Letatsi forthcoming). In the Eastern Cape there was wide variation across schools in the manner in which textbooks were used in classrooms, and significant differences in the breadth of coverage across the learning outcomes and how the specific content is covered (Venkat 2010).

Teacher recruitment, education, development and deployment, critical to better teaching and learning, are being given increased attention. In 1994, 65 per cent of teachers had a matric plus a three-year qualification; 95 per cent of teachers are now so qualified (DBE 2011a). But despite the improvement in qualifications and a long history of in-service teacher development, there seems to be little relationship to learning outcomes. Questions are raised, therefore, about the quality of teacher education and development programmes. Talks of a social compact to bring all stakeholders on board have taken various forms including the establishment of an accord between the Department of Basic Education (DBE), business and organised labour and the finalisation of a protocol through which teacher unions will be able to provide teacher development. This is part of the thrust by the NPC that education must become a 'societal issue', with the active participation and action of all sectors to contribute to better teaching and learning in schools (DBSA 2009; NPC 2011).

In keeping with global trends, South Africa is paying increasing attention to curriculum delivery, pedagogy and pre-service training, and a focus on more detailed prescription of what teachers should do in their instructional time, which is being implemented through the training frameworks in the Curriculum and Assessment Policy Statements (CAPS). There is also much greater emphasis on accountability and performance management. Critical consideration of many of these laudable reforms and strategies suggests that there is much South Africa could learn from international experience of how to provide better assessment and monitoring (Sayed and Kanjee forthcoming), to invest more heavily in teacher education and in teachers themselves as human resources (Tatto 2007, Torres 2008), and to sustain and develop a professional culture in which teachers see themselves as leaders in implementing the curriculum (Taylor 2011). Many challenges remain. The conflation of race with quality schooling still persists (Ndimande 2005); the diversity of classroom contexts is insufficiently considered, even in the Action Plan 2025; and there is very little oversight of the performance of the schools and teachers on a regular basis. Discipline among teachers – from punctuality to preparedness – must be prioritised, including the need for teachers' unions to contribute responsibly to the development not only of their members but also of the profession as a whole; and government officials at all levels of the education bureaucracy must also show the way, to ensure that policies are implemented and that teaching is delivered. The attainment of quality has to be linked to the broader developmental agenda, because all the evidence points to enduring problems of the quality of schooling provided in poor communities.

CONCLUDING COMMENTS

There is increasing agreement over the problems in South African education, and much better diagnosis, supported by rich evidence, of the extent and depth of these problems. In the more recent research two aspects stand out: the unpacking of the black box of classroom practice and pedagogy, and (an aspect less discussed by educationists) the relationship between poverty, inequality in education and the resultant labour market outcomes, which mirror differentials based on race and class. What is more muted in current discussions is the importance of the schooling process, leadership and agency critical to providing the appropriate infrastructure for effective teaching and learning to take place. Moreover, the technicist approaches to improving numeracy and literacy skills and teacher accountability (more prescriptive texts and performance contracts) may be insufficient in providing effective alternatives to the way out of the education crisis. It has been powerfully argued that South Africa seems to accept uncritically global policy pathways, and there is an urgent need for a stronger insertion of the notions of equity and diversity into the education discourse (Tikly and Barrett 2009; Sayed and Ahmad 2011).

In the welter of discussions about pass rates, marks, standards and assessment in the recent past, less focus is given to the purpose of education, and education as a public good with social benefits above the level of the individual. As Lewin (2011) notes, 'poverty reduction is unlikely unless knowledge, skills and capabilities are extended to those who are marginalised from economic activities by lack of literacy, numeracy and higher level reasoning capabilities'. The symbolism of the clamour at the gates at the University of Johannesburg in early January 2011, of students desperately trying to get into tertiary education, was more powerful than any text. Young people want mobility out of poverty, and education attainment is the key to this. Supply and demand for education must be aligned to generate opportunities for reducing poverty.

Finally, although education is high up on the political agenda in South Africa, and democracy gains will be measured by the social indicators of health, education and welfare, what is apparent is that 'political will is a necessary but not sufficient ingredient for the implementation of reforms' (Little 2011). Little points to the importance of a range of nonpolitical technical factors – technically sound and detailed plans of action at multiple levels, adequate finance and human resources to translate plans to action, involvement and a sense of ownership by administrators near the ground, regular monitoring and evaluation and sustained effort. One of the least successful aspects of South African education reform is the decentralisation strategy of devolved governance which has seen the coordination and delivery of policy efforts from national level falter at the provincial level, particularly in less well-off provinces.

South Africa is often presented as a success story of universalising access, and national planners are working hard to translate the global goals of the Education for All strategies and those of the Millennium Development Goals into targets, indicators and actions. However, unless these universal aspirations take root and ownership on the ground, the effective delivery of quality education for the majority of disadvantaged learners will continue to be unsuccessful.

REFERENCES

Ahmed R and Y Sayed (2009) Promoting access and enhancing education opportunities? The case of 'no-fees schools' in South Africa. *Compare*, 39(2): 203-218.

Alexander N (2010) Understanding Language Issues in the SA Context, RNE/DBE workshop, Pretoria. September.

Amsterdam C (2006) Adequacy in the South African context: A concept analysis. *Perspectives in Education* 24(2): 25-34.

Anderson KG (2005) Relatedness and investment in children in South Africa. *Human Nature* 16(1): 3-25.

Bloch G (2009) *The Toxic Mix: What's Wrong with South African Schools and How to Fix It*. Cape Town: Tafelberg.

Carnoy M, L Chisholm and B Chilisa (forthcoming) *The Low Achievement Trap: Comparing Schools in Botswana and South Africa*. Cape Town: HSRC Press.

Casale D and D Posel (2010) Mind your language: The benefits of English proficiency in the labour market. In Hofmeyr J (Ed.) (2010) *Transformation Audit: Vision or vacuum? Governing the South African Economy*. Cape Town: Institute for Justice and Reconciliation.

Chisholm L, S Motala and S Vally (2003) *South African Education Policy Review*. Johannesburg: Heinemann.

Chisholm L (2011) *The Crisis in South African Schooling and What Government Is Doing About It*. Cape Town: Institute of Justice and Reconciliation.

Deacon R and V Dieltiens (2007) OECD South Africa Country Report. Pretoria: Department of Education.

Department of Basic Education (2011) Annual National Assessments. Report to Basic Education Portfolio Committee. 16 August. http://www.pmg.org.za/report/20110816-department-basic-education-amendments-basic-laws-amendment-bill-b36d.

Department of Education (2004) Review on School Governance: Report of the Ministerial Committee. Pretoria: Department of Education.

Department of Education (2005) Grade 6 Systemic Evaluation Report. Pretoria: Department of Education.

Department of Education (2006a) Monitoring and Evaluation Report on the Impact and Outcomes of the Education System on South Africa's Population: Evidence from Household Surveys. Pretoria: Department of Education.

Department of Education (2006b). Amended National Norms and Standards for School Funding. Pretoria: Department of Education.

Department of Education (2006c) Education Investment Review: Key trends and policy implications. 10: Pretoria: Department of Education.

Department of Education (2008) Foundations for Learning Campaign 2008-2011, Notice 306, 14 March. Pretoria: *Government Gazette* No 30884.

Department of Education (2008) Ministerial Committee Report on Learner Retention in the South African Schooling System. Pretoria: Department of Education.

Department of Education (2010) Action Plan to 2014: Towards the realisation of Schooling 2025. *Government Gazette*, No. 33434.

Department of Education (2010) Education/Treasury Sector Overview. 18 April. Pretoria: Department of Education.

Department of Education (2010) Action Plan to 2014: Towards the Realisation of Schooling 2025. Pretoria: *Government Gazette*, No. 33434.

Dieltiens V and S Meny-Gibert (2008) Relative Poverty in South African Schools. Child Gauge. Children's Institute, University of Cape Town.

Dieltiens V and E Ngwenya (2010) Gender and Access, Create South Africa Policy Brief. Education Policy Unit, University of the Witwatersrand.

Dieltiens V, E Ngwenya and S Letsatsi (forthcoming) What do Learners have Access to? In Motala S, V Dieltiens and Y Sayed (Eds) (forthcoming) Access to What? Exploring Meaningful and Equitable Learning in South African Schools. Create South Africa Book, Education Policy Unit, University of the Witwatersrand.

Fiske EB and HF Ladd (2006) Racial equity in education: How far has South Africa come? *Perspectives in Education* 24(2): 95-108.

Fleisch B and S Woolman (2004) On constitutionality of school fees: A qualified defence. *Perspectives in Education* 22: 111-113.

Fleisch B (2008) *Primary Education in Crisis: Why South African School Children Underachieve in Reading and Mathematics.* Cape Town: Juta.

Hanuschek E (2003) The failure of input based schooling policies, *The Economic Journal* 113:64-98.

Hallman K and M Grant (2004) Poverty, educational attainment, and livelihoods: How well do young people fare in KwaZulu-Natal, South Africa? *Horizon Research Summary.* Washington, DC: Population Council.

Howie SJ (2007) Reading literacy in South African schools. In Kennedy A, I Mullis, M Martin and K Trong (Eds) *PIRLS 2006 Encyclopedia: A Guide to Reading Education in the Forty PIRLS 2006 Countries.* Chestnut Hill MA: TIMSS & PIRLS International Study Center, Boston College.

Human Sciences Research Council (2004) Performance scores in international maths and science study reflective of South African inequalities. Media brief. Pretoria: Human Sciences Research Council.

International Institute for Educational Planning (2010) In search of quality: What the data tell us. *IIEP Newsletter* XXVIII(3).

International Institute for Educational Planning, United Nations Educational, Scientific and Cultural Organisation & Southern and Eastern Africa Consortium for Monitoring Educational Quality (2011) Pupil achievement among SACMEQ school systems. Paris: IIEP/Unesco/SACMEQ.

Kraak A (2007) The education-economy relationship in South Africa, 2001-2005. In Andre Kraak and Karen Press (Eds) *Human Resources Development Review 2008: Education, Employment and Skills in South Africa.* Cape Town: HSRC Press.

Lafon M (2009) The Impact of Language on Educational Access, CREATE Pathways to Access Monograph No. 24. Education Policy Unit, University of the Witwatersrand.

Lewin K (2007) Improving access, equity and transition in education: Creating a research agenda. Create paths to Access Discussion Paper, No. 1. Sussex: CIE.

Lewin K (2011) Making Rights Realities – Researching Educational Access, Transitions and Equity. Create/University of Sussex/DFID.

Leibrandt M et al. (2009) Poverty and Inequality Dynamics in South Africa. In Aron J, B Kahn and G Kingdon (Eds) *South African Economic Policy under Democracy.* Oxford : Oxford University Press.

Little A (2011) EFA politics, policies and progress. Create PTA no 13. Institute of Education, University of London.

Luxomo G (2011) Household and social determinants: Parental involvement and participation in children's education. In Motala S, V Dieltiens and Y Sayed (forthcoming), *Access to What? Exploring Meaningful and Equitable Learning in South African Schools.* Education Policy Unit, University of the Witwatersrand.

Meny-Gibert S and B Russell (2009) Barriers to education. Technical report of the National Household Survey. Johannesburg: Social Surveys Africa and Centre for Applied Legal Studies.

Motala S (2006) Education resourcing in post-apartheid South Africa: the impact of finance equity reforms in public schooling. *Perspectives in Education,* 24(2): 79-93.

Motala S, V Dieltiens, N Carrim, P Kgobe, G Moyo and S Rembe (2007) Educational Access in South Africa. Brighton: Create (Consortium for Research on Educational Access, Transitions and Equity), Centre for International Education, University of Sussex.

Motala S, V Dieltiens and Y Sayed (2009) Physical access to schooling in South Africa: Mapping dropout, repetition and age grade progression in two districts. *Comparative Education,* 45, 2: 251-263.

Motala S (2009) Privatising public schooling in post-apartheid South Africa – equity considerations. *Compare*, 39: 185–202.

National Planning Commission (2011) Diagnostic report. Pretoria: NPC.

National Treasury 2007 Overview of the 2007 Budget. Pretoria: National Treasury. http://www.treasury.gov.za/documents/budget/2007/review/chap1.pdf.

Pereira C (2010) Access to Learning – Mathematics Performance in Schools in Gauteng and the Eastern Cape, Create South Africa Policy Brief No 3. Johannesburg/Brighton: Wits EPU/University of Sussex.

Pereira C and R du Toit (forthcoming) Access to numeracy. In Motala S, V Dieltiens and Y Sayed (forthcoming) Access to What? Exploring Meaningful and Equitable Learning in South African Schools. Education Policy Unit, University of the Witwatersrand.

Perry H and F Arends (2003) Public schooling. In *HSRC Human resources development Review 2003: Education, Employment and Skills in South Africa.* Cape Town: HSRC Press.

Psacharopoulous G and YC Ng (1994) Returns to investment in education: A global update. *World Development*, 22(9), 1325-43.

Republic of South Africa (1996) South African Schools Act, Act 84 of 1996. Pretoria: Government Printer.

Reddy V (2006) Mathematics and science achievement at South African schools in TIMSS 2003. Cape Town: HSRC Press.

Rose P (2003) Community Participation in School Policy and Practice. *Compare,* 33, (1)47-64.

Sayed Y and S Motala (2009) Fee Free Schools – Free and Fair? Create South Africa Policy Brief. Education Policy Unit, University of the Witwatersrand.

Sayed Y and R Ahmed (2009) Promoting access and enhancing education opportunities? The case of no-fees schools' in South Africa. *Compare*, 39(2), 203-281.

Sayed Y and R Ahmed (2011) Education quality in post-apartheid South African policy: Balancing equity, diversity, rights and participation. *Comparative Education* 47(1): 103–118.

Shindler (forthcoming) Access: a district perspective in Motala S, V Dieltiens and Y Sayed (forthcoming) Access to What? Exploring Meaningful and Equitable Learning in South African Schools. Education Policy Unit, University of the Witwatersrand.

Soobrayan B (2010) DoE 2010 Action Plan to 2014: Towards the Realisation of Schooling 2025. *Government Gazette*, No. 33434.

StatsSA (2006) Stats in Brief, 2006. Pretoria: Statistics South Africa.

Stats SA (2010) General Household Survey, July 2006. Pretoria: Statistics South Africa.

Strauss J and M Burger (2000) Monitoring Learning Achievement Project. Pretoria: Department of Education.

Tatto MT and DN Plank (2007) The dynamics of global teaching reform. In MT Tatto (Ed.) Reforming Teaching Globally, Oxford: Symposium: 267-277.

Taylor N (2011) Improving the effectiveness of our schools. *HSRC Review* 9(3): 30-35.

Tikly L and AM Barrett (2009) Social justice, capabilities and the quality of education in low income countries. EdQual working paper No. 18, Bristol: EdQual.

Tikly L (2011) A roadblock for social justice? An analysis and critique of the South African Education Roadmap. *International Journal of Educational Development*, 31: 86-94.

Tomasevski K (2006) The state of the right to education worldwide: Free or fee: 2006 global report.

Torres R (2003) Improving the quality of basic education? The strategies of the World Bank. In ER Beauchamp (Ed.) *Comparative Education Reader*, New York: Routledge: 299-328.

Tsang M and W Taoklam (1992) Comparing the costs of government and private primary education in Thailand. *International Journal of Education Development* 12, no.3.

Unesco (2008) *EFA Global Monitoring Report: Education for all by 2015. Will we make it?* Paris: Unesco.

Van der Berg S (2005) How effective are poor schools? Poverty and educational outcomes in South

Africa. Paper presented at the SACMEQ International Invitational Research Conference, Paris.

Van der Berg S et al, (2010) Low Quality Education as a poverty trap. University of Stellenbosch research paper.

Veriava F (2005) Free to learn: a discussion paper on the school fee exemption policy. In Leatt A and S Rosa (Eds) *Targeting Poverty Alleviation to Make Children's Rights Real*. Cape Town: Children's Institute: 267-291.

Venkat H (forthcoming) Examining 'Opportunity to Learn' in a Sample of Eastern Cape Schools. In Motala S, V Dieltiens and Y Sayed (forthcoming) Access to What? Exploring Meaningful and Equitable Learning in South African Schools. Education Policy Unit, University of the Witwatersrand.

Wildeman R (2003) The proposed new funding in provincial education: A brave new world? Idasa occasional paper. Cape Town: Institute for Democracy in South Africa.

Wilson S (2004) Taming the constitution: rights and reform in the South African education system. *South African Journal on Human Rights*, 20: 418-447. <http://www.law.wits.ac.za> [Accessed January 2008].

World Bank (1993) The East Asian miracle: Economic growth and public policy. Washington DC: World Bank.

CHAPTER 12

Health sector reforms and policy implementation in South Africa: A paradox?

Laetitia Rispel and Julia Moorman

INTRODUCTION

The health of South Africans is poor, relative to the country's economic development and health care expenditure (Blecher et al. 2011; Coovadia et al. 2009). The country is faced with the coexistence of 'explosive HIV and TB epidemics, a high burden of chronic illness, mental health disorders, injury and violence-related deaths as well as a silent epidemic of maternal, neonatal, and child mortality' (Lawn and Kinney 2009: 2). Life expectancy has declined over the past decade (largely because of the HIV epidemic), there is insufficient progress towards the achievement of the Millennium Development Goals (MDGs), and health system performance is sub-optimal (Chopra et al. 2009; Rispel and Kibua 2011). Gender, race and geographical location remain the key markers of social and economic vulnerability and of poor health outcomes (Coovadia et al. 2009). Despite many supportive health policies and significant progress in social service development, stark health inequalities remain between the rich and the poor and between urban and rural dwellers (Harris et al. 2011; Padarath and English 2011).

In response to these problems, the minister of health signed the Negotiated Service Delivery Agreement (NSDA) for the health sector in October 2010. In terms of the NSDA, the four strategic outputs for the health sector are: increasing life expectancy; decreasing maternal and child mortality; combating HIV & AIDS and decreasing the burden of disease from tuberculosis; and strengthening health system effectiveness. Figure 1 shows the linkages between intended health care reforms and improvement in health outcomes.

Figure 1: Linkages between intended health care reforms and improvement in health outcomes

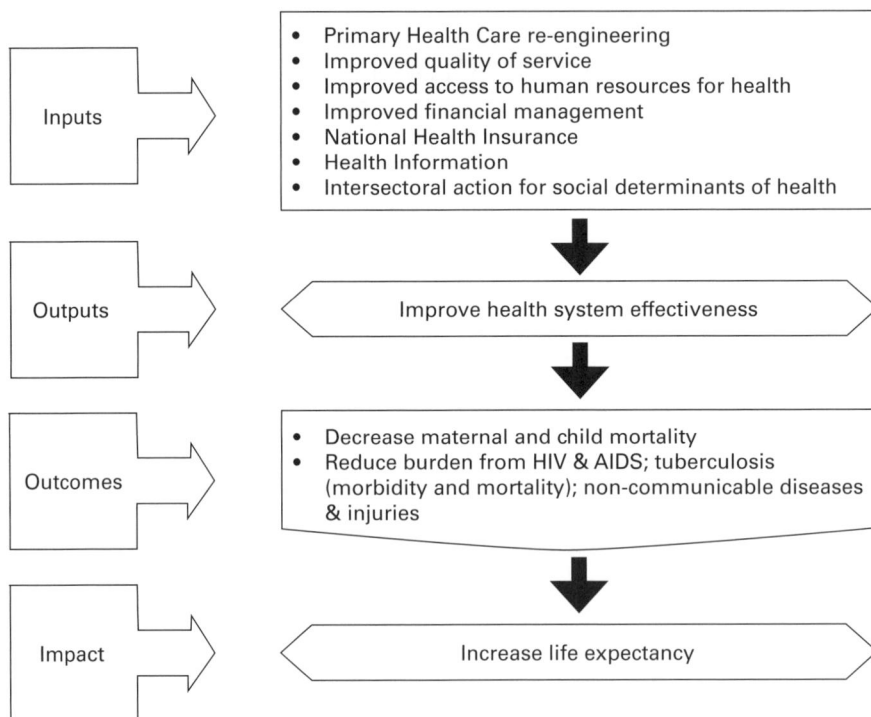

(Source: Adapted from Ministry of Health, 2010)

In the past two years, a number of policy initiatives to strengthen the South African health system have been launched by the national Department of Health. These include the re-engineering of primary health care; improving human resources for health, notably the revitalisation of the nursing profession; the introduction of compulsory accreditation of all health facilities and the proposed national health insurance (NHI) system, the last-named having received the most media attention. As can be seen from Figure 1, these initiatives have their origins in the NSDA.

This chapter is concerned with analysing the content and context of these health sector reform initiatives, the processes, and the contestations around them. The analysis draws on in-depth interviews with ten informants, technical experts or government officials who have a good knowledge of, or have been involved in, the health reforms. Ethics permission was obtained for the interviews, which were conducted during January and February 2012. We analyse the gaps in the proposed policies and argue that the effectiveness of these policies in addressing current health system challenges depends on: managing the tension between political priorities and funding realities; addressing existing health inequalities and the social determinants of health; greater involvement of provincial health departments; and improving the performance of the public health system.

UNDERSTANDING CURRENT HEALTH SECTOR REFORMS

The period since the signing of the minister's NSDA in October 2010 has seen the reintroduction, initiation of, and communication around several health care reform initiatives, the majority driven personally by the minister of health, Dr Aaron Motsoaledi. The key initiatives with which our analysis is concerned are: the re-engineering of primary health care (PHC); the NHI green paper; improving human resources for health, notably an initiative to 'revitalise' the nursing profession; and the establishment of the Office of Health Standards Compliance. Each of these reform initiatives is summarised briefly below.

Re-engineering of PHC
A renewal of PHC in recent years has regained global prominence, in part due to growing inequalities within and between countries, and to a disjuncture between the expectations of citizens on the one hand and the performance of health systems on the other. First enunciated in 1978, the international Alma-Ata Declaration on PHC articulated an overall philosophy, principles and strategies for organising health systems, underpinned by the values of equity, social justice and health as a fundamental right. The main PHC strategies include universal access to good quality essential health care for priority health conditions, intersectoral action at local level to address the root causes of ill-health, and community participation and accountability (WHO 1978).

In South Africa, PHC was embraced at democracy and articulated in both the Reconstruction and Development Programme, and the White Paper on the Transformation of the Health System (African National Congress 1994; Department of Health 1997). Since 1994, several initiatives have been implemented to strengthen PHC and to promote the development of the district health system. These initiatives include: the promulgation of the National Health Act, which formalised the legal status of the district health system; structural and policy changes; removing access barriers through free PHC services and the clinic building programme; and implementation of priority health programmes, such as the cervical screening programme, the expanded programme of immunisation and the HIV /AIDS programme. Successes include increased health care coverage and access for the majority of South Africans, an almost doubling of total PHC expenditure per capita in real terms from R666 in 2005/06 to R1 100 in 2010/11, improved

HIV counselling and testing; and a decline in severe malnutrition and diarrhoea among children under five (Day et al. 2011).

However, many of the early gains and improvements have been compromised by a multiplicity of factors, such as the quadruple disease burden,[1] staff shortages in rural areas, low morale among and sub-optimal performance of health personnel, inadequate management systems and huge gaps between policy intentions and actual implementation (Coovadia et al. 2009; Rispel and Moorman 2010). A critical challenge has been the complexity of achieving a functional district health system. Early documentation on the district health system proposed three governance options for districts: direct provincial responsibility for all district health services; creation of a separate district health authority through provincial legislation; or a local government option with local authority responsibility for all district health services (Department of Health 1997). Because of a lack of capacity at local government level, the third option has not materialised and the majority of districts are functioning as sub-provincial units, rather than as management entities with delegated authority. Hence, the benefits of decentralisation, such as local accountability, community participation, efficiency and coordination of integrated services, have not been realised.

Health outcome indicators such as infant and maternal mortality rates and TB cure rates are poor, and not commensurate with health care expenditure (Blecher et al. 2011; Coovadia et al. 2009). Furthermore, health services remain largely focused on hospital and curative care, quality of care is poor, and financial, infrastructure and human resource constraints have compromised the delivery of effective PHC (Naledi, Barron and Schneider 2011).

The re-engineering of PHC should be seen against this background and is at the core of revitalising and strengthening the health system. It is therefore not surprising that PHC re-engineering is one of the key outputs of the NSDA. The principles of the re-engineered system are: a population orientation to health care; meeting priority health needs in a comprehensive manner; improving health outcomes; a well-functioning district health system; and a focus on the 'upstream' factors that affect health – that is, the social determinants of health.

The three strategies of the PHC re-engineering focus on a proactive approach to accessing households and communities and supporting districts, health care workers and facilities in order to improve health outcomes. The strategies are:

1. Municipal ward-based, multidisciplinary community outreach teams with nurses and community health workers (CHWs) playing critical roles. One community health worker will be employed for every 250 households and they will be responsible for promoting the health of households and the individuals within those households – and will be guided by, and accountable to, communities.
2. Effective implementation of a national school health policy, with one school nurse employed in every school.
3. The establishment of district clinical specialist teams (consisting of medical and nursing specialists) in every district specifically to improve maternal and child health.

NHI Green Paper

Although South Africa spends around 8.6 per cent of its gross domestic product (GDP) on health, this spending is not reflected in good population health outcomes. For example, Blecher et al. have pointed out that 'South Africans could only expect to live, on average, to the age of fifty-one to fifty-five years, twenty years less than Brazilians, who spend marginally less on health as a percentage of GDP' (Blecher et al. 2011: 32). There is a large private health sector in the country that includes health providers (doctors and nurses), private health facilities (hospitals, laboratories), other funding mechanisms such as life and short-term insurance, and traditional health practitioners. The private health sector is dominated by medical schemes funded primarily by contributions from employers and employees. Medical schemes cover about eight million South Africans or 17 per cent of the total population. However, a larger proportion of South Africans use general practitioners and/or pharmacies, with out-of-pocket payments that further disadvantage poor people. In 2009, provincial health spending exceeded medical scheme spending for the very first time, but unacceptable inequalities in health access, quality of care and spending between the public and private health sectors remain acute (Blecher et al. 2011; Harris et al. 2011).

The Green Paper on NHI was released in August 2011 and outlines the intentions to implement the various reforms over a period of fourteen years. The stated principles of the proposed NHI are: universal health care coverage, health care access as a right, social solidarity, effectiveness, appropriateness, equity, affordability and efficiency (Department of Health 2011a). The proposals contained in the NHI discussion document represent the most far-reaching proposal for health financing changes in the country. The objectives of these reforms are to: improve access to quality services; pool risks and funds to achieve equity and social solidarity; mobilise and control key financial resources in an efficient manner; and improve health sector performance.

The Green Paper highlights the links between national health insurance and the other health sector reform initiatives discussed in this chapter: re-engineered PHC services, strengthened human resources for health and the establishment of the Office of Health Standards Compliance. The essential elements of the NHI are shown in Table 1.

The NHI document proposes a single, national fund for health care, thereby pooling risks and funds and ensuring equity and social solidarity. Currently, the delivery of health care in the public health sector is the mandate of provincial health departments that receive a combination of equitable share funding and national conditional grants, whereas medical schemes dominate private sector funding. Contribution to this fund will be compulsory for all South Africans and permanent residents who earn above a certain income level, but details on the fund are lacking in the NHI document.

It is envisaged that the NHI fund will purchase a comprehensive package of health services (that will include disease prevention, health promotion and treatment of disease, including rehabilitation) on behalf of the population, from accredited, contracted health providers that will include public and private hospitals, private general practitioners and district health authorities on behalf of clinics and community health centres. Services included in the benefit package will be commensurate with available resources and will be free for all users of the accredited facilities, with no co-payments (user fees). Health establishments will be reimbursed for the services they provide rather than merely receiving an annual operating budget (such budgets have not, so far, taken into account the volume and quality of services delivered), and the method of reimbursement (not explicitly stated) will ensure efficient behaviour by providers and maximise the efficient use of financial resources.

Initial cost estimates presented in the Green Paper are that the total cost of the NHI will be R255 billion by 2025 (US$28 billion), which needs to be seen against current total health spending. Implementation of the NHI is envisaged to start in the 2012/13 financial year. In February 2012, the minister of finance announced R1 billion for the establishment of ten pilot districts in 2012. The initial phase of NHI will involve testing the new PHC model at district level and strengthening public health services, before contracting with, or purchasing from, private health providers.

Table 1: Essential elements of the proposed NHI

1.	Membership to the national health insurance will be compulsory for all South Africans and permanent residents. Individuals may choose to continue with voluntary private medical scheme membership although there will be no tax subsidies for those who choose to do so.
2.	All employed individuals who earn above a certain income level will make a payroll-linked mandatory contribution to the NHI.
3.	All citizens and permanent residents, regardless of employment or socio-economic status, are guaranteed access to a comprehensive health-care package, which will be free at the point of contact. The content of this package of services is yet to be spelled out and may include some exclusions or co-payments for 'non-essential' services such as cosmetic surgery.
4.	Citizens will be encouraged to use PHC facilities, including accredited private providers, and will have access to disease prevention, health promotion, treatment of diseases where prevention has failed, and rehabilitative services – at all levels of care (from clinic level through to central hospitals).
5.	Population sub-groups with the greatest health needs will be prioritised.
6.	All health establishments (public and private) that render health services will have to meet core quality, service, management systems, and performance standards.

(Source: Department of Health 2011a)

Improving human resources for health

In South Africa there is a health workforce crisis, characterised by critical shortages of all categories of health care workers, an imbalanced skills mix, and unequal distribution between urban and rural areas and between the public and private health sectors. This crisis contributes to sub-optimal health outcomes, and insufficient progress on the Millennium Development Goals (Department of Health 2006; Department of Health 2011b).

The national human resources for health (HRH) strategy was released for comments at the end of August 2011, and was launched by the minister of health on 14 October 2011. In the minister's introduction to the strategy, it is noted that:

> This HRH strategy document is a guide to action. Starting with immediate effect we need to undertake a range of activities, make new policies, develop new programmes, make detailed staffing plans for new service strategies, and manage our health care workforce in ways that motivate them to provide quality health care. These activities need to be undertaken by provincial departments of health, faculties of health sciences, labour organisations, health care managers and professionals (Department of Health 2011b: 7).

The need for a workforce that will ensure the implementation of the health care reforms is explicit in this strategy, which focuses on three themes: the supply of health professionals and equity of access; education, training and research; and the working environment of the health workforce. In addition, there are eight strategic priorities that range from leadership and governance to the promotion of access to health professionals in rural and remote areas. The strategy, like the NHI Green Paper, is a broad statement of key strategic areas that need to be addressed to ensure an adequate supply of health care workers, with appropriate training, the optimal performance of the health workforce, improved access to health care for all and improved health outcomes.

The strategy document highlights a number of human resource challenges: an overall shortage of health care workers in the country with a very minimal increase in the number of health professionals in the past ten years; poor retention of doctors; a gap between public and private health sectors of medical specialists, pharmacists, physiotherapists and occupational therapists; and the poor performance and productivity of many health professionals. Strategies are proposed to alleviate many of these challenges including the creation and training of new categories of health care workers; motivation and retention of the existing workforce; and improvement of the performance of the workforce.

In recognition of the centrality of nurses to the optimal performance of the health system and many of the impending health care reforms, the minister of health spearheaded the National Nursing Summit, which was held from 5 to 7 April 2011 at the Sandton Convention Centre in Johannesburg. Nurses are the largest single group of health care providers in South Africa; some 231 036 nurses are registered with the South African Nursing Council (Department of Health 2011b). It is widely recognised that the challenges highlighted above are even more acute in the nursing sector and this crisis is compounded by an ageing nursing workforce, low staff morale and sub-optimal work performance (Breier, Wildschut and Mgqolozana 2009). The theme of the summit was 'Reconstructing and Revitalising the Nursing Profession for a Long and Healthy Life for All South Africans'. Close to 2 000 nurses and a diverse group of stakeholder organisations, representing all districts and provinces in South Africa, attended. The summit was opened by President Jacob Zuma, and the minister of health, Dr Aaron Motsoaledi, attended every day of the three-day event, which concluded with the adoption of the 'Nursing Compact', a collective call for greater attention, investment and integrated action to reconstruct and revitalise the nursing profession. The key proposals in the Nursing Compact focus on governance and leadership of the nursing profession; nursing education and training; and strategies to improve performance management, support to and working conditions of nurses, within the context of a re-engineered PHC system.

Office of Health Standards Compliance

Quality of care has been a central preoccupation of the government since 1994. The Batho Pele (people first) campaign, emphasising the eight principles of consultation, service standards, access, courtesy, availability of information, openness and transparency, redress and value for money, was a national public sector crusade initiated during the first term of democracy and enjoyed high levels of political commitment. Other government initiatives to improve the quality of public health services have included the development and prominent display of the patients' rights charter, creating enabling environments, addressing staff attitudes through training and enshrining quality of care and service standards in the 2005 National Health Act.

There is, however, a widespread perception (and some evidence) that the quality of care is poor in the public sector and that in some instances it has deteriorated. A 2008 household survey that measured access to health care found that more than half of the respondents (55 per cent) felt that patients at public hospitals are 'rarely treated with respect and dignity' (Harris et al. 2011). The study also found that, among public sector patients, between a third and a quarter were dissatisfied with the overall quality of care received, compared with fewer than 10 per cent of private sector patients.

In response to the chronic quality of care problems, the National Health Amendment Bill tabled in Parliament in November 2011 provides for the establishment of the Office of Health Standards Compliance (Republic of South Africa 2011). Improving the quality of service in public hospitals is one of the preconditions for the NHI implementation and the minister of health has described the National Health Amendment Bill as a revolutionary piece of legislation because it would 'change the way that South Africans see the public health system' (Hartley 2012).

The Office of Health Standards Compliance (OHSC) will be responsible for the setting of standards for all public and private health care facilities and for monitoring compliance with these standards. Health establishments, starting with hospitals, will be accredited every three years. The establishment of the OHSC will ensure that complaints received from health care users or the public are investigated. The Office will also advise the minister of health on the development of standards, norms and quality management systems for the national health system; it will inspect and certify health establishments as compliant with prescribed norms and standards; and monitor indicators of risk as an early warning system relating to breaches of standards.

THE CONTEXT OF HEALTH SECTOR REFORMS

Context, which is important in analysing health reform initiatives, refers to situational factors (a moment in history that affects the intended policy change); structural factors (such as the country's economy); cultural factors of values and beliefs; and exogenous factors (that is, outside the country or health system) (Walt and Gilson 1994). The health care reform initiatives have been informed by numerous interlinked and contextual factors. Although each has a specific context, we focus here on the common factors.

At a political level, there has been increasing concern about research evidence that has shown that, despite supportive policies and health care reforms since democracy, early health gains and improvements have been compromised or reversed in some instances (Coovadia et al. 2009). The evidence also shows that, despite support for the MDGs, South Africa is unlikely to meet the health targets by 2015 (Chopra et al. 2009; Rispel and Kibua 2011).

Following the appointment of Dr Motsoaledi as minister of health in 2009, there was a great deal of political pressure to improve population health outcomes and to improve health system performance. The poor, and worsening, population health outcomes were exacerbated by increasingly negative perceptions of the quality and management of public sector hospitals and a sense of a 'failing' public health sector (Development Bank of South Africa 2008).

In addition, there was a political imperative to improve the image of the Department of Health following the period of intense controversy over HIV & AIDS denialism under the late minister Manto Tshabalala-Msimang. Importantly, in what Ake (1966) called 'charismatic legitimation', Minister Motsoaledi has been able to raise the profile of key health policy issues and ensure relatively widespread support for them at a political level as well as from the private health sector and civil society pressure groups. As one key informant commented:

> Aaron is able to be a champion for the reforms; when he came in [as minister of health] he started looking at HIV prevalence, he was very interested in the maps on HIV prevalence, some very worrying maternal and child health indicators, and the

country's inability to meet the MDGs ... there were talks about going back to the ANC health plan ... Even if there was no controversy with the previous minister, he would still have [more] credibility – he has energy, drive, enthusiasm and is a good storyteller (Informant 1).

Another informant noted:

There is a lot of unhappiness in the nursing profession. We have a dysfunctional nursing council, the profession is not where it was twenty years ago, and the minister picked up on the noise, and did something about it [with the Nursing Summit](Informant 5).

The need for health care reforms is even supported by private health sector allies, albeit for different reasons. In a report that proposes health care reforms that 'will allow the private sector to operate more efficiently, broaden access to its services', the Centre for Development and Enterprise (2011) highlights key imperatives for health care reforms in South Africa, notably poor health outcomes, high private health care costs, inequitable access and poor public health sector design and functioning.

Senior civil servants have found that a more open and conducive environment has allowed for the reintroduction of dormant policy proposals on primary health care, community health workers, national health insurance and an independent quality regulator. Lastly, the rekindling of partnerships with some international donor agencies, which fell out of favour with the previous minister, resulted in increased technical and/ or funding support that enabled international visits to take place and senior managers and politicians to learn from the experience of other countries (such as Brazil) and to take forward key policy proposals on primary health care and national health insurance.

PROCESS, CONSULTATION AND CONTESTATIONS

Despite the minister's charisma and ability to engage with key stakeholders, the process of policy development and consultation has not been without problems, and has varied greatly across the different reform initiatives. Although generally acknowledged to be positive attributes, the minister's drive, energy and enthusiasm, combined with the political imperative to deliver in an impossibly short time frame, has perhaps led to a lack of real engagement with stakeholders and there has been a tendency to push through reforms, regardless of the opinions of colleagues and peers, especially where these have differed from the minister's proposals. Several of our informants commented on this:

'Some of the reforms are very good, such as PHC re-engineering and the Office of Health Standards Compliance. But I think it is a fundamental mistake to put specialists in the district. The minister says all the right things, but I think he has overdone the criticism of the health system. Not everything in the system is bad, and it leaves many public servants demoralised when he keeps on thrashing the [public] health services. The minister is a bit like a steam train, so people find it difficult to raise genuine concerns or problems with some of the reforms.' (Informant 7)

'Dissenting voices were not recognised and it was clear that whatever the minister and the president stated as their opinion at the [Nursing] summit were then put in the documentation as opinions of the majority of nurses, which clearly was not the case.' (Informant 9)

'One of the major problems with the development of the reform proposals is the over-reliance on, and the extensive involvement of, externally funded consultants who are not full-time staff and in many instances have little experience of the public sector, executive management or front-line service delivery. One informant commented: 'We do need external assistance … there is limited capacity at national level, but these reforms need to be led by officials [public servants].' (Informant 8).

A second general concern is that documents, such as the human resources for health strategy, are being presented as new documents but in fact duplicate earlier work.

'The intended outcomes were the same as those articulated more than three years ago when the nursing strategy was developed. The strategy has now seemingly been 'parked', which is a pity as it is basically a sound document – the problem was that there was no commitment on the part of the national Department of Health to implement the strategy. Instead of doing so we have now tried to reinvent the wheel, this time with different people and we have as a result retarded progress even further.' (Informant 9).

PHC re-engineering

Notwithstanding the importance of PHC, there is no documentation on the Department of Health's website on its re-engineering although there are ministerial speeches and media references to 're-engineer' PHC. There was no formal launch of PHC re-engineering, as is usually customary with government initiatives, but the national Department of Health has made presentations to conferences and meetings of professional and nongovernmental organisations.

Although there has been no formal consultation process on PHC, comments made in submissions to the NHI Green Paper highlight concerns that mechanisms and structures have not been established to provide an avenue for community and civil society input into determining what goes into a PHC package. There would need to be inevitable trade-offs and difficult choices in the selection of cost-effective services to be provided.

The lack of consultation with provincial health departments and other important stakeholders – local government, trade unions and civil society – has resulted in uneven uptake across the country of the strategies envisaged to improve PHC delivery and lack of 'buy-in' by provincial and district staff. One informant noted: 'Primary health care is not being implemented in any way that was envisaged … there was no consultation with provincial health departments. We discussed a few things in Gauteng and touched base in the Western Cape' (Informant 7).

There is concern that the process is tied closely to political stakeholders and is essentially top down, leading to very unrealistic time frames for implementation. The NSDA targets are for 2014, linked to the next elections, and there is no doubt that these very short time frames have put extreme political pressure on implementing new strategies. For example, the national Department of Health committed itself to training 5 000 CHWs by December 2011, and is undertaking the coordination of the CHW training itself rather than building on training programmes already under way in a number of provinces. Consequently, the CHW programme is emerging as a vertical programme. Some unintended consequences of the lack of consultation with provinces are listed in Table 2 below.

Table 2: Unintended consequences of lack of provincial health consultation

1. Insufficient attention to all aspects of PHC re-engineering process, such as required leadership, district-based support teams and support to PHC facilities.
2. National DoH is implementing programmes rather than providing support to provinces to fulfill their implementation roles.
3. National DOH is not focusing on its policy and leadership role, which includes clarification of CHW qualifications, recruitment, selection and appointment, CHW core competencies and their scope of work.
4. Undermining of successful CHW initiatives undertaken by non-state actors.

Rushing through activities such as the CHW training also undermines the need for a strong functioning district health system to be in place prior to such initiatives. Without the pillars of strong leadership, strong management and accountability, the initiatives are unlikely to produce the desired health outcomes.

NHI Green Paper
Although the process of developing the NHI Green Paper started in 2007 with an African National Congress (ANC) resolution, and the subsequent appointment of the 2009 ministerial task team on the NHI, we pointed out previously that a transparent process and meaningful public participation have been largely absent (Rispel and Moorman 2010). There are very particular reasons why public consultation around NHI is essential: possible financial implications for tax payers; the multiplicity of stakeholders that will be affected by the policy; public interest and constitutional implications (Van den Heever 2011).

Government saw the release of the document as the start of a consultation process, but civil society groups were of the opinion that consultation should have started much earlier. Following complaints from various stakeholders, the initial two-month period for public submissions was extended until the end of December 2011.[2] A number of discussions have taken place since the release of the Green Paper, involving the minister of health and senior officials in the DOH, mainly with health professional organisations, including the organised medical profession, and medical insurance organisations. In December 2011, an NHI conference was held at which a number of international experts from the World Health Organization, World Bank, Thailand and Australia were invited to share their experiences of countries that have implemented universal coverage policies.

Meaningful consultation was challenging and limited because of the relatively short period for consultation and the lack of detail around certain key elements of the proposal – how the intended benefits of the NHI will be achieved, the exact funding mechanism, the future of the private sector and the components of the various service packages. The submissions on the NHI Green Paper suggest that the confusion and anxiety around the concept have not been alleviated. Without adequate consultation and engagement, implementation will be delayed and difficult. One informant commented on this: 'The Green Paper proposes contracting, which is very complex, and the state health services simply do not have the capacity for that. The CEO of the NHI fund will report to the minister, so I guess the provinces will disappear … but this is not explicitly stated' (Informant 7).

Another uncertainty is that the Green Paper does not fully explain how the transition – from an inequitable health care system with divided public and private health sectors to a national system – will take place over the next fourteen years and there is no clear implementation plan beyond 2015. The Green Paper does not deal with the contentious issue of the regulation of the private sector. Section 137 of the document makes provision for the general public to 'continue with voluntary private medical scheme membership, if they choose to', but there will be no tax subsidies for those continuing with voluntary insurance.

Finally, although green papers are broad discussion documents, the NHI Green Paper has not answered the many questions of civil society or of consumers. National health insurance was reported on extensively in the media both before and after the Green Paper was released. At the same time, the public health sector was often in the news with negative reports about the quality of care and the shortage of health care workers. The release of the NHI Green Paper, and lack of media interest in other policy reforms going on at the same time, encouraged a perception that the NHI would resolve civil society's concerns about the public health system, as is evident from the many questions received about how this financial reform would be implemented in the current environment of poor quality of care and insufficient health care providers. A more coordinated approach to communicating with civil society may well alleviate concerns and negative public responses to such reforms.

Improving human resources for health (HRH)

The HRH strategy was released for public comment at the end of August 2011, and launched by the minister of health six weeks later. At the launch, the minister announced that a process of consultation with general practitioners countrywide about their role as gatekeepers in the provision of health care for the public sector was under way. However, the time period of six weeks to allow for public comment is extremely short. A consultant was contracted to develop the document, but there are concerns that much of the data underlying the proposed strategies is wrong and that the document was 'a cut-and-paste job'. One informant said:

> 'Human resources are the biggest stumbling block to the implementation of the NHI – if we do not have people, we cannot move forward. The consultation process was flawed. They [DOH] first invited doctors, then nurses, and asked for comments to be submitted within two days. We submitted comments, but these were not considered. The consultant said that the document was not perfect, but that there was pressure to get it out' (Informant 5).

One of the most critical concerns – for the health care professions and for the public – is the critical shortage of health care workers, which will impede the success of other reforms. Although the strategy outlines the key elements of an approach to alleviate this critical shortage – training more doctors, improving retention by improving service delivery and conditions of service – the details as to how and when this will happen are scanty.

The national nursing summit was conceptualised and organised by a committee appointed by the director general of health six months prior to the event. The minister took a special interest in the preparations for and the outcome of the summit, which was preceded by nine provincial consultative meetings attended by between 200 and 300 nurses from various stakeholder groups. The summit itself was attended by close to 2 000 nurses. There is a general feeling that there was extensive consultation prior to the summit, but there was insufficient debate on the content of the Nursing Compact, which is now taken as 'cast in concrete'. Although the compact highlights a number of important elements that will revitalise the nursing profession, there was no prioritisation of these elements or any consideration of the financial implications of some of the proposed strategies.

One informant was of the opinion that the summit did not make a significant difference, as critical issues were not addressed. 'I suspect the real aim of the summit was to demonstrate political commitment to nursing rather than to really address the issues' (Informant 9).

Office of Health Standards Compliance

A particular concern with the Office was that the finance minister, Pravin Gordhan, announced in his 2011 budget speech that R117 million had been set aside for the Office prior to any public debate or consultation about the need to establish this public entity. Another concern has been whether the public entity will function optimally, and one informant commented: 'I think it is a mistake to have a public entity. The history of public entities in this country is not a good one' (Informant 7).

Additional concerns relate to the independence of such a body and a lack of engagement with health care workers and the public over the proposed standards. The National Health Amendment Bill states that the CEO and the board, as well as the Ombud's office, will be appointed by, and report to, the minister of health. There is a general feeling that such a body will not be truly independent and will be open to political pressure and influence. Certainly the success of the initiative rests on the clear separation of policy making and oversight, as any regulatory body should be independent and transparent.

WILL SOUTH AFRICA'S HEALTH CARE REFORMS CURE OUR AILING HEALTH SYSTEM?

Collectively, the reform initiatives outlined above are intended to improve health sector performance and health outcomes. There is widespread support for much-needed change in the South African health sector, and one informant noted that 'despite the huge task that lies ahead … there are no alternatives but to do something'.

Notwithstanding the support for, and intentions behind, these health care reform initiatives, the content and process by which they were developed raise several critical questions: how to manage the tension between political priorities and funding realities; whether the reforms will improve health sector performance; whether the reforms will improve population health outcomes; the extent to which the reforms will address existing inequalities; the extent to which due attention will be paid to change management; and whether there will be ongoing monitoring and evaluation.

Managing the tension between political priorities and funding realities

A 2009 study commissioned by Minister Barbara Hogan on overspending in provincial health departments estimated the size of the national health debt at around R7.4 billion, and this was considered an underestimate (Integrated Support Teams 2009). Three factors accounted for the debt: overspending in previous years, which meant that provincial health departments started the new financial year with their budgets minus their overspending in the previous year; significant numbers of unpaid accounts for services and goods; and 'unfunded mandates' – national or provincial political commitments or announcement made, but for which funding was not provided.

In the case of PHC re-engineering, both KwaZulu-Natal and the Western Cape have not agreed to participate in the CHW training provided by the Foundation for Professional Development. The Western Cape has not participated in many of the health reforms, such as the CHW training. This is partly for political reasons, but also because of perceived unfunded mandates. One informant said that: 'CHWs are very expensive when one looks at the numbers that are needed. There is no evidence that they provide good value for money' (Informant 9).

The HRH strategy contains statements on proposed increases in the number of health care professionals without indicating sources of funding for this increase. One informant noted: 'A primary concern for me is prioritisation of these objectives and activities. For example, a number of committees, reviews and expanding medical schools are proposed, but it is not clear how most of these activities will be funded. The key question is whether the Department can afford all these activities, or will we be faced with difficult choices and trade-offs?' (Informant 10).

Will the reforms improve the performance of the health system?

While the goals of the current reforms are supported, they do not adequately address the deeper structural issues that have led to the current health care crisis – the lack of efficient and effective management at all levels of the health care, the lack of effective governance and accountability, and failure to devolve authority and responsibility to districts and hospitals. In particular there is a strong sense that government should acknowledge and take responsibility for previous wrong decisions or past failed initiatives. These include policies of voluntary severance packages that resulted in the retrenchment of health care professionals and the strengthening of the private sector. These problems are well captured by the National Planning Commission (2011):

> The health system is fractured with pervasive disorder and multiple consequences: poor authority, feeble accountability, marginalisation of clinical processes and low staff morale. Centralised control has not worked because of a general lack of discipline, inappropriate functions, weak accountability, lack of adherence to policy, inadequate oversight, feeble institutional links between different levels of services (especially hospitals) and defensive health service levels increasingly protective of turf and budgets.

One informant commented that 'most of the reforms are aimed at the symptoms rather than the root causes of the problem. Some of them will succeed, but I am not sure that they will bring about long-term, lasting changes' (Informant 6).

To a large extent, the success of the reforms depends on the capacity for implementation in provinces. This is captured by a commentary by a senior newspaper editor:

> I cannot fathom why any decent person would oppose endeavours to provide health care for all. It is a no-brainer. But the way the public health system is being run does not inspire confidence. In fact, the thought of placing my well-being in the hands of a system that is beset with mismanagement, corruption and wasteful expenditure frightens me. How did the biggest hospital in the southern hemisphere, Chris Hani Baragwanath, run out of essential life-saving drugs? Even the most basic drugs, like Panado, are hard to come by (Tlhabi 2012: 2).

In December 2011, the provincial health departments of Eastern Cape, Limpopo and Mpumalanga were placed under 'administration'. The majority (78 per cent) of the provincial health departments received either a qualified or an adverse audit outcome for the 2010/11 financial year (Figure 2). In addition to the financial findings, the auditor general found that in the majority of provinces there were weaknesses in the implementation of health information systems (7/9), that reports on HIV statistics were unreliable (7/9), that ambulance staff or vehicles were not available (5/9) and that, in six provinces, new clinics or health facilities were either unutilised or underutilised.

Figure 2: Audit outcomes for 2010/11 financial year

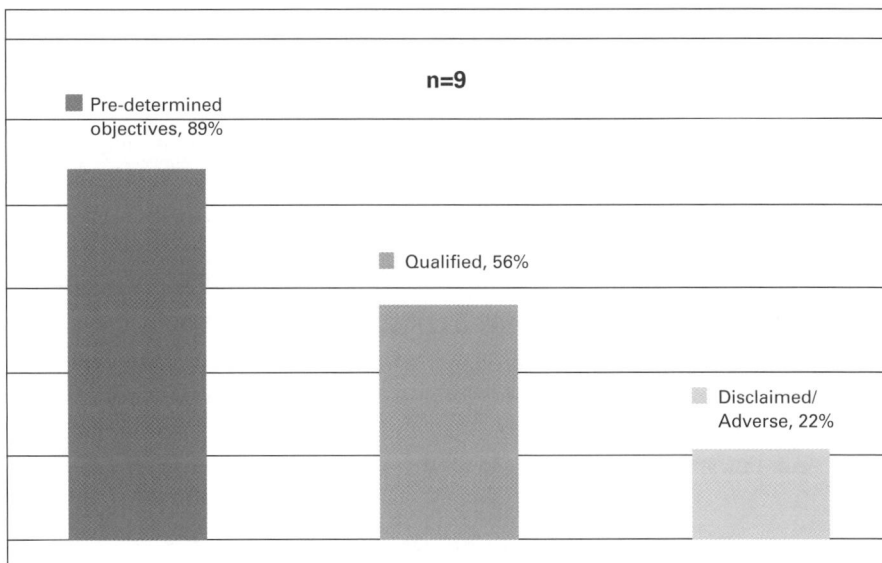

(Source: Auditor General of South Africa 2011)

The auditor general's findings imply that there has not been much progress since the 2009 health system review (Integrated Support Teams 2009), which documented many shortcomings ranging from strategic planning and leadership to financial management and monitoring and evaluation. The review team cautioned against the 'mounting negative consequences' if these shortcomings were not addressed.

The poor performance of the public health system is also seen as a key obstacle to achieving the goals in the NHI document. One submission noted that: 'universal coverage, which technically exists [is] compromised by poor performance' (Van den Heever 2011), and in the inaugural Abu Asvat memorial lecture, Dr Mosibudi Mangena said:

We read, see and hear, almost on a daily basis, about the needless deaths of our people in our hospitals; babies dying in their mother's wombs or in delivery wards; babies being needlessly brain-damaged during birth; the lack of linen, gloves and food in our facilities; filthy hospitals; broken equipment that is not being serviced; the non-payment of medical suppliers leading to chronic shortages of medicines and other essentials; the non-payment of bills at the National Health Laboratory Services … and the long queues at our hospitals for very little satisfaction (Mangena 2012: 16).

The capacity problems in provincial health departments are further compromised by the lack of clarity on the role of provincial health departments. For example, the role of the provinces in service delivery appears to be undermined in the NHI Green Paper by the centralisation of the contracting function of an NHI Fund.

Several informants were of the opinion that there needs to be some prioritisation in the implementation of the various reforms:

If we had the management capacity, financial systems, human resource capacity, good information systems, if the big IFS are fulfilled … then we will have a well-functioning health system like in other countries. But the time frames are short and the challenges big. I think we should focus on getting the basics right, rather than have such an ambitious plan (Informant 7).

I think the district health system system is not working as well as it could and should. We need leadership and management, as well as management and mentoring systems. The systems issues are generally neglected. In my opinion, if the national health insurance does not result in strengthening of the district health system , then in three to four years' time we would have just distracted people from their work (Informant 8).

The extent to which reforms promote equity
Various stakeholders have raised concerns that the current reforms and policies may further entrench existing inequalities in access to quality health care. The Bill of Rights and section 27 of the Constitution place an obligation on government to ensure the progressive realisation of these rights and there is a strong belief that these reforms should prioritise on poor areas and poorer people (Table 3).

The extent to which reforms incorporate citizens' voices
The National Planning Commission has highlighted the importance of community participation and the role of civil society, and the need to revive the 'culture of valuing and respecting the needs of communities'. The previous section noted the contestation around consultation and the processes of the reforms. The People's Health Movement commented that there should have been 'an open and inclusive process where community organisations, health workers, activists and trade unions are consulted on what they would like to

Table 3: Analysing health care reforms from an equity perspective

Initiative	Possible equity implications
Primary health care	Areas with greatest capacity more likely to attract staff, further entrenching poor service delivery and differences in service delivery and health outcomes across districts.
National health insurance	Geographical access in rural areas hampered by lack of health facilities. NHI does not specifically address non-financial access barriers (e.g. poor roads, inadequate transport, etc.). Over 50 per cent of the population in rural formal areas live more than 10km away from the nearest clinic as opposed to under 5 per cent of the population in urban formal areas. Costs of accessing care much higher for rural people (e.g. transport and long distances, lack of affordable and reliable public transport).
Office of Health Standards Compliance	Facilities in poorer districts and rural areas less likely to meet accreditation criteria, exacerbated by lack of clarity on what will happen if facilities are not accredited.

see in a reformed health system' (People's Health Movement 2011). Community consultations have identified people's greatest concerns – shortages of staff, insufficient medication, patient transport and a shortage of ambulance services – and it has been suggested that these issues must be considered when proposing major changes to the health care sector.

One informant also noted that, in the absence of adequate, informed consultation, implementation of the NHI could be delayed once various stakeholder groups understand the details and implications of the reforms, and commented that: 'General practitioners are currently supportive of proposed changes. They think that they will benefit greatly and that they will receive a stable income. The true test will come when they hear what they are going to earn' (Informant 1).

Will the reforms improve the health of South Africans?
Access to good quality health care is only one of the social determinants of health – that is, the circumstances in which we are born, grow up, live, work and age (Commission on Social Determinants of Health 2008). The Living Conditions of Households in South Africa Survey of 2008 /2009 highlights very significant differences in the living conditions of households across provinces and racial groups (Statistics South Africa 2011). Just over 80 per cent of white households fall into the fifth consumption expenditure (the highest), whereas only 8 per cent of black African households fall into this quintile.

Households in the Western Cape do have almost three times the household expenditure of those in Limpopo. Over 37 per cent of the rural population live more than ten kilometres from the nearest primary school as opposed to 2.5 per cent of the urban formal households. Over 25 per cent of households indicated that their food consumption was inadequate, and 29 per cent that their housing was less than adequate. Households in Limpopo spend one-fifth of the amount on health that households in the Western Cape. Achieving health requires a good health care system as well as intersectoral interventions such as good education, adequate housing and food, access to water and sanitation. The health ministry alone will not improve health outcomes.

CONCLUSION

Notwithstanding some scepticism among the informants interviewed about the likelihood that these reforms will achieve their expected outcome, the need for health care reforms is undisputed in light of the overall health system challenges.

None of the documents is explicit about the need to improve governance and accountability throughout the health system, particularly the public hospital and district health system. There are ten *de facto* health departments in operation in South Africa, but details are lacking on the role of provincial health departments, the envisaged district health authorities, and their links to provincial health departments and the current district health system. Difficult issues such as ensuring responsiveness to population needs and strategies to eliminate corruption and mismanagement have not been addressed in any of the reforms. In light of chronic overspending and inadequate financial management, reporting and accountability in many provincial health departments, it is uncertain what mechanisms will be put in place to strengthen financial planning and monitoring systems, particularly in the public sector.

More work is required to decide on implementation priorities, the details of many of the reform initiatives and ways of ensuring that sufficient resources are available. It is imperative that current health resources are utilised optimally, and that the gap between reform initiatives and their implementation is eliminated. Ultimately, the effectiveness of these health care reforms in addressing current health system challenges depends on managing the tension between political priorities and funding realities; addressing existing health inequalities, and the social determinants of health; greater involvement of provincial health departments; and improving the performance and implementation capacity of the public health system.

NOTES

1   The quadruple disease burden refers to four groups of diseases: communicable disease (especially HIV & AIDS and tuberculosis), non-communicable diseases (also called chronic diseases), maternal, neonatal and child deaths, and deaths from injuries and violence.

2   Extension period published in *Government Gazette* Number 34606 of 15th September 2011.

REFERENCES

African National Congress (1994) The Reconstruction and Development Programme: A policy framework. Johannesburg: Umanyano Publications.

Ake C (1966) Charismatic legitimation and political integration. *Comparative Studies in Society and History* 9(1):1-13.

Auditor-general of South Africa (2011) Consolidated general report on provincial audit outcomes 2010-11. Pretoria: AGSA.

Blecher M, A Kollipara, P de Jager and N Zulu (2011) Health Financing. In Padarath A and R English (Eds) *South African Health Review 2011*. Durban: Health Systems Trust.

Breier M, A Wildschut and T Mgqolozana (2009) *Nursing in a New Era: The Profession and Education of Nurses in South Africa*. Cape Town: HSRC Press.

Centre for Development and Enterprise (2011) *Reforming healthcare in South Africa: what role for the private sector?* Johannesburg: CDE.

Chopra M, JE Lawn, D Sanders, P Barron, SS Abdool Karim, D Bradshaw, R Jewkes, Q Abdool Karim, AJ Flisher, BM Mayosi, SM Tollman, GJ Churchyard and H Coovadia (2009) Achieving the health Millennium Development Goals for South Africa: challenges and priorities. *The Lancet* 374:1023–31.

Commission on Social Determinants of Health (2008) Closing the gap in a health generation: Health equity through the social determinants of health. Geneva: World Health Organization.

Coovadia H, R Jewkes, P Barron, D Sanders and D McIntyre (2009) The health and health system of South Africa: historical roots of current public health challenges. *The Lancet* 374:817-34.

Day C, P Barron, A Padarath, R English and N Massyn (Eds) (2011) *District Health Barometer 2010/11*. Durban: Health Systems Trust.

Department of Health (1997) White Paper on the Transformation of the Health System in South Africa. Pretoria: National Department of Health.

Department of Health (2006) National Human Resource Plan. Pretoria: Department of Health.

Department of Health (2011a) National Health Insurance in South Africa: Policy paper. Government Notice: 657 of 12th August 2011, Gazette Number 34523. Pretoria: Department of Health.

Department of Health (2011b) Human Resources for Health South Africa: HRH Strategy for the Health Sector: 2012/13 – 2016/17. Pretoria: DOH.

Development Bank of Southern Africa (2008) *Health Sector Roadmap*. Midrand: DBSA.

Harris B, J Goudge, JE Ataguba, D McIntyre, N Nxumalo, S Jikwana and M Chersich (2011) Inequities in access to health care in South Africa. *Journal of Public Health Policy* 32 (Supplement 1): S102–S23.

Hartley W (2012) Health standards compliance 'vital to NHI plan'. *Business Day*, 16 February.

Integrated Support Teams (2009) Review of health over-spending and macro-assessment of the public health system in South Africa: Consolidated Report. Pretoria: ISTs.

Lawn JE and MV Kinney (2009) Health in South Africa: An executive summary for the Lancet Series. *The Lancet*.

Mangena M (2012) Abu Asvat – A people's hero before his time. *Sunday Independent*, 26 February.

Ministry of Health (2010) Negotiated Service Delivery Agreement. Pretoria: Department of Health.

Naledi T, P Barron and H Schneider (2011) Primary Health Care in SA since 1994 and Implications of the New Vision for PHC re-engineering. In Padarath A and R English (Eds) *South African Health Review 2011*. Durban: Health Systems Trust.

National Department of Health (2010) Service delivery agreement for outcome 2: A long and healthy life for all South Africans. Pretoria: National Department of Health.

National Planning Commission (2011) National Development Plan: Vision 2030. Pretoria: NPC.

Padarath A and R English (Eds) (2011) *South African Health Review 2011*. Durban: Health Systems Trust.

People's Health Movement (2011) The Green Paper on NHI: open discussion document. Cape Town: People's Health Movement.

Republic of South Africa (2011) National Health Amendment Bill.

Rispel L and J Moorman (2010) Analysing health legislation and policy in South Africa: context, process and progress. In Fonn S and A Padarath (eds) *South African Health Review 2010*. Durban: Health Systems Trust.

Rispel LC and TN Kibua (2011) Whither the MDGs? Stewardship for health in Kenya, Nigeria and South Africa. In Kondlo K and C Ejiogu (Eds) *Africa in Focus: Governance in the 21st Century*. Cape Town: HSRC Press.

Statistics South Africa (2011) Living conditions of households in South Africa, 2008/2009. Pretoria: StatsSA.

Tlhabi R (2012) Trying to cure a sick health system – one dead patient at a time. *Sunday Times Review*, 12 February.

Van den Heever A (2011) Evaluation of the Green Paper on National Health Insurance. Johannesburg: Graduate School of Public and Development Management, University of the Witwatersrand.

Walt G and L Gilson (1994) Reforming the health sector in developing countries: The central role of policy analysis. *Health Policy and Planning* 9:3-70.

WHO (1978) Alma-Ata 1978: Primary health care. Geneva: World Health Organization.

—— (2008) The World Health Report 2008: Primary health care, now more than ever. Geneva: World Health Organization.

CHAPTER 13

Cadre deployment versus merit?
Reviewing politicisation in the public service

Vinothan Naidoo[1]

The post-apartheid transformation of South Africa's public service sought to rehabilitate merit as a core principle in a nonracial and politically inclusive society. This is unremarkable. What is worth noting, though, are the practical challenges the country has since faced in attempting to clearly and robustly embed merit standards as a central organising feature of its bureaucracy, an undertaking complicated by the ambiguity and recriminations accompanying the practice of 'deployment', which has been problematically driven by party political incentives. Merit has been an important feature of historical efforts to reform public administration through the introduction of formal measures to competitively evaluate the technical knowledge and fitness of persons seeking administrative office.[2]

Mid- to late-nineteenth century interventions such as the Northcote/Trevelyan report in the United Kingdom and civil service reform legislation in the United States were intended to counter the administrative instability, disorderliness and corruption wrought by earlier patronage or partisan-driven recruitment into the public service (Ingraham 1995; Greenaway 2004). Merit remained a constant goal of subsequent administrative reform periods, from the archetypal early twentieth-century Weberian official to post-Second World War efforts to restructure developing country bureaucracies to promote social and economic development.

The challenge South Africa faces in applying the merit principle stems from the difficulty of marking a clear division between administrative and political reliability, which has traditionally distinguished merit from patronage values. This challenge, however, is neither unique to the country nor historically absent elsewhere. No less a commentator than the former US president Woodrow Wilson ([1913-1885]: 290-291,) who spearheaded late nineteenth-century administrative reforms, remarked on the importance of merit relative to patronage-driven motives in the American bureaucracy. In distinguishing between 'political' and 'nonpolitical' offices, he ascribed to the latter the 'strictest rules of business discipline, of merit-tenure and earned promotion', and associated the former with party political decisions to 'make and unmake, reward or punish'. Importantly, he also held that it may be difficult in practice to delineate these two fields where '[i]n all the higher grades this particular distinction is quite obscured'. Greenaway's (2004) revisionist critique of the 1854 Northcote/Trevelyan report also challenged conventional beliefs about the weight of its attack on patronage. Correspondence between the drafters of the report suggested that a more modest and incremental attempt to reform the patronage system was intended, in which competitive examinations could weed out undesirables among aristocratic elites while preserving their preferential access to higher public service offices. In their influential cross-national surveys of the relative roles and responsibilities of bureaucrats and politicians in Western Europe, Putnam, Aberbach and Rockman (1981: 3) also referred to the evolving Weberian distinction between 'technical effectiveness and democratic responsiveness', the former referring to the merit-defined domain of the public servant and the latter marking the politician's territory. Although recognising a historical tension between these two sets of players, they added that insufficient analysis of the interrelationship between them in practice may mask a more fluid interaction between the values that supposedly distinguished their actions.

These observations suggest that the boundary between merit and patronage/partisan credentials may be more opaque in practice than is generally assumed, and may further imply that the notion of a merit-based public service is, to some extent, a function of politicisation, including the promotion of party political values in the staffing of administrative offices (Peters and Pierre 2004). The issue of politicisation is abundant in the research on public administration and layered in its complexity. Consequently, proposals on how best to introduce, inculcate and expand a merit-driven public service to counter the potentially corrosive effects of politicisation belies the multifaceted character of politicisation, as well as its perceived effects: Are politicisation and administrative fitness (merit) necessarily conflicting values?

The complex relationship between politicisation and merit is salient to the transformation of South Africa's public service, which has experienced significant shifts in party political oversight, a greatly expanded policy agenda and a high turnover of personnel in a remarkably short time. In the immediate aftermath of the 1994 democratic transition politicisation was accorded a relatively wide but temporary berth as a stabilising mechanism in an uncertain process. This resulted in efforts to control the appointment of personnel at higher levels of the public service and was reinforced by legislation requiring employment equity through affirmative action. The subsequent character of South Africa's politico-administrative relations has, however, brought to the fore concerns about the detrimental effects of politicisation, such as clientelism and corruption. A catalyst for these concerns has been the explicit espousal of party strategies to politicise the bureaucracy, most notably the policy of the governing African National Congress (ANC) of installing party members in administrative offices.

Increasing criticism of the ANC's 'cadre deployment' has in effect politicised politicisation, or efforts to consolidate and employ legitimate forms of political control over the public service. This has obscured efforts to analyse the presence – and absence – of merit and its role in developing a career public service in South Africa. This chapter will assess the extent and character of politicisation in the public service. It will review efforts and the attendant challenges of evaluating the scope and the severity of its effects on the application of merit criteria. It will also assess how this issue has affected the evolving relationship between politicians and senior bureaucrats; a union that has traditionally been a useful barometer for gauging the tension between administrative and political reliability.

THE MULTIFACETED CHARACTER OF POLITICISATION

Politicisation refers to the various methods and measures that elected officials have employed to ensure compliance with their political preferences and to exercise democratic accountability over the bureaucracy (Auriacombe and Mavanyisi 2003). This reality complicates the task of explaining what is meant by politicisation. More specifically, is there a uniform or simple understanding of how it occurs? Then, how should we judge or tolerate its presence? Would it be appropriate to outline degrees of acceptability, or should we dismiss politicisation in the public service out of hand? The reality prevents us from doing the latter because politicisation has been, and continues to be, ingrained in how public services function globally. Recalling the historically powerful appeal of politicisation and attempts to regulate it in the nineteenth century, Rouban (2003: 311) noted that '[i]t was … a matter of containing a phenomenon that no one could or wanted to eradicate totally'. The continuing relevance of the practice therefore highlights the difficulty in distinguishing a boundary between political and administrative actions.

In the *Politicisation of the Civil Service in Comparative Perspective*, Peters and Pierre (2004: 2) provide a basic definition of the issue and illustrate the various means and motives behind its existence. They refer to politicisation as the 'substitution of political criteria for merit-based criteria in the selection, retention, promotion, rewards, and disciplining of members of the public service'. The general utility of this definition belies the more complex forms that politicisation assumes in reality. For example, this definition emphasises control and influence over the management of personnel, and in particular the staffing of administrative offices with party political loyalists. Although politicisation is most commonly associated with this practice, it is internally diverse in form and in degrees of acceptability. A contrast is made between the kind of unbridled 'spoils' patronage, in which public service offices were treated as political rewards, and the subsequent evolution of accepted and regulated levels of political appointments within expanded career public service systems, as documented in countries such as the US, Germany and France (Peters and Pierre op. cit.; see also Rouban 2003: 313, Derlien 1996: 155). The German practice, which is also evident in France, of 'political civil servants' is of particular interest because it prompts a reinterpretation of 'substitution of political criteria' and whether this implies a complete or partial substitution of merit criteria. Although this class of official has a party political affiliation, they are recruited from within the career merit system (Peters and Pierre 2004: 2; Derlien 1996: 155-156; Van der Meer, Steen and Wille 2007: 43; Rouban 2003: 315).[3]

The employment of senior public servants representing both partisanship and merit has historically been eschewed in other countries such as the United Kingdom, where career public servants are barred from holding formal party affiliation. Analysis of the UK public service has, however, indicated that the comparative and historical barrier between administrative and political roles has come under considerable pressure in more recent times. This was outlined in a UK parliamentary report on the relative roles of ministers and senior public servants. The report observed that despite, and sometimes because of, a long history of bureaucratic insulation from political involvement, the interaction between ministers and public servants in practice, especially in cases of policy or administrative failures, had resulted in concerns about reduced accountability (House of Commons 2007). These concerns, primarily expressed by politicians, can be traced back decades and, according to Wilson and Barker (2003: 350-351), can be distinguished by several criticisms: quality of the policy advice rendered by public servants; quality of the management capacity of public servants (which took on greater weight in the 1980s and 1990s under politically induced public management reforms); ideological inflexibility; and a public service that was 'inadequately equipped to serve … political needs'. The consequence has been the varied methods employed by elected officials to reassert their political authority over the British bureaucracy, including employing more political advisors (a specific type of political appointee who functions outside the career public service as a ministerial counsellor (Wilson and Barker 2003: 352; Rouban 2003: 315)); the outsourcing of policy advice to think tanks; and the more recent and controversial measure of reforming departmental governing boards, including the appointment of business leaders with the authority to recommend the dismissal of senior public servants (Wachman and Curtis 2010).[4]

Unpacking the concept of politicisation reveals that the issue straddles what Peters and Pierre (2004: 2) refer to as the 'bounds of acceptability', linked on the one hand to a need to ensure political accountability and control and on the other to prevent unethical conduct. The politicisation research is also dominated by the experience of Western industrialised nations, though this may simply reflect the historical roots and continued relevance of the issue there. The experience of these nations should not, however, necessarily be viewed as idealised models, given inter-country differences (Van der Meer, Steen and Wille 2007 on Western Europe). There is also a distinction between the intent and circumstances behind politicisation in developed versus developing countries, which in the former is said to be motivated more by policy control and management, and in the latter driven more by clientelistic exchange – jobs for friends or allies (Peters, Pierre op. cit.; Rouban 2003: 315). A caveat to this distinction suggests, however, that one motive does not lead to the complete absence of the other, but indicates a relative preponderance, for example clientelistic exchange in developing countries, which some have equated with corruption or the risk thereof (for example McCourt 2000: 2; Lodge 1998: 182, with reference to South Africa). Indeed, the contingent circumstances of developing countries or states undergoing major political system changes are also pertinent to evaluating the politicisation-merit relationship because they have a more limited pool of technically as well as politically capable officials for recruitment into the bureaucracy (Peters and Pierre 2004: 8); and what Adamolekun (2002: 375) referred to as overbearing governing parties, in which he cites sub-Saharan African states where '[p]arty militancy was substituted for the merit system as the dominant criterion for recruitment'. He does, however, qualify this by conceding a lack of clarity in how the relationship was measured.

POLITICISATION, MERIT AND ADMINISTRATIVE TRANSFORMATION IN SOUTH AFRICA

The post-1994 politicisation of the South African public service was largely a response to the discredited public service of the past that was highly politicised under entrenched National Party rule. The political-administrative axis that formed under successive apartheid governments is well documented. Posel's survey (Posel 2000: 47; 51) of the ethnic manipulation or 'Afrikanerisation' of administrative appointments is especially revealing of the detrimental effects this had: she observed that the expansion of administrative activity, coupled with discriminatory hiring practices, contributed to reduced capacity and productivity, inadequate training, and concerns about rising mediocrity in the bureaucracy. Still, successive National Party governments were forced to sustain the functional trade-offs resulting from this strategy in order to maintain political control. In practice this meant that the Nats became increasingly beholden to the public service as a reliable ethnic voting bloc while delegating greater decision-making power to bureaucrats to oversee an expanding administrative agenda.

Schrire's (1986) analysis of political-bureaucratic relations under apartheid also cited the increasing power and influence assumed by senior bureaucrats under the premiership of BJ Vorster, which was subsequently curtailed under the leadership of PW Botha.

Post-1994 government policy directed at merit was, in consequence, driven by a corrective. The ANC government's policy position on merit noted that although it was viewed as fundamental, 'the principle … has been eroded and misused in the past by drawing up narrow, exclusive position requirements which discriminated both against external candidates and against certain groups of internal candidates, to the detriment of the quality of human resource capacity within the public service' (RSA 1997a). The principle of merit was therefore unavoidably laced with discredited historical practice that would in turn be used to enlarge the range of characteristics to be considered when assessing the suitability of candidates for administrative office.The subsequent White Paper on Human Resource Management (RSA 1997b) noted that '[s]election criteria … will be based on competencies rather than undue over-emphasis on academic qualifications. Merit must be defined within the context of employment equity.'

This phrasing, which singles out formal academic qualifications from a wider notion of technical fitness, is due to past educational discrimination – it elevates other characteristics such as interpersonal skills, future potential, and a more intimate knowledge of (and affinity with) South Africa's social and economic problems, as part of the merit pool.[5] In reality, the profiling of merit also overlays party political considerations. The Presidential Review Commission (RSA 1998) reported that it was unsurprising that the new ANC leadership viewed the public service with suspicion and immediately attempted to control appointments to its senior ranks. Although the Commission recognised this practice as necessary in the circumstances, its report also pointed to the assortment of candidates[6] this was actually yielding: ' … some of those new appointees have not been able to offer much beyond political loyalty …'. Miller's (2005: 97) comparative assessment of directors general pre- and post-1994 drew different impressions about this post-apartheid cohort; despite their lack of career experience in the bureaucracy (compared with their pre-1994 predecessors) owing to restricted access, they held a range of experience and skills from academia, the nongovernmental sector, and as political activists.

POLITICISATION AND 'CADRE' DEPLOYMENT

Transforming South Africa's public service resulted in efforts by the incoming ANC-led government to control top appointments strategically as well as redefine the merit principle in accordance with political loyalties. The tabling, at the ANC's 50th Mafikeng Conference in 1997, of a policy to manage the personal development and institutional deployment of its members or 'cadres' to state offices, which included the public service, marked a watershed in the politicisation of the bureaucracy. For some, this has resulted in a degeneration of technical knowledge, skills and accountability, whereas for others its existence has encumbered the building of a stable career bureaucracy. I also contend that the apparent pre-eminence of the party's policy has in effect exposed ambiguity in the institutional regulation of political appointments in the public service, enabling party dominance of the process.[7]

Cameron (2010: 686, 687, 698) has suggested that a distinction can be drawn between the motivations behind, and related technical qualities associated with, different waves of ANC deployment, distinguishing the period before and after the introduction of the cadre policy. He argues that the introduction of the policy, marking a second wave of deployees, was more 'overtly' political in its preference for party functionaries in comparison with the diversity of first-wave deployees who shared an ideological consonance with the party's policy agenda. He implies that this had a detrimental effect on 'management' capacity, though he cautions that ' … differences between the first and second wave appointees were not always watertight'. Cameron's research draws partially on Miller's (2005) comparative account of the role and functioning of directors general prior to and after 1994, which emphasised the importance of ideological compatibility in early appointments made by the ANC. Miller did not, however, distinguish periods or related characteristics of political appointees to the DG position, which may be taken as support of Cameron's qualified distinction between the managerial abilities of first- and second-wave appointees. Still, concerns about the quality of deployees have not gone unnoticed, with Plaatjies (2011: 103) revealing that the ANC has also conceded the patchiness of deployment, including those 'who do not even meet the basic requirements for the posts they are deployed in'.[8] A more compelling exposé of the sidelining of merit criteria is given in Cameron's analysis of local government in South Africa, which has revealed more acute spoils-based politicisation in which, enabled by political decentralisation, party and personal loyalties have undermined human and financial administration (Cameron 2011; 2010; see also RSA 2009; World Bank 2011). Drawing on individual research, and corroborated by central government reports, his analysis signals polarisation between political and merit considerations. Cameron (2011: 10) also linked the issue with internal ANC party conflict over cadre deployment, referring to accounts of deployment structures in some provinces clashing with national offices over a proposed parliamentary Bill to regulate the appointment of senior local government officials. Butler (2002: 9) has also alluded to internal party divisions over the management of cadre deployment, noting efforts since 1999 by central ANC structures to assert control over deployment at all levels of government.

Booysen (2011) has given an account of ANC deployment between 1994 and 2011. She documents instances of internal divisions and instability in party governance over cadre deployment, which, as civil society groups have also, elsewhere, argued, threatens to undermine the integrity and public accountability of state institutions (Centre for Constitutional Rights 2008; Institute for Accountability in Southern Africa 2010). Citing more recent introspectively critical pronouncements by the ANC on its deployment experience, Booysen added that party political divisions during the Mbeki-Zuma leadership transition had penetrated the 'state bureaucracy', and she specifically referred (2011: 383-384) to instances of officials altering their decision-making as a result of fear and to avoid potential reprisals by new political principles and senior officials.

Party political divisions over cadre deployment have also overshadowed efforts to regulate clearly the politicisation-merit relationship. Mafunisa's (2003) analysis, for example, cites a provision sanctioning politicisation, outlined in section 195(4) of the Constitution: 'The appointment in public administration of a number of persons of policy considerations is not precluded, but national legislation must regulate these appointments in the public service'. He adds that the intentions of the clause are clear, despite the possibility of its abuse by 'corrupt public functionaries' (Mafunisa 2003: 89). Whether this clause is in fact clear regarding political appointments is open to debate. The reference to persons 'in public administration' and 'in the public service' is, arguably, imprecise as it could pertain to the privilege granted to ministers of appointing 'special advisers' as policy councillors, but who are meant to operate outside of departmental hierarchies and therefore may not be said to be 'in public administration' or 'in the public service'. Or, would this proviso extend to senior public servants who are, as a matter of practice, involved in policy formulation ('of policy considerations'; in terms of the ranks being included; and of the extent to which we can detect and avoid tendencies to misuse or abuse the proviso for clientelistic reasons)? Although the Regulations to South Africa's Public Service Act (RSA 2001) appear clearer on this issue, stating that public servants should not 'abuse' their position to 'promote or prejudice the interest of any political party or interest group' (C.2.7), and refrain from 'party political activities in the workplace' (C.3.7), it is reasonable to suggest that the constitutional proviso remains ambiguous yet nonetheless valid.

This ambiguity is evident in Maphunye's (2005) analysis of politicisation and the roles of senior public servants, conducted through interviews with 180 officials in four provinces. Maphunye examines the effect of appointments 'of policy considerations' and their extension to senior bureaucrats. Referring to one interpretation of politicisation as 'participation [by public servants] in political decision making' (Rouban 2003), Maphunye (2005: 221) states: 'In the South African case, this occurs more at the levels of DGs, deputy DGs and perhaps some superintendent-generals, chief directors and directors in some departments as these officials are known to have been required to take decisions by virtue of their proximity to the elected heads of their departments.'

Of interest here is the potential effect on the appointments process of senior public servants becoming involved in 'political' decision making, distinguishing policy from narrower partisan motives; and possibly by decision making influenced by an official's 'proximity' to elected officials, although Maphunye's reference to proximity may in this instance refer to the official's rank. Maphunye's main point concerning political decision-making stands and is later developed:

> While not openly admitting that the party had deployed them, very few senior public servants boldy stated that in the present democratisation stage in South Africa the country could not afford to have a politically neutral public service. Overall, there seemed to be a quite wide belief that the top three positions of chief director, deputy DG, and DG inevitably would be highly politicised positions … (Maphunye 2005: 223).

Maphunye also pointed to the difficulty of distinguishing 'merit' from political considerations, noting that ' … some interviewee respondents suggested that senior public service positions were being vetted according to [personal or party-related affiliations] … because of the government's drive not to appoint and promote solely according to merit'.

A more recent comparative study for the Organisation for Economic Cooperation and Development (OECD) (Matheson et al. 2007), which assessed the level of political involvement in the staffing of senior bureaucrats, builds on Maphunye's (2005) detection of widening politicisation in the upper echelons of the public service. Though the study confirms the expanse of political control over senior management appointments, its unique if empirically limited findings confirmed the depth of reach that political factors appear to have over post-appointment career management.[9] In the category, 'who appoints', referring to the involvement of elected officials in the appointment of senior officials, South Africa ranked fourth behind the United States, Sweden and Italy on a scale spanning 'more political' to 'more administrative'. Across individual categories, directors general and their deputies are considered 'political', whereas chief director and director appointments are described as 'hybrid', where administrative criteria are combined with 'political considerations' (Matheson et al. 2007: 15). Of potentially greater concern is that the post-appointment career management of senior officials is also widely subject to political considerations, where in all but the category of dismissals, in which administrative protections apply to all but directors general, there is a mixture of political and hybrid factors governing promotions, transfers and performance assessments. This indicates the depth of political factors regulating the career prospects of public servants. It also indicates that these do not operate unchecked from administrative criteria.

Interpreting the extent of political involvement in administrative appointments, Matheson et al. caution that this does not, 'per se, make that appointment … political or partisan', citing the Swedish case in which all appointments are, regardless of other considerations, meant to be subjected to skill and merit criteria (Matheson et al. 2007). This reinforces the difficulty of marking a simple trade-off between political and merit criteria, especially in instances of a hybrid classification. It should reasonably be expected, however, that this is subject to the rigour and transparency of the process.

Kopecký's (2011) more exacting comparative study of politicisation in public appointments in Ghana and South Africa generally supported the extensive breadth of politicisation in public service appointments recorded by Matheson et al. The research was informed by a survey of forty-five experts in each country, including public servants and participants from nongovernmental sectors. The analysis projected the appointment process onto different types of state institutions, including core state departments and various nondepartmental bodies. By aggregating the scoring of responses to questions about the breadth and depth of party control over administrative appointments, Kopecký (2011: 722) found clear but varying levels of control across sectoral institutions which, he cautioned, do not support exaggerated claims of 'total' party political control or unrestricted reach.

A more interesting finding concerns the extent of party political involvement in appointments in core administrative departments. It was highest relative to nondepartmental entities – although this again varied across sectors (Kopecký 2011: 724). Administrative sectors with the strongest levels of politicisation in South Africa included the military/police and the foreign service. The former was broadened to include institutions whose mandate includes state security, such as home affairs and intelligence agencies. This accords with Booysen's (2011: 379, 381) account of what she termed 'institutional domain wars', in which intra-party conflict appears to have adversely affected institutional and personnel stability in the justice and crime prevention sector that functions alongside the state security structures cited by Kopecký. Examples from this sector include the decision, sanctioned by ANC policy, to disband and replace the Directorate of Special Operations ('Scorpions') with a new structure to pursue serious crime investigations ('Hawks'); and the more pertinent case of the controversial dismissal and subsequent replacement of the country's top prosecutor, Vusi Pikoli, with Menzi Simelane, both of whom were subject to disagreements about their 'fitness' to hold office.[10] A further case is the ructions involving resignations of top administrators in state security structures[11] (Jeff Maqetuka, Gibson Njenje and – at the time of writing – speculation about the impending departure of the experienced intelligence operative and ANC veteran Mo Shaik), which have been linked to their resistance to political interference in agency operations exerted by the minister of state security (defenceWeb 2011).

Finally, though Kopecký's (2011: 727) study broadly confirmed the extent of politicisation in the higher levels of South Africa's public service, it also observed a greater emphasis on institutional control (including control over policy) over rewards as the primary motive behind politicising appointments – although motives combining rewards and control came a close second. In the first place, this deviates from the policy control/reward divide distinguishing politicisation in industrialised versus developing countries (as referred to above), and it also suggests that this distinction may be overly crude or at least insufficiently nuanced, whereas the previous examples highlight the destabilising effects of politicisation where policy control appears at least partially relevant. Finally, the cruder rewards-based motive behind politicisation was not absent from Kopecký's findings on South Africa; he pointed to a tendency for rewards-based politicisation to be more prevalent at subnational levels of government (regional and local). This coincides with Cameron's (2011) observations of spoils-driven politicisation at the local government level.

ADMINISTRATIVE RISKS TO THE POLITICISATION-MERIT RELATIONSHIP IN SOUTH AFRICA

The available research on politicisation in the South African public service clearly reveals its expansion into the senior reaches of the bureaucracy. This is not surprising, given the maintenance of party deployment strategies such as the ANC's cadre policy. It is also evident, though, that political criteria have taken precedence over merit in administrative appointments and functioning. The picture appears more troubling at the local government level. I describe below a number of administrative risks that could alter the politicisation dynamic towards greater clientelistic motives and result in a more comprehensive sidelining of merit criteria. These risks also impede efforts to enhance cohesion and stability in the bureaucracy.

Politicisation and its effects were not tackled in the Department of Public Service and Administration's (2007) submission to the South African government's *Fifteen*

Year Review of its performance, which presented a more sanguine picture of an increasingly formalised senior management service (SMS), comprising the highest levels of the bureaucracy, in which greater attention was being directed at competency assessments. The Department's research on the SMS also indicated that a significant majority of sampled senior bureaucrats hold postgraduate qualifications; tertiary education has historically represented a core component of merit. In addition, one could not help but notice the report's ill-advised reference to efforts to improve the 'deployment' of senior managers across the public service, although the implication was clearly that this should proceed on a non-partisan basis (not in the party deployment sense) to regulate the movement of scarce personnel across state institutions (RSA 2007: 24).[12]

Despite clear efforts to create the conditions for greater cohesion and a careerist trajectory in the public service, the susceptibility of the senior management class to clientelistic pressures remains a risk. This relates to the DPSA's acknowledgement, elsewhere in the report, that despite the installation of a performance management system in the public service, 'it was not considered to have led to any improvement in accountability'. Cameron (2010: 693-694) made a similar observation, citing evidence of non-compliance and manipulation of performance management processes. Although no explicit link was drawn to politicisation, and nor was the problem judged as systemic rather than variable, he did recognise that there was a 'reasonable degree of political involvement in performance assessment'. The implication is that performance management manipulation cannot simply be put down to functional pressures or oversights, but could be influenced by clientelistic motives. A more troubling concern with non-compliance was also cited in research by the Public Service Commission (PSC 2008a), which audited selection processes in selected government departments. The study, which sampled the departments of health and public works at the national and provincial levels of government, found that, *inter alia*, a majority of departments lacked job descriptions for advertised posts, and departments were not fully compliant with conducting job evaluations prior to advertising posts. The Commission noted that this 'may lead to the selection of candidates that do not possess the required qualifications, skills and experience', a clear risk to clientelistic appointments.

Sangweni and Mxakato-Diseko's (2008) critique of the developmental capacity of South Africa's public service also exposes possible administrative risks to the politicisation-merit relationship. Most notable is the authors' critique of personnel practices, which they contrast with classic East Asian developmental states, and which would appear to undermine efforts to foster internally robust career experience in the public service while potentially heightening the risk of deployment abuse (this author's interpretation). Sangweni and Mxakato-Diseko (2008: 40, 43), citing Johnson's (1982) work on Japan, argue that the absence or weakness of efforts to inculcate a common administrative and developmental culture and 'grammar' undermine a system in which lateral entry into the public service draws in persons from a variety of nongovernmental sectors. Although it would be inappropriate to suggest that the authors are here critiquing lateral entry *per se*, their remarks, read in the wider context of their essay, suggest a concern for the lack of cohesion in the bureaucracy and an underemphasis on skills derived through vertical career mobility. Their second observation ironically highlights excessive mobility in the public service in comparison with controlled or regulated mobility,[13] in which common instances of rapid movement of officials from junior to senior management ranks appear devoid of measures to assess their minimum readiness (Sangweni, Mxakato-Diseko 2008: 44). Poor incentivisation for internal career experience, and excessive mobility, create further risks of clientelistic motives.

A final risk associated with clientelistically motivated politicisation has been the instability caused by the sometimes tense relationship between heads of department, including directors general at the national level, and the ministers to whom they are meant to account. The occasional but consistently reported unease between them has been a constant feature of public service functioning in South Africa (Mafunisa 2003: 95). A number of reasons have been advanced to explain the tension. Apart from what might be labelled transitional politics, wherein new ANC ministers oversaw heads of department retained from National Party rule (Maserumule 2007: 154), these reasons have included role confusion and discord stemming from conflicting legislated duties over human resource and financial management (Maserumule 2007: 161; Cameron 2009: 921); personal and policy conflicts (the latter reflecting unclear policy roles as well as heads of department assuming a larger role in the policy formulation process (Maserumule 2007: 159; Miller 2005: 110); and the adverse effect of limited term (three- to five-year) contracts on employment security. In the case of the last-named reason, although PSC (2008b: 24) research found that contracts were found to be useful in expe-diting the departure of weak officials according to some heads of departments (HODs) surveyed, Cameron (2009: 928) and Miller (2005: 115) both concluded that the contract instrument could also heighten political control through the convenience of changing HODs when there is a change of minister.

The relationship between ministers and HODs has contributed to an inordinate level of instability in the administrative leadership of the public service, which the PSC has measured through the turnover of HODs. Of particular concern is the finding that contract termination was the single biggest reason (59 per cent) behind the departure of heads in the period between 2003/4 and 2006/7; and as much as 89 per cent of current HODs interviewed[14] believed that their tenure was directly linked to their relationship with ministers (PSC 2008b: x, 9). This may be read with another finding that 61 per cent of current heads believed that a change in minister would precipitate a change in their positions (PSC 2008b: 20). Political factors can therefore be seen as influencing the insta-bility and uncertainty of tenure in top administrative leadership, which could heighten the risk of clientelistic politicisation.

Despite this risk, the appointment process for heads of department is legally regu-lated by the president who, since 1999, has been invested with the authority to appoint heads at the national level (directors general), though in practice the pre-selection and screening is typically delegated to a committee of ministers. On the one hand, Cameron (2009: 926) submits that this 'procedure ensures that the directors general are appointed largely on the basis of political affiliation'. On the other hand, Miller (2005: 88) links this procedure to accountability, in terms of which presidential privilege is meant, *inter alia*, to 'depersonalise the relationship between the minister and director general' in order to mitigate the risks of instability resulting from a breakdown in the relationship. Although this provides greater insight into the rationale attending the appointment process, it still leaves unresolved the question of how to regulate the employment of political criteria appropriately in the appointment of heads of department. The National Development Plan prepared by the National Planning Commission (RSA 2012), an executive body, does suggest one way of doing this, by recommending that a 'hybrid' approach be applied to the staffing of departmental heads, a term Matheson et al. also used to describe the staffing of senior bureaucratic offices. The Commission defines a 'hybrid' approach as subjecting the recruitment of HODs to greater regulation, so that the constitutionally empowered PSC, along with a newly designated head of the public service, would be charged with vetting the administrative suitability of candidates for ultimate selection by ministers (RSA 2012: 414). The intent would therefore be not to eliminate political criteria *in toto* but to regulate their application better.

CONCLUSION

This chapter argues that the interface between politicisation and merit in the South African public service is neither polarised nor, indeed, stable. Although party political control over the appointment and career management of senior officials is clear and explicitly sanctioned, it is not evident that political criteria have completely subsumed merit considerations, amounting to the zero-sum trade-off that is sometimes publicly perceived and debated, and often linked to the effects of affirmative action. A wider body of research, however, persuasively highlights a host of administrative shortcomings that could expose appointment and personnel management practices to greater risk of clientelistic pressures. These pressures could, in turn, sideline and devalue merit criteria in favour of partisan ties, which also appear prone to the destabilising effects of intra-party rivalry and manoeuvring in the context of a dominant party system. Finally, these risks also militate against efforts to develop, over the longer term, a vertically oriented career bureaucracy with levels of cohesion and stability to enable sufficient insulation from political interference.

The challenge facing South Africa is to avoid becoming fixated on the necessary but short-term need to stem the harmful effects of party political abuse and clientelistic pressures resulting from the existing level of political control over senior bureaucratic appointments and functioning. Greater attention should be paid to the longer-term question of how to clearly and legitimately incorporate space for elected leaders to hold the bureaucracy accountable in making and managing political appointments. This would require decisions about where and how to transparently incorporate and regulate space for elected leaders to make political appointments, a process currently constrained by ambiguous statutory provisions. The process should more clearly specify and demarcate (and not just regulate – see the National Planning Commission's recommendations) who constitutes a political appointee. Should this be confined to ministerial advisers or deputants above departmental leadership to steer major policy initiatives, or should the category extend to senior public servants – and if so, to what level? For instance, the NPC's recommendation of a hybrid 'approach' to the appointment of departmental heads does not necessarily result in this position being reclassified as non-political, according to how the term is used in the study by Matheson et al., so that even political appointments may be subject to, and therefore regulated by, administrative criteria. This reinforces the need for statutory clarity on how far political appointments should extend. Above, as well as into, the bureaucracy? The level to which political appointments stretch within the bureaucracy is also important in view of the need to balance political advocacy for, and operational compliance with, major policy proposals, with the need to create a more stable, upwardly mobile and career-oriented public service.

NOTES

1   I wish to thank Linda Oduor-Noah, a Master's student in the Department of Political Studies, University of Cape Town, for her assistance in gathering and cataloguing relevant literature. I am also appreciative of Professor Anthony Butler for commenting on an earlier draft of this chapter.

2   This has historically included tertiary education qualifications, as well as competitive entry examinations.

3   This corresponds with Rouban's (2003: 313) corrective that '... the politicisation of appointments does not necessarily imply a lack of professional competence', where '[p]oliticisation generally seems linked to the idea of an amateurish administration'.

4   The implications for public servants of reforming boards are tellingly evident in an interview with a public servant quoted by Wilson and Barker (2003: 368), in which the official recalled that in the presence of business executives their minister remarked to the executives: 'Shall we tell these bozos [referring to the assembled public servants] what the real world is like?'

5   One could here cite sections 2.5 of the 1998 White Paper on Affirmative Action in the Public Service, and section 3.3.1 of the White Paper on Human Resource Management in the Public Service.

6   Interestingly, correspondence behind the 1854 Northcote/Trevelyan report also lamented the 'mixed-multitude' of candidates generated by the unreformed patronage system in the UK (Greenaway 2004: 8).

7   Plaatjies (2011: 96) makes a similar if broader point when evaluating the ANC's deployment strategy: 'While the architecture and working style of the executive and legislature are embedded in the Constitution, their practice, including setting policies, is swayed by party interests'.

8   Booysen (2011: 362) corroborates this observation, noting that 'from 2010 onward [deployment was] formally recognised by the ANC to have detracted from government performance'.

9   The study was based on one or two expert interviews with current or former senior public servants in each of twelve mostly industrialised countries, along with a review of documentation, and limited its scope to higher administrative offices, excluding political advisors.

10 A Supreme Court of Appeal ruling in 2011 invalidated the appointment of Menzi Simelani by President Jacob Zuma.

11 Seegers's (2010) analysis of state intelligence agencies in South Africa also suggests that officials within these structures have been especially vulnerable to partisan influence and interference.

12   Previous research by the author recorded double digit vacancy levels at middle and senior management levels. See Naidoo, V. 2008.
13   A report by the DPSA (2007: 23, 24) also referred to measures to limit 'job-hopping'. A pull factor may also be high levels of vacant posts at the SMS level, thereby increasing competition between departments for a limited pool of applicants.
14   Based on a 49 per cent response rate.

REFERENCES

Aberbach JD, RD Putnam and BA Rockman (1981) *Bureaucrats and Politicians in Western Democracies*. Cambridge, Mass: Harvard University Press.

Adamolekun L (2002) Africa's evolving career civil service systems: three challenges – state continuity, efficient service delivery and accountability. *International Review of Administrative Sciences*, 68: 373-387.

African National Congress (1997) 50th National Conference: Resolutions – Building the ANC. Available from: http://www.anc.org.za/show.php?id=2427 [Accessed 22 January 2012].

Auriacombe C and J Mavanyisi (2003) Political control over the bureaucracy. *Politeia*, 22(3): 72-84.

Booysen S (2011) *The African National Congress and the Regeneration of Political Power*. Johannesburg: Wits University Press.

Butler A (2002) South Africa's Political Futures: The positive and negative implications of one-party dominance. EISA Democracy Seminar Series, 7 August. http://www.eisa.org.za/pdf/dss_south-africa2002.pdf [Accessed 19 December 2011].

Cameron R (2009) New public management reforms in the South African public service: 1999-2009. *Journal of Public Administration*, 44(4.1): 910-942.

Cameron, R. 2010. Redefining political-administrative relationships in South Africa. *International Review of Administrative Sciences*, 76(4): 676-701.

Cameron R (2011) Patronage in South African Local Government. Unpublished manuscript.

Centre for Constitutional Rights (2008) Letter to the Public Protector of the Republic of South Africa, Re: Alleged unlawful and unconstitutional cadre deployment in the Public Service. http://www.fwdeklerk.org/cause_data/images/2137/letter_to_public_protector1.pdf [Accessed 19 December 2011].

DefenceWeb. Mo Shaik likely to follow Maqetuka's exit. 2 December 2011. http://www.defenceweb.co.za/index.php?option=com_content&view=article&id=21753:mo-shaik-likely-to-follow-maqetukas-exit&catid=49:National%20Security&Itemid=115 [Accessed 6 February, 2012}.

Derlien H-U (1996) The Politicisation of bureaucracies in historical and comparative perspective. In Peters and BA Rockman (Eds) *Agenda for Excellence 2: Administering the State*. Chatham, NJ: Chatham House.

Greenaway J (2004) Celebrating Northcote/Trevelyan: Dispelling the myths. *Public Policy and Administration*, 19(1): 1-14.

House of Commons, Public Administration Select Committee. 2007. Politics and Administration: Ministers and Civil Servants. Third Report of Session 2006-07.

Ingraham PW (1995. *The Foundation of Merit: Public Service in American Democracy*. Baltimore: Johns Hopkins University Press.

Institute for Accountability in Southern Africa (2010) Submission to the Ad Hoc Committee of the National Assembly enquiring into progress with service delivery, prepared by: Advocate RP Hoffman SC on behalf of the board and trustees. http://www.ifaisa.org/ad_hoc_committee_submission.html [Accessed 19 December 2011].

Kopecký P (2011) Political competition and party patronage: public appointments in Ghana and South Africa. *Political Studies*, 59: 713-732.

Lodge T (1998) Political Corruption in South Africa. *African Affairs*, 97: 157-187.

Mafunisa JM (2003) Separation of politics from the South African public service: Rhetoric or reality. *Journal of Public Administration*, 38(2): 85-101.

Maphunye KJ (2005) Re-politicising the bureaucracy to solve apartheid's inequalities? The 'political-administrative interface' in South Africa. *Journal of Public Administration*, 40(3.1): 212-228.

Maserumule HM (2007) Conflicts between directors-general and ministers in South Africa: 1994-2004: A 'postulative' approach. *Politikon*, 34(2): 147-164.

Matheson A et al. (2007) Study on the Political Involvement in Senior Staffing and on the Delineation of Responsibilities between Ministers and Senior Civil Servants. OECD Working Papers on Public Governance. Paris: OECD Publishing.

McCourt W (2000) Public Appointments: from Patronage to Merit. Working Paper No. 9. Institute for Development Policy and Management, University of Manchester. http://www.sed.manchester.ac.uk/idpm/research/publications/archive/hr/hr_wp09.pdf [Accessed 12 January 2012].

Miller K (2005) *Public Sector Reform: Governance in South Africa*. Aldershot: Ashgate.

Naidoo V (2008) Assessing racial redress in the public service. In Bentley KA and A Habib (Eds) *Racial Redress and Citizenship in South Africa*. Cape Town: HSRC Press.

Peters BG and J Pierre (2004) Politicisation of the civil service: concepts, causes, consequences. In Peters BG and J Pierre (Eds) *Politicisation of the Civil Service in Comparative Perspective*. London: Routledge.

Plaatjies D (2011) Values, political governance and deployment. In Plaatjies D (Ed.) *Future Inheritance: Building State Capacity in Democratic South Africa*. Johannesburg: Jacana.

Posel D (2000) Labour relations and the politics of patronage: a case study of the apartheid civil service. In Adler G (Ed.) *Public Service Labour Relations in a Democratic South Africa*. Johannesburg: Wits University Press.

Public Service Commission (2008a) Audit of Selection Processes in Selected Departments. Pretoria: PSC. http://www.info.gov.za/view/DownloadFileAction?id=107872_ [Accessed 24 January 2012].

Public Service Commission (2008b) The Turn-over rate of Heads of Department and its Implications for the Public Service. Pretoria: PSC.

Republic of South Africa (1997a) Managing People in a Transformed Public Service. White Paper on a New Employment Policy for the Public Service, First Draft. Department of Public Service and Administration. http://www.info.gov.za/view/DownloadFileAction?id=70439 [Accessed 14 December 2011).

Republic of South Africa (1997b) White Paper on Human Resource Management in the Public Service. Department of Public Service and Administration. http://www.freetrans.gov.za/documents/unpan005183.pdf [Accessed 22 January 2012].

Republic of South Africa (1998) Report of the Presidential Review Commission on the Reform and Transformation of the Public Service in South Africa. http://www.info.gov.za/otherdocs/1998/prc98/index.html

Republic of South Africa (2001) Public Service Regulations, 2001. As amended by Government Notice No. R.382 of 14 May 2010 with effect from 17 May 2010.

Republic of South Africa (2007) Improving the performance of the public service: lessons of the transformation process. Department of Public Service and Administration. Pretoria: DPSA.

Republic of South Africa (2009) State of Local Government in South Africa: Overview report, National State of Local Government Assessments, Working documents. Department of Co-operative Governance and Traditional Affairs. Pretoria: CoGTA.

Republic of South Africa (2010) Dispensation for the Appointment and Remuneration of Persons (Special Advisers) Appointed to Executive Authorities on Ground of Policy Considerations in Terms of Section 12a of the Public Service Act, 1994: 1 January 2010. Department of Public Service and Administration.

Republic of South Africa (2012) National Development Plan 2030 Our Future – Make it Work. Pretoria:

National Planning Commission. http://www.npconline.co.za/pebble.asp?relid=25 [Accessed 17 August 2012].

Rouban L (2003) Politicisation of the Civil Service. In Peters BG and J Pierre (Eds) *Handbook of Public Administration*. Thousand Oaks, Cal: Sage.

Sangweni SS and N Mxakato-Diseko (2008) It does not matter what slant or take you have on the Developmental State: at the end of the day, a strong, coherent and astute public service is critical. In Turok B (Ed.) *Wealth Doesn't Trickle Down: The Case for a Developmental State in South Africa*. Cape Town: New Agenda.

Schrire R (1986) South Africa: Bureaucracy and the process of reform. *Journal of Contemporary African Studies*, 5(1-2): 145-164.

Seegers A (2010) The new security in democratic South Africa: A cautionary tale. *Conflict, Security and Development*, 10(2): 263-285.

Van der Meer F, T Steen and A Wille (2007) Western European civil service systems: A comparative analysis. In Raadschelders JCN, TAJ Toonen and FM van der Meer (Eds) *The Civil Service in the 21st Century*. Basingstoke: Palgrave Macmillan.

Wachman R and P Curtis (2010) Civil service shake-up will see business chiefs on departments to oversee cuts. *The Guardian*. 16 December.

Wilson GK and A Barker (2003) Bureaucrats and politicians in Britain. *Governance*, 16(3): 349-372.

Wilson W (1913) [1885] *Congressional Government: A Study in American Politics*. Boston: Houghton Mifflin.

World Bank (2011) Accountability in Public Services in South Africa: selected issues. Washington: World Bank.

CHAPTER 14

Traditional male initiation:
Culture and the Constitution

Louise Vincent

——•——

INTRODUCTION

Traditional male initiation has in recent years been the focus of government and media attention as a result of unacceptably large numbers of initiates being severely injured or dying. Between 1995 and 2006, more than 6 500 boys undergoing initiation were admitted to Eastern Cape hospitals, more than 300 died and over a hundred had their genitalia amputated following ritual circumcision (see Apps 2005: 28). The Eastern Cape Department of Health reported that eight initiates had died in the province between early January 2007 and November 2006 although two of these deaths were not directly related to circumcision (one had been murdered and another had died in a fire at a school). This represented a decrease in the number of deaths compared with the same period in the preceding year when fifteen deaths had been recorded. However, multiple problems continue to beleager traditional initiation practices in the Eastern Cape. In 2009 alone, ninety-one newly circumcised men in the Eastern Cape died, fifty-six of those deaths occurring in the mid-year school holidays (Associated Press 2010).

Would-be initiates are mindful of the risks and their sense of uncertainty is compounded by an awareness of the extent to which the reproduction of the custom has become fragile and uncertain. The role prescribed by tradition for families is not always followed where there are many female-headed households, and the certainty of communal bonds and hierarchies implied by the practice have been fractured and become muddled. The social imperative to be initiated is as strong as it ever was, accompanied by an uncompromising set of social and physical punishments for those who fail to abide by it, but the social networks and foundations upon which that imperative once securely rested, and which served to support it, are no longer in place in many communities. This has led to a crisis with multiple dimensions including bogus fly-by-night surgeons and circumcision lodge operators; widespread reports of alcoholism and drug abuse by initiates and by those practising as traditional surgeons and nurses; and under-age boys being abducted into circumcision lodges or taking it upon themselves to be circumcised without the knowledge of their families.

In response, the government has put in place a number of legal and regulatory instruments aimed at bringing traditional initiation more firmly under its supervisory gaze. A comprehensive legislative framework has been matched by massive public outreach campaigns and considerable financial and physical resources devoted to the implementation and monitoring of the new regulations. To the extent that government's newly imposed regulatory regime has been met with resistance, this has come from traditional authorities, who have fought to maintain a toehold on power and influence in the face of criticisms that they are an anachronism in a democratic constitutional state. In this regard, the question of traditional initiation in South Africa serves as a window into a much wider debate concerning the relationship between culture and rights, between traditional and democratic authority, and between customary and formal law. Attempts by the central state to regulate initiation practices can easily be read as intrusions into traditional authority, which echo the dismissive approach to custom during colonialism and apartheid. Ritual male initiation is thus one of several phenomena in contemporary South Africa that have thrown into relief the relationship between traditional (hereditary) and formal (democratic) lines of authority – between the formal, constitutional legal framework and customary law.

TRADITION REINVENTED

The South African amaXhosa, the majority of whom live in the Eastern Cape province, are one of several ethnic groups in southern Africa that practise the ritual of circumcision as part of a rite admitting boys to manhood. Xhosa boys are aware from a young age that initiation is an inevitable part of male life. Some 10 000 Xhosa males are traditionally circumcised annually in the Eastern Cape. In Xhosa custom the ritual is performed most commonly on males between the ages of fifteen and twenty-five – the Eastern Cape's circumcision legislation sets the legal age for circumcision at eighteen but boys of sixteen and seventeen may undergo initiation with the permission of their parents or guardians. The continued circumcision of underage boys, sometimes as young as twelve, has been one key target of government's regulatory attention.

Although the 2005 Children's Act demands parental consent for those circumcised under the age of eighteen, a study conducted in the Flagstaff health district of the Eastern Cape in 2004 found that most initiates (41.66 per cent) did not inform their parents before enrolling in the initiation school. They simply disappeared from home and made their way to the initiation site (Mogotlane et al. 2004: 60). Because custom prescribes that initiation is not discussed at all with female relatives, sons in female-headed households are faced with a genuine dilemma. One informant told the authors of the Flagstaff study: 'I have no father or any male relative. When I felt that I was ready to enrol, I told my mother and I noticed that she was against this ... so I brought myself to initiation school.' There is even a term in the local vernacular describing this: *ukubalekela* (literally, to escape into, meaning to run away from home and seek temporary refuge at the initiation school). Moreover, the circumcision of boys younger than sixteen continues to be widespread. In the Flagstaff study, for instance, informants reported that the age of initiates ranged from twelve to twenty. The informants themselves felt that the most appropriate age at which to be initiated would be eighteen.

Traditionally, the circumcision instrument of choice would have been an *umdlanga* (assegai). In the past, instruments were only rarely sterilised. The Eastern Cape government has attempted to regulate the use of instruments by stipulating what sort of instrument is acceptable and by providing chemicals for sterilisation, and training in the use of acceptable instruments. This is a very sensitive issue, with some traditional leaders baulking at the idea of the traditional surgeon having to obtain permission for the instrument he chooses to use: 'We cannot use any other instrument to circumcise young boys, we just cannot' (interview, Chief Mandlenkosi Dumalisile).

The operation is performed by a traditional surgeon (*ingcibi*), who was customarily a man of standing and status in the community, trusted for his experience in performing the procedure. The custom is for the roles of traditional nurse and traditional surgeon to be handed down within families from generation to generation. Where demand increases and there is a need to introduce new members into this fraternity, the requirements are traditionally stringent: a prospective candidate should himself be a circumcised male for not less than ten years; should not be a drinker; should be a man of discipline; and should be generally acceptable to the community (interview, Jackson Vena, traditional dresser). But recent years have seen the rise of self-proclaimed traditional nurses and surgeons motivated by financial incentives. These 'mushrooms', as they are sometimes referred to, are naturally frowned upon by the established community of traditional nurses and surgeons.

While at initiation school (*ibhoma*), participants are known as initiates (*abakhwetha*). In contrast to dominant Western human rights discourses in which children are singled out for special treatment as vulnerable subjects for whom the possession of rights to humane treatment at all times is especially significant, the initiate is expected to obey instructions and has few rights and little say in what happens to him at the circumcision lodge. Referring to the harsh way in which he was treated by the *ikhankatha*, an initiate explains: 'As a man you do not beg an *umkhwetha*, a Xhosa initiate, into manhood, for he is a subordinate' (anonymous first-hand account).

Initiates are expected to observe strict dietary taboos during their initiation. Originally these included a prohibition on drinking water or eating salty foods in the first seven days after circumcision, presumably to limit urination, which would be painful. However, it is now illegal to instruct an initiate to avoid drinking water, as dehydration has been a primary cause of death and illness among initiates. Two changes in contemporary practice have made dehydration a bigger risk today than it was in the past: first, circumcision is frequently performed in the hotter summer months (presumably to accommodate school holidays), whereas in the past it was most often performed in autumn. Second, plastic sheeting is now often used to build the initiate's hut instead of the traditional leaves and grass, which were much cooler.

Whereas the traditional surgeon is ideally a person trained by his predecessor with skills handed down from one generation to the next, in a contemporary period characterised by much greater social change, mobility and cultural rupture, the training and competence of *ingicibi* are not always assured. Some injuries occur as a result of incorrect surgery – for example, too much skin being removed. Associated complications include haemorrhage through laceration or amputation of the glans and/or the penile shaft as well as removal of too much foreskin, denuding the penile shaft (see also William and Kapila 1993: 1231-1236; and Menahem1981: 45-8). Medical reports suggest that traditional surgeons are largely ignorant of anatomy and commonly chop rather than excise the foreskin. Traditional attendants or nurses are ignorant of aseptic technique or the importance of blood circulation and nutrition in wound healing, as is evidenced by the nature and application of dressings and restrictions on protein-rich foods. Because pain and suffering are regarded by informants (traditional surgeons and attendants) as good for initiates there is no attempt to control or alleviate pain, haemorrhaging, shock or dehydration.

A recurring charge in recent years is that of surgeons operating while under the influence of alcohol or narcotics. Related to the problem of the training and competence of traditional surgeons are questions of hygiene, the correct use of appropriate instruments and sterilisation. Though not trained in Western medical practice, the experienced *ingicibi* would be well versed in traditional practices including, for example, the use of herbal medicines to combat infection, but current reports speak of the reuse of instruments without cleaning or sterilisation, the use of blunt instruments, and a lack of hygiene at many circumcision schools. As a result there are concerns about infection and the spread of venereal disease, and HIV in particular. Septicaemia from poor hygiene can lead to death if not treated with appropriate antibiotics.

At the 2006 hearings on traditional circumcision convened by the Commission for the Promotion and Protection of the Rights of Cultural, Religious and Linguistic Communities (CRL), the South African Human Rights Commission and the National House of Traditional Leaders (NHTL) held at the Qawukeni Great Place in Lusikisiki, Prince Zukisile Makaula, a senior royal member of the AmaBacha, spoke out against opportunists who sought to gain materially from performing circumcisions. The financial incentives are considerable. In a province characterised by very high levels of poverty and unemployment, financial factors inevitably intrude to create incentives other than purely cultural ones for keeping initiates under the control of the traditional school and its leaders. With each initiate being charged a fee by the traditional surgeon, circumcision is big business and there have been reports of boys as young as eight being kidnapped from their homes to increase numbers at circumcision schools. As a result, self-proclaimed traditional surgeons and traditional nurses operate without the sanction of their communities or the chief in authority in a particular area, and they do not register with the government-appointed medical officer. At the 2006 hearings on traditional circumcision, parents and elders also expressed alarm about abductions of young boys who were taken out of their home area to a different district to be circumcised. Members of the public spoke of people 'going around in trucks collecting boys for initiation, without getting permission from parents, and without reporting even to the local traditional leader'.

Widespread unemployment and poverty in the region mean that many families are unable to save enough to pay to send a son to initiation school and as a result some boys leave school early to find work in order to pay for their initiation. Reports of overcrowding and inadequate facilities for shelter at initiation schools are common. The Flagstaff study described a lodge accommodating forty initiates that measured eight strides across and in length. The structures are often not properly roofed or sealed, exposing initiates to the elements. Floors are not cemented so dust and grass often contaminate the circumcision wound.

The hazards initiates face are widely known and spoken of but they are usually seen as far outweighed by the disincentives of a life lived as an uninitiated male. Many social privileges and positions of status are available only to initiated males. These include the right to inherit, the right to take part in family courts, to attend the chief's court, to act on behalf of one's father when the need arises, to attend and participate in feasts and beer-drinking ceremonies without being pushed aside and branded a *kwedini* or child (Momoti 2002: 50). The uninitiated male, even when middle aged, is treated with contempt, and there is no alternative route to the achievement of social inclusion, status and respect. As a result, young boys face enormous social pressure to be circumcised. Peer pressure, avoiding being called cowards, avoiding being ridiculed and harassed, pressure from women and older people to maintain tradition, and the desire to gain respect feature strongly in the self-reported motivations of Xhosa males to be circumcised. Studies in the field of public health (see for example, Tenge 2006; Bottoman 2006) have found that uncircumcised males are traumatised as a result of the ridicule and harassment they experience at the hands of peers and elders who have already undergone circumcision. The risk of ostracism is experienced not only by the uncircumcised boy himself but also by his family, who fear social exclusion if their son has not been to initiation school.

TRADITIONAL AUTHORITY AND LIBERAL CONSTITUTIONALISM

When the British government took over the Cape Colony from the Dutch in 1806, it tried to bring order to the 'eastern frontier', partly by bribing local chiefs, who were in return expected to exert control over their subjects. This set the pattern for the relationship between traditional and formal authority through the colonial, and then the apartheid, years. Traditional authority was pragmatically accommodated to the extent that it was useful; chiefs were bought and those who were uncooperative were simply replaced with more helpful proxies. As a result, the relationship between traditional authorities and the liberation movement in exile – and subsequently the ruling party – has always been a delicate one and many did not expect the institution of the chieftaincy to survive into the democratic era (Van Kessel and Oomen1997: 561). Contrary to expectations, however, in the democratic era we have seen a reassertion by chiefs of their relevance and legitimacy, based in part on their casting themselves as the rightful custodians of 'culture'. This has rendered issues such traditional circumcision, polygamy and virginity testing potentially explosive touchstones for the balance of power between the authority of the state and these more dispersed, localised and traditional lines of authority.

The very idea of hereditary traditional leadership appears to directly contradict the fundamental principle of democratic elections so central to the idea of democracy. But the 1996 Constitution safeguards the institution, although many issues remain unresolved. For example, traditional leaders argue that their power to allocate land to their people should be fully restored. They also object to the 1999 Municipal Structures Act, which outlines local government administration, without a role for traditional leaders, and requires elected officials to implement development programmes. The government is unwilling to compromise on any of these issues.

Although the Constitution and its accompanying Bill of Rights recognise cultural rights and the right of citizens to participate in the culture of their choice, these rights may not be exercised in a manner inconsistent with any provision in the Bill of Rights. The liberal tradition suggests a neutral approach to constitutional interpretation in instances where cultural or group and individual rights – both of which are recognised in the Constitution – conflict, but it is unclear how principles of neutrality or disinterested tolerance assist in resolving disputes. For some, cultural rights are always second-order rights that can only be recognised if they do not violate individual rights or equality norms. Similarly, customary law which gives expression to cultural specificity is regarded with suspicion from the point of view of a discourse of human rights based in individual freedoms. This ranking, however, is by no means neutral. It once again assumes the subordinate status of indigenous law in a manner that replicates the colonial approach: limited recognition of indigenous law under very restricted circumstances. Moreover, colonial and apartheid expediency is replicated too, so that there is a sense in which indigenous law is regarded as representing outdated cultural remnants that will be superseded in time by a superior system of law based on individual rights.

Indigenous law is recognised as part of South African law, subject to the Constitution and protected by it, as well as being subject to legislation consistent with the Constitution that deals specifically with it. However, although there are those who appeal to 'custom' as though it is an unchanging and commonly recognised set of prescriptions in an attempt to resist state regulation of cultural practices, there are no timeless, mutually agreed-upon customs. What often lies behind the appeal to custom is a mixture of sensitivity regarding the historical manner in which the state used and abused traditional authority, concern on the part of traditional leaders about their loss of power and influence to the state, and concern about the potential for loss of control over, and access to, scarce material benefits and resources.

The historical importance and legacy of the relationship between the state and traditional authority structures provide an important framework within which government attempts to regulate traditional circumcision, and resistance to those attempts must be understood. In an attempt to legitimise its interventions, government has argued that, far from undermining tradition, its regulatory regime is the protector of culture in its most authentic form from the corrupting influences of greed, alcoholism and ignorance of tradition associated with contemporary society.

The response by the traditional authorities echoes the historical bifurcation between resistance and accommodation that has always characterised the relationship between the state and these authorities. Some traditional leaders have offered their public support for government regulation. In support of the state, Sibusiso Nkosi, spokesperson for the National House of Traditional Leaders, has argued that the problem is not with traditional initiation itself but with its practice by 'bogus' initiation schools that 'claim the lives of our innocent children … making a mockery of our culture' and bringing 'shame and doubt on traditional practices' (Sapa 2005).

On the other hand, opponents of state regulation have themselves used the language of cultural authenticity to resist what are seen as illegitimate incursions into their sphere of influence. Traditional leaders frame their vigorous opposition to the regulation of circumcision by appealing to the arcane intricacies of the practice, which are frequently interpreted in their most uncompromising form. And gender is, predictably, often an important theme. For example, opposing the Eastern Cape's regulatory regime, the Congress of Traditional Leaders of South Africa (Contralesa) argued that the law was unacceptable because women were on the team that drafted the legislation and according to tradition women must not be involved in any way with the rituals of manhood. Contralesa described the law as 'an insult to our tradition' and vowed to stop medical officers having anything to do with ritual circumcision. The injunction against the involvement of women was taken to a bizarre extreme in the case of one mother, who was barred from attending the funeral of her son, who had died at initiation school after being beaten by the school leader following an attempt to escape from the school.

Arguing that they alone are the rightful custodians of culture, traditional leaders protest that the new regulatory regime fails to provide for them to be included in such processes as the registration of *iingcibi* and *amakhankatha*. The picture is politically complicated by the fact that opposition to state regulation of tradition comes from within the ruling party as much as it does from without. Eastern Cape House of Traditional Leaders chair and ANC MP Mwelo Nonkonyana called the province's Application of Health Standards in Traditional Circumcision Act 'nonsensical' as it stripped traditional leaders of their power to administer the custom and vested those powers in the provincial health minister and 'his doctors' – some who may themselves not be circumcised. Contralesa has argued that the Act is unconstitutional as it infringes on the traditional rights of communities protected by the Bill of Rights.

Although some traditional leaders, such as chief of the abaThembu tribe and ANC MPL Zwelinzima Mtirara, are more accommodating, others have advocated outright civil disobedience in their response to government regulation. Nonkonyana, for example, is on record as saying that 'if an uncircumcised man is found near an initiation school he will be detained and circumcised' and that 'traditionally a woman found in the area near a circumcision school would be killed but because of the human rights thing she's detained and dealt with in another way by the people' (*Mail & Guardian*, 8 December 2003). Nonkonyana has declared that he would be prepared to go to jail rather than comply with the act, and that his own son was illegally circumcised at an unregistered school, although the actual circumcision surgery was performed by a doctor with Western medical qualifications – the important point for Nonkonyana was that the doctor was himself a circumcised man (*Cape Argus* 2003).

Purported 'compromise solutions' such as the Western Cape government's 2004 proposal to establish 'cultural villages' where 'Xhosa people may practise their culture' (afrol news 2004) have been less successful. Billed as 'part of bringing democracy to the people' by providing 'an appropriate facility for people to practice their initiation culture', the R1.2 million initiative met with little enthusiasm from traditional leaders, who pointed out that the burning of initiation huts so central to the symbolism of the rite would not be possible in a designated cultural village consisting of state-owned permanent facilities.[1] Like many rites of transition, physical separation is an essential part of ritual circumcision. Seclusion in the bush and building and living in a temporary lodge that is subsequently burned along with the initiate's personal belongings to mark the end of seclusion and the start of a new phase in the lifecycle and a new status in the community are central tenets.

Although hospital circumcision seems the ideal solution to the problematic rate of death and injury associated with traditional male circumcision, those who attend legal schools or who are circumcised in hospital risk being stigmatised and branded '*amadoda phepha*' (paper men). According to Nonkonyana, 'if you are not circumcised through custom in the mountain, you are not regarded as a man. You are a social outcast. Such people are called *abadlezana*, a woman who gives birth in a hospital ward. He is not a man, he is the equivalent of a woman' (*Cape Argus* 2003).

Advocates of hospital circumcision overlook the reality of the poor access the majority of South Africans have to effective medical care in the formal health sector and the enormous contribution the traditional healing sector makes to public health. South Africa has one doctor for every 1 500 people, but in rural areas, where ritual circumcision is most commonly practised, this figure falls to one in 26 000. There are an estimated 200 000 traditional healers in the country in contrast to some 31 000 'Western-trained' medical practitioners (De Souza 2001: 373). According to the Medical Research Council, between 75 and 80 per cent of South Africans regularly consult traditional healers.

A medical doctor told the Pretoria High Court that hospitals in Limpopo Province 'were so badly run that patients had to be sent home for lack of running water; they had to lie in their own urine for days; equipment was regularly stolen; and essential medication was either out of stock or not provided' (Schlemmer and Wilson 2001: 54). It is, then, somewhat disingenuous to hold up South Africa's public health facilities – which are already groaning under the weight of the country's HIV crisis – as the answer to the medical problems that surround traditional circumcision.

Differences in attitude on the part of medical staff at hospitals can be key to whether or not adult male circumcision services are provided in practice. Staff interviewed at some hospitals took the view that 'we don't do that here; they must go to the *sangoma* for that'. In some cases this attitude is apparently motivated by repugnance for the tradition and a sense that it 'does not belong in a proper hospital', and in other cases it appears that staff are themselves opposed to the idea of male circumcision taking place in a hospital because it offends tradition. Many hospitals consider circumcision, cosmetic surgery and would only offer adult circumcision in cases of medical emergency, for instance, where an injury has been sustained to the penis. Ironically, most such injuries are incurred during bush circumcision.

CIRCUMCISION AND HIV/AIDS

But it is not only traditional chiefs who are contemporary circumcision enthusiasts. Support for the practice has come from surprising quarters. In the context of South Africa's high rate of HIV/AIDS infection (between four and five million South Africans are estimated to be HIV-positive), the risk of HIV has featured prominently in calls for the regulation of traditional circumcision. Whereas government has appealed to the risk of HIV infection through unsafe surgical practices as one of the ways in which it legitimises greater regulation of traditional male initiation, recent research (see, for example, Huff 2000; Silverman 2004: 426) reveals that circumcision offers males some protection against HIV infection. This has resulted in renewed interest in traditional circumcision and whether it might be refashioned to become a significant aspect of South Africa's response to its HIV/AIDS crisis. Added to this is debate about the extent to which the traditional educative function of circumcision 'schools', which has been lost in many areas, might be recovered and an HIV-awareness component inserted into the traditional teachings that are meant to be part of traditional male initiation rites.

Discrepancies in regional HIV infection rates may partially be explained by differing circumcision practices. In most West African countries, for example, where male circumcision is widespread, HIV prevalence levels are between 1 and 5 per cent compared with 25 per cent in many of the predominantly non-circumcising east and southern African nations (Viall 1999). Groundbreaking research among more than 3 200 HIV-negative young men from Orange Farm, an African township south of Johannesburg, found that men who are circumcised are 60 per cent less likely to contract HIV than those who are not. The clinical trial randomly assigned half of the men to be circumcised and the other half remained uncircumcised as a control group. For every ten uncircumcised men who contracted HIV, about three circumcised men contracted the virus. It was deemed unethical to proceed without offering circumcision to all the men in the study.

According to a study published in the *Public Library of Science Medicine* in November 2005, the outcome of these studies suggests that 3.7 million infections could be averted, and 2.7 million lives saved in the next twenty years in sub-Saharan Africa (where circumcision rates are low in many countries) if more men were circumcised. The president of the South African Clinicians Society, Francois Venter, said that this is 'the buzz in prevention circles. If we had a vaccine that powerful, we'd roll it out right away.'

The promising Orange Farm results were confirmed by two studies, conducted in Kenya and Uganda, whose results were released late in 2006. Researchers monitored 4 996 men between the ages of fifteen and forty-nine living in Uganda and 2 784 men aged between eighteen and twenty-four living in Kenya. Half were randomly assigned to be circumcised and the other half served as a control group. The aim was to determine whether circumcision reduced HIV infection. The mechanism is uncertain but it is believed that male circumcision eliminates the cells most vulnerable to HIV. In addition, a circumcised penis develops thicker skin that is more resistant to HIV infection. African countries with low circumcision rates (including Botswana, South Africa, Swaziland and Zimbabwe) have the highest HIV prevalence on the continent. The Ugandan study found forty-three cases of HIV among the uncircumcised men, compared with twenty-two among the circumcised men – a 48 per cent reduction. The Kenyan study found forty-seven cases of HIV among uncircumcised men, compared with twenty-two among the circumcised men – a 53 per cent reduction. So compelling were these results that the trials were halted early and circumcision offered to all participants. There was also no evidence that circumcised men in the studies adopted higher risk behaviours such as unprotected sex or sex with multiple partners.

As a result of these research findings, some South African AIDS activists have advanced a vision of mass 'chop shops' where volunteers are expected to come forward in numbers to have their foreskins quickly removed. Some advocates of circumcision as an HIV-prevention measure have suggested that one way of increasing the numbers of men making themselves available for circumcision would be to offer financial incentives.

Though some have hailed these findings of the apparent protective effect of circumcision against HIV infection as 'the most important breakthrough in HIV prevention since the efficacy of the male condom was unequivocally demonstrated in laboratory and human studies' (Coates 2005), others have pointed out that the United States has a very high rate of circumcision coupled with the highest HIV infection rate in the developed world, whereas Scandinavia, on the other hand, has one of the lowest rates of circumcision in the world coupled with a comparatively low incidence of HIV infection. The argument is, as some commentators have pointed out (see, for example, Milos and Macris 1992; Lagarde et al. 2003), disingenuous. Disease is caused by contact with specific organisms and the spread of disease is prevented by reducing contact with these organisms through education and altered practices rather than through the amputation of healthy body parts. Moreover, advocating circumcision as a protection against HIV can lead to unsafe sexual practices by providing a false sense of security (Lagarde et al. 2003:89).

On the other hand, traditional circumcision has itself given rise to concerns about HIV infection as a result of the common practice of a single instrument being used, without intervening sterilisation, to circumcise several initiates at a time – often in groups of ten or more. This concern arises in the context of the already existing exceptionally high rate of HIV infection among South Africa's children. 'At the end of 1987, 80 000 children below the age of fifteen years were estimated to be infected. Between 1994 and 1997 the number of children infected tripled. Current estimates show that at least one-quarter of all children in hospital in South Africa are HIV positive. In some hospitals 70 to 80 per cent of paediatric beds are occupied by HIV-positive infants' (Davel 2002: 282).

Mongezi Guma, chairperson of the Commission for the Promotion and Protection of the Rights of Cultural, Religious and Linguistic Communities, has cautioned that introducing a mass circumcision campaign as part of a national HIV prevention strategy would pose huge challenges for the traditional circumcision schools. And there are unanswered questions to grapple with. Should health officials target young men or old? The new legislation provides for males older than sixteen but younger than eighteen to be circumcised if their parents specifically request it, but is clearly aiming at the minimum age for circumcision being eighteen.

It is well known, however, that sexual activity begins for many South African men at a much younger age. Would this mean that if the aim is the prevention of HIV infection rather than the regulation of a cultural custom the legislation should be amended to lower the permitted age? This in turn once again raises the problems of consent, the rights of children and parental involvement, which were precisely some of the issues the legislation sought to circumvent by placing the age limit fairly high.

Another question concerns the role public hospitals should play in such a campaign. There are deep cultural sensitivities around men opting for hospital circumcision, and sensitivities around the incursion of state power into the traditional role of chiefs, traditional surgeons and circumcision school leaders. These cultural sensitivities are not eased by the financial dimensions – if a campaign begins to urge young men to be circumcised in hospital to prevent HIV infections it is highly likely that traditional surgeons and traditional nurses will see this not only as a cultural threat but also as an incursion into a vital source of income. The service offered at public hospitals would probably be free. The poor, the main clients of traditional circumcision schools, would now have a financial incentive to bypass traditional schools. Moreover, if free circumcision became widespread it may soon no longer be ideologically viable to brand hospital-circumcised men as 'not real men' because there would be so many of them.

However, it is not only the surgical aspect of circumcision that is of potential benefit to attempts to curb the rate of HIV infection. Circumcision itself is meant to be accompanied by a process of initiation that traditionally had an educative socialisation function, inducting boys into the responsibilities and restraints associated with manhood

(Pitje 1950). In contemporary circumcision schools, much of the traditional educational aspect of the initiation rite has fallen away (interview, Jackson Vena). But in some areas of the Eastern Cape, such as the Makana district where traditional circumcision is very tightly controlled by an established board of traditional nurses and surgeons (the organisation calls itself Isiko Ioluntu or 'rite of passage'), there has been a revitalisation of the educational component of the rite. The motivation has been twofold. Traditionalists in the region are deeply concerned with what they view as the lack of knowledge among the youth of Xhosa culture, which they see as contributing to social problems such as crime, alcoholism and the high school drop-out rate; secondly, concerns surrounding HIV/AIDS have given rise to the idea that circumcision schools could be used to spread the message of sexual health, safety and responsibility.

CONCLUSION

If the state is to take seriously its constitutional commitment to respecting cultural diversity then it cannot simply dismiss the objections of traditionalists who are sensitive to intrusions into what is regarded as one of the most sacred of Xhosa cultural practices. An important feature of the appeal to cultural authenticity to legitimise traditional circumcision is the idea that social order has broken down as a result of the corrupting influence of 'foreign' ideas and practices. Ritual circumcision is thus defended by traditionalists on the basis of its usefulness as a mechanism for the maintenance of social order, particularly in relation to the perceived crisis in youth sexuality marked by extremely high levels of gender-based violence and HIV infection. Young men, once circumcised, are meant to behave differently, to put away childishness and to take on the mantle of responsible and proper behaviour expected of a man. However, as with any mechanism of social control, there are no guarantees. In a society beset by a mesh of illiteracy, conflict, unemployment, violence against women and children, extreme poverty and wealth disparities, masculinity is widely perceived to be in crisis (see, for example, Clare 2000; McDowell 2000). To pretend that ritual circumcision is going to make a major difference to this crisis is disingenuous – as was perhaps most vividly demonstrated by the case in which eight initiates were accused of gang-raping a twenty-seven-year-old woman. They had recently graduated from initiation school and reportedly gang-raped the woman to remove from their bodies a white substance (*ifutha*) that is used as part of the initiation process (Sapa, 31 January 2006).

With few marketable skills and limited opportunities for the assertion of power or status, those who find themselves marginalised in the democratic order see in 'tradition' a limited currency with which to trade for power. State regulation of tradition risks devaluing this currency and those who own it. The resultant conflict is rendered more acute by the fact that the traditionalists frequently neither own nor have ready access to any other currency, and that what they do own is not readily convertible into the coinage of a modern liberal capitalist order. Where the conversion does take place the results are often tragic, with financial gain a key reason for the mushrooming of fly-by-night circumcision schools and bogus traditional surgeons.

Those who style themselves as the rightful custodians of culture claim that pristine tradition is being corrupted by outside influence. In reality, of course, it is precisely the flexibility of African belief systems that accounts for their survival in the face of a history of invasion and political domination. It is ironic that the unhistorical, frozen-in-time view of tradition associated with the maligned Western scholars of Africa is being proposed by cultural entrepreneurs of the present, who suggest that pure, authentic practices are at risk from corrupting outside influences represented by the democratic state.

NOTE

1   On the other hand, Contralesa's Phathekile Holomisa has argued that hut burning has long not been widely practised, with many contemporary initiates living in ordinary houses, and only the belongings of the initiate are burned. 'We must adapt to changing times,' Holomisa is quoted as saying (afrol news, 2 March 2004).

REFERENCES

Apps P (2005) Deaths prompt action on circumcision schools. *Reuters/IOL*. 28 July.
Beidelman TO (1965) Notes on Boys' Initiation among the Ngulu of East Africa. *Man* 65: 143-147.
Bottoman B (2006) The Experience of Indigenous Circumcision by Newly Initiated Xhosa Men in East London in the Eastern Cape Province. Unpublished Master's Thesis, Unisa.
Cape Argus (2003) Eastern Cape circumcision schools rebel. 10 December.
Crosse-Upcott ARW(1959) Male circumcision among the Ngindo. *J R Anthropology Institute* 89: 169-189.
Chanock M (1991) Law, state and culture: Thinking about 'customary law' after apartheid. *Acta Juridica*: 52-70.
Church J (2005) The place of indigenous law in a mixed legal system and a society in transformation: A South African experience. *ANZLH E-Journal*: 94-106.
Coates TJ (2005) The snip could save many lives. *The Star*, Johannesburg, 31 October.
Davel T (2002) The African Charter on the rights and welfare of the child. *De Jure*: 281.
Delius P and Glaser C (2002) Sexual socialisation in South Africa: A historical perspective. *African Studies* 61 (1):27-54.
Funani L (1990) *Circumcision among the AmaXhosa. A Medical Investigation*. Braamfontein: Skotaville.
Gluckman M (1949) The role of the sexes in Wiko circumcision ceremonies. In Fortes M (Ed.) *Social Structure: Studies Presented to AR Radcliffe-Brown*. Oxford: Clarendon Press:145-167.
Green J (2004) Bones of contention for traditional healers. *The Star*, Johannesburg. 27 September:11.
Hambly WD (1935) Tribal initiation of boys in Angola. *American Anthropology* 37: 36-40.
Heald S (1986) The ritual use of violence: Circumcision among the Gisu of Uganda. In Riches D (Ed.) *The Anthropology of Violence*. Oxford: Blackwell.
Hemson D and K Owusu-Ampomah (2005) A better life for all? Service delivery and poverty alleviation. In Daniel J, R Southall and J Lutchman (Eds) *State of the Nation: South Africa 2004*. Cape Town: HSRC Press.
Holredge CP and K Young (1927) Circumcision rites among the Bajok. *American Anthropology*. 29:661-669.
Hosken G (2004) City clinic performs 50 free circumcisions. *Pretoria News*. 28 June.

Huff B (2000) Male circumcision: Cutting the risk? *American Foundation for Aids Research* (August).

Kahn T (2006) What if circumcision saves lives? *Business Day.* 3 August.

Koyana DS (1980) *Customary Law in a Changing Society.* Cape Town: Juta.

Lagarde E, T Dirk, A Puren, R Reathe and A Betran (2003) Acceptability of male circumcision as a tool for preventing HIV infection in a highly infected community in South Africa. *AIDS.* 17 (1): 81-95.

La Fontaine JS (1985) *Initiation.* Manchester: Manchester University Press.

Library of Congress Country Studies. http://lcweb2.loc.gov/frd/cs/cshome.html

Longmore L (1959) *The Dispossessed: A Study of the Sex Life of Bantu Women in and around the Urban Areas of Johannesburg.* London: Jonathan Cape.

Mail & Guardian Online (2002).The Making of a Man. 19 July. http://www.mg.co.za/

Mayatula V and T Mavundla (1997) A review on male circumcision procedures among South African blacks. *Curationis* September:16-20.

Mayer P (1971) Traditional manhood initiation in an industrial city. In De Jager EJ (Ed.) *Anthropological Essays Presented to OF Raum.* Cape Town: Struik:7-18.

Mbiti JS (1978) *Introduction to African Religion.* London: Heineman.

Meintjes G (1998) *Manhood at a Price. Socio-medical Perspectives on Xhosa Traditional Circumcision.* Institute for Social and Economic Research, Rhodes University.

Menahem S (1981) Complications arising from ritual Circumcision. *Israeli Journal of Medical Science* 17:45-48.

Milos M and D Macris (1992) Circumcision: A medical or a human rights issue? *Journal of Nurse-Midwifery* 37(2) March/April:87-96.

Mogotlane SM, JT Ntlangulela and BJ Oganbanjo (2004) Mortality and morbidity among traditionally circumcised Xhosa boys in the Eastern Cape Province of South Africa. *Curationis* May 27(2):57-62.

Momoti N (2002) Law and Culture in the New Constitution with Specific Reference to the Custom of Circumcision as Practiced in the Eastern Cape. Master of Laws Thesis, Rhodes University.

Morris K (2001) Treating HIV in South Africa: a tale of two systems. *The Lancet* 357, April 14.

Mtuze P (2004) *Introduction to Xhosa Culture.* Alice: Lovedale Press.

Ndaba B (2002) Mother of dead initiate barred from funeral. *Saturday Star,* 28 June.

Nhlapo T (1995) Cultural diversity, human rights and the family in contemporary Africa: Lessons from the South African constitutional debate. *International Journal of Law and the Family* 9.

Peires JB (1981) *House of Phalo: A History of the Xhosa People in the Days of their Independence.* Braamfontein: Ravan.

Pitje GM (1950) Traditional systems of male education among the Pedi and cognate tribes. *African Studies* 9.

Russell A (1997) Ancient practice of tribal circumcision divides South Africa. *Daily Telegraph.* 23 January:27.

Sapa (2005) Leaders urge probe after circumcision death. 29 June.

Sapa (2006) Protests after initiates gang rape. 31 January.

Schlemmer L and J Wilson (2001) Social development. *South Africa Survey 2001/2.* Johannesburg: Institute of Race Relations:33-60.

Sefara M (2001) Top doctor urges pre-initiation school medical checks. *The Sowetan.* Johannesburg, 11 July.

Sidley P (2001) Eastern Cape Tightens Law on Circumcision to Stem Casualties. *BMJ* 10 November.

Silverman EK (2004) Anthropology and Circumcision. *Annual Review of Anthropology* 33: 419-445.

Spencer P(1965) *The Samburu: A Study of Gerontocracy in a Nomadic Tribe.* London: Routledge and Kegan Paul.

Tenge S (2006) Xhosa Teenage Boys' Experiences During the Period Prior to Circumcision Ritual in East London in the Eastern Cape. Unisa, South Africa. MA Health Studies.

The Star (2006) Scores of initiates died in E Cape, hearing told. Thursday, 5 October.

Tucker JT (1949) Initiation ceremonies for Luimbi boys. *Africa* 19:53-60.

Turner V (1962) Three symbols of passage in Ndembu circumcision ritual. In Gluckman M (Ed) *Essays on the Ritual of Social Relations*. Manchester: Manchester University Press:124-173.

Van der Meide W (1999) Gender equality versus the right to equality. *South African Law Journal* 116 (1): 100-112

Van Kessel I and B Oomen (1997) One chief, one vote. Traditional authorities in post-apartheid South Africa. *African Affairs* 96.

Van Tromp J (1947) *Xhosa Law of Persons*. Cape Town: Juta.

Viall J (1999) Circumcision may cut the risk of AIDS. *Cape Argus*, 23 November.

Williams N and L Kapila (1993) Complications of circumcision. *British Journal of Surgery* 80 (10):1231-1236.

Wilson MH (1952) *Social Structure*. Pietermaritzburg: Shuter & Shooter.

Wilson M and A Mafeje (1963) *Langa: A Study of African Groups in an African Township*. Cape Town: Oxford University Press.

Wood K and R Jewkes (1998) Love is a dangerous thing: Micro-dynamics of violence in sexual relationships of young people in Umtata. Medical Research Council Technical Report, Pretoria.

Zenani NM and H Scheub (1992) *The World and the Word: Tales and Observations from Xhosa Oral Tradition*. Madison, Wisconsin: University of Wisconsin Press.

SOUTH AFRICA AT LARGE

4

South Africa at large

Roger Southall

Under the presidency of Nelson Mandela, South African foreign policy sought, for the most part, to assume a high moral ground, refashioning itself after the isolation and ignominy of the late-apartheid years by adopting adherence to human rights and international law as its basis. Following clashes with African states over human rights issues (and the criticisms of their domestic policies that this implied or activated), his successor, Thabo Mbeki, opted for a more pragmatic approach combined with a reformist pan-Africanist agenda embodied in the launch of the New Partnership for African Development (Nepad). Subsequently, under Jacob Zuma, South African foreign policy has sought to extend its outreach globally and continentally while consolidating its linkages regionally.

The two chapters that conclude this volume highlight both dimensions of foreign policy under the Zuma presidency: first in Sanusha Naidu's exploration of South Africa's admission into the grouping of 'emergent' economies known as the BRIC (Brazil, Russia, India and China); and, second, by an analysis of relations between the governments of Swaziland and South Africa by John Daniel and Marisha Ramdeen.

Naidu describes the invitation to South Africa to join the BRIC club in December 2010 as a diplomatic coup on the part of the Zuma presidency, a signifier of South Africa's high profile in various international forums as a representative of the global South. However, South Africa's admission as the fifth member country of BRIC was greeted with ambivalence, some arguing that it confirmed the country's status as an influential player globally, others that South Africa had been admitted more for political than economic reasons, noting especially that economically it was dwarfed by the other member countries. Naidu asks what implications joining the BRIC has for South Africa's foreign policy, and whether it marks a culmination of Mbeki's developmental and internationally reformist agenda.

Naidu depicts Zuma's foreign policy as combining elements of Mandela's human rights agenda with an attempt to smooth relations that had been ruffled by Mbeki regionally, notably with Angola, but she sees continuity with Mbeki's goal of strengthening South Africa's position continentally and globally, inclusive of pursuit of greater inclusion of the global South within multilateral forums and notably within international financial institutions. Joining BRIC is presented as in accordance with this agenda, although she goes on to point out that it is not entirely clear what the BRIC grouping is about or even what it is. Is it an economic club? Is it a joint effort among the members to promote trade liberalisation and fair markets among and for its members? Or is it merely a loose grouping speaking in generalities and platitudes?

While noting that the BRIC countries themselves justified the invitation to South Africa in terms of lending African weight to global debates, Naidu notes that as for size and performance there were other more convincing 'southern' candidates (such as South Korea, Turkey, Mexico and Indonesia) for inclusion. Against that, recent years have seen South Africa deepening its economic and political relationships with all the four BRIC nations. From this perspective, the Zuma administration would seem to view joining BRIC as a way of attracting significant investment from the other four nations, while providing a springboard for South African corporations to access new and potentially major markets, thus assisting South Africa to attain the economic growth rate it requires to meet its goals of growth and development. Meanwhile, from the BRIC perspective, South Africa's inclusion will offset criticisms that BRIC's activities have only represented Asian and Latin American interests and have reinforced existing inequalities within the South. Although Naidu endorses South Africa's entry into BRIC as promoting the country's international profile and leverage, she suggests that the strengthening of linkages with China and Russia in particular may come at major cost to any continuing adherence to an agenda of human rights. Naidu concludes that the Zuma government has yet to work out the full implications of its joining the BRIC club. She also suggests that being by far the weakest member of the grouping, South Africa will need to 'punch above its weight' if it is seriously going to make BRIC work for its development goals and those of Africa as a whole.

Whether human rights issues continue to inform South Africa's foreign policy underlies the analysis of 'the South African connection' with Swaziland. Daniel and Ramdeen probe beneath the surface of why Pretoria should have agreed a R2.4 billion loan in mid-2011 to an essentially bankrupt Swazi government when the latter had not only historically allied itself with the apartheid state against the ANC, but also in the present era sustains a constitutional and political order that is profoundly undemocratic and oppressive. They go further to question why monies should be loaned to a state headed by a fabulously wealthy monarch who garners his wealth from the institutions of the state but refuses to pay his way or give back anything in the way of taxes.

The authors note that the democratic transition in South Africa prompted a resurgence of democratic political activity in Swaziland in the mid- to late-1990s, a push for reforms that were broadly supported by President Mandela's leadership role in the Southern African Development Community (SADC). However, despite the official commitment of the monarchy to a constitutional reform process, years went by with nothing to show for it, not least once it became clear that, under Mbeki, South Africa was eager to avoid any action that would allow it to become depicted as an apartheid-style, bullying regional hegemon. Nonetheless, the monarchy was to come under increasing pressure as during the 1990s and the early years of the new century the economy was thrust into a growing crisis by a mix of monarchical excess, drift of investment away from Swaziland to South Africa, declining access of Swazi exports to key overseas markets and, most recently, the restructuring (and reduction) of fiscal transfers to Swaziland under the umbrella of the Southern African Customs Union. For the mass of the population, the consequences were job losses, declining incomes, and increased taxes as the Swazi state has sought to stave off bankruptcy. But for the king, and those around him, little changed. Lavish spending continued amid continuing monarchical involvement in an array of business interests, with increasing resort to state coercion and terror to quell growing popular protest against monarchical repression and the evident inequities of the economic crisis.

On the face of things, the situation is ripe for South Africa to expose the false nature of the so-called economic crisis in Swaziland as one not of revenue generation but of distribution. Should not the Zuma administration be pressuring the monarchy to pay its way and to accept democratic reforms? This is not happening. Instead, the Zuma government is prepared to bail out its neighbour, despite – as Daniel and Ramdeen detail – the history of anti-ANC Swazi state activity in the 1980s. The authors explain this apparent paradox by reference to Zuma's partiality to African tradition and custom and to personal ties with the Swazi monarchy. Another factor, cited by the South African Treasury, is a concern to contain a possible political implosion on its eastern doorstep, and a reluctance to further complicate inter-state relations within SADC at a time when the regional body displays neither the will nor the capacity to confront member regimes that have offended against democracy.

A concern with human rights may not have entirely disappeared from South Africa's foreign policy – but few can now doubt that it is entirely subordinate to what the ANC government considers the national interest.

CHAPTER 15

South Africa and the BRIC:
Punching above its weight?

Sanusha Naidu

———•—

The rationale for South Africa's approach [to join BRIC] was in consideration of a matter of crucial importance to BRIC member states, namely the role of emerging economies in advancing the restructuring of the global political, economic and financial architecture into one that is more equitable, balanced and rests on the important pillar of multilateralism.[1]

SA must not misunderstand the nature of BRIC – it is an acronym dreamt up by orthodox banks based in the global north. BRIC does not have development initiatives emanating from it, unlike the IBSA (India, Brazil and SA) forum; rather it is a grouping about market and economic access.[2]

INTRODUCTION

The years 2010 and 2011 were significant in South Africa's foreign policy outreach. In 2011, Pretoria began its second term as a non-permanent member of the United Nations Security Council for the period 2011 and 2012, and China extended an invitation to the Zuma presidency to attend the Third Heads of State BRIC Summit. This followed a formal invitation from China to South Africa into the coveted BRIC club in December 2010. It was a diplomatic coup for the Zuma administration, and followed months of hard lobbying, and of emphasising the importance and value of South Africa's identity in the global South.

The announcement of South Africa's pending admission as the fifth member of BRICS met with some ambivalent responses. On the one hand, commentators such as Mzukisi Qobo highlighted that South Africa's role globally has 'made substantial contributions to global governance issues and played a very active role in post-conflict reconstruction in Africa. Its voice has been fluent and it's seen as an honest broker in international relations. That would definitely have some influence' (Cloete 2011).

On the other hand, there were reservations about what South Africa's membership would bring to the BRIC forum. Jim O'Neill, the former chief economist at Goldman Sachs who coined the term BRIC, argued that Pretoria was an unsuitable candidate to be admitted into this clutch of resurgent or emerging economies, arguing that it was not entirely obvious to [him] why BRIC should have agreed to ask South Africa to join as South Africa could not be regarded as a big economy (Mashego 2011).

For the sceptics, the concern is really about whether South Africa's comparative economic advantage is on a par with, or complements, that of its fellow members so as to contribute to the rise of the BRIC club as a global economic hegemonic group by 2050. This is because BRIC is seen less as a political forum than as a loose constellation of economic interests with China leading the pack.

For South Africa, the real issue is what its entry into BRIC means for the country's foreign policy direction. Whereas under the Mbeki presidency the need to elevate South Africa's global status as a country pursuing justice and reform of the international regime was a clear mandate, the question now is whether we are witnessing a culmination of these ambitions in the Zuma presidency. Are South Africa's global stature and its Africa policies being redefined through the lens of Southern and global groupings such as the IBSA (India, Brazil and South Africa) alliance, which includes the G20 and BRIC? And how is the sometimes human rights dimension of South Africa's foreign policy expressed, given the motley crew of BRIC partners?

These and other pertinent questions should be considered in order to glean what the overlap is between South Africa's membership in BRIC and the alignment to Pretoria's overall foreign policy strategy. Does South Africa's perceived junior status in BRIC not in fact raise fears that Pretoria's global ambitions are being shaped by a populist mindset of 'punching above one's weight' or 'running with the in-crowd'?

This chapter examines some of these concerns as they relate to South Africa's foreign policy under President Zuma. Why, for example, did he push so vigorously for entrance as the fifth BRIC and how does admission into BRIC dovetail with South Africa's domestic priorities?

FOREIGN POLICY UNDER ZUMA

Following the election of Zuma in 2009, questions were raised about whether his presidency would see a significant shift from the foreign policy doctrines of the Mbeki era. With the exception of the name change of the Department of Foreign Affairs to that of

International Relations and Cooperation (DIRCO) – which, in general terms, could have signified a foreign policy more closely aligned to domestic issues – very little initial differentiation could be discerned around the foreign policy ideals and priorities as defined by the Mbeki regime (Grudz 2009). The primary aims of 'reshaping the current international norms, institutions, and processes to further justice for Africa and the South' (Alden and Le Pere 2004: 283) that were the hallmarks of the Mbeki years remained the pillars that underlined the discourse of the Zuma presidency's international relations and cooperation. There was even a hint that the new administration would bring back the centrality of the human rights agenda that had been something of a trademark in the Mandela years (see Grudz 2009).

This is how it appeared when the Zuma presidency flexed its muscles and summoned the ambassador of Myanmar for a dressing-down after the democratic opposition leader, Aung San Suu Kyi, was placed under house arrest in 2009. Or, for that matter, when it reiterated its support for the Rome Statute even though it supported the Africa position taken in July 2009 to seek a delay to the International Criminal Court (ICC) arrest warrant for the Sudanese leader Omar al Bashir (Grudz 2009). These events seemed to suggest that South Africa was becoming more strategic in its global diplomacy.

Unlike Mbeki's image of an aloof intellectual global statesman, President Zuma's affable nature was seen by regional neighbours as a more endearing quality, particularly in smoothing out regional tensions such as those with Angola, the other potential powerhouse in the region. Zuma's first diplomatic visit after assuming office in 2009 was to Angola; it was seen as a tactful and nuanced departure from the terse relations that underpinned engagements between the Dos Santos government and the Mbeki administration. Indeed, the diplomatic suaveness Zuma displayed during the visit to Luanda was perceived as a way also, subtly, to enlist the assistance of the Dos Santos government in Pretoria's peace efforts in Zimbabwe (Grudz 2009).

In other ways, the Zuma presidency has given signs that its foreign policy stance in practice represents a continuity with that of the Mbeki regime. Perhaps the only difference that is evident lies in the subtle changes of style and the way in which Zuma executes his easygoing charm offensive to capitalise on the platform created by Mbeki's foreign policy kudos. In fact, one could argue that under Zuma there have been concrete steps to strengthen South Africa's position continentally, across the South and globally – a follow-up to initiatives started by Mbeki. For instance, whereas Mbeki positioned South Africa as a member of the Outreach 5 countries that attended the G8 summits to push forward the agenda of a multilateral international system and the inclusion of the global South, today the Zuma administration has upped the ante with its presence at the G20, pushing for a more equitable reform of the global financial architecture following the financial crisis in 2008. Finance Minister Pravin Gordhan has recently called for the international financial institutions to increase the voice of the African bloc within the changing international financial system in accordance with the shift and alignment of the new structural centres of financial power becoming evident in the South.

Similarly, the stance adopted by Pretoria around the Copenhagen climate change meeting in supporting the BASIC (Brazil, South Africa, India and China) group has also elevated South Africa's status as a legitimate African voice to push for a just accord in the global climate change debate.

It is from this perspective that South Africa's formal invitation to the Heads of State BRIC summit in Beijing in April 2011 must be viewed. It reaffirmed Pretoria's commitment towards the overall objective of sustaining the global outreach of its international legitimacy, and recognition by the global community. As Alden and Le Pere highlight, 'since the ending of apartheid, the international community has played a seminal role in fostering the idea that South Africa is marked out for leadership on the continent' (2009: 165). This can also be extended to the way the other four BRIC countries perceive South Africa by identifying Pretoria as the viable African voice to assist them in recasting the power structures of the international system.

WHAT IS BRICS?

Before South Africa joined, BRIC was an acronym coined in 2011 by the Goldman Sachs senior economic analyst Jim O'Neill, in a paper entitled 'Building Better Global Economic BRICS'. In it, O'Neill argued that the rise of Brazil, Russia, India and China highlighted a new constellation of global economic muscle. He noted that by 2050 these four countries would be the four most dominant economies in the world given that together they made up 25 per cent of the world's land coverage, 40 per cent of the world's population, and had a combined GDP (PPP) of US$18.486 trillion.

The euphoria and attraction that surrounded the unveiling of BRIC has, it seems, shifted the balance of economic power away from the traditional G8 countries towards these new 'darlings' of the South. Now there is an unprecedented clamour by almost every nation across the globe to do business with the BRIC countries, and yet it is not clear what the BRIC entity actually entails. Is it an economic grouping? Does it have a set of trade rules that promotes trade liberalisation and fair market access among its members? Or is it merely a loose configuration of countries that speak in broad political and economic platitudes?

In all reality, BRICS is amorphous in nature and substance. The fascination seems to stem from the fact that three of its number – Brazil, India, and China – are among the fastest-growing economies globally, and gaining a foothold in those markets makes for good business acumen. That said, it is difficult to see how becoming a member of BRICS creates overall benefits for the citizens of the member country. The political elites will of course be enthused by being awarded the accolade of international recognition and admission into a prestigious Southern club.

THE YELLOW BRIC ROAD

That China as rotational chair of the BRIC forum took the initiative alone to invite Pretoria to the April summit needs to be contextualised by events that led to Beijing's arriving at this decision. In 2009, President Zuma embarked on a BRIC foreign policy offensive. He visited all four BRIC nations in his first eighteen to twenty months in office,[3] and used each occasion to push South Africa's credentials as a potential member of BRIC by showcasing what he termed the immense trade and investment opportunities that South Africa could offer, as well as Pretoria's geostrategic significance. He marketed the country's well-established economic infrastructure as a significant platform that could be utilised to access other African markets. The visits, of course, also served to drum up support for Pretoria's bid for one of the permanent seats in a reformed UN Security Council. The lobbying paid off when, at the G20 summit in Seoul in November 2010, 'the Russian president Dmitry Medvedev announced that South Africa had "officially" applied to join the BRIC forum' (Freemantle and Stevens 2011: 3).[4]

For Brazil and Russia, it seemed that South Africa's admission would expand the geographic coverage of the forum, especially at a time when China and India were seen to be escalating their footprint globally, in particular across the South and chiefly in Africa. Consider the response by the Russian Ministry of Foreign Affairs to the invitation:

> South Africa's inclusion is in line with the sustainable trends of global development, including the emergence of a polycentric international system. The entry of [South Africa], an active participant in the G20 and the largest economic power in Africa, will not only increase the total economic weight of our association but also will help build up opportunities for mutually beneficial practical cooperation within BRIC (Campell 2011).

Similarly, the Brazilian government affirmed that Pretoria would bring a depth to the BRIC forum that would underscore a strong commitment for political action on issues concerning African affairs and consensus around the international agenda (Campbell 2011). Thus, though South Africa's admission into the BRIC forum was merely a formality at the April summit, it remained unclear to many observers as to whether political or economic issues, or a combination of the two, had informed the decision. We need, therefore, to consider some of the arguments in order to disaggregate the pros and cons of South Africa's admission into BRIC.

ECONOMIC IMPERATIVES

One of the main detractors of South Africa's entry into BRIC is Jim O'Neill, who believes that South Africa does not possess the economic weight to complement the economic identity of the BRIC bloc. According to O'Neill:

> In terms of my thesis of economics, it doesn't make a huge amount of sense. There
> are lots of other emerging nations that have more people and/or considerably bigger
> economies than South Africa. If I were any one of Korea, Turkey, Indonesia, Mexico,
> or even Poland or Argentina, I'd be saying today, 'Why not me?' (see Shira 2010).

In terms of economic muscle, South Africa certainly lags behind the other BRIC nations.

First, South Africa's economy, population and growth rate are much smaller than those of all the other BRIC members. Second, the country's gross domestic product (GDP) last year was US$286 billion, far less than the US$2 trillion of India and Brazil, China's US$5.5 trillion, and even Russia's US$ 1.6 trillion. Third, South Africa has in recent years recorded sluggish economic growth. It has performed at a tepid 3 per cent on average per annum over the last several years, less than Russia's 4 per cent, Brazil's 7.5 per cent, India's 9.7 per cent and China's 10.5 per cent. Finally, the size of the country's population at approximately 50 million people is tiny compared with that of China (1.36 billion), India (1.2 billion), Brazil (201 million) and Russia (139 million).

It is understandable, therefore, that economic pundits such as Razia Khan, head of Africa research at Standard Chartered in London, expressed bemusement about how South Africa 'fits into BRIC' with the size of its economy, its rate of growth, and 'the most controversial aspect' being its 'share of global GDP compared with others' (Woolridge 2011). Hardly surprising, too, that other commentators believe that other and better-performing emerging economies such as South Korea, Turkey, Mexico and Indonesia should have eclipsed South Africa's entry into the BRIC club. These countries have GDP rates that are impressive and outstrip South Africa by a fair margin. South Africa's current GDP is less than half of South Korea's US$832.5 billion, Turkey's US$617.1 billion and Mexico's US$874.9 billion. It is two-thirds of Indonesia's US$540.3 billion.

So, in purely economic terms, South Africa struggles to live up to the economic realities of BRIC. This is further exemplified by the data on South Africa in global terms: 'South Africa's US$330 billionn economy is large in Africa but dwarfed by the US$9 trillion BRIC bloc … Ranked by GDP in US$ terms in 2010, South Africa's economy was the twenty-seventh largest in the world, compared to China (second), Brazil (eighth), Russia (tenth) and India (eleventh) … [in addition] South Africa is only the seventieth wealthiest in the world in per capita terms. And growing slowly: from 1990, South Africa has been the ninetieth (out of 124) fastest growing economy in the emerging world' (Freemantle and Stevens 2011).

On the other hand, South Africa enjoys a fairly good economic relationship with each of the BRIC nations on a bilateral basis and, with each, Pretoria's trading profile has deepened, with some obviously more than with others. With China, South Africa's trade relationship has grown by more than US$13.6 billion since the formalisation of diplomatic ties in 1998. By the beginning of 2009, China was South Africa's main export destination and on the import side Pretoria was Beijing's largest partner. Trade between the two sides increased by 2 per cent from US$16 billion in 2008 to US$16.3 billion in 2009 (Nkosi 2010).

Similarly, India's trade engagement with South Africa has grown exponentially. Total trade has more than doubled since 2004-2005 from US$3.18 billion to US$7.73 billion in 2009-2010. At the same time, 'India was South Africa's largest trading partner in South and South East Asia and one of Pretoria's top ten trading partners globally' (Sharma 2011). Furthermore, both New Delhi and Pretoria are hoping to increase bilateral trade to US$15 billion by 2015.

During his 2009 state visit to Brazil, President Zuma remarked that trade with the South American country had shown significant improvement. Two-way trade had amounted to US$2.52 billion in 2008, a 10 per cent increase over 2007, and in 2008 there had been a 48 per cent increase in the value of South African exports to Brazil' (Nkosi 2009). In the case of Russia, however, and compared with the other three BRIC countries, trade between Moscow and Pretoria is diminutive. By the end of 2009, South Africa's total trade with Russia stood at a meagre US$517 million out of Moscow's total external trade turnover of US$469 billion (Dyomkin 2010).

By joining BRIC, South Africa will intensify its trade portfolio with its alliance partners. However, as much as each of the other BRIC countries identifies South Africa as a strategic economic partner and powerhouse in Africa, the trade component will remain heavily skewed in their favour. Thus, among the challenges Pretoria will need to confront are its trade imbalances with its fellow members, stemming from the bias in the pattern of their economic engagements, by the nature of the exports and imports flows. In the cases of China and India, South Africa remains a primary exporter of minerals and other such commodities and import, *inter alia*, machinery, electrical goods and processed goods. To this end, South Africa needs to diversify its export base towards more value-added production that can act as a catalyst for the economy and achieve the outputs of the New Growth Path and Industrial Policy Action Plan 2 (the latter has been part of the rationale offered by the Zuma administration regarding South Africa's admission into the BRIC).

Alignment between South Africa's foreign policy ideals and domestic economic priorities will be an important intersection. Synergies in the niche areas of South Africa's economic restructuring have been identified by President Zuma in sectors such as the green economy, rural development, infrastructure, food security, mineral beneficiation, agriculture, services and manufacturing. All this means changing the nature of economic engagement with major trading partners, including the BRICs.

The issue is whether being part of the BRIC forum will assist South Africa in addressing the country's economic woes and transforming the country's industrial base into a sizeable and viable economic power that befits the status of a BRIC nation. Theoretically, this is what the Zuma administration is hedging its bets on; attracting investment from the BRIC nations in order to stimulate delivery on the five million jobs the administration has promised to create by 2020.

Whether admission into the BRIC will serve as a catalyst for the South African economy can only be assessed in time. One of the immediate challenges facing the Zuma presidency is to reconcile the interests of domestic constituencies such as labour with that of the corporate sector from the BRIC countries. But for now it seems that, with Pretoria's admission into BRIC, SA Inc is enjoying a comparative advantage over other domestic actors in the economy.

THE CORPORATE FACTOR

Pressure from the corporate sector was a powerful influence in South Africa's drive to join BRIC. Why?

First, South African corporate capital needs access to the BRIC markets and in this regard some progress has been made. For example, Standard Bank has entered into a 20 per cent venture with the Industrial and Commercial Bank of China, Discovery Health has embarked on a joint venture with Ping An health insurers in China, the First Rand Group has opened a subsidiary (First Rand India) in Mumbai, the Airports Company of South Africa has been contracted to refurbish the Mumbai International Airport, Standard Bank and Ashanti Gold have operations in Brazil, and the Russian market has become an important outlet for fruit exports from Capespan.

Second, the commercial knowledge the business sector brings to the alliance in terms of technology, research and development and innovation should be considered as another driving factor for admitting South Africa into the BRIC. It is something to which Chinese public and private corporates both want access.

Third, the experiences that SA Inc engenders, and its willingness to underwrite risk in the African markets, also holds South African companies in good stead for jointly exploiting economic opportunities, not only in Africa markets but also in regional economic environments, which can be seen as equally difficult to penetrate (Daniel, Naidoo and Naidu 2004).

Therefore, as we reflect on South Africa's entry into BRIC, the corporate factor provides an interesting possibility that perhaps we are going to witness the emergence of a new BRICS transnational corporation formation, one that will wield strategic economic power and penetration. In this regard, the argument put forward by Daniel and Bhengu (209: 163) is instructive: in their view, although the footprint of South African capital is notable on the continent and will grow in the future, 'local capital will never be able to match the Chinese or India investors in the size and value of their contractual arrangements'. This intimation suggests that perhaps the real awakening for South Africa's admission into the BRIC is to be found in the emergence of BRIC Incorporated.

THE GEOPOLITICAL ANGLE

In the current international environment, geopolitics is about having a voice at the table that can assist in leveraging influence around significant decisions. It is also about strategic movements that can be cultivated around common interests, especially as they relate to the interplay between power, geography, economics and governance that informs the foreign policies of nations.

Within this context, the timing of China's invitation could not have come at a more opportune moment for the BRIC countries to boost their capacity to capitalise on the rise of the South in the global arena. Moreover, with the establishment of the G20 to oversee the coordination of the global financial system, the role of the G8 has become somewhat reshaped. It is no longer obliged to play this strategic role on the financial front, and there is uncertainty about whether the engagement with the Outreach 5 (O5) countries will still wield a significant seat for the O5 at the G8 summits, especially now that BRIC has initiated its own annual summit among member states.

With these normative issues still ambiguous, South Africa's inclusion into BRIC had a number of push factors. One, South Africa's 2011-2012 two-year nonpermanent seat within the United Nation Security Council was seen as giving added weight to the BRICS' voice on the Security Council post-2011 when all five partners had sat on the Security Council. Then, even though BRIC had become the new 'buzz' in the lexicon of international relations, it could not claim to be a true representative of the South without the African bloc's being represented and so the geographical deficit represented by Africa's absence meant that South Africa's global credentials provided a 'win-win' outcome for the BRIC members.

But South Africa's geostrategic relevance can be appreciated in other respects.

THE CHINA FACTOR

China's decision and timing to invite South Africa to join BRIC was a masterstroke on its part. First, it flagged the fact that Beijing was moving expeditiously to build its political capital in Africa and to stamp its footprint on key decisions affecting the continent. One of these related to its support for a referendum on Southern Sudan's future. With the outcome predictable, China gained the support of a reliable oil-producing African state, and one so weak and in need of aid that it could easily be turned to favour China's political will and whims.

Second, the fact that South Africa is perceived as a gateway into the markets of the Southern African Development Community (SADC) and beyond served Beijing's interests in the south of the continent and its corporates. The 'going out' strategy of Chinese companies is certainly being boosted by joining forces with South Africa corporates in exploring and exploiting market opportunities in African economies (Naidu 2008).[5] That South Africa is a willing partner in this venture by China and its corporates is illustrated by the 2011 visa debacle surrounding the Dalai Lama's visit and the comprehensive strategic partnership agreement signed in 2010, which offers more commercial ties with, and investment from, China.

Lastly, it enables Beijing to demonstrate its global leadership qualities, especially in the South and the developing world. In fact, this move reflects one of the four cornerstones of

China's foreign policy priorities, namely its ensuing engagements with the Third World (Naidu 2010).

THE INDIA FACTOR

It is difficult to see why New Delhi's reaction was muted about Pretoria's entry into BRIC. Perhaps it is in part aligned to how China once again leveraged its geostrategic status and outmaneuvered India in projecting itself as championing the voice of Africa and the global South. Or maybe it is because once again China has overshadowed the political and economic distinctiveness of IBSA, in which India plays a much higher-profile role and enjoys a tactical offensive *vis-à-vis* its other alliance members. Whatever the reason for India's tepid response, New Delhi still has an opportunity to influence some of the posturings within the newly configured BRICS set-up.

India can use its position within IBSA to shape a common consensus within BRICS around critical global governance decisions, development cooperation and policy interventions. Moreover, IBSA has more of an institutional identity than BRICS. Whereas BRICS is attractive and appealing because of its economic leverage (especially to big business), IBSA on the other hand tends to represent more of a construct around social development and development cooperation priorities – as is evident from the development fund and the social development programmes the trilateral espouses.

Taylor (2009) has highlighted the potential importance of IBSA in view of the World Trade Organisation (WTO) negotiations around the completion of the Doha Development Round. He argues that, given the small band of countries with capacity and bargaining power, IBSA is identified as part of this group, with India a vocal actor on the reform of the global trade order and trade distortion measures that limit access to Northern markets and across the South.

This compartmenalisation between IBSA and BRICS suggests that each operates within different dimensions. For IBSA, this indicates that the developmental agenda is perhaps better placed to enhance South-South cooperation and the championing of the voice of the South in international forums such as the WTO (see Agarwal, Besada and White 2010).

Second, India does have a comparative advantage because it now has a strengthened democratic currency within BRICS, which it can use to its own advantage *vis-à-vis* China and Russia. Third, as much as New Delhi may feel eclipsed by China, this may also be in India's favour by working behind the scenes to give BRICS a critical identity and a more cohesive strategic distinctiveness. It can play a role in answering a number of questions. Is BRICS a political alliance? Is it an economic bloc? Or is it merely some kind of Musketeers Club? Nobody knows how to define what BRICS really is because of its amorphous nature.

Finally, the India factor could have a positive influence on the direction that BRICS follows because it is clear that New Delhi shares a like-mindedness and synergy with all its alliance partners (albeit one more tenuous with Beijing). But this is something to be explored in further depth by New Delhi and South Africa as partners.

NOT ALL ROADS ARE PAVED WITH GOOD BRICS

At the beginning of this chapter questions were raised about whether and how admission into BRICS would shape South Africa's foreign policies. It was also implied that perhaps the invitation would turn out to be a defining moment in the Zuma administration's foreign policy ambitions.

In 2010, China's *People's Daily Online* of 30 November editorialised that '[by] joining the BRIC countries, South Africa also hopes to become the gateway for the BRIC countries' entry into Africa ... South Africa has the ability to promote agendas related to Africa on the international arena ... This is an important factor that makes South Africa valuable as a BRIC country.'

Although this often expressed view may reflect a normative and rhetorical approach to how South Africa is perceived by the international community (namely as representing the African voice in multilateral forums), it is by no means clear whether the African bloc itself actually sees South Africa in this way. Partly, this is due to the ambivalence Pretoria demonstrates in its Africa policy. Post-apartheid South Africa explicitly stated that its political relationship with the continent would be defined by the building and consolidation of partnerships, stitching together alliances with African states and rejecting 'the go-it-alone' posture of the apartheid government. In essence, however, democratic South Africa's relationship with Africa has been defined more by Africa's underdevelopment and the continent's impending economic regeneration, which Pretoria explicitly located within what it saw as its multilateral role in global institutions. As Landsberg (2003) notes, 'South Africa has positioned itself as a key player in resolving issues of interest to the global South'. In effect, it was this position that resulted in South Africa's taking up the challenge of promoting more equitable relations in the WTO and the Bretton Woods Institutions, committing itself to the Millennium Development Goals as well as placing Africa's dire economic situation on the agenda of the G8, the WTO and the Monterey conference for effective redress. In short, the country's perceived strategic geopolitical importance dovetailed with Pretoria's view of reconciling its position on the continent with redressing Africa's developmental challenge on the world stage.

Yet the perception in practice is that this has not always been the case. The struggle for South Africa has always been to maintain the balance between commitment to the African development agenda – with its new-found post-apartheid status of international legitimacy – and the position it takes within these global institutions. These are not always interpreted as intersecting with the interests of the African voice. And then there is the penetration of South African capital into African markets, which underlines a parochial suspicion that South Africa's political relations with the continent are structured to advance the interests of its corporate sector (Naidu 2004). This opinion is exemplified by Dot Keet, who argues that:

[it is] not lost on other African countries that South Africa – with its banks, private companies and even parastatal corporations keenly looking for investment opportunities in Africa and elsewhere – has its own 'national interests' in promoting the kind of 'global rights' of corporations in all countries and (almost all) sectors that an investment agreement in the WTO is aimed at (2003:12).

It is evident that Pretoria's attempt to push forward the African agenda could in reality create a backlash because of post-apartheid South Africa's inherent prejudices as found in displays of xenophobia against African migrants. Moreover, the behaviour of corporate South Africa and its links to Southern transnational corporations could be interpreted as furthering what Patrick Bond (2006) calls South Africa's sub-imperial capitalist agenda in southern Africa, and across Africa, through BRICS.

So to assume that South Africa and the continent speak with one voice is presumptuous to some extent, particularly as there has been a quiet African reaction to the news of South Africa's admission into BRICS, seen by some African countries as a way for South Africa to embed itself further in African markets through the use of its international legitimacy and membership in Southern institutions such as BRICS and IBSA.

South African corporates will have more to gain through market cooperation with counterparts from the other BRIC countries, which seem in any event to have had little trouble investing in African markets on their own. In fact, African governments have welcomed such investment, which is seen as much larger than that of South Africa's outward investment, so it is rather doubtful that South Africa's admission into BRIC will really augment the presence of the BRICS corporates in the African landscape. Maybe it is more about sharing resources and striking economic alliances that could prove to be lucrative and useful for economic elites, networks and pacts.

On another front, there is the possibly innocuous belief by Pretoria that through BRICS it can explicitly maximise opportunities in the African market to revitalise its domestic economy recovery. This is what the minister for economic development, Ebrahim Patel, revealed where he succinctly stated that unlocking the continent's potential would be the key to job growth in South Africa (Davis and Terreblanche 2011). This is reminiscent of the Mbeki years when it was argued that South African prosperity was intimately tied up with Africa's development.

A second point, as South Africa contemplates its role and duties, is that it is vital to evaluate how these will intersect with its interests in the IBSA forum and the G20. Becoming a member of BRICS has produced an overlap in membership and a contradiction in behaviour and outcomes. How will Pretoria decide which club takes precedence? Which decision will override the other? What kind of rationality and harmonisation will there between belonging to several groupings? These issues must be given consideration because they will affect the global governance concerns that BRICS seeks to reshape and the polycentric world order that it wants to create.

Then there is the question of whether BRICS is becoming the equivalent of the G8. Will membership to this premium club stop with South Africa? Or are we likely to see more members being added to the club? Will the African membership increase? There are definitely other countries waiting in the wings, including the Next 11[6] or CIVETS[7] (minus South Africa) (see Shaw et al. 2009). If so, then are we going to witness a new era of South-South cooperation in which BRICS will be expanded and will follow the same evolutionary path as the G8? And will we see another set of countries challenging the dominance of the BRICS as we saw when the G8 invited the Outreach 5 countries to attend their summits?

A fourth concern is that, in spite of the common thread of the reformist agenda underpinning the BRICS forum, it is important to ask the awkward question of whether BRICS does indeed speak with one voice. On the completion of the Doha Development Round and the removal of trade-distorting measures protecting domestic economic producers, the penetration of the BRICS economies into each other's markets poses serious constraints to South African exporters trying to enter and gain market traction. For instance, there is a 40 per cent tariff barrier for value-added goods trying to enter the Indian markets. Similar constraints exist in China. More recently, wine exporters from South Africa faced a 30 per cent tariff duty on their exports because the Indian wine association is trying to protect its local wine industry.

The sensitivity surrounding the export of agricultural products will be a cause of concern for agri-business in South Africa, as Brazil, China and India have instituted protectionist measures in this sector against competitive imports. In addition, South African fruit exporters face non-tariff measures such as sanitary and phytosanitary (SPS)[8] when exporting to China. SPS remains a grey area, and a sensitivity, in the agricultural cooperation between South Africa and China. In the past, the Chinese have used it against South African orange and other fruit exporters, claiming that the products pose a risk of contamination to the Chinese fruit industry.

Finally, consideration must also be given to preferential/free trade agreements between and among BRICS member states. With each of the BRICS countries trying to strengthen market access into the economic environments of member states, negotiated preferential trade agreements such as the pending SACU-India free trade agreement or the SA-Mercosur free trade talks may be interpreted as contradictory and unfair trading advantage under the trade liberalisation policies of the WTO. If one of the BRICS member states believes that they are being prejudiced by South Africa's preferential trade agreements, whether under the economic partnerships greements (EPAs) or through the Southern African Customs Union (SACU), it would be interesting to see whether this BRICS member state will lodge a dispute at the WTO over unfair trading practices.

Brazil is one of the BRICS members to have responded negatively to the preferential market access granted to the African, Caribbean and Pacific (ACP) countries by the European Union (EU) for agricultural exports (especially bananas and sugar) to enter the EU market. Brazil argues that this is a contravention of the WTO rules on trade liberalisation. It is not clear whether Brazil is going to lodge a dispute at the WTO, but what it does signal is that Brazil, also an exporter of these products, wants the playing field to be levelled.

China prefers bilateral trading partnerships. How Beijing responds to these trade measures will be critical in determining whether the Chinese will shift towards engaging in free trade agreements.

Similarly, it is not clear how such tensions between BRICS members will be resolved or whether there will be some overall trade preference mechanism that will inform the intra-trade relations of the BRICS countries. But, more importantly, what position South Africa will take as such issues emerge will be significant, as it will affect Pretoria's own domestic economic restructuring and its relations with regional economies. Consideration must be given to the rules of origin issue, especially if South Africa's membership of BRIC enables the dumping of goods by other BRICS countries into the Southern African markets.

CONCLUSION

The admission of South Africa into BRIC has been a significant moment in the trajectory of the Zuma government's foreign policies. In a sign of continuity with the Mbeki years, it could reasonably be argued that the Zuma administration has extended South Africa's global outreach by joining the heavyweight division of the South – which has increased Pretoria's global prestige and recognition, and its status in the international community.

But has it been worthwhile? Belonging to a group like BRICS denotes a level of responsibility. It is not enough merely to acquire membership; it is what you do with that membership that defines whether admission into the club was the right choice. Thus far it is debatable whether the Zuma presidency apprehends how to carve out a niche for itself within the BRICS.

Being the weakest member of the alliance means that if South Africa is to be heard and respected it must start punching above its weight. Additionally, not only must Pretoria live up to the confidence its BRIC partners have shown in its membership, it must also illustrate to the South African people the efficacy of being part of BRICS. Alliance politics should not only be about multilateralism and a kind of musketeer ideology. It should also be directly linked to how our domestic challenges and aspirations are going to be addressed through the BRICS club, especially those challenges and aspirations related to unemployment, a viable industrial policy and social development.

There is another consideration that underscores South Africa as the fifth BRIC: an obsession by the foreign policy mandarins and the presidency with becoming a 'group junkie'. Admission to the various global groupings such as IBSA, G20 and G77 is fine but there is the risk of overstretch and of inadvertently moving away from the overall objec-tives of foreign policy. This is certainly a danger to the moral high ground that South Africa has chosen to occupy and definitely a threat of Pretoria's moving further away from the African agenda. Therefore, the greatest challenge for South Africa is to start making BRICS work for itself, while at the same time meeting the expectations of its BRIC partners, including promises and trade-offs President Zuma may have committed to them during his lobby visits to muster support for South Africa's entry into the forum.

POSTSCRIPT: TOWARDS THE 2013 BRICS SUMMIT[9]

In 2013, South Africa will host the fifth BRICS summit and assume the position of the rotating chair. Although Pretoria has indicated that this will provide South Africa with an opportunity to exploit its membership of the club to address domestic priorities such as investment in infrastructure, it will also focus the spotlight on what the Zuma presidency brings to the table to strengthen the African agenda and promote a reformed international order.

The major issue South Africa will certainly advance at the summit is the creation of a BRICS development bank. As one of the co-sponsors, with India, of the proposal adopted at the 2012 summit in New Delhi, South Africa will seek to push ahead with the bank's framework.

A side issue in Pretoria is who will be given oversight of South Africa's BRICS agenda: the DIRCO or the National Treasury.

With the government's BRICS strategy adopted by Cabinet, notwithstanding the election of Nkosazama Dlamini-Zuma as the newly elected chair of the African Union Commission and the pending operationalisation of the South African Development Partnership Agency to replace the African Renaissance Fund, understanding the alignment of the different agendas in South Africa's presidency of the BRICS club will be critical.

NOTES

1   Maite Nkoana-Mashabane, South African minister for international relations and cooperation: DIRCO press brief issued 24 December 2010. The briefing is available at: http://www.dfa.gov.za/docs/2010/brics1224.html.

2   Lyal White, director of the Centre for Dynamic Markets, Gordon Institute of Business Science. Interview, *Times Live*, 1 January 2011.

3   President Zuma launched his BRIC tour with a state visit to Brazil in November 2009. This was followed by a visit to India in June 2010, Russia in August 2010 and China at the end of August 2010.

4   It was reported that in late 2009 Minister Maite Nkoana-Mashabane had made a formal request to the BRIC member states to consider South Africa as a member of the grouping.

5   The 'Going Out' strategy was a national plan adopted by the Chinese authorities around 2000 to enhance the outward expansion of Chinese state owned enterprises (SOEs). The purpose was to make these SOEs globally competitive and acquire appropriate technology and other innovation expertise, which could be used to contribute towards the industrial outputs of the Chinese economy.

6   The Next 11 (N11) are a set of countries that Goldman Sachs identified as new modes of influence in the changing nature of the international system. The countries include Bangladesh, Egypt, Indonesia, Iran, Mexico, Nigeria, Pakistan, the Philippines, South Korea, Turkey and Vietnam

7   This is an acronym for a group of countries that are identified as the new set of emerging markets after the BRICS. Coined by Robert Ward, the global director for the Economist Intelligence Unit, the group is made up of Colombia, Indonesia, Vietnam, Egypt, Turkey and South Africa. With South Africa now formally admitted into BRICS and Egypt having to rebuild its economy following the social protests that ousted the Mubarak regime, it will be interesting to monitor whether there will be another African country that will replace these two as the African bloc. The countries of the East African community could be an interesting regional grouping.

8   Sanitary and phytosanitary (SPS) measures, or the SPS agreement, are safeguards adopted under the WTO trade rules. The agreement was negotiated under the Uruguay Round of the General Agreement on Tariffs and Trade (GATT), and came into force when the WTO was established in 1995. The SPS agreement applies a set of basic health and safety conditions that must be adhered to in respect of exports and imports that relate to food, animal and plant products. Although the standards are enforced to safeguard industries in importing countries against the transmission of diseases, the SPS measure are being implemented as a non-tariff barrier to protect local industries against cheaper imports from other countries.

9   For more on BRICS, see the knowledge hub on the South African Foreign Policy Initiative (SAFPI) programme website: http://www.safpi.org/knowledge_hubs/brics .

REFERENCES

Agarwal M, H Besada and L White (2010) Social challenges and progress in IBSA, *South African Journal of International Affairs* 17(3): 333-360.

Alden C and G Le Pere (2004) South Africa's post-apartheid foreign policy: From reconciliation to ambiguity? *Review of African Political Economy*, 31(100): 197-283.

Alden C and G Le Pere (2009) South Africa in Africa: Bound to lead? *Politikon: South African Journal of Political Studies*: Special Issue: Africa's Relations with Emerging Powers: Charting a New Direction in International Relations 36(1):145-170.

Bond P (2006) 'South African sub-imperial accumulation' in *The Accumulation of Capitalism in Southern Africa*, Rosa Luxemburg Political Education Seminar. Available at http://www.arts.yorku.ca/polscirsaunder/courses/2008/4575/readingspercent20postedpercent20topercent20site/4575percent20ONDpercent20SApercent20Imperialismpercent20andpercent20Nepadpercent20(2006).pdf [Accessed 20 January 2011].

Campbell K (2011) Bric becomes Brics, but will this be good for South Africa? *Polity.org,za*, 14 January. Available at http://www.polity.org.za/article/bric-becomes-brics-but-will-this-be-good-for-south-africa-2011-01-14 [Accessed 12 February 2011].

Cloete K (2011): South Africa prepares to head into the BRIC fold. IPSNews, 7 January. Available at http://ipsnews.net/news.asp?idnews=54055 [Accessed 15 January 2011].

Daniel J, V Naidoo and S Naidu (2004) The South Africans have arrived: The post-apartheid corporate expansion into Africa. In Daniel J, A Habib and R Southall (Eds) *State of the Nation: South Africa 2003-2004*. Cape Town: HSRC Press.

Daniel J and N Bhengu (2009) South Africa in Africa: Still a Formidable Power. In Southall R and H Melber (Eds) *A New Scramble for Africa? Imperialism, Investment and Development*. Scottsville: UKZN Press.

Davis G and C Terreblanche (2011) The disconnect of Afro-Trade. *Sunday Independent*, 20 February.

Dyomkin D (2010) Russia inks new Uranium deal with South Africa. *International Business Times*, 5 August. Available at http://www.ibtimes.com/articles/41216/20100806/russia-inks-new-uranium-deal-with-south-africa.htm [Accessed 1 February 2011].

Grudz S (2009) Foreign policy under Zuma: Change of style or substance. *The Growth Magazine*, 21 December. Available at: http://www.saiia.org.za/governance-and-aprm-opinion/foreign-policy-under-zuma-change-of-style-or-substance.html [Accessed 15 January 2011].

Freemantle S and J Stevens (2011) Beyond the Diplomatic Applause: Threats and Opportunities underlying South Africa's Bric Invitation. *Standard Bank Research Reports: BRIC and Africa (Economic Strategy)*, 26 January. Available at http://ws9.standardbank.co.za/sbrp/DocumentDownloader?docId=3437 [Accessed 15 February 2011].

Keet D (2003) Proposal on the role of trade within the New Partnership for Africa's Development (Nepad) – Challenges and Questions. Paper presented to *Workshop on African Trade Unions* hosted by the National Labour and Economic Development Institute (Naledi). Johannesburg, 22–23 May.

Landsberg C (2003) Hegemon or pivot: Debating South Africa's role in Africa. Debate hosted by the Centre for Policy Studies, August. Available at http://www.sarpn.org/documents/d0000620/P611-Pivotalstate.pdf [Accessed 5 February 2011].

Mashego T (2011) Analysts skeptical over BRIC invite. Times Live, 1 January. Available at http://www.timeslive.co.za/business/article832044.ece/Analysts-sceptical-over-Bric-invite [Accessed 15 January 2011].

Naidu S (2004) South Africa's policy: Mixed messages. In Sidiropolous E (Ed.) *Apartheid Past, Renaissance Future: South Africa's Foreign Policy 1994-2004*. Johannesburg: South African Institute of International Affairs.

Naidu S (2008) South Africa-China relations: Balancing a strategic partnership. In Ampiah K and S Naidu (Eds) *Crouching Tiger, Hidden Dragon? China and Africa: Engaging the World's Next Superpower*. Scottsville: UKZN Press.

Naidu S (2010) China in Africa: A maturing of the engagement. In Harneit-Sievers A, S Marks and S Naidu (Eds) *Chinese and African Perspectives on China in Africa*. Oxford: Pambazuka Press.

Nkosi B (2010) South Africa-China trade ties to strengthen. 23 August. Available at http://www.mediaclubsouthafrica.com/index.php?option=com_content&view=article&id=1920:china-230810&catid=45:economynews&Itemid=114 [Accessed 15 January 2011].

Nkosi B (2009) South Africa, Brazil cement ties. 13 October. Available at http://www.mediaclubsouth-africa.com/index.php?option=com_content&view=article&id=1362:sa-brazil-131009&catid=44:developmentnews&Itemid=111 [Accessed 5 January 2011].

Sharma A (2011) Huge untapped potential for investment and trade between India and South Africa. Address to India Business Forum in Johannesburg. 11 January. Press Release by the Department of Commerce, Government of India. Available at http://commerce.nic.in/PressRelease/pressrelease_detail.asp?id=2711 [Accessed 20 January 2011].

Shaw T, AF Cooper and GT Chin (2009) Emerging powers and Africa: Implications for/from global governance? *Politikon: South African Journal of Political Studies*: Special Issue: Africa's Relations with Emerging Powers: Charting a New Direction in International Relations 36(1): 27-44. [Guest Editors: S Naidu, L Corkin and H Herman].

Shira D & Associates (2010) South Africa joins Bric nations at China's request. 29 December. Available at http://www.2point6billion.com/news/2010/12/29/south-africa-joins-bric-nations-at-chinas-request-8291.html [Accessed 15 January 2011].

Taylor I (2009) The South will rise again? New alliances and global governance: India-Brazil and South Africa. *Politikon: South African Journal of Political Studies*: Special Issue: Africa's Relations with Emerging Powers: Charting a New Direction in International Relations 36(1): 45-58. [Guest Editors: S Naidu, L Corkin and H Herman].

Woolridge M (2011) Will Brics strengthen South Africa's economic foundations? *BBC News Online*. 5 January. Available at http://www.bbc.co.uk/news/mobile/world-africa-12113830 [Accessed 10 January 2011].

CHAPTER 16

The Swazi Nation, the Swazi government and the South African connection

John Daniel and Marisha Ramdeen

Singing, swaying, dust and heat,
Glistening bodies damp with sweat,
Rhythmic noise of beating feet,
Coloured cloth and plastic beads,
The tension of the crowds rises,
The shrill piercing cry of the crowd
Tells us outsiders the King has arrived

(Thembi Russell 1986)

The bare-bone facts of the Swazi political economy are well known: an undemocratic no-party state presided over by an unelected and autocratic monarch who in his reign of twenty-six years has accumulated a personal fortune estimated by *Forbes Magazine* in 2010 (7 July) to be in the region of US$100 million, making him the fifteenth richest monarch in the world, albeit some way behind Africa's richest king, Mohammed 1V of Morocco, whose fortune was put at US$2.4 billion. Beyond the Swazi king's thirteen palaces, just over two-thirds of his citizenry live at or below the poverty line and its government is unable to cover its monthly wage bill and other costs to the point where in 2011 it sought a R2.4 billion bail-out from South Africa. Landlocked, Swaziland depends on South Africa for about 80 per cent of its imports and sells South Africa 60 per cent of its exports; GDP growth has declined through the first decade of the century to under 1 per cent in 2010, and the annual revenue pay-out from the Southern African Customs Union's common tariff pool has slumped by nearly two-thirds. This, combined with rampant state corruption and the monarchy's lavish lifestyle, has generated the current economic crisis in the kingdom, one that, however, barely impacts on the monarch and his vast aristocratic network, the Swazi Nation. 'They are flying, we are dying' is a common expression mouthed in opposition circles in Swaziland.

Yet in the face of glaring inequality, vast poverty and no meaningful political rights, opposition is not widespread and what there is, is easily, though often harshly, contained. Even so, by modern African standards Swaziland is not a Zimbabwean or Sudanese-type tyranny – but then it does not need to be. King Mswati is neither a candidate for arraignment at the International Criminal Court (ICC) and nor, it seems, need he fret at the possibility of a North African-type 'Swazi Spring' or any form of decisive regional or international intervention.

In its examination of the modern Swazi state, this chapter examines the relationship between the South African and Swazi states and attempts to understand why the government in Pretoria should have agreed to a fiscal bail-out request and why it attached what can only be described as feeble conditions to the loan. What makes this soft stance towards the *status quo* in Swaziland so remarkable is: first, the late apartheid era's history of relations between the African National Congress (ANC) and the Swazi government in which the latter allied itself with the apartheid state against the political and military wings of the ANC; and, second, the fact that the so-called Swazi economic crisis is not at root a fiscal crisis but a manufactured political problem, something that must surely be apparent to the Zuma administration.

In analysing the situation in Swaziland, this chapter will:

a) dissect a constitutional system that enshrines all power in a network of unelected and democratically unaccountable institutions, the network locally referred to as the 'Swazi Nation' and currently headed by King Mswati III (born Makhosetive Dlamini in 1978);

b) analyse the political economy of Swaziland to demonstrate how the King personally – and the Swazi aristocracy more widely – has accumulated vast wealth while the common people go hungry and die from an HIV/AIDS pandemic that has since independence in 1968 reduced Swazi life expectancy from around sixty years of age to below forty (hence, the slogan 'They are flying, we are dying');

c) demonstrate how a pervasive socialisation process emanating from an 'ideology of tradition' has in effect depoliticised the Swazi people to the point that they remain essentially politically passive in the face of rampant injustice; and

d) look at the role of some important corporate actors in the Swazi drama. Among these are: i) the Swazi affiliate of the South African telecommunications company MTN; and ii) an investment arm of the Swazi Nation, the Tibiyo takaNgwane[1] (the Wealth of the Swazi Nation) Fund, of which the ANC's Chancellor House group is a pale imitation. The board of the fund is appointed by King Mswati and is answerable to him (Booth 2000:114-15).

THE ORIGINS OF THE SWAZI STATE

The modern Swazi state originated in the early decades of the nineteenth century, a time of regional state formation and dissolution triggered by the Shakan revolution or *Mfecane* (Daniel and Vilane 1986; and Matsebula 1972).That state was considerably larger than the current entity and included parts of present-day Mpumalanga province, including the former kaNgwane homeland, and parts of southern Mozambique, including the port of Maputo.[2] To counter the threat posed to the youthful Swazi kingdom from the emerging Zulu state, the Swazis sought to guarantee their independence through alliances with either British or Boer forces in the area. On four occasions between 1864 and 1876, Swazi soldiers fought with the Boers in campaigns against indigenous forces, and in 1879 it was actually the Swazi army that secured victory for the British in their war with the Pedi (Bonner 1983).

The defeat of the Transvaal Republic in the South African War of 1898-1902 resulted in a British takeover of Swaziland. Pursuant to the development of a settler mode of agriculture, a wholesale land appropriation (decreed in 1909 and implemented in 1914, one year after a similar process in South Africa) deprived the Swazis of two-thirds of their territory. This 'forced removal' eroded the power base of the Dlaminis and their allied clans but the British did not allow that loss of power to go too far. From the outset, the locus of domestic political power within the emerging Swazi state resided in the royal lines of the Dlamini clan and even in the era of British colonial rule – which ran from the early twentieth century up to independence in 1968 – the supremacy of the monarchy in regard to traditional affairs was acknowledged, albeit in only that one-third of the country in which the Swazi were then allowed to reside after 1914. Thus, for example, the monarchy encouraged Swazi chiefs to act as labour recruiters for the South African Chamber of Mines and to levy a capitation fee per Swazi recruited. This facilitated a process of capital accumulation on the part of the Swazi royalty, a process further abetted when the British permitted the monarchy to impose a range of fines over the Swazi peasantry. As Daniel and Vilane noted (1986:56), 'gradually over time, the Swazi aristocracy emerged as a petty-bourgeoisie within the colonial capitalist state – a class with certain comprador characteristics'.

The South Africa Act of 1909, by which the British government united their four South African colonies into a single state in 1910, made provision for the eventual incorporation of the three so-called High Commission Territories (HCTs) of Basutoland, Bechuanaland and Swaziland into the white-dominated state. It never happened for reasons not discussed here, but it was only in 1964 that the South African government backed off the incorporation idea and agreed to a decolonisation of the HCTs (Hyam 1972). Swaziland's independence, however, was delayed for two years beyond that of Lesotho and Botswana in 1966, as the Swazi monarch, Sobhuza II, delayed the process by demanding monopoly control over the administration of Swazi law and custom and all mineral rights and the royalties derived therefrom. By that time, deposits of iron ore, asbestos, coal and diamonds were either being mined or were known about. Eventually the British acceded to the demands. To administer the mineral rights, Sobhuza created a special development fund – originally little more than a bank account – known as Tibiyo takaNgwane. It was into this initially modest instrument of royalist capital accumulation that, from 1968, mineral revenues were deposited.

INDEPENDENCE AND THE MAKING OF THE 'MODERN' SWAZI CONSTITUTIONAL ORDER

The hegemonic authority of Swaziland's traditional rulers was threatened by the British imposition of a Westminster-type constitution on the country at independence. This made provision for free party political competition and regular elections by secret ballot for a central Parliament. In this new order, the Swazi monarchy was relegated constitutionally to a largely ceremonial status. Here, however, Sobhuza revealed his political adroitness by adapting to the requisites of modern political processes through the creation in 1966 of his own party political vehicle, the Imbokodvo National Movement (INM), which won all parliamentary seats in elections held prior to independence. Thus it was that Sobhuza ensured that the now independent Parliament did nothing of which he did not approve.[3] According to the first post-independence premier, Prince Makhosini Dlamini, this is as it should have been. 'It is the king, not I, who leads the people,' stated Dlamini, asserting the principle that to this day remains the central tenet of the traditional or monarchical conceptualisation of Swazi political culture (Daniel and Vilane 1986: 56).

In the first post-independence elections held in 1972, the INM's monopoly in Parliament was dented when an opposition grouping won three out of the available twenty-eight seats. This setback for the king coincided with the High Court's declaring a parliamentary enactment in regard to a citizenship and immigration issue unconstitutional. At this point, the monarchy's flirtation with Westminster-type politics came to an end. The INM had done its job and now it was time to revert to business as usual, to the ways of the monarchical order of old.

On 12 April 1972, Sobhuza summoned his people to the royal cattle byre at Lobamba, the then seat of the monarchy, and declared a state of emergency (which *de jure* remains in force today, forty-one years later). He then announced the dissolution of Parliament, the suspension of the 1968 Constitution, and the banning of all political parties including his own INM. Sobhuza justified this outlawing of political parties, by declaring them 'alien' and 'undesirable', inconsistent with Swazi custom and the importers 'of undesirable political practices … designed to disrupt and destroy our own peaceful and constructive and essentially democratic method of peaceful political activity' (Daniel and Vilane, op. cit.). The fact that political parties remain banned today, despite the introduction of a new constitution in 2005, suggests that this hostile view to political parties is shared by Sobhuza's successor, Mswati III. It also suggests that for the Swazi monarchy to concede the democratic principle that all Swazis should have the right to organise themselves politically would be a paradigm shift ideologically on its part, and one it shows no signs of being willing to make.

Into the political vacuum, the king inserted the traditional institutions of the precolonial era, namely the monarchy and its key advisory institution, Liqoqo, comprising senior Dlamini princes and other trusted male confidants of the king. It is to the institutions of the monarchy that the term 'Swazi Nation' applies and it is here where supreme executive, legislative and judiciary power is now vested. Six years later in 1978, Sobhuza introduced a semblance of democratic consultation with a new electoral system. Again, he reverted to a traditional consultative form, *tinkhundla*, modifying it as the instrument through which a new parliament could be elected every five years.

In this electoral process, candidates run only as individuals and not as representatives of any party or grouping. The number of candidates per constituency is limited to three, and their nomination is subject to a local screening process conducted in public by a show of hands by the local chiefs in the area. The franchise is open to all adults over the age of eighteen, and votes are cast by secret ballot. Despite the quasi-democratic form of this electoral process, it does not conform to the widely accepted 'free and fair' criteria for democratic elections.[4] The ban on party political activity limits the range of political choice. So too does the local screening process, which inevitably has the result that the vast majority (if not all) of candidates are linked to, or sympathetic to, the royalist structure. Finally, balloting is for only fifty-five of the eighty-five parliamentary seats, which means that about 35 per cent of legislative seats are non-elective and the prerogative of the king himself. He appoints ten members of the fifty-five strong House of Assembly and twenty of the thirty-member Senate. Thus, even in the improbable eventuality that a majority of elected members turned out to be reformists, their capacity for change would be neutralised by the nominated bloc of royalist-aligned members of Parliament. Under current circumstances, therefore, a lawful or constitutional change of power in Swaziland is impossible.

The sham nature of this gesture to democracy and the toothless nature of the Swazi parliament was revealed in October 2012 when, in a rare show of defiance, the body passed with a three-fifths majority a motion of no confidence in the Cabinet in regard to a matter relating to the telecommunications system in the country. In terms of section 68 (5) of the 2006 Swazi Constitution, the Cabinet must either stand down or be dismissed by the king. Neither happened. The king refused to meet with the speaker of Parliament to receive an official communication on the issue, and the prime minister, with the support of the attorney general (both non-elected monarchical appointees) rejected the decision. In response, the Parliament, instead of dissolving itself, in effect said 'sorry' by rescinding its original decision. Like the Natives Representative Council of the apartheid era in South Africa, the Parliament confirmed its status as a 'toy telephone' into which it speaks while no one listens.

The predominant role of the king in the traditional system has often led to Mswati's being described as an 'absolute monarch'. This suggests that he rules alone and is all-powerful, which is not strictly correct. It would be more accurate to apply the term 'absolute' to the Swazi traditional order, which comprises an intricate network of royal clans in which the Dlaminis are just one, albeit the largest and most influential. At the monarchy's apex sits

the king and his mother, the queen regent, who has a set of functions and potentially countervailing powers to that of her son. Then there are the king's brothers and uncles, the sons
of the previous king. Given Sobhuza's longevity, the uncles are numerous. Many of them
are elderly and consequently influential, although to differing degrees. The most influential of these princes sit on the Liqoqo, along with, at times, some prominent commoners.

The king does not therefore rule alone but in concert with Liqoqo, although as he gets
older the balance of power within the monarchy and Liqoqo tilts more and more in his
favour. Mswati has not yet reached the age and level of seniority at which he can rule at
whim. And this monarchy is not a homogeneous entity. Like any large family, it is riven
with rivalries, jealousies and grievances, real and imagined. The stresses within the king's
immediate family are such that three of his thirteen wives have fled Swaziland and one
has been banished to her family home after being exposed as romantically involved with
a Cabinet minister and former close confidant of Mswati. She, it is said, will never be
'visited' again by the king and has to have his permission to see her children.

The 1990s democratic transition in neighbouring South Africa prompted a resurgence
in political activity in Swaziland with various political groupings – notably the Swaziland
Youth Congress, the Peoples United Democratic Movement and the Swazi Federation of
Trade Unions – pushing for democratic reforms along the lines of those introduced in
South Africa. This reform thrust was also supported by President Nelson Mandela in his
capacity as chair of the Southern African Development Community's (SADC) Organ on
Politics, Defence and Security.

After apparently failing to persuade a respected critic of the regime to head a constitutional review commission (CRC), the king appointed one of his brothers. It laboured
behind largely closed doors for eight years, during which it became clear to the Swazi
establishment that its powerful neighbour had no intention of pressuring it in any democratic direction. By that time President Mandela had retired and his successor, Thabo
Mbeki, had larger continent-wide foreign policy goals and was also keen to shift away
from South Africa's 'bully boy' image of old towards the region. So, pressure on the Swazi
monarchy eased as South African foreign policy moved away from a primary concern
with human rights in favour of pragmatic self-interest and non-interventionism.

The CRC's final product in the form of a new constitution took effect in February 2006.
Although it introduced some limited reforms in areas such as women's rights, it affirmed
the political *status quo* of monarchical supremacy, along with the continuing prohibition
on political parties. A challenge to the continuing ban on political parties by a coalition
of civil society groups, which argued that it violated the constitutional right to freedom
of association, was rejected by the Supreme Court. It produced a memorable quote from
the chair of the Swazi Elections and Boundary Commission, Chief Gija Dlamini, that
freedom of association in Swaziland applied to the right 'to join a soccer club, rather
than to form a political party (ACTSA 2010: 4). In response to the court outcome and
this assertion by the chief, Jan Sithole, then president of the Swazi Federation of Trade
Unions, made the pertinent observation that Swazis were 'squatters in our own country'
(http://www.iol.co.za/news/Africa 12 October 2003).

What the Swazi constitutional order represents is something unique in sub-Saharan Africa: namely, a situation in which the feudal rulers of the precolonial/precapitalist era have not only survived but also managed to capture – or, rather, recapture – political power, and devise a means to exercise it in a largely unfettered way. Simultaneously, it has also enabled them to free themselves from the limited ways of capital accumulation the British permitted and to engage post-independence in an untrammelled process of capital accumulation. This aristocracy, the 'Swazi Nation', is *de facto* a state within a state, populated by a capitalist class of considerable wealth. The rest of the Swazi population, the commoners, live a very different existence. Nearly 70 per cent of them are poverty-stricken and about 25 to 30 per cent of them – an estimated 190 000 – are afflicted by the AIDS pandemic. Their welfare is the responsibility of that other part of the Swazi state, the subordinated government of Swaziland.

THE SWAZI POLITICAL ECONOMY

The Swazi economy grew steadily, albeit unspectacularly, in the decade and a half after independence, driven largely by an expanding sugar sector that enjoyed preferential access to the US and European markets. Complementing sugar were modest but prosperous timber (paper and pulp), citrus and cotton operations. The mining and manufacturing sectors grew steadily and South African tourists flocked in growing numbers to enjoy the 'forbidden fruits' of gambling, interracial sex and cheap but potent marijuana. The annual revenues generated by disbursements from the common tariff pool of the Southern African Customs Union (SACU) constituted a 'cherry on the top'.

Despite the internecine squabbles that afflicted the royal family in the years from Sobhuza's death in 1982 and Mswati's installation in 1986, economically things got even better in the decade of the 1980s and early 1990s. Real per capita GDP growth rates in the period 1980-94 averaged 2.7 per cent annually. This was in large part because as unrest grew in South Africa foreign investors abandoned the apartheid arena and, attracted by a generous bouquet of incentives such as five-year tax breaks, some of these divestors moved into Swaziland (the largest of these were Coca-Cola and Cadburys). The result was that from the mid-1980s new foreign investment in manufacturing boosted economic growth rates and the reduced value of the local currency, tied as it was to the South African rand, which slumped in value after PW Botha's disastrous 'Rubicon speech' of 1986,[5] served only to boost the competitiveness of Swazi exports and dampen the growth of imports.

The advent of democracy in South Africa in 1994 marked the beginning of the end of the economic good times in Swaziland. Some of the new investors of the 1980s shut up shop and returned to South Africa, the tourist flow declined, and the South African mining sector turned to local labour and cut the number of migrant recruits from its neighbours. The notable exception to the cluster of corporate returnees was the Coca-Cola Corporation, which has steadily grown its operations in Swaziland since 1990 and is now the single largest manufacturer in the economy. Another plus in the 1990s was the entry into the economy of a number of textile groups – mostly Taiwanese – that took advantage of the tariff discounts offered by the US Growth and Opportunity Act (AGOA). Even so, in the 1990s the country incurred a number of small trade deficits.

The first decade of the new century produced more economic shocks and in that decade Swaziland was the worst-performing economy of all the ten SADC states. Among the shocks was a decline in foreign direct investment as well as a process of divestment with the withdrawal in the second half of the decade of most of the textile plants that had moved into the country to take advantage of AGOA, with the resultant loss of over 20 000 jobs, held mostly by women. This coincided with the phasing out of Swaziland's sugar concession with the European Union, so that the value of its exports of raw and processed sugar declined. At the end of the decade, and following a fire that destroyed about 60 per cent of one of the world's largest cultivated timber plantations, the Usuthu Forest, its South African owners announced the closure of its operations in Swaziland, including its huge paper mill at Mhlambanyati, with a loss of about 600 jobs.

One of the government's responses to the job losses of the late 1990s and early 2000s was to expand the size of the public sector, primarily by swelling the ranks of the police and army to the point that by 2006 Swaziland had one of the largest civil services in Africa in relation to population and GDP (*Mercury* 29 December 2011). This is still the case. In these circumstances, Swaziland's reliance on its annual disbursements from SACU soared to the point that it constituted by 2009 around 60 per cent of total government revenue. Hence, the crisis generated when the size of that disbursement tumbled late in the decade by about two-thirds from R6 billion in 2008 to R1.6 billion in 2010.

But although the crisis for the Swazi government and most of its people is a real one, it is only part of the story because in gross economic terms this is not a real economic crisis but a manufactured one, a product not of the negative factors cited above but of the undemocratic and unaccountable nature of Swaziland's political order. The solution is not to be found in IMF reform packages or South African bail-outs. It lies at home in the abolition – or at the least a radical reform – of the politics and economics of the Swazi Nation.

That most African economies are characterised by dualism in the form of formal and informal sectors is commonplace. Swaziland is no exception, at least in regard to the open, visible part of the modern economy. However, in Swaziland the concept of a 'dual economy' has a whole other meaning, for just as the monarchy – the Swazi Nation – operates as a state within a state, so too does the monarchical economy. What we have in Swaziland is a private sector coexisting with a largely hidden economy that operates above and beyond the remit of the Swazi government. Of these two economies, the one is currently in difficulties, unable to pay its way, struggling each month to meet its wage bill as well as the critical needs of the health, education and other sectors. The other is flourishing, awash with cash, up there in wealth terms with some of the monarchical economies of the oil-rich Gulf states.

This so-called economic crisis in Swaziland, which the South African government is willing to ameliorate, is not one of revenue generation but of distribution. Above all, it is a political crisis. The Swazi monarchy does not pay its way. Instead, it functions as a parasite on the modern economy, sucking out of it ever-increasing annual disbursements to fund its palaces, its lavish lifestyle, its frequent shopping forays abroad, the private school fees of an ever-larger number of princes and princesses. In the annual budgets in 2011 and 2012, the royal household received from Parliament grants of R210 million, an increase of 23 per cent over 2010 and 63 per cent over 2009. Hardly evidence of an austerity crisis. The household itself makes no contribution to its running costs, not a single cent, because members of the royal family (and their numbers run into the thousands) and its institutional 'cash cows' are exempt from the payment of taxes. For the Swazi monarchy, it's all take and no give.

The rise and growth of this royal economy is largely the story of the Tibiyo Fund. As noted earlier, Tibiyo's origins lie in the eve-of-independence British concession that gave the monarchy – and not the government – monopoly control over revenues generated from mineral rights. These constituted Tibiyo's original capital base and were used to buy freehold land from non-Swazis, much of which was developed into royal-owned maize and dairy estates. Tibiyo then moved into the retail sector, establishing a range of small but profitable businesses: butcheries, liquor stores, taxi operators and the like. By the late 1970s and under the stewardship of a commoner but close confidant of the king, Simon Sishayi Nxumalo, the fund had generated sufficient capital to begin acquiring equity (usually in the range of 40 per cent to 49 per cent) in foreign companies operating in the economy. These have included the large agro-industrials in the sugar, timber, citrus, and fruit, processing industries, large wholesalers, banks, mining, manufacturing, and hotel companies.[6]

In this way, Tibiyo has spread its net into all sectors of the economy, establishing a solid partnership with foreign capital, the dividend payments from which became Tibiyo's principal source of revenue. It has also been the means by which the Swazi aristocracy has acquired for itself a considerable material base in the modern economy, complementing their control of the traditional agrarian sector, achieved through its monopoly over the right to allocate and withdraw land tenure rights. In other words, as Daniel noted (2006: 526), 'the Swazi aristocracy ... is not just a privileged elite but a modestly wealthy capitalist class for whom regime change or even a significant democratisation of the system, could have negative consequences.'

That term 'modestly wealthy' would seem now to be an understatement in regard to King Mswati. His father Sobhuza was an old-fashioned traditionalist, an autocrat in political terms, but his priority was never personal aggrandisement and he lived a modest lifestyle by modern standards. His son could not be more different. He is very much the modern African head of state, grossly consumerist, flamboyantly rich and committed to an aggressive path of personal accumulation. Although details of the king's fortune or the nature of his investments are not publicly known, his wealth is clearly considerable. Mswati has taken control of Tibiyo and used its resources to invest widely and, in the process, built enough of a personal fortune to catch the attention of the compilers of the Forbes rich lists.

Tibiyo's website describes itself as one of the main players in the Swazi economy. This is an understatement. The *Mail & Guardian* (23-29 September 2011) reported that it held one-third of all privately held assets in the country. In 2010 it reported a profit of R150 million – and 2010 was not a strong year for investments. Clearly, he who controls Tibiyo is a major player and prosperous to boot. That player is King Mswati.

So, just how rich is King Mswati? What is the value of his royal treasure trove? Few know. In 2008, *Forbes* magazine estimated Mswati's net worth as in the region of US$160 million based on the value of his land holdings and investments. Two years later, that amount had slipped to approximately US$100 million, reflecting the slide in share values as a result of the global meltdown experienced by all but two of the top fifteen richest monarchs. And where are these investments? Certainly in Swaziland, through Tibiyo, but also further afield. We know this because, in response to media criticism of his lavish expenditures, the CEO of the king's office told the media that the king 'earns a high salary as head of state, has investments inside and outside the country and owns an unspecified amount of shares in different companies within Swaziland' (http://en.wikipedia.org/wiki/Mswati_111). One of these is the South African mobile telephone operator MTN, which has a monopoly on mobile telephony in Swaziland.

MTN Swaziland, in which MTN South Africa had a 30 per cent shareholding, was launched in 1998 with a licence to develop a mobile telephony operation. The majority shareholder at the time was the state-owned landline operator, Swaziland Posts and Telecommunications (SPTC), with a 51 per cent share, and the other 19 per cent was held by an entity known as the Swaziland Empowerment Group. Though small by global standards, the local MTN operation grew rapidly so that by mid-2008 it claimed to have 457 000 subscribers or nearly half the Swazi population. With high charge-out rates, it is a 'cash cow'.

In the face of such profits, SPTC decided a few years back to enter the mobile telephony arena and developed a rival cellphone service with lower charge-out rates. At the time, SPT claimed it had transferred 41 per cent of its holdings in MTN to the ministry of finance and 10 per cent to the king. MTN disputed this and claimed that SPT was in violation of its arrangement with MTN by going into competition with it. Litigation followed, and in March 2012, the International Court of Arbitration ruled in MTN's favour.

The Swazi government responded by, in effect, nationalising MTN, taking over its 30 per cent shareholding and announcing that it would run the cellular operation in competition with MTN, but at lower rates. Although this could be seen as a popular and sensible economic measure, the suspicion is that the new entity will be developed as a cash cow for the Swaziland government and that its profits will become part of the exchequer, a new source of government revenue. Indeed, this may already be the case and SPTC's cash resources may have been used either to pay the monthly wage bill or as collateral for an anonymous entity channelling funds to the government in the wake of the failure to secure the loan from South Africa. A report tabled in Parliament in February 2012 by the Finance Committee referred to an 'entity' making loans to government worth

R1.4 billion. The *Swaziland Newsletter* of 17 February 2012 quoted a report in the local government-owned newspaper, the *Times of Swaziland*, to the effect that 'in order to pay these salaries [government] had to clinch a deal with an entity and put down shares in SPTC and MTN as collateral'.

WHY DO THEY PUT UP WITH IT? THE IDEOLOGY OF TRADITION

Swazi political culture has, since the 1920s and the assumption to the kingship of Sobhuza II, been dominated by an ideology of 'tradition'. This is a set of ideas that should not be confused with 'conservatism', which is associated with resistance to change and a desire to keep things as they are, to preserve old ways and customs. Tradition can sometimes mean that but, as Macmillan has shown (1985), in the Swazi context it has been anything but. Instead, it has been dynamic, constantly adapting to changing circumstances, amending custom and the old ways of doing things with one end in mind – to restore and then preserve the political dominance of the royalist elite. Tradition as an ideology in Swaziland dates back to the 1920s when the recently crowned Sobhuza – well educated, with a keen understanding of history and with politically canny advisers such as the ANC founder Pixley Ka Isak Seme – began to be acutely aware of the threat to royal hegemony from both British colonialism and the spread into Swaziland of commercialism.

He thus started a shrewd political game of manipulating the colonial administration to his ends (even threatening at times to abdicate if he did not obtain certain gains) but without alienating them, and also by encouraging educated members of the elite to move into the commercial arena. He undertook a process of documenting – which at times meant re-interpreting, if not inventing – Swazi law and custom, and established a cluster of 'Swazi national schools' for the education of largely, but not exclusively, the sons of the royal elite and of the chieftancy. As Macmillan put it (1986: 110), 'traditionalism … in the eyes of Sobhuza, was not a question of clinging to the past and attempting to recreate a lost world, but rather of selection and adaptation'. The end result, Macmillan argues, was that a 'rural elite – whose original power stemmed from the distribution of the land which remained in Swazi occupation under customary tenure – has established exclusive political control over an increasingly complex society' (op.cit.: 122).

What Macmillan does not emphasise is that this ideology of traditionalism has been accompanied by a relentless socialisation process geared to persuading the ordinary Swazi, the rural commoner, that the dominance of royalty is the natural order of things and that the king knows best and has the best interests of the nation at heart. It has been brilliantly successful. It is this that accounts for the fact that the political opposition, composed of modest numbers of politically active tertiary students, a small urban elite and trade unionists, has been unable to develop a mass base simply because it has not been able to mobilise the rural majority. In short, the opposition has not been able to undermine the power of tradition through a trans-class alliance, even in the face of poverty and worsening rural conditions and in the context of a democratising region.

This raises the issue of South Africa, a regional hegemon, now ruled by a party that would *prima facie* seem to have no reason to feel any affinity for Swaziland's rulers.

THE SWAZI-SOUTH AFRICAN RELATIONSHIP

The Swazi-South African relationship over the past century and a half has, on the part of the Swazis, been characterised by pragmatism and a narrow concept of self-interest. As in the case of its post-independence foreign relations, Swaziland has not been driven by commitment to any ideological notions such as anti-communism or a sense of African or black solidarity. Its primary concerns in the nineteenth century were survival as a nation and, in the twentieth century, the regaining of sovereignty as well as the as yet unfulfilled ambition of regaining territories ceded by King Bhunu in the land concessions of the late nineteenth century (Bonner 1983).

As noted earlier, in the nineteenth century the Swazi monarchy forged alliances with powerful white groups in the region and cooperated with them against indigenous black interests. A century or so later, and alone among the states of southern Africa, independent Swaziland sided actively with the apartheid state against the ANC. Today, Swaziland continues on a maverick path, for example as one of only two African states to maintain full diplomatic ties with Taiwan in preference to mainland China (Malawi is the other). And it does so because, to put it crudely, 'it pays well' in that the Republic of China is a generous donor.

Even though it was under British rule for two-thirds of the twentieth century, Swazi politics in that period was shaped largely by King Sobhuza II. Declared heir to the throne in his infancy in 1901, he was sent to Lovedale College in the Eastern Cape where he received 'the best secondary education then available to a black South African' (Macmillan 1985:107). This was at the time of the founding of the ANC and Sobhuza was among its early members and close to its first president, Pixley Ka Isak Seme, who also acted as his lawyer in a case the Swazis took to the Privy Council in London in the early 1930s.[7] Unsurprisingly, therefore, Swaziland was hospitable to the first wave of South African refugees who entered Swaziland after Sharpeville and the banning of the ANC and the Pan Africanist Congress (PAC). That community remained small, however, given Swaziland's landlocked status and the fact that it was surrounded by neighbours hostile to African nationalist aspirations: South Africa and the then Portuguese-ruled Mozambique.

That all changed in the mid-1970s with the coming to power in Mozambique of a then Marxist-oriented and pro-Soviet government and the Soweto uprising in South Africa. Virtually overnight, Swaziland became a haven to thousands of young South African refugees, many eager to join the armed struggle, along with a new cadre of exiled ANC leaders – among them Thabo Mbeki and Jacob Zuma – with a mandate to construct a political underground in Swaziland and to reconnect it to ANC clusters in Johannesburg and Durban. Even though ANC president OR Tambo and Sobhuza negotiated an arrangement whereby the ANC could establish a political presence in Swaziland, the relationship between Swazi security and the ANC was always uneasy, if not hostile, worsening over time as Swazi security was increasingly penetrated by South African security.

In 1977, the Swazi police arrested Mbeki and Zuma, along with another ANC cadre, Albert Dlomo, and, after telling the three that they were being deported to Mozambique, tried to put them on a flight to South Africa. The three refused to board and created a huge disturbance, running all over the airport shouting for help and alleging they were being sold 'to the Boers'. Eventually, the embarrassed police contingent relented and returned them to police cells. They were later moved to Mozambique and safety (Simpson 2009:102-3). It was in the wake of this incident that the agreement with Sobhuza was negotiated. That arrangement specifically prohibited the ANC from using Swaziland for military activities, either in the country or in transit. It was routinely ignored by the ANC, and by the end of the 1970s Swaziland had become an important forward staging area for both political and military operations. Members of Joe Slovo's 'special ops' unit operated out of Swaziland in the early 1980s and many of the unit's spectacular 'armed-propaganda' operations of the early 1980s (the attack on Sasol and the military base at Voortrekkerhoogte in Pretoria, as examples) were carried out by cadres who were either based in Swaziland or who moved through it in transit with their weaponry. It was in this context that South African security in the early 1980s referred to the 'eastern front' with Swaziland and Mozambique as 'leaking like a sieve'. Until 1982, Sobhuza and his security forces largely 'looked the other way' in regard to ANC operations.

South Africa did not and, in the early 1980s, launched a counteroffensive. This took the form, in the case of Mozambique, of recruiting, training and arming a 'contra' force in the form of the Mozambican National Resistance Movement (Renamo) which in the next decade would wreak economic havoc in Mozambique, force the government to expel the ANC from its territory and reduce the country to beggar-bowl status (Hanlon 1986; Minter 1994).

In the case of Swaziland, the approach was different. Rather than use force, it exploited the last great objective of the now ageing Sobhuza, the regaining of the 'lost lands'. In 1981, the South African government suddenly indicated that it was interested in discussing border adjustments, involving the possible transfer to Swaziland of the KaNgwane home-land as well as the Ingwavuma district of northern Zululand, a strip of land that would give Swaziland direct access to the sea. It was a brilliant manoeuvre and it worked when, in February 1982, Swaziland signed a then secret pact with South Africa in which it agreed to crack down on the ANC and, more significantly, to give the South Africans the right to intervene in Swaziland (Daniel 1989:12). Within weeks, the ANC's longstanding political representative in Swaziland, Stanley Mabizela, was forced to leave the country (Davies and O'Meara 1985). For the ANC, worse was to follow.

Six months after signing the pact, Sobhuza died. A period of internecine strife followed within the royal family, which ended with power being seized by a conserva-tive clique hostile not only to democracy but also to everything the ANC then stood for. It shared Pretoria's view of the ANC as 'Soviet surrogates' and, in 1984, Prime Minister

Prince Bhekimpi Dlamini banned the ANC from operating in Swaziland, describing it as a 'foreign scourge' and branding ANC President Oliver Tambo 'a liar' (Daniel and Vilane 1886: 64). Mass deportations of known ANC members and suspected fellow travellers followed; some operatives were killed in shoot-outs with Swazi security and South African security personnel were allowed to abduct some key guerrillas and take them to South Africa (some were neither seen nor heard of again).[8]

In 1985, Swaziland and South Africa forged diplomatic relations, with the establishment in Mbabane of a South African trade mission. With the insurgency in South Africa intensifying and the international community increasingly supporting the democratic forces, the Swazi government distanced itself from the campaigns for sanctions and disinvestment and issued an appeal to 'give South Africa a chance …we have been really impressed by what South Africa has been doing for the last years … [South Africa] is on the right track as far as we are concerned' (Daniel and Vilane 1986: 63).

Most commentators interpreted this state of cooperation with South Africa as one in which the Swazi government had no choice, given its dependency on South Africa. A handful took a different view and argued that the decision to side with apartheid was the choice of the Swazi ruling class, one that reflected the fact that 'even in the imperialist context of Southern Africa today [mid-1980s], there are options and degrees of submissiveness and collaboration, and that economic domination and coercion … should not be seen as the sole determinants of the region's relations with both the government of South Africa and the liberation movements opposing it' (Daniel and Vilane 1986: 55). What was argued was that South African coercion only established the parameters within which the small states of the region could operate and that the Swazi position in the mid-1980s reflected a historical continuity of its accommodationist posture toward imperial capital, a position that had ensured both its survival and its modest prosperity. With the crisis of the apartheid state maturing, this was simultaneously a crisis for the ruling royalist class in Swaziland and the decision was again to seek an alliance with white rule. It was a logical political decision on its part. It was not to know then that it would have little to fear from a change of regime in Pretoria.

Initial Swazi fears of ANC-ruled South Africa seemed borne out when President Mandela took a pro-reform position in regard to Swaziland. Despite his ties to Swazi royalty through one of his daughter's then marriage to a Swazi prince and his own family ties to the traditional aristocracy in the eastern Cape, Mandela was critical of the lack of change in Swaziland and used his position in SADC as chair of its Organ on Defence, Security and Politics to apply pressure on Mswati. It is likely that Mswati initiated the constitutional review process in 1996 in response to this pressure. But everything changed when Mandela handed the reins of governmental authority to Thabo Mbeki with the collapse in late 1966 of the Government of National Unity. Non-interference in the affairs of other states – even rogue states – became one of the operating credos of Mbeki's Department of Foreign Affairs. Mbeki was also motivated by the desire to show that the bad old days of 'Pax Pretoriana' were over and that South Africa would no longer play the role of 'regional bully-boy'. This position has been perpetuated by his successor.

How ironical it is that the two who in 1977 had had to beg the Swazi authorities for their security, if not their lives, should two to three decades later cosset the very same rulers of that state.

In this context, it is not surprising that the South African government should have agreed in principle to bail out the Swazi state. The memorandum of understanding (MOU) drafted in regard to the loan was conditional on the Swazi authorities agreeing to open and broaden a dialogue process to include all stakeholders and citizens in the country, so as to determine appropriate reforms. It also stipulated that the process take place in an open environment and be one that would enjoy legitimacy among the people of Swaziland and the region. When one considers the kind of conditions laid down by the European Union for its bail-outs, this was tame, but, even so, it was too much for the king. Although he did not criticise the conditions himself, Mswati's older brother, Prince Mahlabu, described the terms as 'like selling your wife for a hundred rands'. A report in one South African newspaper, however, the *Sunday Star*, described the stumbling block as being a demand from Mswati for a R400 million negotiating fee to be paid to himself. No other paper carried the story and it must be regarded as unconfirmed. Nonetheless, it would not have been out of character for this accumulationist monarch.

The South African government justified its agreement to the loan request as being to prevent an implosion in a border state that could have resulted in a mass inflow of Swazis into South Africa. The MOU between the two parties was never signed and, nearly a year on, no such implosion has occurred or even seems likely. That was a fig leaf of a rationale. The real reason probably has much more to do with President Zuma's links to Swazi royalty in that he was once, and some claim he still is, engaged to marry a Swazi princess and at base he is also a cultural conservative, a traditionalist in terms of African custom. Like Mswati, he is a practising polygamist. On such factors sometimes can matters of state turn.

WHAT OF THE FUTURE?

So what is likely to happen in Swaziland in the year or so ahead? Will the present economic difficulties of the government generate a wave of protest and concerted action? Are the days of royalist hegemony numbered? In our view, the answer is no. Swaziland does not stand poised on the brink of regime change or even of reform. In fact, what is likely to happen in reform terms is nothing, just more of the same. There will be demonstrations and marches, all broken up by the police, some strike action but no Arab-like Spring, no concessions, no political reforms, and no early end to the current economic difficulties. As an illustration, the most organised of Swaziland's unions, the Swazi National Association of Teachers (SNAT) went on strike for nearly two months in mid-2012, demanding higher wages. The government was recalcitrant and refused the demand. Ultimately, the king ordered an end to the strike and the teachers complied. What is extraordinary is that, even with tens of thousands of schoolchildren idled by the strike, they never mobilised or took to the streets. But, although the government pleaded an inability to grant a 4.6 per cent wage hike, sixty-six members of the royal family, including three queens, reportedly, in July 2012, left on Mswati's new private jet for a 'shopping' trip in Las Vegas where they will stay in ten luxury villas (*Swaziland Newsletter* 27 July 2012). The 'let them eat cake' analogy inevitably comes to mind.

So why then will the crisis not mature into the possibility of meaningful political change? Four reasons:

One is the weakness of the domestic opposition and the inability of the urban-based opposition to mobilise the countryside and those bonded by the feudal nature of the rural order. The heavy-handed nature of chieftancy rule should not be minimised. Swazi chiefs have the power to expel from their areas any commoner who is seen as 'crossing the line' of politics and or culture – and it is a power that is used. In March 2012, the Swazi High Court rejected an appeal from an evicted commoner, Sandile Hadebe. The Court ruled that the king made all decisions about how land was used and that he ruled through the chiefs, and in this regard 'Hadebe had no rights'. The judge ruled 'that the Swazi Constitution played no part in this case. In terms of Swazi law and custom, Khumalo [the chief in question] has a right to evict him from the chiefdom for defying his authority (*Swaziland Newsletter* 29 March 2012). Given the draconian rule of the chiefs, the sheer struggle to survive the poverty of rural Swaziland, and the crippling effects on the rural sector of the AIDS pandemic, it is little wonder that rural Swaziland is politically quiescent.

Two is the continuing loyalty of the army and police and the fact that they seem able to act with whatever level of force is required, or to which they feel inclined, and with impunity. Although the loyalty of security forces can never be fully guaranteed, Mswati takes pains to ensure that beyond the monarchical fringe they are an especially privileged sector. Wages are good, and they have been the first in line when monthly payments have sometimes been delayed due to the current public sector salaries difficulties. Members of the army also receive special food and clothing monthly allowances. Similarly, the police have in recent years been able to operate as a law unto themselves. Even in the face of evidence of widespread torture and the occasional death in detention, no action has been taken to rein in the police or to discipline any officials. Impunity is an intoxicating cocktail and it seems to have produced a blind loyalty to Mswati on the part of the one internal element with a capacity to threaten the *status quo*.

Three is the fact that South Africa, the only regional power with the muscle to induce real change in Swaziland, is unwilling to do so while the regional instrument, SADC has its hands full grappling with the situations in Zimbabwe and Madagascar, and has no stomach to tackle yet another intractable regime.

Four is because, at the end of the day, the monarchy has the financial resources, as well as some reliable corporate and other wealthy financial allies, to help it if necessary through the current difficulties until such time as the global economy recovers and revenue from SACU returns to the levels prior to the global downturn of recent years. In April 2012, Mswati celebrated his forty-fourth birthday. As in recent years – although not in 2011 when the fiscal crisis was maturing – this was marked by an expensive and elaborate party. But, as the government claimed it could not pay for it, the people had to pay through a 'request' to the nation's chiefs to acquire 'donations' from the people. Of course, Mswati could himself have paid for the festivities many times over but that is not the royal way. Instead, the Swazi way is that the politically battered and impoverished people must. Can there be a clearer message that even in the direst of times, for the aristocracy, the Swazi Nation, it is business as usual?

NOTES

1   Ngwane is the name for Swaziland in the Siswati language.
2   An official approach by a Swazi government representative deployed by King Sobhuza II in regard to the claim to southern Mozambique was rejected by the newly independent Mozambican government. The so-called 'lost lands' in South Africa are claimed by the Swazi state to this day and remain a source of unresolved tension between the two governments.
3   There is evidence that in formulating his pre-independence strategy Sobhuza received advice from prominent white National Party politicians in South Africa and from Carl Todd, chair of the European Advisory Council (EAC), a body elected by the whites of Swaziland to channel white views to the British colonial authorities. For the two elections held prior to independence, the INM and EAC formed an electoral alliance that received funding from right-wing sources in South Africa. See Halpern 1965, Potholm 1966, Simpson 2009 and Stevens 1963.
4   A Commonwealth Observer Mission to the 2008 elections described them as neither democratic nor fair, and they could not declare the process 'credible'. A mission of the Pan-African Parliament took a broadly similar position. See ACSA 2010.5.
5   This was the speech in 1986 in which President PW Botha dashed expectations at home and abroad of meaningful reforms by adopting a 'so far and no more' posture. The result was a specatacular fall in the value of the rand and an accelerated rate of capital outflow.
6   Some of the Swazi-based companies with which Tibiyo has formed joint ventures are: Swazi Spa, an affiliate of Sun International (39 per cent); Swaziland Brewers, an affiliate of SAB Miller; Ubombo Ranches, the country's largest beef company (40 per cent); Royal Swazi Sugar Corporation (34.2 per cent); Nedbank; Illovo Sugar (50 per cent), Swaziland Development Corporation; Standard Bank; the *Swazi Observer* newspaper (100 per cent); Royal Swaziland Insurance.
7   Sobhuza's grandmother, Queen Regent Labotsibeni, became a financial backer of the newspaper *Abantu-Batho*, edited by Pixley Ka Seme, to promote the ideals of the newly formed South African Native National Congress, later renamed the ANC.
8   On 14 April 1984, four members of Umkhonto we Sizwe's (MK's) special operations unit were abducted from a small police station in the Swazi town of Bhunya, close to the South African border. At the time of the abduction by members of the Eastern Transvaal security police, the police station had been left empty and unattended as the Swazi police claimed they had been called out on an operation. In 1986, a senior MK intelligence office, Glory Sedibe (aka Comrade September) was abducted from a Swazi police station and taken to South Africa where he 'turned' and collaborated with the apartheid police. According to the Final Report of the South African Truth and Reconciliation Commission (1998; vol.2, p. 128), 'three Swazi police officers were paid a total of R150,000 for their assistance in the abduction'.

REFERENCES

Action for Southern Africa (ACTSA) (2010) *Briefing Paper on Swaziland*. London: ACTSA, September, 1-22.

Bonner P (1983) *Kings, Commoners and Concessionaires: The Evolution and Dissolution of the Nineteenth-Century Swazi State*. Johannesburg: Ravan.

Booth A (1983) *Swaziland: Tradition and Change in a Southern African Kingdom*. Boulder: Westview.

Booth A (2000) *Historical Dictionary of Swaziland: Second Edition*. Lanham, Maryland: The Scarecrow Press.

Daniel J (1989) *Destabilisation: Swaziland and South Africa's Regional Strategy*. Roma, Lesotho: Institute for Southern African Studies, National University of Lesotho.

Daniel J (2006) Swaziland. In Repucci S and C Walker (Eds) *Countries at the Crossroads: A Survey of Democratic Governance*. New York and Washington DC: Freedom House.

Daniel J and J Vilane (1986) The Crisis of Political Legitimacy in Swaziland. *Review of African Political Economy*, 35, 54-67.

Davies R and D O'Meara (1985) *Swaziland: A Profile*. London: Zed.

Government of South Africa (1998) *Truth and Reconciliation Commission of South Africa Final Report*, vol.2, Pretoria: Government Printer.

Halpern J (1965) South *Africa's Hostages: Basutoland. Bechuanaland and Swaziland*. London: Penguin.

Hanlon J (1988) *Apartheid's Second Front: South Africa's War Against its Neighbours*. London: Penguin.

Hyam R (1972) *The Failure of South African Expansion, 1908-1948*. Basingstoke: Macmillan.

Macmillan H (1986) Swaziland: Decolonisation and the Triumph of Tradition, *Journal of Modern African Studies*, 643-66, reprinted in Daniel J and M Stephen (Eds) (1987) *Historical Perspectives on the Political Economy of Swaziland: Selected Articles*. Manzini: Social Science Resarch Unit, University of Swaziland, 104-25.

Matsebula J S M (1972) *A History of Swaziland*. London: Longman.

Minter W (1994) *Apartheid's Contras: An Inquiry into the Roots of War in Angola and Mozambique*. London: Zed.

Potholm C (1966) Changing Political Configurations in Swaziland, *Journal of Modern African Studies*, 4, 3 November, 313 – 22.

Russell T (1986) 'The Reed Dance', poem published in *Phoenix, Annual Magazine of Waterford Kamhlaba College*, Mbabane, Swaziland.

Simpson T (2009) 'The Bay and the Ocean': A History of the ANC in Swaziland, *African Historical Review* 41 (1), 90-117.

Stevens R P (1963) Swaziland Political Development, *Journal of Modern African Studies*, 1, 3, September, 327-50.

Contributors

Stephanie Allais is Senior Researcher at the Wits Education Policy Unit, researching education and the labour market.

William Attwell is an M Phil candidate in Public Law, University of Cape Town, and Fox International Fellow, Yale University.

Susan Booysen is Professor in the Graduate School of Public and Development Management, University of the Witwatersrand.

Jacklyn Cock is Professor Emeritus, Department of Sociology, University of the Witwatersrand

John Daniel is the retired Academic Director of the School for International Training in Durban.

David Fig is an Honorary Research Associate in the Environmental Evaluation Unit, University of Cape Town, and a Fellow of the Transnational Institute, Amsterdam.

Dick Forslund is Economist and Researcher, Alternative Information and Development Centre, Cape Town.

Paul Maylam is Professor Emeritus, Department of History, Rhodes University.

Julia Moorman is Senior Community Health Specialist, School of Public Health, University of the Witwatersrand.

Shireen Motala is Director of the Postgraduate Centre, Research and Innovation Division, Faculty of Education, University of Johannesburg.

Prishani Naidoo is a lecturer in the Department of Sociology at the University of the Witwatersrand.

Vinothan Naidoo is Senior Lecturer, Department of Political Studies, University of Cape Town.

Sanusha Naidu is Senior Researcher in the Democracy, Governance and Service Delivery Programme, Human Sciences Research Council.

Martin Nicol is former practice leader, Applied Research and Economic Development, Research at ODA (Pty) Ltd, a Cape Town-based consultancy.

Devan Pillay is Associate Professor and Head, Department of Sociology, University of the Witwatersrand.

Marisha Ramdeen is a researcher with ACCORD, the African Centre for the Constructive Resolution of Disputes, in Durban.

Laetitia Rispel is Professor and Head of the School of Public Health, University of the Witwatersrand.

Roger Southall is Professor Emeritus, Department of Sociology, University of the Witwatersrand and, during 2013, the Van Zyl Slabbert Visiting Professor in Politics and Sociology at the University of Cape Town.

Ahmed Veriava is Associate Professor, Department of Political Studies, University of the Witwatersrand.

Louise Vincent is Professor of Political Studies, Rhodes University.

Index